BY **NAOMI ODENKIRK**

Thank you...

Chris Bilheimer and Henry H. Owings
for the book's amazing design and the key to the printer's back door.

Stephanie Courtney
for your tireless assistance with the episode guide.

Virginia Vanover
for all your assistance, always.

All at HBO for the go ahead, especially:
Carolyn Strauss, Chris Albrecht and Michael Lombardo

Likewise,
Bernie Brillstein, Brad Grey, Sandy Wernick, and Tim Sarkes at Brillstein Grey Entertainment.

Universal Studios Consumer Products Group.

Globo-Chem Pan-Universal Products.

Michael Gendler and Marc Golden at Gendler-Kelly.

Layne Dicker and Joel Mandel at The Management Group.

Ari Emanuel and Brian Lipson at Endeavor.

Daniel Greenberg.

Adam Timrud Photography.

And **Troy Miller** for his granting generous access to the archives.

Photographs featured in the book are courtesy of:
Adam Timrud, Wendy Wilkins, Marina Chavez, Bill Odenkirk, Naomi Odenkirk, Claudia Kunin, Jenine DeShazer, Susie Cross, Bob Odenkirk, David Cross, Troy Miller, Brian Posehn, Jill Talley, Mike Upchurch, Mike Reynolds, Eban Schletter, Museum of Television and Radio of Beverly Hills, and Famous Mortimer.

Original material provided by:
David Cross, Bob Odenkirk,
Brian Posehn with an assist from Eban Schletter.

Additional original material by:
Chris Bilheimer, Heather Miller, Scott Aukerman, Jay Johnston, Bill Odenkirk, B.J. Porter, Dino Stamatopoulos, Paul F. Tompkins.

And to my family:
Bob and Nathan and Erin for their support (Durgaya, too).

And everyone else who contributed their time, stories, photographs and other artifacts to this tome of silliness:
Scott Adsit, Scott Aukerman, Peter Bagge, Jack Black, Louis C.K., Jerry Collins, Susie Cross, Andy Dick, Lauren Dombrowski, Paula Elins, John Ennis, Dave Foley, Brent Forrester, Janeane Garofalo, Tom Gianas, Bob Goldthwait, Eric Hoffman, Jay Johnston, Karen Kilgariff, Tracey Krasno, Beth Lapides and Greg Miller, Dan Manella, Vahe Manoukian, Adam McKay, Heather Miller, Jerry Minor, John Moffitt, Conan O'Brien, Bill Odenkirk, Brett Paesel, B. J. Porter, Brian Posehn, Mary Lynn Rajskub, Dave Rath, Dave Reynolds, Mark Rivers, Eban Schletter, Garry Shandling, Tom Sherren, Sean Shul, Sarah Silverman, Joyce Sloan, Robert Smigel, Tom Snyder Productions, Dino Stamatopoulos and his father, Ben Stiller, Jill Talley, Becky Thyre, Paul F. Tompkins, Mike Upchurch, Bill Utterback and Kelly Leonard of The Second City, Tonyia Verna, Steve Welch, Wendy Wilkins, Lisa Valenzuela, Al Yankovic.

Chris & Henry wish to thank:
Hillary Goerig, Marina Chavez, Eric Levin and Sarah Jacobson with very special thanks to Lillian Lai Hughes and Garth Johnson for work above and beyond any reasonable call of duty.

And most especially...

Bob Odenkirk and David Cross

Thank you all for your cooperation and contributions.
This book could not have been imagineered without you.

MR. SHOW – WHAT HAPPENED?!

Copyright © 2002 by Naomi Odenkirk. All rights reserved. No part of this book may be used or reproduced in any form or by any electronic or mechanical means, including information storage and retrieval systems without express written permission from the author or pertinent copyright holder except in the case of brief quotations embodied in published articles or reviews.

For information, address:
The Management Group,
9100 Wilshire Blvd, #725 East,
Beverly Hills, CA 90212

All sketches and other original "Mr. Show with Bob and David" material are reproduced by permission of HBO and Universal Studios, the owners of all rights in such material, none of which may be used or reproduced in any manner whatsoever without written permission.

All photographs used by permission and are copyrighted by their respective owners.

Design: Chris Bilheimer & Henry H. Owings
Cover Photography: Marina Chavez

Printed by Westcan Printing Group
84 Durand Road
Winnipeg, Manitoba
Canada R2J 3T2

First Edition

ISBN 9713597-8-4

www.bobanddavid.com

TABLE OF CONTENTS

Foreword by Janeane Garafalo	4
Foreword by David Cross	6
Foreword by Adolf Royce Hitler	7
Note From The Author	8
Introduction	10
Birth Of Mr. Show	12
Bob Before Mr. Show	22
David Before Mr. Show	30
Who?	39
Writing The Show	66
Production	76
Season One	90
Season Two	114
Season Three	142
Season Four	192
Acknowledgments	247

FOREWORD BY JANEANE GAROFALO

Damn it, I've got to write a foreword for the *Mr. Show* book. God forbid Americans be denied "the definitive guide to the *Mr. Show with Bob and Dave* experience." How could a coffee table not have its top graced with the aforementioned book? Every internet devotee and conspiracy theorist will rush to Barnes and Noble grab the book and shout: "I told you episode #37 had a continuity gaffe in sketch #34!" They will rally 'round their newfound Bible and discuss episodic theory whilst playing "Magic" or waiting on line to see *Mean Streets* and *Betty Blue* at their local revival theater. (You know the theater with the broken seats that smell vaguely of humus and stale socks.) They shall place the book lovingly in their over the shoulder messenger style bag amidst *HATE* comics and Radiohead C.D.'s and bootleg Phil Hendrie tapes. Know the audience and give them what they want. What they want is a book about the gentlemen who gave them sketch comedy that tickles the "alternative" funnybone, a bone located behind your Buddy Holly-style glasses. (The traditional funnybone also known as "The Reitman," for the masses.) Let them eat shit cake. (My goodness, I'm a rebel.)

If you ever get the opportunity to attend a live taping of *Mr. Show*, I urge you to seize it. It's a wonderful feeling to sit amongst the predominantly white male audience and feel their joy as they realize that being a social retard in high school can lead to an Emmy and dinners with Tracey Ullman and Garry Shandling. It is also exciting to note that the lion's share of the audience resembles Bob and Dave. The smattering of female fans with Louise Brooks bangs are drawn to either the well-heeled non-threateningly handsome God-devoting Bob or the ethnic (read Jew) casually attired David. Fire and Ice they are, so choose your poison and identify at your leisure. I personally have a love-hate relationship with both. I love them for who they are and hate them for being infinitely more talented than I am. I take comfort in the fact that they have busted their collective ass for years to produce sublime comedy for those in the know, and yet they remain largely unsung. All I had to do was get dragged by a big dog on roller skates and flirt with Ben Stiller at a deli on Fairfax circa 1991. In fact the only productive show business thing I've ever done is introduce David Cross to Bob Odenkirk in hopes that David could play a little Sunday afternoon basketball. Naturally Bob rebuffed him in his pre-therapy socially brusque manner. Bob is a lot nicer now, luckily he was always extremely witty and well read. Their first meeting was uneventful but fortunately for you they eventually and enthusiastically fell in love. The romance began at the Montreal Just for Laughs Comedy Festival in, as luck would have it, Montreal. Due to scheduling they were forced to share a hotel room, by day three they were giggling like school girls and napping in one another's arms. French speaking Canadians were honored to have borne witness to the new Martin and Lewis. After Montreal they moved in together and sired three beautiful children, one black and two Episcopalian. All three now attend private school in Scotland with Prince William. I hear they are unhappy with the rigorous academic program and the cold morning showers. In 1997 Bob joined the Scientology cabal and was awarded Naomi Yomtov for his efforts. David still suffers the after effects of a man to man love affair gone bad. Fortunately, his pain fuels some of the best comedy anyone has ever seen. My admiration for them grows seasonally as they display strength and commitment in their fight against Lou Gherig's disease.

I love you,

Janeane Q. Garofalo

August 4,
in the year of Xenu,
75000000000002

Hello, everyone. I am writing this from my bed in room 6-A at the Center. Things are looking up I'm told. And although I am in a great amount of pain, and my movement severely limited by the tubes and wires running in and out of my wallet, I will get this foreword done! (Life Maxim #8: "Pain cannot prevent action, it can only inactivate an active dis-actionable." LRH) I have been asked to reflect, and comment on The Mister Show days. Days in which I was a wastrel. Days in which I was a constant source of de-positivity, bearing no more weight than some random false spiritful. After much thought, and knowing the danger of using my RE-active mind to call up such non-times (Life Maxim #11: "At no time of non-time can one truly be of a time-time." LRH) I have decided that "yes," I will do so one last "nowtime" for the sake of my old friends, regardless of their neglect and inner toxicity.

The Mister Show. What can be said that hasn't already been said by a stranger in an on-line chatroom, or at least is being in part, covered in this book? I don't know, because I won't talk about it, be in the same space as someone talking about it, or read this book. I do not like to look at such things or hear them being looked at. Seeing somebody looking at someone who is hearing somebody looking at these things creates a hurting deep within me that can only be tempered by one thing, a pizza party. (Life Maxim #27: "The raising of the bridge to sanctity is brought about by the convergence of a thetanic uprising, a pre-post-clear, and a pizza party." LRH) Pizza it is then. I would like a large, half "cheese-lovers," and half…do you have fresh tomatoes? You know, like sliced tomatoes? Hello? Hello? I'm not getting an answer. How very rude.

Where was I? Oh, pizza. I absolutely adore pizza. If pizza were a person it would be the Olson twins, suspended in time, forever young and precocious. If pizza were a bird, it would be the auburn spotted "Dapplepie" with its excitable trills and carefree song stylings. If pizza were an ancient Greek it would be the ancient Greek mariner, hard at work in a boat on the cobalt blue Aegean Sea. If there is anything better than pizza, then I don't know what it is, except maybe a thick, rock-hard, 9-inch cock, but other than that, pizza. Am I right about the cock thing? I keep hearing about how women and gay men love a big, thick cock, so I would think so. Have you seen "Sex and the City"? Is it still on? Probably not anymore, huh? What's on HBO now? I'm curious. But not curious enough to expose my decelerated, invisible spheres to such somatics and other barriers. (Life Maxim #3: "Postulates, and considerations can stand independently of mental mass." LRH) (Note to reader: My Auditor says this latest visit to the Center is a huge wake-up call on all my Dynamics!!) So, no HBO for me, although I am allowed to watch "Farm Sex 12" and "Arli$$," HBO's new prison drama.

I'm sorry, I've gotten way off "track." I was writing about The Mister Show. A rather coarse, and unflattering exercise in bacchanalia. To become Clear is to understand the infantile and toxic qualities that made this show a danger to humanity. As I stated before, I refuse everything The Mister Show…for it refused me. While I am comforted by the under whelming number of people who actually saw it, I am still locked in a bitter court case with Odenkirks and HBO's and others to have it "erased." I hope for your sake that I will prevail. Well, my Auditor has informed me that we are ready for another session, so I must now leave you. I hope I have given you some valuable and exclusive insight into the goings on at The Mister Show. Just remember, we are at the end of a 5 million year cycle of civilization of a particular type! Learn the tech of Ethics with the Golden Age of Tech Drills! Use Flag Auditing to progress to OT (Arbitraries Cancelled!!) The Bridge Acceleration Package is normally $25,410. Sign up now for only $13,975!!

David Cross
As dictated to Lorimar Miscraviege, Star Warrior (angel), Level 4

La Questra Inn
Buenos Aires, Argentina

Well, it seems like everyday, somebody, somewhere, is putting out a book and wants me to write a foreword! And once again, I find myself asking, "Why me?" Is it because I, too, once wrote a book, (and only one book), and therefore I can sympathize with the young author's jangling nerves!? Honestly, I don't know.

I am very old now. Very old. Life in and around Buenos Aires, Argentina is slow, yes, but not nearly slow enough for me at my advanced age. The carnival season is particularly hectic. But nothing takes me out of the hustle and bustle like a good book. Lately, I've gone in for memoirs. "Angela's Ashes" was great. I'll read anything (so long as I have my glasses — I've had two eye operations... the most recent being laser surgery — a gift from God!) I'll read a catalog, the ingredients on canned soup, or even a book that lists the sketches on a TV program I've never seen. I love the activity of reading, the communal moment hosted by simple words on paper (or these days, a computer screen). So, buy this book, take it home like your last piece of warm bread, and eat. But chew slowly, dear reader, make it last, because when you've finished reading it, you'll have to fight me for the soup can and catalog!!!

Good luck, and I'm sorry about that thing I did. It was just plain wrong.

Humbly,

Adolph Royce Hitler

Hi.

Who am I? Well, yes, I am married to one of them, but I was a fan first. I love *Mr. Show*. I love watching it, thinking about it, talking about it. I guess I am a *Mr. Show* nerd. It didn't escape me, for example, that Nostradamus accurately predicts that his lover will perish in the great NY quake of 2003, and then the Apocalypse happens while Smoosh is on the moon. (Think about it.) And I appreciate that the music behind that touching moment — where Alexis first reveals himself to Nostradamus as the one who placed the personals ad — is the melody from the *Second Wind* theme song. And so on.

I was fortunate enough to have come to L.A. just as the newfangled 'alternative' scene was percolating. I moved from the Bay Area, where I was a comedy snob. I was heavily involved with the San Francisco comedy scene. In the late 80's there were a lot of great little clubs and one-nighters (Holy City Zoo, The Other Café, The Punchlines, Tommy T's, Cobb's) and scores of local fans supporting the scene and fostering inventive comics. At 22, I was hired as general manager at the newest "legendary" Catch a Rising Star Comedy Club, in Palo Alto, California (which closed six months later). I opened the next newest Catch in Reno, Nevada on the casino floor at Bally's. (This was a great room but is closed now too. Even Bally's sold to Hilton.) I loved comedy, and had consumed so much of it that first 26 years that very little impressed me.

I arrived in L.A. in 1993. I had no job, and only two friends (well, one friend and his roommate). That roommate-guy was a comedy agent at APA (a mini-major talent agency), and he took me to the Improv for an agency showcase, where they line up all the comedians they represent for an audience of invited industry-types. The emcee introduced the first act: "Our first comic tonight is an amazing impressionist, please welcome, David Cross." I'd never heard of David before. His first bit – I remember this clearly – he offered, "I wonder what it would be like if Jack Nicholson was your dentist?" He briefly half-turned his back to the audience as though he was going to come out presenting one of his famed impressions. Instead, he took another beat. And another. I got it right away. I recall being the first and sole person laughing. Soon a few others caught on. David stroked his chin, "Hmm I wonder. What would that be like?" And of course, everyone was with him by the end. He fooled everyone. Now, I was new to town; but what was their excuse for not knowing David Cross?!! The rest of the showcase was a predictable disappointment to me – some were funny, but none of the others were doing anything that interesting. I told you, I'm a snob. But David's set had excited me very much. I made an urgent call to some comedy friends in S.F. who had not made the move to L.A. yet. "You should see what's going on out here! They get smart stuff!"

Reinvigorated, I couldn't consume enough comedy. I was working at the William Morris Agency as an assistant in the comedy department. I went to all the clubs, sometimes 2 or 3 a night to catch specific people's sets. If there was an unfamiliar name in the lineup, I'd be there to learn who they were. Even if they were no good, I was glad to see them. It drove me crazy to think I may be missing someone I would love, another David Cross. And then I went to the *UnCabaret*.

I don't remember how I heard about the *UnCab*, but it must have been going on for a little while before I clued in. These weekly Sunday shows were the complete antithesis of what I hated about comedy. Performers didn't play down to the audience. Their material was more like unscripted personal stories, which I liked to believe were all true. My first time there, I saw Bob Odenkirk, although I didn't know it. He and Andy Dick did not use their names (not that I had ever heard their real names before anyway), and they were in drag. They did a bit where they were actors presenting some

Me at "Blind House" waiting to interview David for this book.
© Adam Timrud Photography

scenes from a new two-person show entitled, *The Two Marilyns*. One as Marilyn (Bob, I think) and one as Norma Jean. It was pee-in-my-pants hilarious. I came back to the *Uncabaret* every week, and eventually I saw Bob Odenkirk. He told some great stories about his father — like how his dad had taught him sarcasm. Wow. He was great. (There's a whole other personal story here that I won't get into now, but suffice it to say, that by the time we actually met, years later, I was in love and he wasn't aware of me.)

Naturally, I was at the Diamond Club shows, and the *Mr. Show*-type shows at the Upfront. I would not miss any of them. It was all so incredible. So many funny performers, and smart, silly, exciting ideas. When Bob and I started going out, he and David were shooting the pre-taped video pieces for the first four episodes. I remember being so excited to visit them on the set, late at night, while he, David and John were shooting the street scene (link to *Asshole at Party* #101). But more than that, I remember how exhilarated Bob was. He couldn't stop talking like some excited kid, about the things they were shooting. We met up one night and he told me they'd just shot Expert Truck (#104) with Jack Black lying down on the top of a pick-up truck, jubilantly waving his cap in the air. Bob was amazed and titillated with their silliness; that they were committing this stuff to video, for their *TV show*. "What gives us the right…?" he marveled.

By the fourth season, I thought there ought to be a book. As you would imagine, I was hearing first hand about all the various escapades that went on as the show progressed. There were so many scenes and so many ideas in every episode, all with entertaining stories behind them. So I hope that you enjoy flipping through this book, and that it serves its purpose as a little archival time caplet for comedy nerds of the future.

Signed

Naomi Odenkirk

"I try not to judge people based on what kind of comedy they like, but it's kind of impossible."
- Ben Stiller

When Bob and David got together in the early 90's with a shared vision to create a comedy show with their like-minded cronies, the result was a sketch show like no other since *Monty Python*. The series lasted four seasons on HBO (1995-98), residing in the remote time-slot of Fridays at midnight, often partially pre-empted by a sports-chat program that ran too long. In some cities, the show's listing actually read, "sometime after 11:30 P.M." And for their fourth season, viewers were challenged to find the show at all. Someone at HBO made an eleventh-hour decision to switch it to the vigorously obscure slot of Monday at midnight. This inspired late-night sketch show has been credited as having "reinvented the genre from the bottom up," yet *Mr. Show* resides in the realm of the Underground. Has anything on TV ever been so lauded yet so utterly unheard-of?…What happened? This book takes you on the insider tour of how the show began, what went into it, and, what everybody always wants to know: why they quit.

TV JUST GOT A LITTLE LESS WORSE…

Garry Shandling: "*Mr. Show* was absolutely 100% inspired. Most things are derivative. Whereas *Mr. Show* is completely unpredictable, and will surprise me. And so there's very few places I can turn in comedy and still be surprised, and that's one place. And that's not something I would take for granted."

Conan O'Brien: "To me the funniest comedy is where you get a bunch of really smart, funny people in a room, who have a similar sensibility, and they indulge themselves. A lot of people think that indulgence is a negative word, it has negative connotations. I think the best thing about *Mr. Show* is they'll indulge themselves: they'll take a thread, and they'll just follow it and follow it and follow it to an insane level. They have this confidence, they go by their own compass. They're not trying to be edgy, they're not trying to be cool, they're just doing their own thing, and that's what makes it so funny. That's what makes the show. You look at the show, and you know that they're not responding to any external stimuli, they're just doing the show that they really want to do."

Dave Foley: "When I first saw an episode of *Mr. Show* it got me excited again about the potential of sketch comedy. There were still new things to be done."

Bob Goldthwait: "*Mr. Show* is a great show, one of the best shows that's been on TV. Bob and David's passion to get something made, where it wasn't a compromise — I was surprised that anyone can pull it off, and not want to get liquored up and shoot a studio office full of executives. It's a Rubik's cube I've never been able to figure out: how to get something on TV that you would actually watch."

Mark Rivers (comedy writer): "*Mr. Show* seemed so simple to me at the time, and I'm realizing now what a novelty it actually was. I'm seeing now why most TV is shitty. And it's not because there aren't talented people. But the talented people are usually drowned out or over-ruled by the untalented ones. It's that old story. 'Wow, the executives generally screw things up, and with *Mr. Show* they didn't. They let Bob and David do what they wanted. How unusual is that.'" ("There were very few notes that I could give them that they didn't already come up with themselves," says Carolyn Strauss, executive for HBO's Original Programming.)

Adam McKay (comedy writer): "*Mr. Show* — it's a mixture of cohesiveness and complete digression at the same time. It's a feeling of anything can happen at anytime."

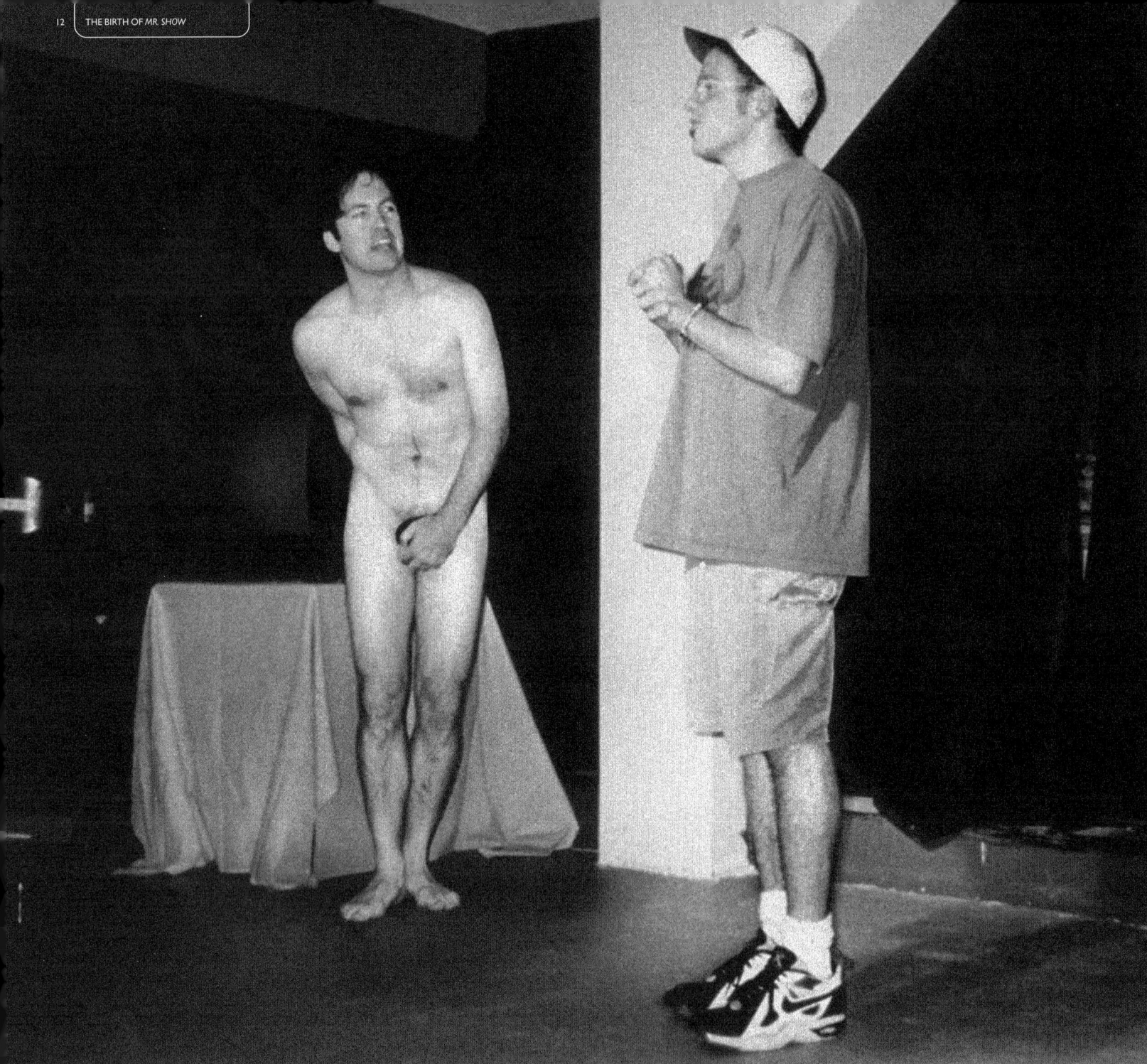

Bob and David performing Naked Phrase Guess at the Diamond Club in Hollywood.

BIRTH OF MR. SHOW

The first few times Bob and David met, there was no appreciation. No indication of the magical-fantastical collaboration soon to come. Once they caught a whiff of it, of the rare ease and enjoyment of writing with each other, it was an immediate decision to work together. Their discovery came out of the budding alternative comedy scene in L.A. circa 1994, in the back room of a loaned-out Hollywood disco club. From that moment, the story goes, they knew they were going to do a show for HBO.

Janeane Garofalo put it together before anybody. She knew David from the fertile Boston days, when they were in college and did open-mic comedy together. She had met Bob on her first *SNL* audition (at 24), and the two later became friends through Chicago guy Jeff Garlin, her L.A. roommate. "I believed the guys would really like to know each other, and tried to set them up," she explains.

"Dave was staying with me at my house on Curson," tells Janeane. "He wanted to play basketball. And I said, 'Oh, my friend Bob, he's a really funny guy, and I know he plays basketball on Sundays. I will walk you the one block over to Bob's house.'" David recalls, "I had the basketball, and we walked up. It was literally around the corner. So she brought me to the screen door, Bob's there, you could see him watching TV. We knocked: 'Hey. What's going on?' 'Nothing.' 'This is my friend, David, he wants to play basketball.' 'No, I'm busy. I'm working.' 'Okay. Well, nice to meet you.' 'All right. Bye.' And that was it."

The next time they met was on the on *The Ben Stiller Show,* which David joined mid-season. There, although both were writers on the short-lived show (13 episodes were made, only 12 of which ever aired), the two didn't collaborate on much.

It wasn't until after *Stiller* was over, when they saw each other perform live, that they took any real notice.

David was doing stand-up at the now-shuttered Santa Monica Improv. He noticed that Bob was doing his one-man show at the neighboring Upfront Theater and decided to kill some time and check it out. "I just loved it," David recalls. "What Bob was doing was very similar to what I was doing in my stand-up at the time in the sense that he took one thing and totally broke the reality, and revealed the layers of a concept." After the show, he invited Bob to see his set at the Improv. "I thought he would like it because I don't do standard stand-up."

Shortly after that, Dave Rath got the Diamond Club together.

Everyone's First Manager

Dave Rath is a talent manager, handling the careers of Brian Posehn, Janeane Garofalo, Patton Oswald, Mary Lynn Rajskub, and many others. In the early 90's, Rath was a young independent talent manager with many of these same clients, but nobody had heard of them yet. At night, he ran the showroom at the Santa Monica Improv. He was also the talent booker for FOX's *Comic Strip Live*, one of the stand-up comedy shows that were proliferating on your airwaves as a result of the late-80's comedy boom. Rath, a rare type in his business, was able to recognize true talent early on, before most other industry executives, and he genuinely wanted to help everybody.

Rath soon found himself surrounded by a circle of new-to-L.A. comics who were *different* — like Janeane Garofalo, Margaret Cho, Mary Lynn Rajskub, Patton Oswalt and David Cross, none of whom were 'traditional comics.' "It was hard to be objective because these people were my friends," says Rath, "but I knew that they were all much better talent than most of the people who were getting stage time in the [L.A.] clubs. But I also knew, commercially, there was a reason for what was happening." Rath put his focus and energy into their cause. "I tried to get David Cross on *Comic Strip Live* for over a year before they agreed to book him. It was a running joke there, because I always pitched these comedians who were not 'TV comics' — Cross was doing material like the tuna thing and the retarded bit [an old Cross joke where he tells of an audience member who corrected him on his bit about the hypocrisy of eating dolphin-safe tuna: "Mr. Comedian, we do not not eat dolphins because they're cute. We do not eat them because they're intelligent." He extrapolates that thinking to conclude that we should eat the retarded. From there, he takes it further and further until everyone is offended, delighted, or gone.] — and they would say, 'We can't put him on, are you crazy?' But I fought for him and others, and they would slowly get booked."

The "Alternative" Comedy Scene

No one really likes to use the term "alternative" to describe the scene that was growing in L.A. at the time (that's why it's in quotes). That, however, is exactly what was happening. In the wake of the late 80's stand-up comedy explosion, in 1992-93, dozens of smart, thinking performers and non-conventional stand-ups were suddenly emerging. In fact, the reason for this seemingly sudden boom in alternative comedy was that within about one calendar year, many performers of this type of moved to L.A. for the first time, mostly from San Francisco, New York and Boston.

Janeane recalls, "It was actually really difficult if you weren't 'passed' at either the Improv or the Comedy Store. You auditioned for Budd Friedman at the Improv, and Mitzi Shore at the Comedy Store. And there was also the Laugh Factory, and you would audition for Jamie Masada. And you either passed or you didn't. Also at the time, you had to pick between the Improv and the Comedy Store; you couldn't do both. So there were basically, like, three places to do stand-up."

Over time, alternate venues were found, and an "alternative" comedy scene began to form, populated by Janeane Garofalo, Dana Gould, Laura Kightlinger, Andy Dick, Margaret Cho, Brian Posehn, Patton Oswalt, Andy Kindler, Craig Anton, Mary Lynn Rajskub, Karen Kilgariff, Taylor Negron, Rick Overton, Judy Toll, Kathy Griffin, Greg Behrendt, Jeremy Kramer, Laura Milligan, Bob, David, and others. Most in this set generally resented typical comedy club audience. What those audiences responded to, these comedians were not interested in delivering (and some couldn't even if they wanted to). In a 1996 interview, David told *Rolling Stone Magazine*, "Not to get sappy about it, but this is a real special time to be out here. All these frustrated people who didn't have an act that was necessarily stand-up friendly, yet were funny, now have a place to go."

"'Alternative comedy' is a strange phrase," says Janeane. "I've always been doing stand-up, and Laura Kightlinger and David Cross have always been doing stand-up, the same way. And if you're going to do it that way, which is more meandering and verbal, not quite as jokey, then you're gonna have a harder time. The average comedy club goer — I'm not talking about alternative comedy clubs, I'm talking about the average suburban comedy club — it's not like you've got intellectual giants sitting out in the audience. So they need it kind of easy. And they need a certain voice inflection, and a certain pattern of comedy that they're comfortable with. So if you vary from that pattern, especially throughout the 80's and early 90's, which we did, and there was a handful of comics who did, you suffered for it. But when you find your audience, you find pockets of hard-core supporters. When people liked you, they *really* liked you."

Many of the performers appeared regularly at the new and very hip *UnCabaret,* a comedy show held every Sunday night in the intimate downstairs showroom at Luna Park, a restaurant/night club in West Hollywood. The *UnCab* was (and still is) hosted by Beth Lapides, arguably the birth mother of the alternative comedy scene in Los Angeles. Lapides started the weekly underground show the night after she and her friends (including Dana Gould and Kathy Griffin) put on a comedy show — true story — for lesbian artists who were reluctant to go to the comedy clubs. Lapides explains, "We did a couple of shows based on the fact that there was this audience that wasn't being served in the comedy clubs." Lapides next set out to create a weekly room where performers could do the things that didn't fit into the customary rooms. "I saw good work at the clubs that the audience just wasn't getting. I knew there was another audience out there." "The *UnCabaret* was the exactly the perfect meeting of venue and comic and audience," adds Janeane.

The *UnCab* fostered a less structured approach to stand-up — closer to storytelling, always with a strong point of view. Every Sunday, four or five performers would each do a twenty-minute set (a lot of stage time for L.A., known as the home of the seven-minute showcase-oriented spot). The performers would bring their written notes on stage and take their time. The type of material varied, as each performer had their own style — and the audience immediately caught on. They knew they would hear about the minutiae of Taylor Negron's week, bitter rants about the blatant idiocy in Hollywood from Andy Kindler, personal dirt, self-derision, and intimate disasters from Margaret Cho, Judy Toll and Kathy Griffin, respectively — and there was always a surprise from unpredictable Andy Dick. Bob and David performed there very often. Everyone had their favorite comic, but more importantly, the audience became fans of the *show*.

Lapides had two stiff rules for performers on her show: the material couldn't be "jokey," and, because the audiences kept returning, the material had to be fresh. Lapides also encouraged true stories, and would often chat on the phone with the people she booked, indirectly grinding them for possible subjects: "Why don't you talk about *that* on Sunday?"

Performers would tell involved, linear stories if they wanted to, starting a story one Sunday and continuing the narrative on a subsequent appearance, or "update" the audience on any new developments as things actually evolved in their lives. It was personal stuff, and very involving. (The "horrendous year" told about in Julia Sweeney's one-woman show/feature, *God Said, 'Ha!',* was intricately dissected and continually unfolding in a long string of *UnCab* sets.) *UnCabaret* fans became regulars, returning Sunday after Sunday to keep up with the various sagas; there was a feeling that if you missed a show, you *missed* something. This helped to create the

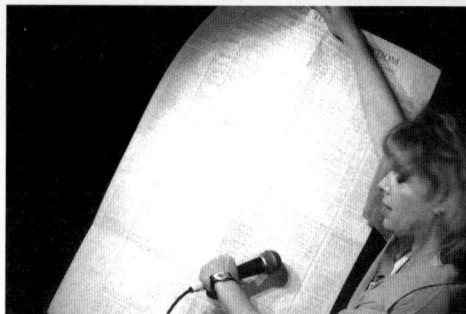

(left) New partners in comedy, 1994; (top right) Andy Dick and Bob fooling around for a few minutes during Bob's set at the "UnCabaret"; (bottom center) Janeane Garofalo, a regular before she moved to New York for SNL; (bottom right) Judy Toll tells an "UnCab" audience about her ridiculous stint as a Scientologist and gives away all the coveted cult-y secrets – one of the more memorable "UnCab" sagas told on stage. Photos by Claudia Kunin. March, 1995. (below) Original "UnCabaret" flyer listing the first regular performers at the weekly show, 1993.

perfect environment for the *UnCab* performers. All of them loved performing there, because the audiences seemed smarter, more interested, and were willing to stay with their long stories where the pay-off was never immediate — audiences that actually listened. "It's just smart comedy for smart people, basically," Janeane sums up.

David's two cents: "The *UnCab* was an almost perfect room. The only thing negative about it was that the audience was so good, too good really, that they tended to make performers lazy. With the exception of Andy Kindler and sometimes Bob, people were ill prepared. Now, most of these people were extremely good at that form of stand-up, but some were not, and that would suck. Who the fuck wants to see/hear someone whining about their pilot deal at FOX falling through for twenty fucking minutes — it's excruciating. But the *UnCab* was, to use a much-employed analogy, like therapy. I could go up there and tell stories about my fucked-up childhood or my asshole dad but instead of being bitter or trying not to come off sad or pitied, I was being funny and that was both helpful for me and entertaining to the suckers — I mean, audience."

(top to bottom) Jeremy Kramer narrarates the story of Jesus and Marshal at the Diamond Club, 1994; Tenacious D's guest spot performing "Tribute" at the Diamond Club, 1994; Postcard flyers from "The 3 Goofballz" at the Diamond Club in Hollywood, 1994, the first shows Bob and David wrote together.

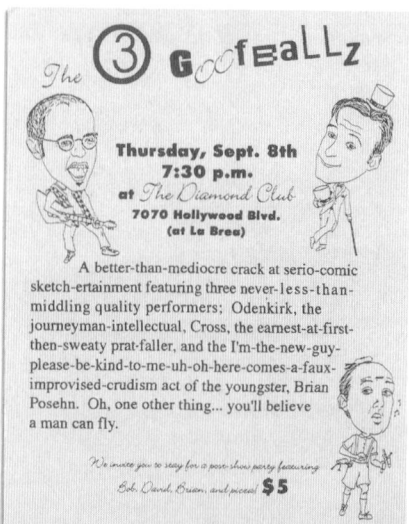

During that time, the alternative comics made up a very tight social bunch. Or, as Lapides puts it, "there was a certain sense of family and community." People were interested in each other's work, and would show up at their friends' shows. But more than that, a group of them hung out together every day, drank together every night, and many dated within the group. To outside observers, it was a very apparent clique. Karen Kilgariff once convinced someone that the 'group' was nicknamed *The Wildcats*. "There was always talk of the 'Posse,' or whatever it was. That's my way of highlighting the stupidity, like, 'who gives a shit in the first place,'" she says. Adds David, "I had people ask me if I was part of the 'Posse' or 'The Wildcats.' There was nothing much you could do except just stare at them until they figured out what your icy silence meant."

Lapides and her co-producer/husband Greg Miller felt that not every performer was right for their room. For better or for worse, they were extremely particular about whom they booked. They used a regular rotation of people. Their preference was to keep working with performers who could come up with a lot of new stuff. This made it nearly impossible for comics outside the group to get a slot, including many from the younger set that Dave Rath was pushing. (Performers like Mary Lynn Rajskub and Brian Posehn, though Wildcats, did not make the cut at *Uncab*.) So, in 1994, from necessity, Rath created an *alternate* alternative venue: The Diamond Club. He explains, "The Diamond Club was great, because it was so frustrating trying to get regular spots [at the comedy clubs] for these people, so it was all about manufacturing stage time."

Some Coke Addict's Disco Dream

The Diamond Club was not an obvious place to put on comedy shows, as Rath describes: "There was this New York night club guy that I met through [New York comic] Mark Cohen, named Scarduzio — we always made fun of him. He was very 'New York,' always putting on loud, sleazy shows: lingerie shows, bad cheesy cigar parties. He took over this strip joint at the bottom of a high-rise on Hollywood Boulevard and made it a nightclub [with business partner Slim Jim Phantom of *Stray Cats* fame]. We paid him $100 to use the back room, and started doing shows." Immediately, there was an underground scene — they were back there, putting on character-based theme shows and sketch shows, a new one every week, competing against the noise from the disco parties in the next room. The audience sat on crazy mismatched parlor couches and chairs.

"The Diamond Club — it was the 'alternative comedy movement' situation. It was a little bit of a scene there. It was like, 'Hmm, you can tell something's going on.' It wasn't your usual people going up and just doing a bunch of hacky stand-up. There was a lot of creative little 'scenelettes' and funny little original bits of business," provides Jack Black, who, with Kyle Gass, made guest appearances at the little club. "The Diamond Club shows were the best shows that ever happened, because they were totally ridiculous," offers Mary Lynn Rajskub. "Everything was always falling apart, like when you watch somebody and go, 'Ooh, you should have worked that out,' or, 'Ooh, that was kind of a bad idea.' But somehow, everything was really good there because it seemed that a lot of people were meeting each other."

Each show was written and produced by someone different, and everybody performed in everyone else's shows. It was here that Bob and David discovered that they really liked working together.

Whoever wanted "in" on Thursday night at the Diamond Club could put a sketch show together. Bob did the first night, and David did the third show two weeks later. David remembers, "We decided to write a couple things together, just some things we had riffed on at parties, and it was just effortless, and fun. It was so easy; it was weird. I've enjoyed writing with a lot of different people, but Bob and I had an unspoken understanding of where we were going; we were building on each other's ideas. It is very rare, and it was really comfortable. The pieces we wrote really stood out in the show." Bob felt the same way about the collaboration: "I've worked with a lot of people, and it's mostly been great, it depends on the project, but David is the best."

Eager to continue working together, they constructed a stage show and spent their own money to produce it. The result was called *The 3 Goofballz,* premiering at the Diamond Club about a month or two later. Bob describes it as the first version of *Mr. Show:* "We did some stuff on video, and some live sketches. The cast was all our friends and people we'd worked with before. We opened with a song, it was with [comic/writer] Jeremy Kramer [as Milosc Seekely], and we each popped out of a box, but Jeremy didn't pop out. He had died. And David and I were going to go on with the show 'to honor him; he would want us to go on.' And then you heard the voice of Jeremy's ghost, 'No, I wouldn't. If you want to honor me, *don't* do the show! I want you to *mourn* me!'"

From there, Bob says, they immediately knew they had to write a show together. "We didn't have a lot of conversations about it, we just said, 'Let's do it.'" David agrees, "We knew it would be good and it would be fun. And Bob's the one who took it from this cool idea of something to do on stage, and spearheaded the idea 'This is going to be a TV show someday.' He said, 'We're going to do this, then that, and we're going to invest our money in it.' He had the whole plan. Whether he said it or not, he was thinking steps ahead, and I was just enjoying what it was." David was going to the Montreal Comedy Festival that week to write things for the HA! Channel (the comedy channel that preceded Comedy Central) — little blurbs for celebrities to say on camera — and he invited Bob to come along. ("Because I love blurbs," says Bob.) Each night, the two performed together at the festival's late-night showcase. ("Another great example of the marginalization and disrespect of alternative comedy. Stick it at the end of the night because it's so 'crazy' and inaccessible," grumbles David.) One night they did *Fartin' Gary*, inspired by a star attraction at that year's fest — a guy who farted, that was his act. Other nights they went up with *Naked Phrase Guess*, and *Heckler Convention.*

Our Talents Compensate For Our Horrible Weaknesses

It was obvious from those shows that David and Bob were perfect for each other; comedically, they complemented each other remarkably well. As different and individual as they were stylistically, they had a shared sensibility. Their material was smart and inventive and it had an energy to it. Rath explains, "They were coming up with really prolific stuff — it was funny on so many levels, really heady and really silly all in the same breath." It was very exciting to see, because you knew something special was happening.

David performing Fartin' Gary at the first Aspen Comedy Arts Festival, 1995.

Tim Sarkes, David's long-time manager, adds, "David's strength is his instincts. He knows what's funny. He knows what works and what doesn't work. With *Mr. Show*, it was an immediate thing; with Bob and David there was instant chemistry."

They did the show again in September with some new sketches and with Brian Posehn as the third "Goofball." David and Bob worked on more material, spent more money, and in early 1995 moved over to the Upfront Theater in Santa Monica. They did the show a few more times over the next few months, always with fresh material. The name was changed to *Mr. Show;* later it became *Grand National Championships*, briefly, and then *The Cross/Odenkirk Problem*. The show still featured pre-taped videos and a cast of friends

(left) David and Bob take their show from nightclub to theater; (right) Running order of scenes in an early incarnation of the live show, briefly dubbed "Grand National Championships."

(including Tom Kenny, John Ennis, Jill Talley, Mary Lynn Rajskub, Jack Black, Laura Milligan and Jeremy Kramer). However, once they went to the Upfront, David points out, there was a defining change in the show. "It felt like more of a show, there was more structure, a real start time, and it was at a real theater, not some coke addict's disco dream."

HBO seemed interested pretty early on. Carolyn Strauss, then HBO's Director of Development seemed interested pretty early on. She came informally to see them at the Diamond Club. "I had a relationship with Bob because of *The Ben Stiller Show* [which was produced by HBO], and we developed this thing with him called *Life On Mars*," Carolyn explains. Bob says that from the start, Carolyn earned his respect. "She also came out to my one-man show in Santa Monica, she was so great. She was smart and cool, and I wasn't intimidated by her." Sarkes adds about Strauss, "Carolyn trusted the guys' creative instincts."

Carolyn says she was impressed. "We weren't necessarily looking for a sketch show. We were looking for something good. Bob and David had really taken this form and made it really unique to them; they borrowed from *Monty Python,* but it was the combination of the sensibility and the structure that really stood out to me."

Sarkes explains that with *Mr. Show,* there was actually some difficulty in selling it as a TV show. "The problem was that it was so different. The way you get it is to see it. So when we initially got development money from HBO it was to [continue to] develop a live stage show, not just a script."

Basically, their deal meant that HBO liked the show. They got very lucky, because HBO was really the only place to take it. *Mr. Show* was not suited for the broadcast networks for obvious reasons; the linking scenes (no room for commercials), and the swearing. ("We like to swear, and as it turns out, we're not allowed to do that on television," says Bob.) Also, and perhaps most importantly, Bob and David needed the creative freedom that HBO offered in order to do the show they wanted.

Development money from HBO also meant that Bob and David were no longer doing it out-of-pocket. By this time, at $2000-$3000 per show for shooting and editing the video pieces, Bob and David had already invested in the vicinity of $18,000 of their own money in the productions of the live shows.

Bernie Brillstein — The Godfather of Mr. Show

HBO runs an annual comedy festival in Aspen, CO, where TV and film executives from all over the country ascend to ski (and see new comedy talent). 1995 was the first year of that festival, and Bob and David's show was invited to perform. Unsurprisingly, Aspen is an unusual environment in which to showcase a live sketch show, and *Mr. Show* in Aspen was not a slam-dunk. "It didn't go over well in Aspen," Rath agrees, "but Bernie Brillstein was still behind it. Bernie was the key to that show getting on the air."

As Bernie Brillstein will tell you, this whole business is instinct; you either have it or you don't. Bernie has it to spare. Bernie's the guy behind many innovative TV shows that helped shape a culture: *Hee Haw*, *The Muppets*, *Saturday Night Live*. As a personal manager, he's stewarded the careers of Jim Henson, John Belushi, Dan Aykroyd, Gilda Radner, Martin Short and *Saturday Night Live* producer Lorne Michaels. Bernie came into the *Mr. Show* picture when he took over as Bob's manager at Brillstein/Grey Entertainment, his giant management/production firm. "I was always a sucker for Bob, but I only knew him as a writer and sometime performer," Bernie admits. "I had no idea who David Cross was."

Bernie recalls the guys' show in Aspen: "It was the first night of the comedy festival; I knew HBO was interested [in the show]. Bob and David did *Naked Phrase Guess*, and they really

David and Bob with Bernie Brillstein at a Mr. Show *panel, Museum of Television and Radio, Beverly Hills, February 1999.*

A NEW COMEDY DUO

When David and Bob originally developed the show, their concept was to share the performing with everybody. "Bob and I talked, in the very beginning before we even shot a thing, about creating a show sensibility that does not necessarily have to have Bob and me as a life force. That's why we called it *Mr. Show*, we didn't want to call it *Mr. Show with Bob and David*. We weren't interested in trying to pad a resume. We wanted to make a really funny show, and that's the best way to do it." "We never hesitated to use other people," adds Bob. "The ideas were always paramount on *Mr. Show*. So anybody could be doing them if they're good ideas." But both Bernie Brillstein and HBO told the guys that they must have an identity on the show; the argument was: 'People relate to people on American TV, they don't relate to a general idea.' "That's kind of true," admits Bob. "And we were willing to compromise and put ourselves out there. So we ended up going in this direction of using ourselves more often than we thought we would. But even now, I don't think people think of it as 'The Bob and David Show.' It's *Mr. Show*."

David: "You've built this identity for yourself and you find yourself sharing it with someone else, who up until a few years ago was a complete stranger, you never even heard of the guy. And now, all of a sudden, for better or for worse, the two of you create this really great thing. And to find yourself after being strong-minded and individualistic for so long, it's weird to realize that you're half, not whole. It can be a sacrifice."

Bernie Brillstein: "Bob and David each loved what the other did; they each respected the other for taking chances. When they go out there individually, the audience is going to be in for a good ride, or a bad ride, but they're never gonna sit there without an opinion. So there's a big risk that putting them together: it could dilute what they each do. But they did it, and the risk paid off. This was a situation where collectively, they had a really great affect on the audience. And amazingly, they have maintained their individuality."

David: "There's a reason that a number of people say we're like a married couple. As much as I hate to believe it and almost feel a little emasculated by it, it's true, we act like a married couple sometimes. And also he fucks me."

```
                    7/11/95                    1

                         SHOW OPEN:
                         THE CROSS/ODENKIRK
                         PROBLEM

    FADE IN:
    INT. STUDIO

                    DAVID/BOB
              Hi, everyone. Welcome to the
              show

                    BOB
              We thought we'd try something a
              little different and start
              tonight and tell you a little
              bit about ourselves.

                    DAVID
              Yes, so you can get to know us
              before we do our sketches.
              Start us off, Bob.

                    BOB
              Yes. Okay. Well...this is very
              hard...I'm not gay, I'm not gay.
              But sometimes, when I'm making
              love to a woman, I imagine
              there's a man, in the corner,
              watching, and touching himself.

                    DAVID
              What the fuck is wrong with you!
              Use some discretion! Nobody
              wants to know that!

                    BOB
              Huh? Well, y'know, forget I
              said it.

                    DAVID
              That's impossible! Now, for the
              rest of the show people are
              going to have that image in
              their heads. Geez! Alright,
              I'm from Atlanta, my family
              moved around a lot, and my
              favorite pig-out food is
              pizza...that's it.

                    BOB
              David, could I try one more?

                    DAVID
              No.
```

```
                    7/11/95                    2

                         SHOW OPEN
                         (Cont'd)

                    BOB
              Come on. I want people to think
              of me in a good light.

                    DAVID
              Okay.

                    BOB
              Alright. I'm an Imperial Wizard
              of the KKK.

                    DAVID
              That's horrible! You're a
              racist?!

                    BOB
              No, that's not implicit. The
              only people I hate are these
              Slackers.

                    (INTO: ASSHOLE SKETCH)
```

```
                    7/11/95                    33

                         NATURAL BORN DRUNK -
                         THE RONNIE DOBBS STORY
                         (Cont'd (17))

         ANOTHER PSA

                    BOB
              Hi, I'm Bob Odenkirk. By the
              time you see this, I will be
              dead. Why? I don't know. But
              they promised not to show this
              video until I passed away. Now
              I am going to read to you a list
              of people I hate, I hope they're
              sad, now that I'm gone. "David
              Cross. David J. Cross. D.
              Cross. David James Cross. D.J.
              Cross..."

         Bob comes out of the crowd.

                    BOB
              Turn that damn thing off!
              Goddamnit! They promised me!
```

From "The Cross/Odenkirk Problem." Show opener and a funny pre-taped video bit that followed Ronnie Dobbs' Entitilitus PSA.

hooked me, because that sense of humor is really my sense of humor. The balls — to be able to do what they did on stage. It really made me laugh. But their show that night really went into the crapper. They were really tanking."

Bernie realized that because David and Bob were not well known yet, they shouldn't attempt such avant-garde material without the audience knowing who they are. "It's asking way too much from the audience," Bernie explains. "I felt they were playing for the band, and I don't believe you get anywhere playing for the band. I think that works for a while. Everyone says, 'Boy are you hip. No one understood it.' But if you decide to make a living doing this, you better let the audience in on your secrets."

The next show was going to start in a few minutes, and Bernie made up his mind to talk to them. "I knew David's reputation of blowing up at business people, but I took a chance and told them, 'The audience doesn't know who you are. They've never heard of you, they don't know what your relationship is to each other, or to comedy.' I told them if they just did five minutes at the front of the show, just letting the audience know who they are, it would help a lot. I think the guys got it right away. They came out for the second show and they did five minutes — which is really what they ended up doing in the beginning of the TV show — that they had just made up. And maybe it was just luck, or maybe it was what I suggested, but the show went through the roof."

There was still no green light from HBO. Back home from Aspen, HBO wanted to see more material, a sign that they were not quite convinced — although Carolyn Strauss says that the premium cable channel was already committed. "From the beginning we always felt like we would make the show. We felt that this could really be something. [Asking Bob and David to showcase more material] was more getting the show in shape to shoot it."

In weeks, Bob, David and friends were back at the Upfront Theater in Santa Monica performing new sketches for an audience that included Strauss and Chris Albrecht (who was then HBO's Head of Programming). "We were standing out in the street, outside the theater," tells Bernie. "Chris asked me, 'Are you really behind this?' 'I wouldn't be here if I wasn't. What, do I like to come out to Santa Monica to visit? Of course I am.' And we proceeded to get a voluminous four-show order. But with very little money."

Bob's L.A. apartment on Sierra Bonita Drive where Bob and David wrote their live shows (and all of Season 1).

"As a company, HBO was not that interested," Bob admits. So basically, let's not say HBO wanted the show. Chris Albrecht and Carolyn Strauss wanted the show, and they were HBO execs and they had access to money." To quote Troy Miller: "It's not a normal show. The show wouldn't exist without Carolyn Strauss and Bernie Brillstein."

Technically, the first season was comprised of a four-episode pilot done on a two-episode budget. Troy explains, "The initial order from HBO was only for two shows. In doing the budgets early on we saw that we could go for two almost normal-budgeted shows, or four very tight-budgeted shows for this number." As Bob explains, their drive was to deliver as many shows as they could. "The more the better. The more that we could reassure them that, 'This show is going to be good, just trust us. We can produce this material and we can create this show.' What we were trying to do was create a show with very little structure. And with *Monty Python* as our guide — if you showed one episode of *Python* to a network and you said, 'So there's the show, what do you think?' I think they would rightfully say, 'It was funny, but what do you do next week? Are you going to see those same characters next week?' And if your answer is (as *Python's* would have been, as ours was), 'No, you won't see those same characters,' the network would want to know what *will* be the same each week. 'Well, those guys will come out and say, 'Hi.' And that's it. Everything else will be different.' Then the person ordering the show might not trust it: 'I understand that you made one episode and it was funny, but I don't trust that you can make another.' What we wanted to do was a show where the only thing that's going to stay the same is our sensibility, and us saying, 'Hi.' That's it. It will be funny; it will feel like a show. But beyond that, nothing is the same. So we wanted to take that opportunity to show HBO, really inundate them with our perspective on things and our sensibility."

The credit for stretching that already tiny budget across four episodes goes to Troy Miller. "It could never have been done with out Troy," says Bob. "He is an incredibly resourceful producer. He was able to make things happen cheaply, and we were able to produce four shows for that money. It's incredible what we did."

"NAKED PHRASE GUESS" AND "HECKLER CONVENTION"

Naked Phrase Guess, a sketch from Bob and David's earliest collaboration. The set up: Bob is eager to try improv for the first time. David happily obliges. He explains that a volunteer will escort Bob out of the room. While he's out of earshot, the audience will suggest a commonly known phrase, and Bob has to guess the phrase through the improvised scene with David. As Bob is being led out, David reminds the volunteer, "make sure he can't hear us, and he takes off all his clothes." Bob stops, "Huh? I have to take my clothes off?" "Yeah," replies David. "It's called *Naked Phrase Guess*, it's a very popular improv game. That's the way *The Groundlings* do it!" And, yes, Bob comes out completely nude, at once terrified and thrilled to finally be doing improv.

Bob: "To me the great thing about *Mr. Show* is that it was that it just was funny. There's really funny jokes and silliness. They're not overly clever, they're not absurdest, they're not shocking to no end. And *Naked Phrase Guess* was a scene that I think was just shocking to no real end. At the core of it, it's just a status thing where David is using his status to embarrass me. And it's really only about taking your clothes off in a room full of people, and how shocking that is and how much people get off on that. Not me, but audiences. So it's always going to work, because there is a naked guy there and it's always going to make people hoot 'n' holler. But it's not genuinely funny. We wrote it up for the first season of *Mr. Show*, but it just didn't work. But it makes people laugh, and it's fun to do live, so we saved it for a big dumb live show. And we did it for Comic Relief, which is a big, dumb live show."

Heckler Convention is a fairly elaborate scene they performed at the Montreal Comedy Festival in '94 and years later at the Aspen Comedy Festival, with 'plants' in the crowd. David gets introduced as popular college comic, Brad Klein, and does his inane, high energy act. "Are you ready for *the magazines*?!!" He wheels out a table stacked with magazines, and tells a dumb story using magazine names, holding them up as he goes. He is heckled from the audience — but it's just guys in town for the Heckler Festival (including Posehn and JB+KG at the Aspen performance). Brad pleads with him to stop ruining his act. The righteous heckler (Bob) argues, "Do we hurt or do we help?" He shows a video of all the pseudo-charitable work "Insults That Care," the hecklers' charitable organization, selflessly provides. The two shake hands, realizing they are on the same side.

David: "The Brad Klein character was something I did a couple of times at various places. It's based on a real comic named Brad Stein. He's this way over the top 'high energy' comic, but taken to ridiculous proportions. I'm actually not in shape enough to do it as crazy as he does it. He's like Robin Williams on crystal, which oddly enough, is something that Robin Williams might actually say. But regardless, that guy was/is a bad, bad comic."

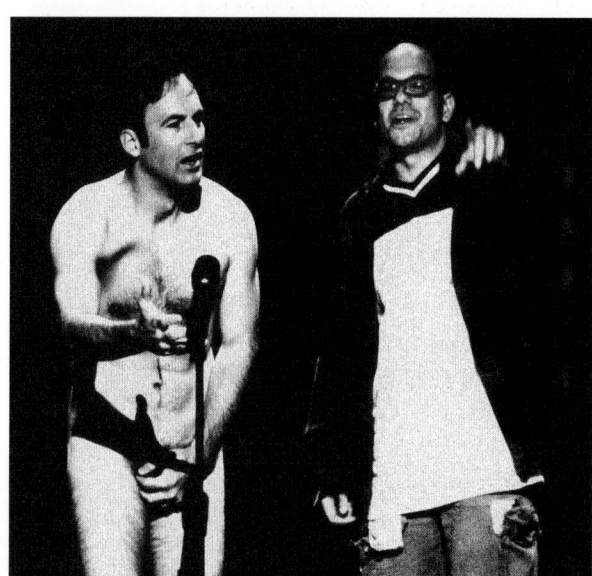

Bob and David on stage at Comic Relief '98, Radio City Music Hall, New York. (photo courtesy HBO and Comic Relief)

BOB BEFORE MR. SHOW

(left) College Days. One of many forays into facial hair. (middle) Lincoln Look. This was not a fake beard; (right) Robert Smigel, Dave Reynolds, Doug Dale, 1985, in the Chicago apartment on Wrightwood shared by roommates Bob, Smigel and Dale (among many others throughout the years).

Comedy Enlists Another Awkward Nerd

Unlike many of his generation, Bob wasn't raised in the glow of the family-room television. He grew up in Naperville, IL, the second oldest of seven kids, and his family just didn't have the TV on that much. They almost never went to the movies. "We just didn't watch a lot. We watched the *Mary Tyler Moore Show, The Carol Burnett Show,* and my dad liked *Hee Haw.* And that's about it. So the idea of becoming a performer, doing it for a living, was just ludicrous. But my brother Bill and I would perform at the dinner table every night; we'd get up and act out stuff. We wrote sketches in the basement."

Hee Haw aside, there were a few comedy shows that did make an impression on young Bob. When he was twelve, he loved a BBC program on PBS called *The Goodies.* Later, his favorites were *SCTV*, and Bill Murray and John Belushi on *Saturday Night Live.* And then, of course, there was *Monty Python.* "It amazed me. I still think it's the best show ever." An important turn for Bob occurred when he was taken to Chicago by his friend's parents to see The Second City's stage revue. It "planted the seed of a brutal dream" in his tender mind.

How, then, did this awkward kid living outside the realm of pop culture find his way into entertainment? College radio. During his college days at Southern Illinois University, a friend named Dan Manella offered him a radio show on the campus station, WIDB (W-Inter-Dormitory-Broadcasting). What resulted was *The Prime-Time Special.* (Bob explains, "It was on every Thursday at midnight; it was neither prime time, nor a special.") Bob's radio show on the closed-circuit station was, as Manella describes, "heavily influenced by *Saturday Night Live* (still in its early years), and *Monty Python*." The format of his show was basically *Mr. Show* on radio.

His routine went like this: after classes on Mondays, Bob would find an empty classroom, and sit down for two or three hours to write sketches and ideas. The next night, he'd meet with the other guys from the show and they'd brainstorm. On Thursdays at midnight, they took the bizarre little show on the air. Bob soon realized that each week, he was taking blank sheets of paper and filling them up with comedy.

That's when the notion of a "career" in comedy sprouted its wobbly legs. ("Before that, I didn't know what I wanted to do. Maybe be a DJ. A terrible thought.")

Seeking Something Other Than Magic In Chicago

Before he graduated, Bob set out to explore his options. Under the guise of a radio-show interview, he went to Chicago to ask Joyce Sloan, producer at The Second City, what it actually took to get on their stage. "It was depressing," he laments with self-pity. "All of her stories were *success stories*, very magical tales. When I asked her how John Belushi got started, she told me something like, 'Well, John walked in here and said, 'I want to be on the Main Stage!' He was delightful. We put him right up there!' Joe Flaherty's story was, 'Joe took a bus from Cleveland to Chicago, knocked on the door, and said, 'I'm gonna be on the Main Stage!' We thought he was hilarious, and a week later, he was on the Main Stage!' Well, I knew that wasn't me, that *magic*." Bob left the interview depressed. (When asked, Ms. Sloan says she does not recall this early meeting with Bob, but adds: "I'm always in love with all the actors, and you know how they get there: by working very, very hard.")

Immediately after that experience, he wandered into a bookstore down the street and spied Del Close. Del Close was the legendary stage director from The Second City. He had served as a mentor for many of the comedic greats (Bill Murray and Harold Ramis, among others). At that time, Close had just left The Second City to focus on acting and teaching.

Hesitantly, Bob approached Close, and asked if he would do an interview. The two talked over drinks at a bar, and then went to Close's "shitty apartment." Del Close inspired Bob. "His version of the creative life was *exciting*. But more importantly, it was real, lively, human. It wasn't so much what he said — it was, here was a guy who'd actually done it, and he was happy about his life. I realized that *people* do these jobs, not magical creatures." Bob was moved to try himself.

At the end of the '83 school year, just three credits shy of graduating, Bob moved to Chicago and jumped right in. He signed up for the

Three O's so they don't get sued. Robert Smigel's popular "All You Can Eat and the Temple of Dooom" ran at the Victory Garden Theater in Chicago, 1983-84.

Players Workshop of The Second City, writing and performing scenes. He performed every chance he could and began important friendships.

At the Workshop, Bob met Tom Gianas, a frequent collaborator. "We were cast into a children's theater show," Gianas remembers fondly. "Bob was a cowboy, and I was Goldilocks' father. It was a crazy show in front of a bunch of kids. But it was stage time."

Smigel, Dooom, & Saturday Night

By 1985, Bob was fully ensconced in his new pursuit. He started doing stand-up comedy as a local opener, and was producing and performing in several live shows. He wrote a one-person show (which Gianas directed), he produced and starred in a play, and he performed in various improvisation groups. One such sketch show, called *Yuk Shack* (an offshoot from Chicago's Practical Theater Company of which Brad Hall and Julia Louis-Dreyfus were members), was where a young Bob Odenkirk first impressed another young writer/performer named Robert Smigel. "I knew Bob from the Workshop," explains Smigel, "but *Yuk Shack* was the first time I'd seen Bob in a real show that people paid to see, and he was a complete stand-out, hilarious."

When Bob had arrived in Chicago, Smigel was in a hit show, called *All You Can Eat and the Temple of Dooom,* featuring Smigel, Jill Talley, Doug Dale, Todd Lambert, Dave Reynolds, Hugh Callaly and Debby Jennings. Bob was impressed with the show co-written by Smigel. They were a hit. "Every performance, the theater was packed," Bob recalls with amazement. "In a town with lots of established theater and improv, it was a big deal."

It was *Dooom* that led to Smigel's, and subsequently Bob's, first big break: getting hired at *Saturday Night Live*. It went like this: former *SNL* writers Al Franken and Tom Davis were casting their new movie project, *Another Saturday Night.* Dave Reynolds, cast member in *Dooom,* landed a lead as the dumb jock, and Bob took over some of Reynolds' parts in *Dooom*. Then, as Smigel admits, "it was just like dropping a big luck bomb; Dave Reynolds is a very sociable guy, and he charmed Al and Tom, ultimately, into coming and seeing our show. That was a very exciting night. We all wanted to be seen by Franken and Davis. But that was it. That was all we were looking to do: see what they thought, and have two people in show business who we knew. But it was great; they had a great time, and we all went out to dinner afterwards. They were very friendly and very complimentary about the show; they liked everybody. And that was that. And then about a month later, I was reading *TV Guide*, and it said that Lorne Michaels was coming back to *SNL*, and was hiring Al and Tom to produce. And we all got very excited very quickly." Franken and Davis recruited Smigel as a writer at *SNL* for the 1985 season.

Through Smigel, Bob began submitting material to *Saturday Night Live*. "Once Robert got in, we all had a purpose," says Reynolds, "and Bob was a machine; he was unbelievable. He started writing; he'd go into the backroom of his apartment, and he would just come out for air. I never saw anybody write more funny, interesting stuff." Bob wrote over the phone with Smigel, and sent in his own jokes and scripts. Some of it even made it onto the show. Bob remembers, "I was working as a food-runner at Ed Debevics in Chicago. I wasn't even a waiter. I was bringing hamburgers out to a table when Dennis Miller read my joke on the air for the first time. ('The statute of limitations on respecting Bob Hope for his earlier work ran out this week . . .')"

Smigel was one of the few writers to get rehired at *SNL* for the 1986-87 season, and he got Bob a meeting with Lorne Michaels.

In his interview with Lorne, Bob made a conscious choice to try not to come across as too eager, which, as he later admitted, was not a smart choice. "Of course I wanted a real job and I wanted to work there, but I went in there thinking Lorne would respect me more if I didn't rave about the place, like, 'Oh, I've always wanted this more than anything!' Later, I talked to other people who got hired there, like Mike Myers and Bonnie and Terry Turner, and they had all told Lorne it's all they ever wanted to do their whole life, their biggest dream. So I learned you're supposed to cream your pants when you go in to meet for *SNL*."

Bob's problem was a general lack of respect for authority. His whole attitude towards Lorne probably hurt any chance the two had at getting along. "I basically was a waiter and a stand-up, and I didn't respect anybody who was in power, and in this case it was Lorne. I just saw him as the guy who told people, 'No'. I didn't see him as the 'cool producer,' a guy who likes comedy, likes writers. He was just the money guy. I was the only person who saw it that way. And much later, I learned that I was not entirely correct."

Robert Smigel was relieved to have other writers of his own age on the SNL staff. "Bob, Conan O'Brien, and Greg Daniels filled a gap for me that season; we were all coming from the same place, comedically. A slightly sillier place, a little less directly satirical. When those guys came, they had less respect for the show than I did, and they made me feel more confident about my own sillier instincts. Before then, I tended to try to shape my style toward what I thought SNL was supposed to be."

Bob shared an office at SNL with other new writers: Ben Stiller, and later Conan O'Brien. "I remember Bob having really strange ideas," says Conan. "Bob and I would waste hours making each other laugh with just crazy stuff, and it was a complete waste of time, because it was never anything that could be turned into a sketch for Saturday Night Live; there was no internal logic to it."

Bob fought it out on staff at SNL for four seasons. "For me, being at SNL was so soul-destroying, and I couldn't get an idea on (the show) that was my own, and I felt so alone and so worthless in that city. I pushed myself so hard and took it so seriously. Too seriously, which probably hurt my writing more than anything. I took it all so personally."

Uphill Climb To Perform

At SNL, Bob was establishing himself as a writer, but wasn't given a chance to perform. However, during a hiatus after his third season on SNL, Tom Gianas put him in The Second City's Main Stage show, *Flag Smoking Permitted in Lobby Only*. Gianas was now the company director, and, at 29, he was the youngest director the Main Stage had ever known. "A number of people resented the both of us," Gianas explains. "Not only had I never directed at a Second City stage and went right to the Main Stage, but Bob never performed with Second City — usually performers work their way up to the Main Stage: two years with the Touring Company, then some time with ETC (the farming team), then, maybe, they get selected for the Main Stage. But I did it for the good of the show. I knew Bob was that good."

Joyce Sloan, The Second City producer who hired Gianas, explains, "I did not know who Bob was. It was enough that Tom wanted him. I trusted Tom so much as a director." Sloan admits that hiring an outsider for the main company was not the usual procedure. "There was no precedent set for this — and was there resentment? Yes. There were actors who were very jealous of Bob going to the company when they thought that they should have. But we made the decision and that was it. And we knew he'd be here until SNL started again, so he was going in just for the summer."

Bob and Conan O'Brien. The early days of developing Conan's new "Late Night" show, 1993.

HAPPY HAPPY GOOD SHOW

Summer 1988. During the writers' strike, Bob, Conan and Smigel took their material that didn't pass muster at *Saturday Night Live* and performed it in a live show called *Happy Happy Good Show* at the Victory Gardens Theater in Chicago. "None of us had done anything real, substantial as performers," says Bob. "I remember some scenes we did. There was the *Nude Beach* scene which Robert and Conan had written — it was on SNL the next year with Matthew Broderick — which was a bunch of people at a nude beach covering their genitals so we can be on TV, or in this case it was in the theater, and talking only about penises – just obsessed with each other's penises and genitalia. We did a sketch about a eunuch, that Conan wrote, who gets hired as a temp in an office, and we did the orignal *Super Fans* (Chicago Bears fans) sketch. The show didn't do that well — it got just so-so reviews. But it did well enough; we got to be in that theater. The reviews didn't hurt our feelings too much. We were just trying to have a good time, and the show was pretty fun to do."

Conan O'Brien: "Going way back to 1988, Smigel, Bob and I were all interested in the same thing — none of us needed to be the biggest star in America. We just wanted to go someplace and do our thing and have people who like it get a chance to see it. And the nice thing, is we all get to do that now."

(top) Early "Conan" writing staff, 1993. From left: Bob, Dave Reynolds, Robert Smigel, Conan O'Brien, Andy Richter, Marsh McCall, Louis C.K., Dino Stamatopoulos, Michael Gordon; (bottom left) Bob and Dana Carvey at "Saturday Night Live," circa 1990; (bottom right) The Second City, Chicago, Main Stage. Tim Meadows, Bob, Jill Talley, Chris Farley, Farley's last show before departing for SNL, summer 1990.

Aside from some lingering resentment, the show went extremely well. Bob joined a work in progress. All summer he wrote scenes with and for Jill Talley, Tim Meadows, Dave Pasquesi, Holly Wortell, Tim O'Malley and Chris Farley, including Farley's 'motivational speaker,' which became an instant favorite when Farley did it on *Saturday Night Live*. "I wrote that all out in one sitting. Just the way it went. That doesn't happen very often, where it flows out of you. I came in to rehearsal, and I just handed it to Farley: 'Here. Try this.' I knew he could make it infinitely funnier than I could. And he made it great. The first time he read it, that character just poured out of him. He was such a great performer."

Getting A Life In L.A.

In 1991, after his fourth season on *SNL*, Bob had plans to go to L.A. to consider a permanent move to the West Coast. On his way, the unexpected happened when he stopped in Austin, TX, to visit his friend Steve Meisner. "Meisner was a huge *Get A Life* fan, so every night we watched these episodes he had on tape. And after, like, the third night, we'd watched four episodes, and the next morning, Steve said, 'You got a phone call, it's your agent.' It was, indeed, and he asked me, 'Do you want to write for *Get A Life*?' And I responded, 'Hell, yeah!' Steve was happy for me, but here we were in his shitty little duplex in the outskirts of Austin, and I get an offer to write for the show we'd been watching every night, laughing at. It was strange, fun, and a bit unreal."

Bob grabbed the chance to make the official move to Los Angeles, job in hand. Once in Hollywood, Bob focused on performing his own show every week at the Upfront Theater in Santa Monica, the owners of which (Jeff Michalski and Jane Morris) he already knew from Chicago. "It wasn't really a formal show; I went to Santa Monica every week, and got on stage for an hour, and did whatever the fuck I wanted to do. Andy Dick was in it. It was constantly evolving." His friends Janeane Garofalo, Ben Stiller, and Judd Apatow would sometimes come by. Janeane recalls, "I would go to Bob's one man show because I enjoyed it so much. Plus, I was still friends with [mutual friend, former roommate, and comic] Jeff Garlin, and then I met Andy Dick. I had met Conan O'Brien and Robert Smigel through Bob. It was a comedy group of people who just intrigued me. There were just a lot of funny people."

Andy Dick remembers hooking up with Bob at The Upfront: "Bob was doing a one-man show and I was doing my one-man show, *Andy Dick's Circus of Freaks*, and Dino [Stamatopoulos] was in that, and my friend Tom Bell, and a bunch of other freaks. And it was hosted by a character that I play called, 'Chester the Retarded Bachelor.' And that was my show. It was not very well received. My show started at midnight, but Bob's show was earlier, his had an audience. Sometimes my shows had more people on stage than there were in the audience. So sometimes Bob would stick around and watch our show. He loved it. And I then I started coming early to watch his show, and we started making up bits with me in his show. In one bit, we would pretend that he also taught improv and that I was his only student right now, and I was taking my final exam and I had to do these improv games in front of the audience, solo, led by him. Where he would take suggestions and then he would throw them at me and then I'd have to perform them. And he'd do them more and more rapid fire until I finally went nuts, and was screaming at him, 'Why the fuck would you do this to me?! It's impossible. No one could fucking do this!! You're an asshole!' And he would say, 'I think I know someone who just passed!' And then I just went off crying. And eventually it just became Bob's show that featured me."

Bob's initial acting break was on Dennis Miller's first talk show, the nightly, late-night network one. "Dennis Miller put me on his show, doing monologues, little pieces; he gave me my first chance. And that counted for something when I got *Stiller*; it probably helped Ben make the choice to use me as a performer."

```
                                          MOTIVATION - 3

BOB:       Hey, Matt, we're ready for you.  His speech is called,
           "Go For It."  Make him feel like there's a crowd.
           (SHOUTING)  Matt?!  Now, buddy!

JILL AND TIM MEADOWS BEGIN TO CHANT AS IF THEY WERE A CROWD AT A
ROCK CONCERT.

CHRIS ENTERS AS MATT FOLEY--MOTIVATIONAL SPEAKER.

CHRIS:     All right.  As your father probably told you, my name is
           Matt Foley, and I am a motivational speaker.  Let's get
           a little, better acquainted by letting me give you a
           little bit of a scenario of what my life is all about.

           First off, I am thirty-five years old, I am divorced, and
           I live in a van down by the river.  Now you kids are
           probably gonna go out there and think, "Hey, I'm gonna
           get the world by the tail.  I'm gonna wrap it around,
           pull it down, and put it in your pocket."

           Well, I'm here to tell you that you're probably gonna
           find out, as you go out there, that you're not gonna
           amount to JACK SQUAT!  (TURNING TO TIM)  Now, young man,
           what would you like to do with your life?!

MEADOWS:   Well, Matt, I'd like to become a writer.

CHRIS:     Weeellllll, la-di-frecken-da!  So we got ourselves a
           writer here.

BOB:       Well, actually Matt, Kate and I have encouraged Byron in
           his writing.

CHRIS:     Dad, I wish you could just shut your big, YAPPER!!  I
           wonder... from what I've heard Byron, you're using paper,
           not for writing, but for rolling doobies.  Now you can
           do a lot of doobie rolling, when you're living in a van
           down by the river.  (TURNING TO JILL)  Well, young lady?
           What do you want to do with your life?

JILL:      I'd like to live in a van, down by the river.

CHRIS:     Well, you'll have plenty of time to live in a van down
           by the river, when you're living in a van down by the
           river!  Now, you kids are probably asking yourselves,
           "Matt, how can we get on the right track?"  Well, there's
           only one real solution to that.  And that is to move my
           gear in and I'm gonna bunk with you, buddy.  I'm moving
           in and we're gonna be BUDDIES!  We're gonna be PALS!
           We're gonna WRESTLE!  Old Matt's gonna be in your shadow.
```

```
                                          MOTIVATION - 4

CHRIS EXITS TO COLLECT HIS GEAR.

JILL:      No...

MEADOWS:   No, Matt, you don't have to do that!  Look, we'll never
           smoke pot again.

CHRIS STICKS HIS HEAD BACK IN THE DOOR.

CHRIS:     I don't give a rat's behind, because I'm moving in.  I'm
           sick and tired of living in a van, down by the river!

THE FAMILY ALL STARE AT EACH OTHER IN SHOCK.

BOB:       Lock the doors!
```

Original "Motivational Speaker" scene, written by Bob for Chris Farley at Second City. (inset) Bob with Chris Farley at Second City, 1990.

(top to bottom) Utterback poster for Second City, Chicago Main Stage Review, 1990. (Front: Odenkirk, Talley, Meadows, Farley. Back: O'Malley, Wortell, Ruby Streak (musical director), Pasquesi. (Original art courtesy Bill Utterback and The Second City); "Half My Face is a Clown," Bob's one-man show. Performed summer of 1989, during second year hiatus at "SNL" at The Second City's ETC stage, directed by Tom Gianas. (characters from this show: Bazooka Joe comic, and Lincoln); Show-Acting-Guy at the Upfront Theater in Santa Monica, 1992.

Andy Dick says Stiller hired his cast on the spot: "Ben came and saw me and Bob live at the Upfront Theater and said to us, 'You're in my show. I want you in my show, no audition, the end!'" "I'm sure it happened like that,' laughs Stiller, regarding Andy's recollection of the atypical way *The Ben Stiller Show* was cast. "There was no network approval or anything like that. Nobody at FOX knew or cared what we were doing. This whole idea of the show – whenever I think about it I can't believe they let us all do what we were doing. We all came and said, 'Look this is what we want to do, and this is the ensemble: Andy, Bob, me and Janeane.' I wanted Bob to be in the cast because I was really impressed with him. I met him at *SNL*. He was such a strong sketch writer, and I knew he was really funny and looking to perform more."

"I was in a great space in a lot of ways with *The Ben Stiller Show* in that Judd (Apatow, co-creator of the show) and Ben gave me a lot of respect. So I had a great freedom and I felt great about the opportunity creatively. I had a lot of fun doing it," says Bob. "The only observation I have about the show – it was very short lived, obviously, and it was getting better as we were doing it, but it never really got to become a whole show. I think almost every single piece had its merits and was funny in its own way. It just didn't necessarily hang together. Which was a result, maybe, of not having enough time to do the show. I think it was getting closer to a sensibility in its later episodes. Overall, though, it was an amazing opportunity and a great time."

When *The Ben Stiller Show* ended, Garry Shandling gave Bob the part of 'Stevie Grant,' Larry's young-turk agent on *The Larry Sanders Show,* Shandling's inspired HBO series. Bob was plainly grateful. "I thought it was a great show; I was really excited to do it. And it was a strong choice for Garry to make." Bob clearly recalls that audition: "Garry took me aside and worked with me, which most of the time people don't do at auditions."

"I don't remember being interested in anyone else for that part," tells Shandling. "My instinct about Bob was that he is an actor. He's extraordinarily bright, and I had no doubt that he would grow into being the actor that he was on *Larry Sanders*. I suppose one of the elements I like to incorporate is the writer/performer aspect of someone, because in *The Larry Sanders Show,* going week to week, it would be great to have someone who could also contribute to the writing of their own character, and think of funny things, and have their own funny ideas. And he did all of that as well."

(above) Bob's "Show Acting Guy" at the Upfront Theater in Santa Monica, and joined by (right) Andy Dick and Ken Campbell, 1992. (below) Bob at the UnCabaret in West Hollywood, 1995. Photos by Claudia Kunin.

Certainly one of the most interesting projects Bob has undertaken is *Life On Mars*, a low-budget, half-hour comedy pilot he developed for HBO with Dino Stamatopoulos. *Mars* was a low-key, high-brow sitcom about friends hanging out in a hip coffee house called Mars (this was a year before *Friends*). It starred Bob, Janeane Garofalo, and Jack Plotnick. Bernie Brillstein, Bob's manager, remembers it well: "I think *Life on Mars* is probably one of the best things Bob's ever done. I love it, and if was shown today, it would get on the air. It was just two years too early."

Bob had to figure out what was next. "Somebody once said 'You don't create something because you want to do it — when did anything good ever come from tinkering around and dabbling? You do it because on some level you *have to* do it.' That's what *Mr. Show* was for me: I felt, 'I gotta write this goddamn sketch show — I know I've done sketch shows, I've done them for years, but I've never really done them right, the way I wanted to, and I've got to try. I know I've got a better show in me.' I always had ideas of a great sketch show — having the sketches intermingle, having a theme, having a tight group of performers. Where it's more about the energy of the show, it comes and grabs you pretty quick — in a minute, you're into the sketch. And where the ideas are as much the stars as the performers. It's not about celebrities (cast members or guest stars) — it's about the *show*."

AFTERTHOUGHTS

Conan O'Brien: "With *Mr. Show*, Bob didn't change to get people to like what he was doing, he just did what he wanted to do, and it's like, 'If you build it, they will come.' And the fans came to *Mr. Show*, and got to know Bob (and David), and got to understand that sensibility and really like it on its own terms. That seems more like the key. I never thought either one of us were people who could walk in front of an audience that didn't know us that well, and blow them away. They sort of had to figure out this weird rhythm first."

Bernie Brillstein: "Bob is competitive, but mostly with himself. He came up to me during a taping, and said, 'This is really not one of our good shows.' Meanwhile, the show's hysterical. He's always picking on himself. Probably a Catholic thing."

David: nine and a half years old. Photo courtesy Susie Cross.

DAVID BEFORE MR. SHOW

"David always lived by the seat of his pants," says Mark Rivers, struggling musician turned comedy writer and David's friend since age 16. "He couldn't earn what he needed, was always borrowing, then trying hard to pay it back — and still he was uncompromising [about his art and his lifestyle]. I always thought, 'Why does *he* get to live like that?? I have to compromise. I work this shitty job.' But David wouldn't bend. It's funny to think — you would never have guessed it about David that he would go far."

David Cross, however, just never questioned that he would achieve success. Never. Being in Boston eventually allowed him to survive off of stand-up comedy and not have a day job. "I didn't live well, but I didn't have to work in some mailroom. There were times when I was frustrated: 'When is it gonna come?' and 'I'm getting tired of being poor.' But I just never questioned that I would one day be here."

He attributes much of his success to luck. "I know a lot of people who are funnier than I am, more talented than I am, who are not as successful. I think a lot of it is right place, right time, good attitude, good people around you. Luck. But I honestly don't think I would have been able to obtain the success without some level of compromise if it weren't for *Mr. Show*. As much as I hate to admit it, I know myself well enough to know that I would have been seduced into doing a sitcom. At some point I would have broken down, compromised, and then been able to find a way to justify doing it."

Loud, Obnoxious, Jokey Kid

There was no single pivotal event that drew David to comedy — but he had an early awareness that it was the only thing he could do. "I couldn't do anything else creative. Couldn't create music, or draw. But it worked out well, because I liked it." He describes himself growing up as always kind of a loud, obnoxious, jokey guy. He admits, "Sometimes my humor was just shock-value comedy or confrontational to authority figures. But always humorous."

Throughout his youth, his father continually moved the family around, and David had to cope with constantly being the new kid, the strange kid. "You have about four seconds to make that impression if you don't want to get beat up." He dealt with things by not taking much seriously, and that's where the tone of his sense of humor developed.

"My dad got fired a lot. He did everything and anything — although I question most of the stories I grew up with. But he got fired a lot, or quit, knowing he was going to get fired. My Dad doesn't take to authority figures at all. He doesn't like anybody telling him what to do. The family would pay the cost for his ego and pride... and he had nothing to back it up. He sold women's clothing; he worked in the restaurant industry; the hotel industry; he was a sales rep. A lot of easy money schemes. I don't know what's true and what are bullshit stories. But I know we were the bane of his life. We held about as much fascination to him as a ViewMaster. I don't think we meant anything to him in real terms. He faked being a Dad."

David was born in Atlanta, but six months later they left for Florida. He and his younger sisters were then taken to New York, where they bounced around the state for five years. Next was Connecticut. You get the picture. Ultimately, the family returned to Atlanta, where they shacked up anywhere they could — sometimes at a Holiday Inn, sometimes getting evicted.

In Atlanta, David turned ten and stayed until he was nineteen, finally laying down some roots. He discovered the punk scene, enrolled in the School of the Arts, and hung out with a group of like-minded friends. He even started doing stand-up comedy at open mic nights, but it was nothing he was pursuing as a career; it was more of a way to meet people.

Pathetic & Cross Comedy

The day after high school graduation, he left for New York. He had no plan; he was just floating. By this time, he had made an art out of meandering through life. He lived hand to mouth, never with any goals in mind. In fact, he actively avoided making any potentially limiting choices. He went to Boston to start at Emerson College, which he promptly dropped out of. He wasn't really trying. At anything. But before long he hit on a couple of biggies: partying and sketch comedy. Both, perhaps in combination, gave him direction and focus that would guide his life and create a career. "I was really straight, I didn't really party that much until college. I started experimenting with a much more concerted effort. I found I had a high tolerance. I just loved it."

High school production of "West Side Story," summer 1980.

David joined a college sketch group, called *This is Pathetic*. Other players included Laura Kightlinger, John Ennis, and Anthony Clark. He also started to perform as a stand-up more regularly. Janeane Garofalo recalls their prolific open-mic days in Boston: "We were the same age, seniors in college, doing open mics. Those were the days where you could do stand-up seven nights a week, and there were a million places to do open-mics and to do paid gigs, which is not the case anymore. There was an unbelievably fertile comedy community, which sustained that kind of fever pitch, until around '92-'93, and then it went bust."

For David, though, it was not particularly easy. He never fit the types of acts they were booking at the Boston clubs. In 1990, a cool scene emerged at Catch A Rising Star comedy club. It rose directly out of what was lacking in the Boston comedy scene. The Boston scene at the time was "a loud, dumb, pandering, racist, homophobic type scene," as David describes it. "There was a lot of really bad comedy because the scene supported it. People were doing open mics for about four months, and then — boom — getting work as stand-ups. They were all copying other comics. Really unoriginal, really dumb. It was the loudest scene in Boston, so it got the most attention. And then there was Catch, this tiny, little, great club in Cambridge that always had headier acts. It was like the snobs vs. the slobs."

At Catch, Monday and Tuesday nights belonged them: David, Louis C.K., Janeane Garofalo, Sam Seder, Chuck Sklar, Marc Maron, Laura Kightlinger, Jonathan Groff, and Jon Benjamin, among others. David was hosting the Tuesday night open mics there. After a couple weeks, he approached the club manager and was given the night to do something different. "We really took over, sometimes in a good way, sometimes in an obnoxious way," says David.

David pulled together a group of about twelve writer-performers (including John Ennis and Paul Kozlowski), and started what became *Cross Comedy*. They combined elements of theater, performance art, and stand-up comedy, and they took risks. What quickly evolved was an off-beat show that David describes as being very similar to *Mr. Show* in structure: a seamless flow of scenes and ideas, with themes and links between otherwise unrelated scenes, but "not as fully realized."

"A big part of David's vision for the show was to suck the audience in — making them think one thing, and then have something else happen," says John Ennis. The group would introduce 'fake' comics, and generally keep the audience on edge so they were never sure what's real. Ennis recounts one of his favorites: "We would start with [group member] Cary Prusa being introduced as an open mic comic. Some of us were planted in the audience, we'd start cheering — the audience didn't know who we were. He tells an unfunny joke, and we howl — 'Tell the one about Mrs. McGully by the water fountain!' So he starts doing jokes about 'work,' and it's making us, his 'co-workers,' laugh, but the rest of the audience hates him."

"The audience started catching on and really getting into it," says David. "We got to do another show the next week. We really found the show. We did characters and videos; we would segue stuff in; it had a beginning and an end. And it was different every week, for better or for worse. Some things were really good, and some things were really bad. But it was very democratic; we would vote as a group [on which pieces made into the show]; everyone got a chance to put their stuff up. It may have suffered because of that."

Ennis emphasizes that David's role as producer was not an easy one: "There were 16 people, very tight, trying to fill an hour and a half. So there was an incredible amount of jockeying from people to get their bits in. And so, every week, it would be all these complainers, and everyone wondering, 'Why wasn't I in this scene?' and, 'Why didn't this happen?' and David handled it very well. During that two-year period, David grew up more than I ever saw him grow. He was not just in charge of people that he thought were funny, but people that he *loved*. And he's gotta somehow juggle all that, and he really did it well. People respected him more and more with each show."

Comedian/writer and then-roommate of David's, Louis C.K., adds, "Up to that point, David was just a rebellious stand-up who drank a lot and smoked pot and hung out with a certain group of guys. He was very funny but very difficult; he didn't like any clubs or any comics. That's who he was. But then when *Cross Comedy*

(all) Summer of '85. One of David and John Ennis' vagabond Boston to L.A. road trips.

came around, he became deadly serious, and he focused on it, and he became so into the details and putting the show on right. It changed him completely."

Tim Sarkes, David's manager since the Boston days, describes *Cross Comedy* as "a really raw type of a thing, all over the map," but says it was the inevitable next step in the town's creative cycle. "The Boston scene had become creatively stale; the whole process of being experimental was gone. *Cross Comedy* was on the right road, but it had a long way to go." Louis C.K. adds, "There wasn't anything like it at the time on TV, and it was way better than sketch comedy anywhere. It was just Tuesday night at Catch; there wasn't a lot at stake. So the only thing left to do is do it your favorite way, and try to make the show really work, just that night. And then go to the bar and drink."

Their audiences were usually great. "We didn't have a huge fan base, but we had a loyal fan base," remarks Ennis. *Cross Comedy* started as this weird, alternative, late night thing, which at first drew only a small portion of Boston's comedy audience — those who were looking for something that didn't stink. And eventually, through word of mouth, a larger audience found them. Ultimately there was a ton of publicity. They were booked to headline the whole week at Catch and other clubs. Very soon they were able to book themselves into a 500-seat theater, four weekends in a row. They used live music, hiring a different band for the show each weekend. "For a very short, brief time, it became a very big thing," David recounts. "It definitely peaked."

Sometime collaborator Mark Rivers feels *Cross Comedy* never really got its due. "It was unbelievable that they had all these incredibly talented people, but their audience was mostly an underground following of their musician friends, comedian friends, and bike messenger friends. They just couldn't gener-

1986. No money for headshots.

Failing At Nothing In L.A.

David stayed in Boston for nine years. He did make a couple of trips to Los Angeles. According to David, the trips were relatively pointless, never having any objective. John Ennis, who was with him on those excursions, says maybe David remembers it that way because they *failed* on those trips: "The way that I remember it, we were going out [to L.A.] to see what we can do." Either way, the result was just more aimlessness, and more drinking. It was his "most unhealthy period of drinking," David admits. "I was just fucking around. I lived in a car, then on this guy's floor, then in the back of the kitchen in a frat house. I spent all my money on entertainment." As friend Louis C.K. puts it, "Dave was choosing his own lifestyle. He was kind of a nomad."

Ennis tells of one brilliant slapdash venture the guys conjured up on one trip to L.A.: "David went down to Venice Beach, he had watched people make earrings, and realized, 'Oh, I can just buy this stuff, and make 'em and sell 'em.' So that was our plan. But the glue that we used was improper, and it began to melt. So these people were walking away with earrings for $8.00 — and we fully worked out this whole comedic spiel while we're sitting on the beach — and while we were trying to sell the earrings to someone else, they'd come back, 'These earring are melting!' And the person buying puts them down and walks away, and this woman wants her money back. And we said, 'you know, we sold four, that's $32.00, let's get out of here.' It took us all day to sell four pair. David would come home every Friday, with a bottle of cheap, bullshit whiskey, but we loved it, and we'd go get a Fatburger. That was our big, end of the week, 'we'll get through another week' thing."

Tired Of Being Poor

In 1992, Boston pal Janeane Garofalo was in Los Angeles, and she was lobbying for David to be a writer for the new Fox sketch comedy show, *The Ben Stiller Show*. But David was having a good time in Bean Town with his sketch group. He wasn't ready to face any of the opportunities that may have been springing up, and he declined. "He was reluctant to leave Boston and that lifestyle, and basically running comedy, being a huge fish in a small pond," grants Janeane.

"The only thing that mattered to David was his craft," says manager Sarkes. "Two things he didn't care about: the politics of the business and making money."

ate the kind of excitement that they deserved." Louis C.K. offers a different perspective: "Especially with comedy, people always have this feeling that every show that's good has this obligation to be an enormous success. I always felt that *Cross Comedy*'s level of success was perfectly appropriate — Catch used to always be packed, they had their audience who loved them. *Cross Comedy* got exactly as big in Boston as it was meant to be. I think that it's great that it just did that and then it died."

(left) "Cross Comedy," 1990-92. Front: Ed Driscoll, Helene Lantry, David, Jon Benjamin. Back: Cary Prusa, Lauren Dombrowski, John Ennis, Jim DeCroteau, David Waterman, Chris Scheeno, Jonathan Groff. (Not pictured: Sam Seder, Paul Kozlowski and Mike Lee); (right) David and John Ennis, from "Cross Comedy"; (below) Pages from a "Cross Comedy" scene, written by David Cross, Lauren Dombrowski and David Waterman.

A few months later, though, David got another call from L.A. A slot had opened up on Stiller's writing staff: would David join the show in mid-season? He reconsidered, and sent a writing submission. It was Friday when he got the offer. The job was his, but he had to start Monday. "I thought, 'Y'know, I'm sick of being poor. Just sick of it.' I made the decision... And that's why moving to L.A. was such a big deal. Even if I didn't say it out loud, I knew this was where I cut the shit. After all those years of just floating, I knew my life would change." Any regrets? "I have no regrets, but I do miss a lot of the carefree times." David loaded up his '76 Chevy Malibu, and drove to Los Angeles in 3 1/2 days.

As writers on Stiller, David and Bob met for the second time. The two had their first opportunity to work together, but, once again, no sparks were ignited. Quite the opposite, actually — Bob wasn't particularly congenial toward him, and the two merely tolerated each other.

When he arrived, David didn't know anyone on the show except Janeane, but she wasn't a writer, and therefore, she wasn't around. "It was kind of intimidating," David confesses. "I was a little cocky — I had come from this experimental theater, and what they were doing on Stiller wasn't exactly my cup of tea. In fact, I didn't like parody at all, and the celebrity impersonation thing I don't really write for. It took me a while to get into the mind-set of the show. Also, I came in mid-season; everybody else was already established there. Some of the writers, Rob Cohen, Brent Forrester, were really nice. Bob wasn't that nice; he was just not interested (in me). But he did fuck with me a couple of times. I felt like I did all through my life, when I would always be the new kid in school, and kids would fuck with me, and I knew they were fucking with me, and they knew that I knew they were fucking with me, and you have to do the little dance. On my second day, there was this writers' meeting, and Ben wanted to do a take-off on A Few Good Men. Everyone's trying to come up with angles, and I didn't give a shit. They're pitching ideas like 'traffic court,' and so on, and I just piped up and said, 'What if it's Boy Scouts — you take all that drama and you just reduce it to Boy Scouts.' Ben liked the idea. Then, Bob stood up (as to end the meeting) and said, 'That's great, David, write it up.' And everyone left the room. Bob just pushed the whole thing off on me; he knew exactly what he was doing. And I didn't want to write it. I spent the first week watching that fucking movie trailer. That's how I spent my whole first week on the show."

```
                    THE JUST-BEEN-DUMPEDS
         BY DAVID CROSS, LAUREN DOMBROWSKI AND DAVID WATERMAN
                         DAVID
          YOU KNOW, SPRING IS IN THE AIR, AND YOU KNOW WHAT THAT MEANS,
          NEW RELATIONSHIPS, AND YOU KNOW WHAT THAT MEANS, THE PAINFUL
          END OF THOSE VERY SAME NEW RELATIONSHIPS.  AND COINCIDENTALLY,
          THREE OF OUR CAST MEMBERS WERE ALL DUMPED ON THE VERY SAME
          WEEKEND, WHICH IS ALWAYS A HOOT.  ANYWAY, WE DECIDED TO WRITE
          A SKETCH ABOUT IT.  IT'S CALLED THE JUST-BEEN-DUMPEDS, AND
          HERE IT IS.

          BLACKOUT.
          LIGHTS UP ON DAVID IN BATHROBE STARING AT THE PHONE.
          THERE IS A LONG PAUSE.
                         DAVID
          FUCKING BITCH.

          ENTER EARL IN BATHROBE.
                         EARL
          ANY CALLS.
```

DUMPEDS TWO

EARL
WELL, HEY, MAN, WE'RE BACHELORS AGAIN.

DAVID
ALRIGHT, MAN.

EARL
YOU KNOW, WE CAN HANG OUT AND DRINK BEER.

DAVID
ALRIGHT, MAN. (THEY TRY TO HIGH FIVE AND MISS. ENTER LAUREN IN OVERCOAT).

LAUREN
(IN SHAKY VOICE) HI GUYS. WHAT'S UP.

EARL AND DAVID
HEY LAUREN.

LAUREN
DRINKING ALREADY? (SHE TAKES OFF COAT TO REVEAL ROBE).

DAVID
IT'S SEVEN O'CLOCK.

EARL
IT IS? OH, PUT ON "GOOD MORNING, AMERICA". (DAVID TURNS ON TV)

VO
THIS MORNING ON "GOOD MORNING, AMERICA", EVERYBODY'S IN LOVE.

ALL
TURN IT OFF!!

DAVID
WANT A BEER?

LAUREN
NO. GOT ANY WHISKEY?

DAVID
YEAH, HERE. (HE GIVES HER A WHISKEY, SHE TAKES OFF SUNGLASSES TO REVEAL EYES STAINED WITH STREAMED MASCARA)

EARL
HEY, ARE YOU OK?

LAUREN
YEAH, I FEEL REALLY, REALLY GOOD ABOUT IT. I MEAN, AT LEAST I KNOW WHERE I STAND NOW. BY THE WAY, I HAD MY CALLS FORWARDED HERE. DID YOUR PHONE RING AT ALL?

DUMPED THREE

DAVID AND EARL
NO.

LAUREN
ARE YOU SURE?

DAVID
YEAH, I'VE BEEN SITTING HERE.

LAUREN
WELL, MAYBE IT RANG WHILE YOU WERE OUT OF THE ROOM.

DAVID
NO, I'VE BEEN SITTING HERE THE WHOLE TIME.

LAUREN
WELL, MAYBE IT RANG WHILE YOU WERE IN THE BATHROOM.

DAVID
NO (HE HOLDS UP JAR) I'VE BEEN PISSING IN THIS JAR.

LAUREN
WELL ARE YOU SURE THE PHONE IS WORKING?

DAVID
YEAH, WHY, WHO ARE YOU EXPECTING A CALL FROM.

LAUREN
OH, IT'S A REALLY IMPORTANT CALL FROM MY...CABLE COMPANY.

DAVID
OH, YEAH, OF COURSE. SO, YOU'RE FEELING OK?

LAUREN
I FEEL REALLY POSITIVE ABOUT IT. I MEAN, THERE'S SO MUCH MORE ROOM IN THE BED NOW, AND, I DON'T HAVE TO SHAVE MY LEGS IF I DON'T WANT TO, AND...HEY CAN YOU GUYS USE A BOX OF CONDOMS?

DAVID AND EARL
NO.

EARL
ANYBODY NEED SOME SCENTED CANDLES?

DAVID AND LAUREN
NO.

DAVID
ANYBODY WANT MY COPY OF ROXY MUSIC'S AVALON?

LAUREN AND EARL
NO.

DUMPED FOUR

LAUREN
ANYBODY KNOW HOW TO REMOVE A TATOO?

DAVID AND EARL
YEAH. ANALGESIC ELECTROLYSIS THERAPY. (THEY RUB THEIR ARMS)

LAUREN
ARE YOU SURE THE PHONE IS WORKING? MAYBE YOUR ANSWERING MACHINE IS FUCKING IT UP.

EARL
YOU KNOW, WE HAVE TO MAKE A NEW MESSAGE ANYWAY. (HE RECORDS INTO THE MACHINE) HI, YOU HAVE REACHED 628-3392, THE HOME OF DAVID AND EARL. WE CAN'T COME TO THE PHONE RIGHT NOW, THAT'S BECAUSE WE'RE OUT, MAYBE DANCING, OR AT A PICNIC WITH SOME SPECIAL FRIENDS. BUT JUST REMEMBER, WHEN YOU CALL HERE, YOU'RE CALLING FOR A PARTY!

DAVID
(INTO MACHINE) YEAH, SO FUCK YOU!!

LAUREN
YOU KNOW, I'M THINKING, MAYBE MY CALL FORWARDING ISN'T WORKING. I'M GOING TO CHECK MY MACHINE. (SHE DIALS PHONE AND WE HEAR LAUREN'S VOICE..) HI THIS IS LAUREN. I'M NOT HERE TO TAKE YOUR CALL, BUT RIGHT NOW I CAN BE REACHED AT 628-3392. IF YOU CAN'T REACH ME THERE, I'LL BE HOME BETWEEN TWO AND FOUR MONDAY, THURSDAY MORNING TIL 11;30, AND ALL WEEKEND LONG, FRIDAY, SATUDAY AND SUNDAY. AND I'LL BE AT A CONFERENCE ALL DAY MONDAY BETWEEN NINE AND FOUR, BUT I CAN GET OUT OF IT, I MEAN IF YOU WANT TO TALK, OR YOU WANT TO DO SOMETHING. I USUALLY SHOWER BETWEEN 8:00 and 8:10, BUT I DON'T NEED TO SAY THAT, BECAUSE YOU ALREADY KNOW THAT, DON'T YOU. SO LEAVE A MESSAGE... IF YOU... PLEASE...(THE BEEP CUTS HER OFF) (ALL THREE HEAVE A BIG LONG SIGH)

EARL
HEY, WHY ARE WE SO DOWN IN THE DUMPS? I MEAN, WE SHOULD BE LIVING THE GGOD LIFE NOW. LET'S FORGET ABOUT THE PAST. LET'S GET OUT THERE AND ENJOY OUR LIVES!

DAVID
YOU'RE RIGHT.

LAUREN
WE'RE JUST FEEDING INTO OUT OWN MISERY. I MEAN, WE STILL HAVE EACH OTHER, RIGHT? I MEAN, FRIENDS ARE IMPORTANT, TOO.

DAVID
LET'S GET ON WITH OUR LIVES! I KNOW IT SOUNDS TRITE, BUT THERE'S A LOT OF PEOPLE OUT THERE. WE ARE THREE DESIREABLE PEOPLE, SO LET'S ENJOY OURSELVES.

Pages from a "Cross Comedy" scene, written by David Cross, Lauren Dombrowski and David Waterman. (inset) Cross Comedy publicity shot number two: Prusa, DeTroteau, Cross, Scheeno and Bob Wilson.

David Cross offers beer to the audience as a consolation for his bad jokes.
Reid Hecker/Tartan Photographer

A Man in Pain. Actual opinions in an actual review from David's appearance at Carnegie Mellon University. © 1993, The Tartan, Carnegie Mellon's student newspaper.

THE TARTAN
(SPRING 1993)
CARNEGIE MELLON UNIVERSITY COMEDY SHOW REVIEW

On Friday night, the first comedian on the agenda was Taylor Mason. This versatile comic entertained us with song, ventriloquism, and side-splitting comedy. He thanked the band for the introduction, and then he went on to comment on everything from college (how the bookstore rips students off) to sports (war in the Middle East should be replaced by the Middle East Basketball Championships).

Between moments of commentary, he sang about a wide range of topics while accompanying himself on the keyboard. In his songs, he celebrated big hair (E=mc2 actually means elevation = mousse x conditioner), did rock and rap star impersonations (R.E.M., Bob Dylan, Sir Mixalot, and LL Cool J, to name a few), and sang a song dedicated to President Clinton (is that Bill or Hillary?)

The highlight, however, of the act was the ventriloquism. Romeo (Mason's dummy) cracked us up with his raging hormones (do dummies have hormones?), tales of his other jobs (one of them as a dummy at Walt Disney World), and his devil-may-care attitude. Later in the act, Juliet was introduced and Mason concluded the act with a song done by the trio – quite an amazing feat.

Next on the lineup was David Cross. I only need one word to describe his act: bad. Actually, I may need more words than that. Terrible, horrible. He crashed and burned, and no wonder. He started out with an imitation of ventriloquism and the show went downhill from there. (But at least he had an introduction.)

In an attempt to get people to stay, he gave away free beer and whined to the audience that he was bombing (and in a big way). He got very few laughs, and when they did come, it was out of pity for a guy who was on stage dying. By the end of his act, the tent had emptied considerably.

Saturday night, the comedy took a turn for the better when Al Romero and Michel Lauziere showed up. These comedians almost made me forget about David Cross.

Al Romero came on first and regaled us with stories about being a Cuban in Miami, and the culture shock he experienced when he moved to New York. He then slammed on several different ethnic groups. But his saving grace was his theory that deep down everyone is the same because we all do the same stupid things (like pushing the button on elevators even though they are already lit up)...

STAND UP

David: "I wasn't really articulate or likable, and I did stuff with the intention to shock. I'd easily lose sight of entertaining people. I just hated the audience; I had such contempt for the type of comedy they were laughing at. I was definitely a comics' comic, and would play to the other comics, which really slowed my learning process as a stand-up. I think I can do stand-up well now, but it took a long, long time just because of my own stubbornness and strong-headedness of just not wanting ever to do anything remotely close to 'acceptable.' And then, after years and years, you sort of figure it out subconsciously, and then you have to reconcile with the fact that, 'Oh, wow, I'm actually doing well. Am I everybody I hated?' You figure out a balance — how to do enough of this stuff that you don't like so much so that all this other stuff will go over."

John Ennis: "David's stand-up was never just stand-up. He was always fucking with the medium, making people wonder if he was for real. So he was never playing to the audience — he was playing to the smart people in the audience. He had an intelligence to his humor that seemed effortless. He'd been a wiseass his whole life, and now he gets to do it in front of people."

Tim Sarkes (David's manager): "David is one of the greatest stand-ups I've ever seen. He is a guy who will go out there night after night and take chances, rather than rely on what he did the night before. He won't put a solid 20-minute set together and then go out with the same set five nights in a row. He will continually take chances, and that's what makes it exciting. If it dies, it dies a violent death, and if it scores, it scores a glorious high. But there's really no in-between. I know how passionate he is."

Concert poster from "The Pride is Back," David's HBO one-hour stand-up comedy special, 1999. (Original poster art by Frank Kozik).

tropolitan Gazette p.24

ERSONALS! FIND YOU

ID SAD

WRTRS SEEKING SKTCH SHOW

Hi! Do you like smiles and good times? Do you like the art of "Clowning"? Than call me. I'm a Professional "Clown" who can help you to create "characters" and "alternate frameworks of possibility" helping you to "self-organize your 'Human' mind". I have been legally recognized as one of the "top ten of Clowns" in North America, and in three of the last five years, safety has been my number one concern. So get off the couch, give me a call and catapult yourself to higher dynasties of understanding with me, a professional clown ... who knows, you might even get on t.v.!
David-Box 500071

Me? I'm a 33 yr old SWM. You? You're a SWF with who likes long walks. Length and duration of walks is negotiable. I'm flexible up to a point and as long as costs are discussed ahead of time. Anything else, you're paying for. Willing to go to couples therapy, too. Do I sound like your "Prince Charming"? Then call!
Bill-Box 43511

Wrter seeks show. I love to laff! Srching for show on which to swear a blue strk, to gain cult fllowing, and to acheive minor clebrity. Look frward to spnding hours in stuffy room arguing about whether or not Santa would still do his job if he were hld hostage. Could u bee the 1? Pls say "yes"! Oh. also, not vry gd at splling.
Bob-Box 41090

SWM with ADS seeks SWF with same for everything all the time.
Box 4723

SWM comedy writer, early 30s. not gay! Hate almost everything except video games, weed, dumb-ass action movies and METAL!! Work habits include coming to work late, arguing, making gay jokes, ordering food, complaining about food when it arrives, pointing out other people's shortcomings, talking shit about other TV shows; especially Arli$$ (even though it hasn't aired yet because I'm writing this in '96, but I have a feeling it will suck). Looking for like-minded assholes to make humor for television.
P.S. No gay fags!
Brian-Box 3738

SWM, 30, w/drink.prob. Emotionally dead, Hollow inside/full of ground glass, spiders. Won't you fix me?
Paul-Box 6266

SWM in search of fat, Single Sketch Show. Seriously, the fatter the better. A Pig not a Twig. I will be the head-over-heals Laurel to your sultry and seducing Hardy. Me: Chaser. You: Chubby. I really want you to sit AROUND my house. I can see us now ... taking long walks on the beach, reading Shakespeare out loud, and me watching you not get through the kitchen door. Please let me be your Papa Cass. I will definitely push your cushion. Other than that, physical appearance unimportant, except of course your feet should be extremely small because nothing grows in the shade. No fatties.
Dino-Box 4932

SWGM (the G is for Gregarious!) Enjoys candle-lit dinners and long moonlit walks to buy candles. Seeks position on hilarious, ground-breaking comedy show -- Big tits a Must!
Scott-Box1007

UP,MNIJ. Unimployed person, my name is Jay. Need job fast. Enjoy eating food, surviving, paying rent. Please, no hitting.
Jay-Box 64230

Me: Pining for you and hung like a donkey*
You: High paying writing job on quality TV show.
Me, "Let's hook up baby."
You: "Yeah, whatever..."
Me: "Fuck you, twat."
You: "Real charming, honeydripper." RU4ME?
BJ-Box 22371
*(Donkey with average-sized human penis)

Are you a girl who doesn't take the "dating thing" too seriously? You are? Well then you're wasting my time! And as a SWMWLRAJ, it's obvious that I already have my hands full. Long walks, live shows and movies ain't the half of it, sister. I got sh*t to do and it ain't with you. Only serious inquiries, please.
Box 4423

Sick of the "personal ad scene"? Me too.
Box 4231

Are you a "girl" with a deep, dark secret? So deep you can't share. it? Do you feel trapped in a life which doesn't suit you? Is every day Halloween with you? Then how about we hook up for some weird and, wild fun and games. Please, no transvestites; he/shes; she/hes or trans-gender.. people going either way.
Box 4356

I'm a 33 yr old SWM. Are you a SWF? Then you're my type. Leave message at 4453. Not interested? Then FU, you choosy bitch!
Box 30601

TEST FROM GLOBO-

WRITERS, CAST & CREW | 39

WHO?

WRITERS, CAST & CREW

John Ennis
cast member - all seasons

John is old friends with "Li'l Davey Cross." They met in 1983, at Emerson, when David auditioned for the college sketch group called *This Is Pathetic,* which John was in. They were the Campus underdogs, basically the people who didn't get into *Comedy Workshop*, the big deal on campus: "Fuck them, let's do our own!" was precisely the attitude that would attract David. John and David, at that first audition, realized they would be working together a long time. "We could just tell," says John, "the two of us right from there knew we were totally in sync. We really hooked up. I sort of thought David was a wise-ass up until then." David adds, "We were basically strangers, and we clicked. The only other person I can really relate it to was when I first started writing with Bob, how effortless it was. It was cool. It immediately sealed our everlasting friendship." Of course, they became the hip group on campus. Other sketch groups followed: *The Kids You Used to Hate* — which was formed only for a show at John's sister's college ("Hey, I can get us a gig!") — *Flurby Humans*, and, ultimately, *Cross Comedy*.

A young actor's dream, being "discovered," happened for John when he was only 17. Or so he thought. He was picked out by Larry Brezner, Joe Piscopo's manager, at a taping of HBO's *Young Comedians Special,* where John and Joe Murphy (from *This Is Pathetic*) were invited to perform a sketch. "He said, 'You're great! You're going to be big!' He told me to grow my hair long and come out to L.A. in the summer, we have an audition for you for this film. So I did. When I got there, I thought it was going to be a lot of limousines; it was a lot of buses. I came into their office, they were talking on the phone to Woody Allen. I thought, just sitting in there, 'Oh, God, this is it! I've made it!' Then they told me the movie had already been cast. I didn't understand the business at all, when they had told me 'come out this summer, we've got a film audition.' They were almost like, 'Holy shit, we didn't think you really were going to come out.'"

David joined John on a slipshod trip to Los Angeles in the summer of 1985. True vagrants, they slept where ever they could. "We lived in a frat house room, and we asked if we can go down in rent," recalls John. "They said, 'There's another, shittier room in the back.' 'Yeah, we'll take that.' It was behind the kitchen where we could steal their food without them knowing. If you laid down, you filled the room. And we shared a fan. Every hour, the other guy would wake up and turn it back towards him." The two lived for a while in a car, sneaking into basement garages at night for a cool morning. "We rolled towels up in the windows, so nobody could see us, and would pretty much just drink ourselves to sleep. It was a very bizarre summer."

Back home in Boston, John was in a group performing sketches for keg beer in front of an audience of bike messengers (where, he brags, he met his wife) when David started *Cross Comedy*. "He said, 'The underground thing is cool, but who the fuck is seeing us here?'" David put a group together and took over Tuesday nights at the Cambridge Catch A Rising Star. When David finally left for a career in L.A., John followed, accepting David's offer to take a part of a television pilot he'd co-written (*Today's Army*). Again, John came to L.A. believing he had work. This time, though, he and his wife quit their jobs and drove across the country with the kids. The work turned to dust. David had John and his whole family live with him for a month.

It wasn't until he performed at the Diamond Club that John warmed up to being in L.A. "I realized everyone was not my rival. When I first arrived, I felt the backlash of the competition that we felt in *Cross Comedy*. So, I felt competitive with all these people I was meeting — 'How am I going to make it in a place where there are so many talented people?' David was the one who said, 'There's room for everybody. Everyone's different, and all these people can be valuable to you — as friends, and also as performers.' And that really helped me, because I started looking at the whole group differently."

The Diamond Club instantly became David and Bob's petri dish, and, naturally, John was included. "John is a very likable guy," offers Bob. "He has a warmth to him that neither David nor I have. There's not a lot of warmth in the show, so John is a relief."

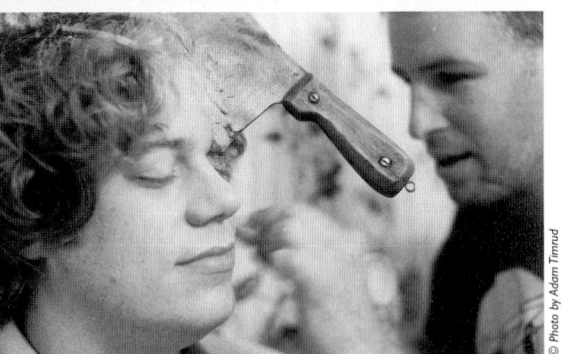

David:

"I was going out to L.A. and I have no money, no prospect for a job. I have $48 and a plane ticket. John gives me an envelope before I leave, and he says, 'Don't open this until you're on the plane.' And I'm in my seat, reading a magazine, and I remember, 'Oh, shit, John gave me that letter.' I open it up, and it has $500 cash and a note that said, 'Get some chili on your fries.' I started crying. I was amazed. I had nothing. Through my own behavior, I had no money. I'm going out to L.A., I don't even know where I'm going to stay. It took this little gesture that made everything okay. Not that he was this rich guy; he was phenomenally generous. He knew the difference between having $48 when you land and $548 is monumental. And it meant that I didn't have to worry. It was really nice and important, and that's the kind of guy he is."

Jill Talley
cast member - all seasons

Jill Talley is the only girl on the main cast of *Mr. Show*. "And that points up what a go-to person she was for us," says David. "That is so valuable when you are writing sketch — to have someone like Jill, who can do a broad range of characters, big and small. She's extremely talented. She really was great to write for. One thing you didn't have to worry about — you have this character that might be difficult — Jill could nail everything. She's amazing."

Jill is married to fellow cast member Tom Kenny. The couple met years before, on another sketch show, *The Edge*, when both were in relationships. "I flew home every weekend to Chicago. I refused to live in L.A. and dig my feet in," Jill admits. "My attitude was, 'I live in Chicago. My family's there, my husband's there, that's where I live.'" All that changed, though, when *The Edge* was over. Jill got divorced, and, in 1994, moved to Los Angeles. To put it in a *Mr. Show*-centric time-perspective, she began dating Tom about the same time David and Bob were courting HBO.

Jill met Bob Odenkirk in mid-80's Chicago, when he was integrated into the working cast of *All You Can Eat In the Temple of Dooom*, Robert Smigel's popular sketch show. "That's where I got to know him well. All those guys, Robert, Bob, Doug Dale, lived on Wrightwood in this apartment; it was kind of a revolving series of roommates. And I didn't live downtown, I lived on the South Side, so after rehearsing our shows, I would always end up crashing on their couch. And extra people always stayed there. It was a really filthy, disgusting place."

"I went right from high school, and — this is so embarrassing — but I did stand-up extremely briefly," Jill explains about her start. "I saw a notice that they were looking for people, 'Maybe I should go down there, I think I have some jokes.' I did really well, but I hated it. I hated being on stage by myself. I was only 18, and I'd never performed before in front of people. I literally vomited in the bathroom before I went onstage, because I was so nervous." Most of her act was character driven, which led to the suggestion that she should take classes at Second City. Jill forayed into sketch and improv, and she found her voice.

The momentous event, quitting her receptionist job, came after only a couple years. Smigel asked her to be in his show, *All You Can Eat…*, which became a long-running hit. "I got a studio apartment, and, because I wasn't on the South Side anymore, I started to get more involved. I was able to stay out and go places, meet people. There was a whole scene happening at the Deja Vu — the Vu on Lincoln — it was a club just a stone's throw away from the Bob/Robert/Doug apartment. We would do shows there, just making shit up and go onstage. It was so crazy, it was so half-ass and so ballsy. There were all these improv groups in Chicago; it was a really exciting time. *Sons of the Desert*, *Friends of the Zoo*, *All You Can Eat*…all these groups, and we all knew each other, and there were different shows going on everywhere. Every year, there was this thing called *Improv 'Til Dawn*, and you would just go down and improvise all night long with different people. When it got late, the only people in the audience would be other actors, other improv groups. We'd come offstage, and they'd go up. It just got stupid. We were drinking the whole time; it was more like a party. It was an interesting time, because improv was kind of new. The people I was involved with, it was more rag-tag — it wasn't real organized groups. It was just people coming together to do shows, then, 'See ya next time.'"

Jill joined the Second City Touring Company, then moved up to the Second City E.T.C. stage. In between, she did *Happy Happy Good Show*, which was a compilation of scenes Bob, Smigel, and Conan O'Brien had written for *SNL*, which didn't make it on the show. Eventually, inevitably, Jill was promoted to Second City's Main Stage, where she worked with Bob again when he joined the cast, which also included Chris Farley and Tim Meadows.

Naïve but resolute, Jill came out to Los Angeles on her own for pilot season, "like an idiot, with no connections and no nothing," she says. "I was determined to come out to L.A. — 'Hey, I know a little bit of improv. I can get an agent.' I had no business being here. It was very un-romantic to eat tomato soup every night and not have any money. None. I came out here with my savings; it went so fast. But I look back, and I am proud of myself that I did it, even though it accomplished absolutely nothing, and it was a big waste of time and money."

Jill has been an important part of *Mr. Show* since the live presentations at the Upfront Theater in Santa Monica, before it was a TV show. But, as she will attest, the roles for women were not abundant. "The show is written by guys, and that's the bottom line," Jill resigns. "The parts for me were usually small, but what I liked about doing *Mr. Show* was, I think they trusted me enough where they'd let me do whatever I wanted, make the character my own, put my own little switch on it. I was happy I got to do all different things. And that's where I had fun, and that's why I stuck with it."

You don't have to look too closely to notice that Jill was pregnant during the show's third season — her altered state was put into action in *Fuzz: The Musical* (#303). "When I told the guys I was pregnant, I was so scared; I was so sure they were they were going to replace me. The whole way driving there, I was very sad, because, at that point, I was having such a good time on the show. I was so happy when their reaction was, 'Of course, you're still going to work!' Eventually they had to not use me towards the last months of my pregnancy, and I certainly understood it, because I was huge. In fact, I think they used me longer than they should have. They had no idea how giant I would get."

Brian Posehn

sometime performer - season 1
writer/cast member - season 2, 3, 4

You notice Brian Posehn. He is odd. He's smart. He has a lot of attitude. As a writer, he's known for coming up with the dark, twisted stuff. As a performer, he's most often cast as the weird guy, who walks in and says some jackass thing.

"I remember the first time I even *saw* Brian," says Bob. "He was at the Virgin Megastore, and he was wearing his Sub Pop 'Loser' jacket. With the word 'Loser' where the name should be. I thought that was a really cool jacket and really funny. But I didn't know who he was, but, of course, you notice Brian. He's...which guy is Brian?"

"Brian wrote a lot of dark stuff," says Paul F. Tompkins. "He came up with just great ideas. And always from kind of a twisted standpoint." Brian learned sketch writing from consuming a lot of comedy, and from knowing what he likes. "I'm not trained. I didn't go to Harvard or anything like that to become a writer. I learned to write sketches from watching *SCTV*, my favorite sketch show ever. I come at things from loving comedy over the years." Brian actually didn't like *Monty Python* when he was a kid, because his mother's boyfriend liked it. Which says a lot about Brian. "As a rebel, I wouldn't like things that older folks liked. I didn't like *Python*, basically because I found other things on my own. I found *SCTV*, so I felt like that was better because I found it. And because this older person was trying to turn me on to *Monty Python*, I said, 'Whoa, that's not for me. That's for older people.' But I gave *Python* a chance once I was in college and found a lot of it really, really funny."

Starting out as a stand-up in Sacramento, Brian soon relocated to San Francisco and became part of a whole contingent of comedians, who are still friends today — Greg Behrendt, Laura Milligan, Patton Oswalt, Blain Capatch, Doug Benson, Margaret Cho. There was a strong comedy scene in San Francisco. Clubs in and around S.F. (including the dark, tiny Holy City Zoo) thrived at that time, independent of any "comedy boom" of the late-80's. There were plenty of open mic nights, welcoming new comics and experimentation. That's where he first met David Cross, when David would come up and work the S.F. Improv. Early on, Brian looked up to David, because his style of comedy was so different from what a lot of people were doing.

Brian followed others from S.F. in moving to L.A. in the summer of '93. His first writing job was for MTV, on *Trashed*, a game show with sketches. "It was a bad show, but I got my foot in the ass of Los Angeles."

"I was already a fan of Bob's from *Stiller*," says Brian. "I thought he was hilarious. Especially his *Manson/Lassie* piece — that was genius." Brian got to know Bob, not through performing, but from hanging in the same social pack. "I got signed by manager Dave Rath, who also was managing Janeane Garofalo and about a hundred other comics. I was roommates with Rath. We all started traveling in the same circle."

Early on, Bob brought Brian in to audition for his HBO project, *Life on Mars*, although, at the time, Bob hadn't seen him act, and the two hadn't even talked much. "I guess I liked his bad attitude," Bob explains. "He's got a lot of character in him, because he's such a bitter fuck, and it's right there in his voice. And that's something that most comics share. A lot of comedy can come from anger, from feeling like you're not a part of things, conventional things, and you think people are stupid and they should be ridiculed. Which is true." The part on *Mars* went to Jack Plotnick, but Brian was pleased he was given a chance — "That was really encouraging." Brian ended up as an extra on the pilot and was "glad to do so...I would have done craft services, or even been a fluffer, if he had asked me."

The "alternative" set of comics and performers began doing live shows together at the Diamond Club, "a cool stage space" Rath started, which

© Photo by Adam Timrud

housed an underground scene for sketch shows. Bob and David put together a show using their friends. It was called *The 3 Goofballz,* which was the template for *Mr. Show,* and they used Brian. "The second time they did *Goofballz,* I was supposed to be the third Goofball popping out of the box, and instead it was [comic] Doug Benson in there smoking pot, and they go, 'Where's Brian? He's supposed to be in there.' And that led into the *Slackers* video, which was redone for season 2, in *No Adults Allowed* [#203]. I was the main slacker that David later played [in the episode]."

Inspired by *Goofballz,* Brian put together a sketch show of his own for the Diamond Club, *Only I'm Funny.* "Bob played a part in one of the sketches, and he also did some free consulting on the writing. These were some of the first sketches I had ever written, and he was very supportive."

Posehn, like most who witnessed Bob and David's early live shows, sensed what was developing, and he was excited to be included. "I wanted to be involved with these two guys because I thought they were so great. And even if HBO slept on it [regarding making the show], I knew that something would happen, and I would be part of this group."

After a stint in New York writing on MTV's *The Jon Stewart Show,* Brian returned to Los Angeles. Just weeks later, Bob and David called him — they had sold their show to HBO, four episodes (which were already written), and Brian would be included as a performer.

"Then, I had a year of starving before Season 2," tells Brian. And even then — because Bob and David only had it in their budget to hire three other writers (Bill, Jay, and Paul) — Brian didn't get hired outright. He felt let down. "Instead of hiring me, David and Bob were just going to buy sketches off me. They were both really apologetic and cool, and told me they would hire me when they could. They approved the NAMBLA thing [*Ad Awards,* #203], and the four voices in my head [*Subway,* #206]. And then they figured out it would be the same amount to just hire me."

David admits that at first, he was not as confident in Brian as a writer as Bob was. "I questioned his devotion, his work ethic. It was one of those things where Bob convinced me, and we took a chance on him. And, obviously, we're glad we did."

"Brian was pretty consistent in a way. He had two big sketches in every year," Bob says of Brian as a writer. "He's amazing in that he's come up with really funny ideas that we've used, not always in the form he's pitched them. His desire to piss people off and make them uncomfortable can just obscure any comedy. Of all of us, he and David are the ones that push the envelope of taste, crude or dark. And that can be really good. The show's distinctive because of that."

Midway through the fourth season, Brian left *Mr. Show.* "A lot of my decisions are based on whether I think I'm gonna have fun," Brian explains about his choice to take a role on a new sitcom. "*The Army Show* [on the WB network] had a bunch of actors that I was really good friends with (including Mary Lynn Rajskub, Craig Anton, Toby Huss, and Dave Higgins), and I wanted to be around those guys. The way it worked out, I was going to be able to finish the first five episodes, and that was important, and I knew I had the option of getting other pieces in the final five [*Weeklong Romance,* #410]. But once I got into the sitcom, I was really missing *Mr. Show.*"

David, Brian and Bob. Losers at HBO post-Emmy Party, 1998.

B.J.:
"Perhaps Scott is the only person on this earth who can comfortably share an office with Brian, as he's very partial to listening to loud speed metal while he writes."

Brian:
"Since Season 2, all of the on-camera members of *Mr. Show* have had a growing number of instances where they've been recognized by fans. I myself have benefited in a fair amount of pussy. All from guys, of course, because as it turns out most of our fans are guys or, suspiciously, women on the internet. (Fat male fans pretending to be fat female fans? You tell me.) Some kidding aside, most of my run-ins have occurred at comic book/sci-fi conventions, or 'nerd-fests.' I noticed it first at the San Diego Convention, one of the biggest in the country, in August of '97. In a two-day period, I must have had at least 20 guys approach me while I was on the convention floor being a fanboy myself. I got Lou Ferrigno's autograph and met a Chinese actor who was in *Big Trouble in Little China.* What impressed me was that I had not had that much screen time at this point — these nerds were really paying attention. The following year, Bob and Jay and Bill came down and met me at the Con, and we all got recognized, especially when we were all standing together. It turns out we have exactly the same fan base as *Ice Pirates.* But, really, thank God for nerds; their voracious appetite for *Mr. Show* made us all not very, very rich."

Brian:
"I consider myself so lucky to have been involved with such an amazing show and to have worked along side Bob and David and the other writers and performers. We all worked our asses off, and it was the most fun I've ever had working (including dosing on acid during a shift at Tower Records). So remember that, kind reader, when, in the description of my involvement with *Mr. Show,* I sound negative or disparage someone or complain about my mistreatment. Or when I describe how one day I'll get my revenge on Bob and David and everyone else on the staff who crossed me. Just don't warn any of them, I trust you."

Bill Odenkirk

contributing writer - season 1
writer - season 2, 3
writer/producer - season 4
sometime performer - all seasons

David on Bob and Bill:
"They're family. They're both hyper-sensitive to each other. But the flip side to that is, when Bob and Bill were clicking — they clicked so well. When those guys would get giggly with each other it was really fun to watch."

Dino:
"He's so much like an old man. In fact, once, Bill walked by the office humming 'The Daring Young Man on the Flying Trapeze.' Bob just shook his head — 'Bill is such an old man. Why would anyone whistle that?'"

"William Odenkirk, or 'Bill' as he is known to people in a hurry," never imagined he would be writing comedy. "If Bob hadn't done this, there's no way I would have pursued it," he says. "It wouldn't have entered my realm of thought." His plan was to finish college and go directly to graduate school (to study inorganic chemistry, of all things), then possibly go into teaching. But when older brother Bob began writing comedy — first for a college radio station and, eventually, for *Saturday Night Live* — Bill's talent began to emerge, and he unwittingly embarked on a career as a comedy writer. "Bill is really funny and very quick," Bob says of his brother. "He came up with stuff right from the first season of *Mr. Show*. He was the only other writer who contributed material for the first season."

Bill was still a high school boy in Naperville, Illinois, when he would visit Bob to help on his college radio show. When Bob moved to Chicago, Bill met a lot of his brother's Chicago friends: Robert Smigel, Doug Dale, Jeff Garlin, Tom Gianas — all comedy writers and performers. "It was great to get out of Naperville and to be exposed to that," says Bill. Although he performed a bit with Bob, it was clearly Bob, Bill admits, who had more drive to perform. "He was a lot more brave than I was. Because even now, when I think about doing stand-up, I can't. I couldn't take the failure."

When Bob made it to *SNL*, Bill was attending college at Loyola, and the two collaborated long distance. "We started working over the phone. We'd talk about scenes he was writing. Once in a while I'd pitch a scene idea, then we'd work on it. And once in a while, I'd visit him in New York and help him on the show. One of the scenes we worked on was my idea that actually got on the air — about George Bush shaking off his lightweight image — they opened the show with my scene."

Once Bill was in graduate school, he and Bob were on the phone two or three times a week, talking about scenes. "I loved it when he called, especially when graduate school turned into hell for me," Bill says emphatically. "Bill would take a break, which was rare, but he would take a weekend from his horrible job in the lab, and he'd come out and help me at *SNL*," says Bob. "And otherwise, he'd be in hell back at the chemistry lab. It was like he went back to prison. He hated it there, the professor treated him like shit, he hated the work. It was oppressive. It was fourteen hours a day, even weekends. He was living in a shithole, not making any money."

Bob adds that Bill's visits to *SNL* made a big impression: "Bill got to know all the other writers, Robert Smigel, Conan O'Brien, and they appreciated his wit and his talent." In fact, when Conan O'Brien got his own show, Robert Smigel (then co-creator of Conan's new show) and Conan asked Bill to submit material to be a writer on the show. It was very competitive, though, and Bill didn't get hired. Smigel said he was reluctant to hire Bill partly because he didn't want Bill to give up graduate school and all he'd worked for. Instead, Bill came out to New York a few times to work with the writers.

Around his fourth year of graduate school, Bill started to seriously doubt his choices. "It was one of those things, where you commit to something very big, and then you slowly discover that, well, it's really bad. And it's not going to get better. And even though I've come this far, and I can do it, I don't think this is what I should be doing. It really makes me miserable to think about it. I remember thinking, 'When this is done, I'm going to be I don't know how old, but if I'm going to try comedy writing, this is the time. But I still had around three more years of graduate school left. It was very hard. I still have dreams that I'm not done with graduate school. And the single thought I have is, *'When am I going to finish this? I'm never going to finish this.'*"

Eventually, Bill finished, but when he came to L.A., there were new hurdles. He was Bob's younger brother, and most of the friends he had were Bob's friends. He was living in a back room of Bob's apartment. Furthermore, this was right when the first season of *Mr. Show* was underway, so Bill was also working on Bob's show. More than anything, Bill wanted to work in comedy, but also have his own identity. His talent definitely warranted it. "Everybody wants to establish themselves. It's hard enough to come to Hollywood, and you're seen as attached to someone else's success in someway," says Bob about his brother's predicament. "Every real artist, every person with ego, wants to be known for their own work. And Bill has since established himself, separate from me. [Bill became a writer/producer on the Matt Groening program, *Futurama*.] But back then, there was no way around it — Bill's last name is Odenkirk, and I established myself first. It is an annoying truth, because he belongs doing this as much as me. And what he's doing, he certainly deserves to do and should do because it's organic to him. I think to compound matters is, that in a lot of ways, *Mr. Show* is a comedy writer's dream. It is not a show that is going to come a long very often for any of these writers. And even though Bill hadn't had a lot of experience, there was this awareness — 'Why did my brother have to co-create the coolest show?'"

Bill admits, "Being in Bob's apartment, psychologically, was extremely traumatic. Not Bob's fault at all, he was just living his life. And he certainly was helping me enormously. I was living there for free, and he was letting me use his car, any number of things, you name it. But I was sort of back-tracking over my life, and going, 'I just got my Ph.D. in chemistry from the University of Chicago, and I'm living in someone's back room, and I don't know when, or if, or how I'm ever gonna get a job, or if anything's gonna happen out here.' And, on top of it, to see Bob, who was doing great. He was doing *Larry Sanders*, he had friends established out here, contacts, all kinds of people wanting him to do all kinds of work, movies, shows. The comparison was a little bit hard to live with day in, day out. I think a lot of people would have that reaction, especially in my situation. It's not like I was some sort of dropout trying to get my shit together."

Bill was the obvious hire for Bob and David when HBO ordered a second season. "Bill was the first guy to bring on as a writer," says Bob, "because anything I wrote I ran by him, for years. And he would always pitch me ideas. He'd basically been writing with me for years when he finally got hired."

As Dino Stamatopoulos admits, being Bob's brother was something for everyone to overcome. "When I first met Bill, I was a little put off. The whole 'Bob's brother' thing. And I respect Bob's opinion, but they're *brothers* — maybe Bob's opinion was a little colored. But Bill totally won me over. Once he becomes comfortable with someone, he is really funny. And he's a good writer, very smart. Bill constantly makes us laugh."

Being Women

David: "We almost never played women in the show. That was actually a conscious decision. I think it takes you out of the sketch. You realize, when you see the sketch, you see a guy dressed as a woman, and that's what you think about. And we wanted to service the sketch in the best way we could, and that's usually getting a woman to do it. We knew a lot of great women who could do comedy."

Bob: "*Python* would play full-on female characters with long scenes. And they did a good job. They were playing comic characters that were batty old women. And when they had a young woman they would use Carol Cleveland. And *Kids in the Hall* played women; they'd play young women and older women and everything. I think it's a Canadian/British thing. Americans — it doesn't work on the same level. But we also knew on *Mr. Show*, we were not going to do that. Obviously, when we're getting into real parody or something, we would get into some unreal situations, but there was always an element of sort of gritty reality in our scenes. That's why people would swear or use really common language. And then there's scenes — like the basketball recruiters [*Recruiters*, #205] — which I think are really close to Waiting for Guffman or *Spinal Tap*-type fake documentary played real. So, us playing women in that tone, it didn't work at all. And I never liked the element of it that, to some extent, you're getting some juice out of the fact that it's men playing woman. It's just kind of artificial."

John Ennis as Morgangeline The Puckering Moron (#403).

Jay Johnston

sometime performer - season 1
writer/cast member - season 2, 3
writer/cast member/producer - season 4

Jay Johnston does not think linearly. Or so he's been told. "That's something Bob's said, which is news to me. I'm not aware of *that*, everything seems very appropriate to me. If you can't think of the word, make it up." This, Bob and David have pointed out to him, is expressly what he offers in the writers' room. Jay explains, "If people are going from real hard jokes, or a real hard line, and they're trying to get from start to finish, I will sort of *tangentialize* the conversation so people look at the journey in different ways, or with different possibilities."

From a young age, Jay had been encouraged to look at things in different ways. He was raised in Chicago, a couple blocks away from Wrigley Field in a two-story Victorian house, which he describes as a "lean-to shack with a rake holding up the ceiling in one room and a porch ready to take a hike at any moment. It was a little run down, but it had character." He went to school in a compound, a reformed convent, behind Wrigley Field. "There were five teachers, forty kids, and three grades. It was the best. The headmaster's philosophy was to let the kids learn at their own rate. I found my own ways to learn, instead of being told how to learn."

At the curious school he went to, they also did plays. Jay got cast, and, from then on, he always pursued that type of thing. In high school he was in musicals, always getting the biggest part which didn't require him to sing. But not writing, Jay confesses. "Writing isn't something I thought I would do."

At the insistence of his father, Jay went to college, Columbia College in Chicago, and that's where he found his niche in comedy, but not right away. His academic strategy was to cover the basic requirements, then take classes he liked again and again. Every year, he enrolled in the same acting class, tackling a different genre each time; eventually, he got to comedy. "I was never into comedy. I thought that must be the hardest thing in the world. I didn't understand why people would do that. I didn't know *how* they did it. I tried everything else that I didn't want to do: Shakespeare — because I didn't understand or identify with the material that much; Ibsen — all that shit that seems like a big yawn when you look at it from the outside; then, finally, comedy. I waited until the last minute to do the comedy thing. I was just absolutely annoyed by all the people in comedy I ever met. I thought they were idiots, just joking around all the time, and not being funny, usually."

Ultimately, Jay took a course titled 'Comedy Workshop,' which basically was an exploration of sketch comedy. The curriculum included scenes from *Kids in the Hall* and *Monty Python* to illustrate constructions that worked, or didn't. "It was interesting and certainly a challenge," Jay recalls. "And the thing is, when I was in grade school, I watched *Python* all the time, and I enjoyed it. But I didn't ever think it was something I wanted to pursue. Since I got into school, I'd been in trouble non-stop for fucking around. By the time I got interested in comedy, everyone said, 'Yeah, already. We knew that you would do that.' But I was the last to know. Much like fellas who are gay and come out, and you say, 'Yeah, I knew that ten years ago.'"

At the urging of the department head, he went to check out Second City. "I took classes at Second City and didn't do so well; I did just okay. Then, I auditioned for their touring company. And one of the biggest battles I've had at that place, and probably at *Mr. Show*, is that I'm no mental giant. I'm no 'king of references,' no 'political tornado.' And Second City relies heavily on current affairs and topical shit. And I am always ignorant of that stuff; it's my own fault. So, at the audition, they throw things at you — 'How would you solve the deficit problem?' I just made up a story that was absolutely ridiculous, about war, Canada taking over, defending our borders. Nothing to do with anything in the last 100 years. And what amazed me is, of course, that's what they were looking for, the ability to be creative outside of the facts. So, I joined The Second City Touring Company."

Jay also performed Friday nights with the *Annoyance Theater* in Chicago, in a late-night sketch comedy show called *The Bean Can Tour*. The revue was renowned for its "anything goes" philosophy: performers can do whatever they want onstage. Where most people used that liberty to do "blue" or crass material, Jay moved quickly past that. "Well, I can do anything, but what do I *want* to do, and what would be fun to watch? It was a real interesting experiment of making snap judgments — that you need this, this and this, at least and then from there you go. And I don't think anything could've hammered that in more than that experience."

The more traditional forms of comedy at Second City posed a difficult adjustment for him after he had been sans reigns in *The Bean Can Tour*. But a new producer came aboard — Kelly Leonard, who allowed The Touring Company to do their own material. "I don't know that what we did was that groundbreaking, but we always at least would make each other laugh," says Adam McKay, *SCTC* cohort who went on to become a head writer on *SNL*. "It was incentive to stay in the Touring Company, because we got to try out this fun material." Their "fun material," however, didn't go over on every stage. McKay explains, "It was a bit risky, because

---

John Ennis:
"I respected Jay so much because I saw the work ethic he had. Everyone's getting tired, and at the end of the day, Jay's still going. He still has something for it, he doesn't want to leave. There's an energy to Jay."

David:
"When Jay tells a story, he really gets into it. Some people are good at all the minutiae and the details, but he will actually act out the story as though you are slightly deaf and maybe not from this planet, and he's trying to describe it to you. He must be very good with retarded children because he really lays it out. The way he tells stories, it's so fucking funny. It's got to be annoying at this point, because I make him tell this one story over and over again. But if you ever see Jay in a bar, make him tell you the 'shit factory' story."

David:
"Jay looked out the writers' window and saw that his car had been 'booted' because he had not paid a bunch of tickets. These are virtually impossible to get off. So he said, 'Aw, shit! They booted my car.' And on his lunch break, he got a tool box and took the boot off his car. The common man should not be able to remove that boot. Yet, Jay was out there on his back, in about three minutes flat got it off, went back inside and had one of his traditional 17 pound lunches."

David:
"Jay built some of the props we needed for the show. He just figures the way to make things work in kind of a Rube Goldberg-esque kind of way, where he'd grab whatever is laying around: rubber band, wax candles and a copy machine. And the next thing you know, he's built a car that can travel to the sun and back."

one moment you're in Omaha, and then the next you're in Boston. And it would change from crowd to crowd what they'd think was funny. But we didn't care. Jay and I would do stuff where we couldn't stop laughing. And it would almost become like an insult to the audience, the two of us would be onstage for a five-minute stretch, just laughing. And we would be sure that we would get in trouble, but they never would call." Soon, though, Jay noticed that everyone around him was being promoted to the stage revue. Realizing the inherent limitations, he left Second City. "It dawned on me that I couldn't do what I really wanted to do there. I said, 'Forget this safe, comfortable shit,' and I moved out to L.A."

When Jay got to Los Angeles, McKay put him in touch with stand-up comedian from Philly, Paul F. Tompkins. McKay admits that this sort of third-party set-up is usually awkward, "but I told Jay, 'this is one you actually should do, because I know you would like this guy.' I think it was a lazy connection — they're both funny, they both own Zippos." Jay recalls vividly: "For the next three days, it was like a whirlwind love affair. Paul and I just stayed up almost 24-hours a day talking and laughing. It was insane." A few days later, Paul was given a spot at *Tantrum,* a weekly alternative comedy show held at the Diamond Club, and Jay talked him into doing a sketch instead of stand-up. "It did great. I think everyone was really surprised. So we decided to put a sketch show together, *The Skates*. The cool thing about that show was that it didn't rest on material. It was totally my and Paul's relationship onstage. Somehow, we have a great rapport. We are very charactery and very opposite and very compatible in that." McKay describes Jay and Paul's collaboration as "having that rambly, energetic kind of style, and it just seemed to fit kind of perfectly."

Through McKay, they got Bob and David to check out their show. "They gave us notes on our show and told us they would use us as writers, if their show got picked up for a second season," recalls Jay. "I thought 'Yeah, whatever, buddy. You're full of shit.' People always say crap like that. So I didn't think much of it until like a year later, and they hired us." Jay remembers the first day he and Paul were asked to meet with David and Bob: "They said, 'Bring some ideas if you want to.' So we go in there, and somehow that 2:30 meeting turned into us staying there until 8:30. No one told us that we'd start working. And the scene we worked on that day was what ended up being the *F.F. Woodycooks* crime scene [#201]."

"It was a learning experience," Jay says of his tenure at *Mr. Show*. "At first it was great, but I didn't know what the fuck was going on. I didn't have much writing experience for suddenly getting paid $700-$800 a week to be there doing it. Even though that's not much at all," he laughs. Once Jay's first year (Season 2) got underway, however, he still felt tentative about certain things, about ideas. He was acutely aware that his sensibility was notably different. "I don't know what it was like for the other guys, but writing *Mr. Show* was a really hard job for me."

"Jay has this insecurity about being smart, about not being intelligent enough to convey his idea or participate in the discussion of a sketch," says David. "He's a lot smarter than he seems to think he is; he's very smart and observant. He's not reading the paper or something like that, but that really has nothing to do with it."

Over the seasons, Jay figured ways to work in his inventive take on scenes. "I learned a lot about how those guys saw comedy," Jay says of David and Bob. "Coming at it from a real outsider's perspective, I always try to think, 'What about the guy who doesn't get the reference? Can't the scene stand on the idea of the characters, or something else?' Because one thing I've always disliked was reference-heavy comedy, or things that you need another set of rules to understand what's going on. That's why I identify more with character relationships or behavior scenes, because they're universal. So that's something I tried to stand up for. What I'm always looking to do — and it's insane chasing this rainbow — is what will appeal to everybody. Not to water something down, but what is something that doesn't exclude anybody. I think that's why I like physical comedy. It's not language-based, and it's not of the time. It's emotional and situational."

"Jay would come up with really wild stuff, and he was fearless in that way," says Paul. "He would let his mind go off in crazy directions and come up with some really inspired, nutty stuff. I think that's what he was best at — bringing surreal elements and silliness to things." "I cannot believe I was able to do the physical comedy on the show, because of what kind of show it is," adds Jay. "I learned my first season that the writers had a very strong reaction to physical comedy, and usually it was not very good. And I'm not saying they're all idiots, and they don't know. It depends on execution; it seems so base when you explain it. Slowly, I was encouraged to pitch more of those ideas, after it was apparent Bob and David were enjoying some of the physical stuff. The small percentage of the more physical things I pitched that made it into the show doesn't seem like much, but, looking back over the seasons, it is a huge accomplishment."

Jay dealing craps on a craps table he built.

Jay on Jay:
"On a more personal note, and it may be none of your business, but Jay rarely reads and enjoys hobbies such as carpentry and working on his car and living like the biggest pig you ever saw. He recently finished building a craps table. He also loves to gamble. Mostly craps. Fuck Poker. Poker can suck my dick."

Dino:
"The two attributes of Jay — he's clumsy and he eats a lot. The best scenario for him would be to fall into a mound of food."

Tom Kenny
cast member - season 1, 2, 3
sometime performer - season 4

In his hometown of Syracuse, Tom Kenny started as a comedian with Bob Goldthwait. They were both about 15. "In our town, there was no comedy club, there was no comedy anything," recalls Tom. All we knew about comedy scenes in big cities was what we read about, books like *The Last Laugh* [Phil Berger's book about stand-up]. We thought, 'Wow, we can actually maybe get some of this stuff going here in our shitty, boring town.'" "We were waiting for our friend to get his driver's license," adds Goldthwait.

As high school teens, they answered an ad — comic Barry Crimmons was looking for more acts to start a comedy night. "Crimmons didn't realize we'd just escaped puberty," says Goldthwait. "We showed up for his open mic night, and they didn't have enough comedians, so he put us up, despite our being so young." "He used to call us the 'kiddie corps,'" Tom laughs, "but we always did well. It was good for my confidence, which was never my strong point." Crimmons also nicknamed the two — Tomcat and Bobcat. Later, around 17 or 18, they started a sketch group called The Generic Comics. ("This was a lot funnier in 1979 when we worked in grocery stores," Tom disclaims.) The six-person Generic group gained a local following. "We became this huge thing within our area code — doing shows at a broken down, Mafioso-owned rock bar called Lost Horizon," tells Tom.

Kenny and Goldthwait bonded through comedy. "Goldthwait was the only other kid I knew who was interested in listening to Carlin albums and Cheech and Chong albums, and going to Marx Brothers and Woody Allen movies when they would be showing at the dollar day at the crummy little fourth-run movie house in our town." Their big inspiration was *SCTV*, which they "pirated" from Canadian airwaves. In Syracuse, they were close enough to Canada that they could tune in CKWS, the station that ran *SCTV*. "We were able to see *SCTV* about two years before it ever ran in the U.S.," says Tom. "We just couldn't believe it. The rest of Canadian TV was so crappy. Low budget Canadian soap operas and game shows. And then there was this show that had these reference levels and great characters. The cast just seemed like people you could hang out with."

Tom Kenny is the only *Mr. Show* guy ever to have made a living as a road club comic (40 weeks on the road each year). But, at the time, Tom seriously lacked the confidence to really pursue it. "I had a hankering. But Goldthwait was much more into it and much more fearless about performing it than I was. I would write stuff, then not have the balls to go out and be a stand-up by myself. I would give him the jokes." When Goldthwait left for Boston to do comedy, Tom stayed in Syracuse to play in a punk-pop band called Tear Jerkers, the local opener for touring bands like the Go-Go's, Nick Lowe, etc. In 1983, though, Tom was prepared to move on. "The band was winding down, and bagging groceries at the Price Chopper isn't really the fabulous career I envisioned for myself." Goldthwait encouraged Tom to do more stand-up: "I always felt Tom was much funnier than me. So I thought it was a shame that I was working, and he wasn't."

So, Tom went to Boston, just as Bobcat was relocating to San Francisco. Bob left Tom his apartment and his roommate (comic Dan Spencer). In retrospect, Tom says there was something to his decision to move to Boston after Goldthwait had already left: "It was probably based in a subconscious desire to not have that association. We were almost like a comedy team in Syracuse. I wanted to be me." Goldthwait acknowledges that Tom was concerned about being in his shadow, but adds: "The thing about Tommy and me, we're really close friends, but very rarely do we work together onstage. There's not a straight man amongst us; that's the problem. That's why we're never like a team. 'You're the fat one and you're the skinny one.' People used to always say that. Yeah, I'm the fat goofy one, he's the tall, skinny goofy one."

Boston was somewhat disappointing to Tom. "I thought I was moving to a hipper place. I was thinking, 'Harvard, bookstores, this is gonna be great.' But a lot of the hip didn't filter down to the comedy scene. You were playing these jughead rooms, and it was all 'bully' comedy. I was really disappointed. It was like the bullies had taken over stand-up — the jocks! But there were a couple of people who were different — Dan Spencer, Paul Kozlowski — and we started hanging out, and we realized that what we really wanted to do was sketches." They put together a three-man sketch team, Uncle Stinky's Dipsy Doodle Review, and performed all around Boston. Soon, Goldthwait invited them out to San Francisco as his opening act on a string of shows. "Like Goldthwait, we did much better in San Francisco than we did in Boston, so we made the move." After a short while, Spencer and Kozlowski returned to Boston where they were established as stand-ups, but Tom stayed in San Francisco. "That's when my stand-up really bloomed. I was making good money. I was paying cheap rent. I was living in San Francisco. It was great."

"I loved his stand up," says David Cross, who remembers Tom from those early stand-up days. "He had this great energy. There was really no one quite like him."

Tom came to L.A. in 1991 to do Goldthwait's cult-ish movie, *Shakes the Clown*. "I'm completely lucky — I've never not worked," Tom says of his move to Los Angeles. Julie Brown, who also worked on *Shakes*, hired him for her Fox sketch show, *The Edge*, on FOX. He met his future

---

© Photo by Adam Timrud

David:
"The one thing about Tom — you can not shut him up. I've never ever seen anybody talk as much and as rapidly as he does. It's amazing. If words were currency, Tom would be broke."

Tom:
"I remember when I turned 32, thinking: 'I'm finally at the point, where for half my life, I've been entertaining random strangers at bars.'"

wife Jill on *The Edge*. "In the first thing that we shot together, they cast us a couple with a new baby." "Platonic pals" on the close-knit cast (which included Wayne Knight, Jennifer Aniston, Julie Brown, Carol Rosenthal, and James Stevenson III), Tom and Jill went back to their respective cities after the show ended. "She was married at the time. I didn't see her again until two years later, when we were both back in L.A., and both free. The friendship blossomed into a romance on *Mr. Show*. We just started hanging out, and it became this unlooked-for romantic thing — it was like suddenly Ralph realized Norton was really beautiful, and he wanted to date him."

People notice that the fourth season of *Mr. Show* featured much less of Tom. His voiceover career "went through the roof," and, basically, he was faced with a scheduling problem. "Bob and David had a show they have to cast, and there's eight animated shows dependent on me. And so it was the work clock conspiring against me, I guess." (Tom lends his voice to characters on: *Rocko's Modern Life, Powerpuff Girls, Dexter's Laboratory, CatDog, SpongeBob Squarepants,* and *Futurama*.)

"For Tom, it got frustrating when they starting bringing in other cast members," Bill explains. "He'd watch other people get parts that used to be his. It got really hard for him. It didn't make sense to do another season of *Mr. Show*. It was really sad, because he so wanted to be involved with the show." John Ennis, who was the only other person on the original cast along with Tom and Jill, was particularly sad to see Tom leave. "I missed Tom terribly. He has so much to offer on so many levels. I looked up to Tom and Jill in those first two seasons, because they were right there on the edge. When he left, it was a shock to me."

Bob and David worked Tom in whenever possible that season. "I was always thrilled that they would throw me a lot of the voiceover stuff," says Tom. "It allowed me to still be involved with a show that I really loved. I missed being on a show that I thought was the best on TV. Jill and I were always aware, from The Upfront on, that these were the best sketches, ever. This was the funniest shit ever. It's untouchable. And I'm sure *Mr. Show* will have the same cataclysmic effect on younger people thinking about getting into comedy that *SCTV* did for us. Where you see it, and it just blows your mind and forms the rest of your life. I can definitely track *SCTV* as being the thing that put my life on a whole other path. It's like a religious experience. Almost like when people are born again or something. It was that powerful — and probably more lasting than other people's spiritual careers."

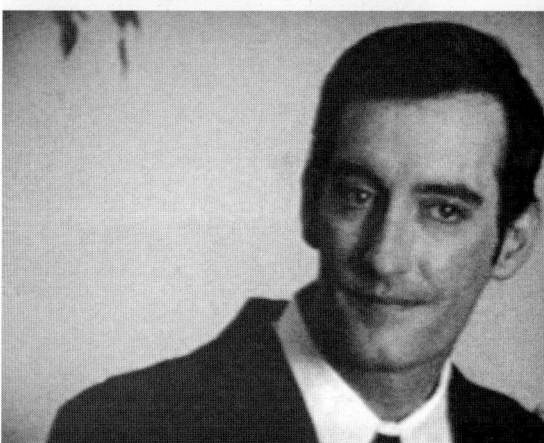

Becky Thyre
cast member - season 4

Becky Thyre was added as a regularly featured performer in the show's fourth season. Becky had met Bob a long time before, through Chicago friends. Most notably, she was Marcia Brady in *The Real Live Brady Bunch* and performed as a beauty contestant in a show called *The Miss Vagina Pageant*. The latter of which astounded Bob: "A group of women wrote it and performed it. It's really funny. And to see a whole group of women be that fucking funny was amazing and great. Becky was great."

Becky performed with *Mr. Show* cast members at various junctures on her resume. Ben Stiller hired her to do *The Ben Stiller Show*, in the Woody Allen *Husbands and Wives* parody. (She was the Bride of Frankenstein/Mia Farrow.) And she was in the 1992 pilot for *The Edge*, a sketch show for Fox with Jill Talley and Tom Kenny (on a cast that included Jennifer Aniston and Julie Brown and Wayne Knight). The pilot went on to series, but without Becky. "I was stupid at the time. I was really involved with my group of people that I worked with on *The Brady Bunch*, and I was afraid to do something away from them. So I wouldn't sign the [standard] five-year contract at *The Edge*. I had some things to learn about my career. I was 24."

ized to take it seriously. "It was mostly a show that
Dino Stamatopoulos
guest writer/sometime performer - season 2
writer/executive producer/sometime performer - season 3, 4

Dino Stamatopoulos has an over-developed adventurous streak. He admits to having a reputation in every aspect of his lifestyle — the drugs, the drinking, the long hair, the motorcycle. And he never tries to down-play any of it.

As Dino describes, his ideal set-up would be to live as a hobo — travel around, take odd jobs, no real responsibility. In Chicago, he lived a whole year off of giving sperm and baby-sitting. He earned $100 a week, which more than covered his $300 rent. "It was the best time in my life," he brags.

A gawky kid, Dino wrote for his high school variety show — and was astounded that he could get laughs. He went to Chicago's performing arts college, Columbia College (with Jay Johnston, Andy Dick, Scott Adsit, and Mike Stoyanov). "I wrote and performed. But I liked writing best." Around that time, one of his best friends was Andy Dick. They started doing comedy, little scenes together for the lunch crowd in the cafeteria. They parlayed this into an open mic bit, which begat a larger stage show. "We did a show at the Roxy, a bar/theater type place, tells Dino, "and we did half stage, half video stuff. It was an 'anti-comedy' show. We were sick of all the comedy that was going on, and we would just make fun of comedy." Or "ca-mo-day," as they would always say, embarrassed to take it seriously. "It was mostly a show that other comedians would like."

The pair performed at the alternative performance spaces in Chicago: "I remember Dino and Andy had a stand-up act," says Bob. They would do their bit about a ventriloquist where Andy was the ventriloquist and Dino was the puppet. It was really funny. They also did their *Who's On First* routine, where one of them slaps the other really hard every time he gets it wrong. They made me laugh. But I didn't know either of them that well." Dino's elaborates: "Andy was the dummy, and he spoke for himself in a very low energy way, like he was drugged. Then, you find out he actually took a bottle of sleeping pills or something. I remember this bit vaguely. I think we only did it a couple of times. The *Who's On First* routine was ultimately filmed by Troy Miller for the *Stiller Show*, but it never got on. I think it worked in a live setting. The audience response was always huge because Andy would really smack me hard. Now, when I say 'response,' that doesn't mean 'laughter,' necessarily."

"The audience would just go crazy, it was so violent," adds Andy Dick. "And then I dropped all comedy — 'C'mon. We went over this, remember? Why don't you tell me the guy's name on second base.' And Dino'd say 'Who?' And I'd just fuckin' rail him again with an open fist. I wouldn't hold back. He'd be shaking. He told me that he lost his hearing in one ear, because I missed his face and actually boxed his ear. The bit was so twisted and so dark that sometimes it went over very well, and sometimes it just freaked everybody out. Another bit we did was a video bit in 'Smell-O-Rama.' We put scratch 'n' sniff stickers on index cards and passed them out to the audience. And as stuff was happening on the film, it would say, 'scratch #1.' And it would smell minty as I was brushing my teeth. And then my armpit would be pepperoni pizza, and the whole audience would go, 'Eeewwww!' — they don't know it's pizza. They see my hairy armpit up there, and then they smell this sharp pepperoni and it just seems we got an armpit smell. The show was called *Dino and I* (after *Withnail and I*). At the time, it was cool."

Jay Johnston remembers Dino from the Columbia College days: "For years, when I was in Chicago, it was, 'Dino had left Chicago and was out, just doing it.' Everyone was always saying that he was a great sketch writer. I never thought I would work with him someday. He was one of these guys that you were always chasing after the things he'd already accomplished."

Andy Dick persuaded Dino to submit to *The Ben Stiller Show* his *Simpsons* spec script (which he had written just out of love for the program). It got him hired.

Dino felt that, although there were strong performers at *Stiller*, the show's perimeter was too tight. "*Stiller* was all parody, where you needed to know the reference. Also, I felt that at *Stiller*, they were too precious about material. I felt like the stuff would be performed really well, but it was very narrow on what you could write. Bob's stuff was the best, why we won the Emmy." (The award-winning episode of *The Ben Stiller Show* featured three pieces written by Bob Odenkirk.)

Very quickly, Dino became disillusioned by TV. He shared a great example which illustrates how he doesn't easily fit in: "Ben Stiller one time looked at me, shook his head, and said, 'You scare the hell out of me.' And I didn't say anything, but I felt, 'Yeah. I'm scared of him, too.' So we were scared of each other. We were just so different as human beings."

So after *Stiller*, Dino was planning to take a cross-country motorcycle trip. Instead, he moved to New York to work on *Late Night with Conan O'Brien* (where Bob was already on staff). Dino explains, "I liked the idea of an unknown getting a show. Plus, I heard from Bob that Conan was a funny guy. So I was excited." Robert Smigel, who was co-creating the new *Late Night* show, hired Dino: "He was the easiest hire, the quickest hire. He had an amazing packet of ideas for the show. I always tell people that Dino and [comedian/writer] Louis C. K. had as much to do with forming what that show was as I did or Conan or Andy Richter. I really believe that. They created an awful lot of recurring bits and the kinds of ideas that defined what the show is." For Dino, writing for the late-night show was an ideal gig, because, he says, "We got to do anything we wanted (like on *Mr. Show*). Also like *Mr. Show*, the *Conan* people were fun to hang around with. Conan would fuck around and be silly." Conan likens his relationship with Dino to the early relationship he shared with Bob at *Saturday Night Live* — "Dino and I would just spend a lot of time, like retarded twins, trying to make each other laugh with weird bits." "I'm sure Dino had a great time," Smigel adds. "We gave him a lot of rope. His strength was going off and coming up with ideas on his own. And he wrote and produced really interesting visual bits — *Tomorry the Ostrich, Slim Organ-Body Guy,* and *Skull Juice*. And he came up with this thing, 'Crunk' — a cuss word you can say on TV, an all-purpose cuss word. It would cover anything."

Next for Dino was writing on *Letterman* and, then again, for Smigel on *The Dana Carvey Show*, which Dino concisely describes as, "Both miserable for different reasons."

Bob worked again with Dino before *Mr. Show* — they did *Life On Mars* together, a comedy pilot for HBO. "I love Dino, he's brilliant and he's great to work with. He has a strong sense of fun, of having a good time, and he has confidence in his funniest ideas. And he's very intelligent. He can respect other kinds of comedy, other than what he does; he can like other people's pieces. He's a great guy to have in the room. I always thought, sensibility-wise and experience-wise, he's the guy I wish all three of us would've done *Mr. Show*. David and I asked him to be partners with us in the second season. He didn't want to. He was living in New York and doing other things."

"I'm not a good person to be in charge," Dino admits. "I'm good at pitching funny things and just thinking laterally, but it's really hard for me to just sit down and write a well-structured scene. For me, it's usually inspiration, rather than knowing the rules."

They got Dino to come on for a few weeks during the second season for *Jeepers Creepers* (#203), a musical scene about a messiah, who lacks a point of view. It was initially an idea Dino wrote for *The Ben Stiller Show* that never got done. "Bob and David sent me all the shows, and, as soon as I saw the first one, I was like, 'Wow. This is the best thing I've seen in years.' So I definitely wanted to be a part of it. But I was also living in New York and didn't know if I wanted to move." At the third season pick-up by HBO, David and Bob made a more aggressive play for Dino. "They made a lot of concessions for me," Dino admits. "It was really flattering that they wanted me there so much. I feel like I got away with a lot of shit because they both really wanted me there. I tried not to take advantage of it. I got lazy at certain points — and I didn't get yelled at, like I would on other shows."

Dino's work ethic necessitates that he team with someone who will push him. "I work well with Bob. He's pretty driven. I am not driven. I like free time. But it's a really fun show, so it's usually not like work. We sit down and we laugh, and we analyze why we laugh, usually because we're bored, and we come up with why it's funny." One strategy to get work done involved some early mornings. "When there's a lot of people around, I like to go out and hang out with them, joke around and just have fun. So, for my job, when I have to write something, I like to come in early, when there's no one else there, and actually get some work done."

There was a small-scale power struggle on the show when Dino arrived full-time for the third season. Everyone was already established, and here was Dino, brought in as a producer — a producer with opinions and good ideas. The attitude was a bit stand-offish. So, Dino went through the third season as Nice Guy, trying to accommodate this attitude.

David says that he and Bob leaned on Dino to be the mediator: "Bob and I are both very opinionated, and we would pout or stomp our feet. Dino was the tie-breaker. He was the arbiter. And that was really important. I don't mean to diminish all the other great things he did — he's a funny, unique person, and he came up with clever stuff — but he saved us a lot of arguments."

Dino:
"I don't know why Bob and David always try to get me to perform in pieces. I just don't think I'm that good onstage."

Dino:
"Coffee really affects me, because I don't use it a lot, only when I have to get up and write. So, it's just a great drug for me. Any drug helps to write."

Bill:
"Of all the people there, that show benefitted the most from having Dino there. Dino is arguably as funny as Bob or David. You have so much confidence in him, in his opinion. He would read a lot of other people's scenes, give notes. If you get stuck, he'll come up with something really brilliant. He was a great guy to work with."

David:
"Dino's kind of sybaritic, which I really gravitate toward. He's about having a good time, about seeking out decadence and enjoying it and valuing it. He was the only guy on the whole staff that I could really commiserate with about drugs, and we'd go and take acid together. There was this one time that we went to San Francisco for the weekend, just to drop a whole bunch of acid and walk around for a few days. And it was a blast, and I couldn't have done it with anyone else on that staff."

Some classic Dino sketches:
Audition (#404)
Young People & Companions (#305) (with Brent)
Pre-Taped Call-In Show (#309) (with Brent)
Druggachusettes (#304)

These scenes kind of stand out — they are the most intricate mental puzzles on the show, and those were Dino and Brent pieces. And they were helped along by drugs." (Except for *Druggachusettes* which, oddly enough, was not.)

© Photo by Adam Timrud

Mary Lynn Rajskub
cast member - season 1, 2

Mary Lynn was raised outside Detroit and went to art school in Detroit. She started stand-up, accidentally, as an assignment in her "performance art" course. "You do your basics: you learn 'sculpture,' then 'figure sculpture,' and then you learn about 'conceptual sculpture' — sculpture that 'can't even be composed.'" Her sculpture was stand-up, of sorts: "I went to open mic with my boyfriend, and I just wrote down a bunch of things that were like punch lines, with no joke attached to them, and said them all in a row. And people thought I was a big freak. And they were kind of laughing a little bit, because I kept going on, delivering them like they were punch lines. I did it in class, and my teacher said, 'You need to take an acting class, and that's not comedy.'"

Her varied stand-up act — where she gets onstage, a plain, affable girl, and launches into a protracted, seemingly stream-of-consciousness monologue, speaking with an authoritative air — may not be an act at all. Leaving that to question is deliberate. "That's what I'm interested in," she explains, "the line between something when someone's putting it on, and you can't tell if it's really them or not."

In 1993, Mary Lynn moved out to San Francisco, where she met comedians Blaine Capatch, Patton Oswalt, Ron Lynch, and Jeremy Kramer. "Comedy clubs were closing, so people were performing at open mic poetry things. It was pretty happenin' for a while; it was really exciting. And I remember being really attracted to the comedians who did longer, meandering stuff. I was more interested in the clownish aspect of it. People who are putting on airs."

Mary Lynn was 24 when she came to L.A. with then-boyfriend Jeremy Kramer. "I had no business coming here. I had $200 and no car." She signed up with a manager Dave Rath ("I did a torch song version of 'Cop Killer,' and I think that was the thing that won them over."). She shaped her meandrous performing style on L.A.'s budding alternative circuit. "The first time I went up at the Diamond Club, what I was saying made absolutely no sense at all. I can't even believe I got onstage. It was seriously little scraps of paper with random text on it." She started dating David Cross and was a part of the *Mr. Show* cast from its origins. "Everything was really exciting," she marvels.

Friend Janeane Garofalo was instrumental in her being cast on *The Larry Sanders Show*, easily her biggest break at the time. "Janeane helped by telling the producers she wanted to work with me. They wanted to keep her on the show. She told me, 'they dangled you like a carrot in front of me.' We did that first show where she was training me to take her place, and they got her to do another episode."

David Cross says of Mary Lynn: "She is one of those people, as I listen to her make decisions and interact with people, I wonder, 'Does she have any idea just how smart and funny she is?' I know she knows she's smart and funny — that has been confirmed by people's reaction to her, and telling her as much — but does she really know how exceedingly smart and funny she is? And totally unique, too. She's also the only cast member I fell in love with, which flavors all this."

Mary Lynn and David split after more than two years, just before the third season of *Mr. Show*. A difficult break-up, the two couldn't work together any longer. "I tried working with Mary Lynn," David asserts. "She came to the first read-through, we had written sketches with her in them. I fully intended to say, 'Too bad it didn't work out and everything. We're still friends.' But that took a lot longer than I expected; it was too hard to see her there. I truly regret not being able to get my shit together." "It was sad," says Mary Lynn. "I couldn't even watch it after that. I went to a couple tapings, but then I had to stop." Feeling nostalgic, she adds, "The Diamond Club was a really cool time, because a lot of people were sort of in the same place. There is the same group of people, but we don't see each other that much any more."

Karen Kilgariff
cast member - season 3, 4

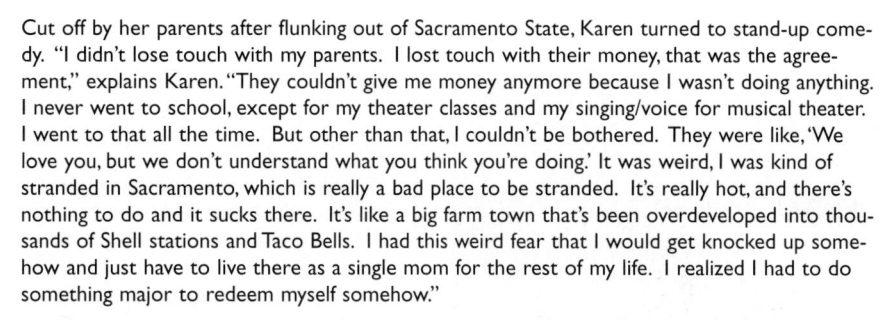

Cut off by her parents after flunking out of Sacramento State, Karen turned to stand-up comedy. "I didn't lose touch with my parents. I lost touch with their money, that was the agreement," explains Karen. "They couldn't give me money anymore because I wasn't doing anything. I never went to school, except for my theater classes and my singing/voice for musical theater. I went to that all the time. But other than that, I couldn't be bothered. They were like, 'We love you, but we don't understand what you think you're doing.' It was weird, I was kind of stranded in Sacramento, which is really a bad place to be stranded. It's really hot, and there's nothing to do and it sucks there. It's like a big farm town that's been overdeveloped into thousands of Shell stations and Taco Bells. I had this weird fear that I would get knocked up somehow and just have to live there as a single mom for the rest of my life. I realized I had to do something major to redeem myself somehow."

She sought redemption through comedy. She started going up at an open mic night run by a friend in Old Sacramento. By 22, she'd moved to San Francisco. Thanks to San Francisco comics who met her in Sacramento during a comedy competition, she went straight to the Improv, "the coolest room." And there's where she saw David Cross for the first time. "We didn't really like each other," she admits. "I thought he was stuck up, and he thought I was a bitch. It's really hysterical that we both had the same impression of each other."

Next came Los Angeles, where again she was warmly welcomed by the local scene. She performed at the *UnCabaret* (weekly "alternative" comedy room), which was an exact fit for her admittedly off-beat stand-up style. She fit in perfectly both stylistically and personally — "It was really cool to have all those people around. It was very cliquey."

Sarah Silverman
sometime performer - season 1, 2, 3

Although Sarah Silverman was not involved with the live stage show that begat the HBO program, she was a part of the *Mr. Show* family from the very first season. For someone who was never a cast member, she was used often and always turning out memorable performances, like Chrysalis (the VJ with *Smoosh*); and Fran (the woman in *Indomitable Spirit*).

Sarah might have been the sole female writer on *Mr. Show* — she was officially propositioned by the guys to join their "Boys' Club" for their fourth season. However, it wasn't to be. Sarah had a prior commitment to co-star in a feature film (*Screwed*) and had to turn them down. "I was so honored, and I was so excited that they asked me. But I said, 'I know I want to act more than I want to write.' I never had a part like that — I gotta do the movie." She didn't know they were facing the last season *of Mr. Show* (no one knew). "It was a huge mistake," she readily admits. "I was so mad at David. I called him and told him, 'I'm going to do this movie instead because I want to be an actor.' I said it was a Norm MacDonald movie, and he said, 'Why do they bother releasing those? Why don't they go straight to video?' I'd hate to say that he was right. Lordy."

In 1993, Sarah spent a year writing and performing on *SNL,* but was not asked to return for a second season. "I had no confidence for a while, like a year," she confesses. Then, when that was over in '95, she came to Los Angeles. Sarah hung out with the same big group of friends as Bob and David. "It was all the Dave Rath-party kind of time, and Fellini's Bar — everyone would go to at night. My roommates were Mary Lynn and Tracy Katsky. It was just kind of like this community, every night was a hang out. And right before they used me on *Mr. Show*, I remember one time we were at Fellini's, and Bob — I was a huge Bob fan, but he didn't really give me the time of day — he came over to me and said, 'I just gotta tell you I just think you're really funny. I never thought you were funny before, but now I totally think you're funny.' I was so happy, but I was also like, 'Hey!'"

Paul F. Tompkins
sometime performer - season 1
writer/cast member - season 2, 3
cast member - season 4

"Season 2 was my first season as a writer on the show. At the time I was hired, I had been out of work for about two months, having been fired from my last retail job. Bob and David called me and Jay Johnston — with whom I'd done a stage show called *The Skates* that got their attention — in for a meeting and offered us jobs on the show. We said, 'Yeah, we'd love to work on the show!' and those guys said, 'Great!' And then we started talking about sketch ideas. My head was swimming. I thought I would pass out or something. I just couldn't believe it — that that was all there was to it, that I really *did* have this amazing job now. I just sat there in a daze, trying to act cool and throw out ideas. Then Jay and I went out to dinner with Bob, Dave, and Bill. I was still out of it. I think I left before everyone else did and walked home. When I got home, I sat on the edge of my couch for a little and just smoked and shook with excitement. I called my parents, and my mother said what she says about anything I tell her having to do with my career: 'Oh, honey, that's great!' Finally, Jay called me up, and we just screamed at each other on the phone — 'Can you fucking believe it?!' Jay told me he was going through the exact same thing I was. We later went out to the Snake Pit on Melrose and had a few beers with David. When we left the bar, Jay and I gave each other a big congratulatory hug. We were writers on *Mr. Show*."

For Paul, it was always going to be show business: "I always loved comedy when I was a kid. I would watch *Carson*, and I would laugh, and I didn't even know what I was laughing at, but I always loved comedians and comedy." Everything was serendipitous in Paul's slide into the biz. "I had a vague idea I wanted to be a stand-up, but I didn't know how to go about it," Paul says. "It was [high school friend] Rick Roman, who got me to do it. Rick came back to Philly, where he had performed a couple of times, and asked if I wanted to do an act together. That was how I got into show business." Paul and Rick split up after a year and a half, because they started to hate each other. "That's what happens with teams," Paul offers. Rick Roman moved to Chicago to do improv; Paul stayed in Philly and started hitting the open mics by himself.

In 1994, Paul came to Los Angeles, and for the first two years — all the way up to right before he started at *Mr. Show* — he was still working the day jobs. That is, until fate intervened, and he was "dismissed" from what would be his last. "It was at Tower Video, in '96. And I got fired from that job for a very good reason," confesses Paul. "I was fired for stealing video tapes. That's a thing that definitely happens in the world of retail, but I was way too old to be doing that. When you work retail, and you do something like that, it's so easy to rationalize it — 'They expect you to steal.' But you're fucking stealing! There's no rationalization. It started out as the occasional film, and, after a while, friends of mine would come in and just fill up a bag — a bag full of movies — and just walk out. Someone ratted on me, and I got caught. That was the last vestige of my immaturity in a way, because that really woke me up. When you're threatened with jail, that will make you think about things, and it will kind of put things in perspective. And you realize you can't be as stupid as you had been for a long time. I was kind of in a state of arrested development for a while, because my life really had not changed that much. I come out to L.A., and I'm back working in a retail store. And once I started really working in comedy, I started to see how things could be, and what was important…what kind of life I could have."

Paul knew almost nobody in L.A., so Adam McKay (his Chicago friend through ex-partner Rick Roman) hooked him up with Jay Johnston for a blind date, of sorts. The two hit it off. Paul marvels, "That never works out, that two people, who have one person in common, meet and actually get along. How rare is that? The fact that we clicked right away, that's really wild to think about. We hung out more in the first three months we knew each other than the last five years. Jay and I fell for each other hard."

Together, they created *The Skates*, a sketch show infused with their shared "out there" sensibility, and to which they wisely invited Bob and David. "They came to our shows and were always very complimentary, but I had no idea there was ever a job to be had," says Paul. "But that was the big break. I am hugely indebted to Bob and David for that job. I honestly do not know what I would be doing now. If I hadn't met Jay, etc., would I still be trying to sign up at the Improv, or sitting on a folding chair all day, in line trying to get a spot at the Laugh Factory?"

David recalls being very impressed by Jay and Paul's collaborative work: "*The Skates* was the funniest sketch show I'd ever scene. Really funny, very clever ideas. It was really surprising, almost jarring, to know that they had just met. The sketches were so funny and weird and

---

Adam McKay:
"Paul dresses like he's 58. Anyone with a cigarette case, you immediately assume is over 40. And I think Paul had a cigarette case when he was about 16."

David:
"I don't understand the suits. I don't get living in the desert and wearing a suit, when you don't have to. Maybe if it were the 1920's, I could understand it a little better. But it's not the '20's, and it's L.A. where it's more casual. Maybe that's why he does it — to retain some shred of dignity. Maybe it's like that guy in *Slaughterhouse-Five*, who goes to the bathroom every day at 9 in the morning, on the clock, because he wants to retain his dignity and doesn't want to let the Germans take that from him."

```
                    RICH
That's the spirit!
                    RICHARD
(NOTICING SOMETHING) Has this
rhubarb been here the whole
while?
                    RICH
All day long!
                    RICHARD
Mmmmmmmm, I love rhubarb.
                    RICH
And it's great in pie.  What
could be more refreshing?
                    RICHARD
Very little!
                    RICH
Speaking of very little, I was
very little upset yesterday when
a flight I was taking was
delayed for over an hour.  I
hate to wait; it makes me feel
so... "not-that-excited".
                    RICHARD
Yes.  How about we take a look
in my... "toolbox"?

THEY LOOK TO THE MONITOR.

CUT TO: VIDEO.  THE GRAND, MARBLE STEPS OF A GOVERNMENT BUILDING.
RICHARD IS SHAKING HANDS WITH THE PRESIDENT OF THE UNITED STATES.
                    RICHARD
```

Page from "Tintrell," the first scene Jay and Paul wrote together for their sketch show "The Skates." Performed in L.A., 1996.

crazy, and they complimented each other real well. And because there were no rules — it wasn't TV, it was just a small, 100-seat theater — you can get away with a lot, as well you should. The concept of the scene constantly changed, and it was really fun. It kept going out there and getting crazier and crazier, and they always pulled it off."

For the fourth season, Paul did not return as a writer. "I was always more interested in performing than writing, just 'cause it's easier. Because writing is a pain in the ass. It's easy to say the fourth season was the most fun, because, for me, there wasn't as much work involved." Paul was relieved that Bob and David continued to use him in a lot of scenes and asked him still to be the live audience warm-up guy. "First of all, it was very flattering and was something that I needed personally for my ego, to be thought of as a good performer by those guys. And also because I left the show — you never know if there's going to be hard feelings. It was such a relief and a pleasure that they wanted me back. I was proud to be associated with the show. It was almost bragging to say, 'Yeah, I was a writer on *Mr. Show*.'"

Scott Adsit
cast member - season 4

Scott is a Second City, Chicago guy, who, in college, unregrettably spent "far too much time" with Dino Stamatopoulos. The two were at Columbia College together, both "kind of unemployed and not happy," says Scott, "except when we would get together and make each other laugh. We'd hang in his apartment, which was just a basement room with a mattress and a computer. And some fries. We'd sit in there and write little shtick and improvise with each other, just make each other laugh. We'd get his guitar, and we'd go and act like we worked at outdoor restaurants and serenade people. We'd ask for requests and just sing some song we wrote earlier. It was a great time."

Dino left Chicago to write for *The Ben Stiller Show* and disappeared out of Scott's life until years later, when he hired Scott away from Second City to work with him on a TV show for Barry Levinson, a project Dino undertook between seasons at *Mr. Show*. The project fell through a few months later. With no job in Chicago, Scott and his girlfriend moved to L.A. Scott was promptly invited to do a scene on *Mr. Show*, which led to more appearances throughout the fourth season.

Jack Black
sometime performer - season 1, 2

Jack Black is featured in the first two seasons of *Mr. Show*, including the spectacular turn as *Jeepers Creepers*, the indecisive messiah (#203). He was a part of Bob and David's early 'presentation' shows for HBO, and before that, with The D, was a guest at the experimental Diamond Club shows. And, before that, they'd never met.

"Me and Kyle started as actors together, we met at the Actors' Gang Theater," Jack says of his unification with Tenacious D bandmate, Kyle Gass. "And he became like my big bro. He was like a father. A grandfather. And we started hanging out. He'd teach me to play the guitar. And then we decided to write a song together. And we wanted to write the greatest song in the world. And we worked on that for a really long time. Like two days. And we realized, you can't. You can't write the greatest song. So we wrote a tribute. And that's where it all started."

Jack and Kyle were around for the magical days of the Diamond Club shows. They had just started the two-man D, "the greatest band on earth." "I remember it like it was yesterday," says Jack of those early days. "Kyle and I actually played our first gigs at a place in downtown Los Angeles called Al's Bar. We only had a couple songs at the time, "Tribute," and "Kyle Quit the Band," and a song about OJ. We discontinued that one. When David Cross came down, he came down with Laura Milligan, and I think we just played "Tribute" that night. And he said, 'Hey, man, I want you guys to do that song with us when we do our show.' And we said, 'Yeah, man, yeah.' But little did we know that he was introducing us to a whole new world of possibilities. I had no idea who he was. I thought he was a schmo."

David has a little story from when he and Jack first met: "I'd already seen Jack and Kyle at Al's Bar, and they were going to appear in our show at the Diamond Club. And Jack and I were talking about what we would do. I lived in a shitty, really hot apartment on Vermont, and I'm just sitting in my apartment with all the windows open. I'm on the phone with Jack about some ideas, and then I hear an ambulance drive by my window. And then, 15 seconds later, I hear a continuation of the ambulance noise from Jack's phone. Then we both paused, and said, 'Hey, did you hear that ambulance?' And he was going through the same thing, 'Yeah, yeah, I did.' 'Where do you live?' '1823 Vermont Avenue.' 'Holy shit! I live on 1804 Vermont Avenue!' We both go to our windows, and we just started waving to each other. We'd been having these phone conversations, and we were literally two buildings away from each other."

Brett Paesel
sometime performer - season 2
cast member - season 3, 4

Brett was new to L.A. and had never seen *Mr. Show* when she was thrown into the cast. "It happened fairly quickly. They needed to replace Jill in a sketch, because she was getting married. I have constantly considered myself very lucky. I can't believe that I fell into this right after I moved to L.A. I think there's so much bad TV out there. And, suddenly, I was doing a great TV show with people I really respected. In a way, it was kind of like, 'Wow, how'd that happen?'"

An import from England and Germany, where she was a "theater fag," she came to the States in 1986 to study theater at Indiana University, where her focus was not comedy. "I thought I was going to be a 'regular' actress doing Williams and Chekov and Shakespeare. I moved to New York, and then to Chicago, with that in mind. And the whole time, I always did comedy as this late-night, guilty thing. It wasn't until I did the *Real Live Brady Bunch* — with [fellow *Mr. Show* cast member] Becky Thyre, oddly enough — that I started realizing maybe I can make a living doing this, and I'm probably not going to make a living doing Shakespeare."

Brett ended up in L.A. after she and others from the tour decided they were tired of being Bradys after three years. (Brett was "Carol.") "So, we created a show in San Francisco called *Not Without My Nipples: The Made for TV Musical*. It was a musical stage show written by Faith Solloway and Ben Zook about a bunch of has-been actors, who make a TV movie-of-the-week. Somebody invited us to perform it in L.A. Suddenly, I was in Los Angeles, and I hadn't even planned on it."

HBO's Carolyn Strauss suggested that Brett fill in for Jill on *Mr. Show* that second season after seeing her perform in her one-woman show, *Don't Call It "'Nam" Unless You've Been There*.

Of her roles on *Mr. Show*, Brett is most proud of portraying housewives. "Most of the time, to be honest, I would be cast as prostitutes and whores. So, suddenly, for someone to see me as a housewife was really fun. Usually, I'm playing some bitch with a heart of gold, or something like that."

Jerry Minor
cast member - season 4

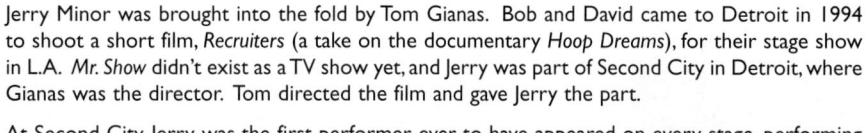

Jerry Minor was brought into the fold by Tom Gianas. Bob and David came to Detroit in 1994 to shoot a short film, *Recruiters* (a take on the documentary *Hoop Dreams*), for their stage show in L.A. *Mr. Show* didn't exist as a TV show yet, and Jerry was part of Second City in Detroit, where Gianas was the director. Tom directed the film and gave Jerry the part.

At Second City, Jerry was the first performer ever to have appeared on every stage, performing with the Second City in Detroit, Chicago, and Toronto, for a total of 10 stage reviews. He began doing open mics in the Detroit area at age 19, getting his first spot by lying about his experience. He was picking up steam as a stand-up when the comedy boom of the 80's began to fade. "And then I dropped out of comedy. I dropped out of college, too. It's like I lost interest in everything then," he explains. "I got married. I had a really good job that I thought I would have for a long time. I was working at General Motors, as a computer programmer (basically data entry). But, y'know, it paid well — what I thought was well. And then I got laid off, and so did my wife. It was pretty devastating." He immediately went back into comedy. For money, he did odd jobs, cleaning at a factory, working shifts starting at 2 A.M. so he could perform at night.

Getting laid off at GM was the impetus Jerry needed: he became very serious about performing. Seeing a show at Second City Chicago inspired Jerry to pull together a sketch group in Detroit with his stand-up buddies, *The Other Level*. They performed all around town, a few colleges. "I think the group still exists, with different people," he adds. Soon, there was word of a new Second City stage opening in Detroit. They held an open audition, and he got in. "They picked seven people out of seven hundred," he boasts.

While in Toronto, Jerry saw Bob and David for the first time since *Recruiters* was shot two years earlier. It was already their third season of *Mr. Show*, and the guys were there to promote *Mr. Show's* run on the Canadian Comedy Channel. "They were doing *The Mike Bullard Show*, which was right across the street from Second City, so I went over there to say hello," recalls Jerry. "And Bob remembered me, and he said, 'Hey, you should come and do more sketches for us.'" "There was a piece we had written [*Lifeboat* #401] with a part I thought he'd be really funny for," says Bob. "And we just wanted him out here. So we promised Jerry he'd be in every show if he came out." Bob and David kept their word. "Even if it is the picture in the background, I think I made my way into every show that season," Jerry points out with pride.

Mark Rivers
theme song creator
sometime performer - season 4

The hauntingly catchy theme song — the one with the drum beat open that starts the show — was penned by David's longtime friend from Atlanta, Mark Rivers. "David called me up, for some reason he was speaking in whispered tones, 'Listen, I think we might be doing a show, so write a few theme songs and send it to us.' Okay. So, I went over a friend's house and threw down a few songs on a home 8-track. I sent them about four ideas, and they picked one. It was the easiest thing in the world."

Mark Rivers met David Cross at 16, when Rivers was the drummer in a "really ridiculous prog-rock band," where the guitarist was a friend of David's. "Oddly, David and I kept in contact," says Rivers. He moved to Boston at David's urging. "He said, 'I'm having the best time out here!' I transferred up there, to Berkeley College of Music — probably one of the best decisions I've ever made — to get out of Atlanta, go someplace completely new, meet a whole new group of friends." But Mark only lasted one semester before he ran out of money. "I wound up working in a mailroom at a law firm, and met a guy I started a band with. We were together for seven years, and we ended up doing pretty good, The Cavedogs. And we all worked in that mailroom. All of the band and David, plus other friends of ours, all musicians and comedians. It was a blast. We would joke around and supposedly work all day. Then go play music and drink at night. And just laugh all day. It was probably the happiest I've ever been in my life, and I was 22 years old."

Rivers finally made it out to Hollywood. During the fourth season of *Mr. Show*, he worked as a production assistant. He jumped at the chance to contribute creatively, writing and recording music for the occasional scene (including the song by the unintentionally homoerotic band *Wyckyd Sceptre* (#403), and pieces for '*Taint* (#406). He can also be seen in #410 as *Info Jimmy*, the human link, where he walks with a clipboard from the end of one scene to the next, giving people their time cues (to a couple going at it in a motel: "Okay, pull out…Now!").

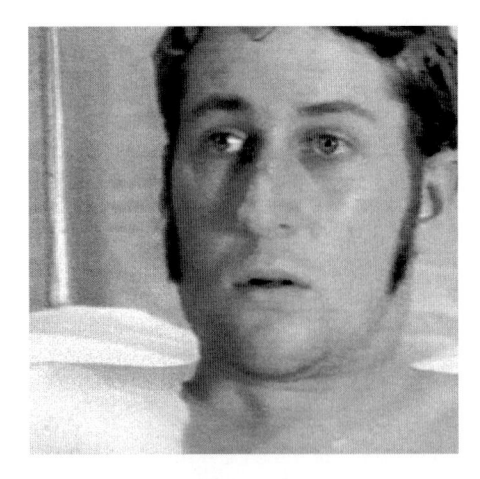

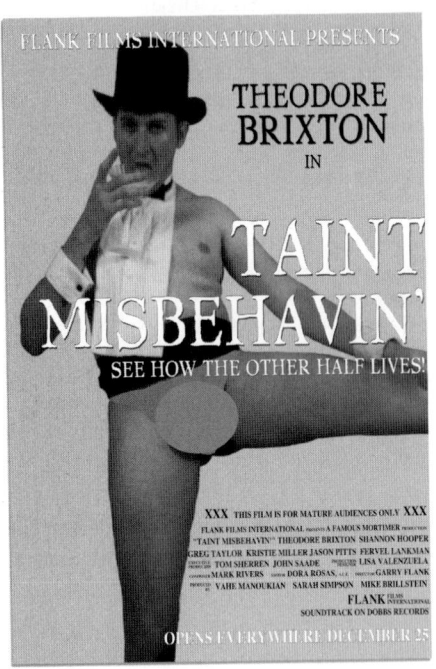

David:
"I was immediately impressed with Scott — not only in is his articulation of an argument, but the fact that he was willing to argue immediately."

Bill:
"Scott is a highly opinionated man, and tends to let people know his opinions."

Scott Aukerman
sometime performer - season 2, 3
writer/cast member - season 4

"It was a mixed blessing," says Scott Aukerman of the fact that, for years, he and his writing partner, B.J. Porter, could not live down the name, *The Fun Bunch*. "The fact that we were called *The Fun Bunch* was kind of a mistake," explains B.J. "The first time we performed together, we did this bit where we were pretending to be from an improv team called *The Fun Bunch*, because we hate what's done with a lot of improv — the dumb games they play and call it a show. We were going to make fun of that. But then people started calling us 'Fun Bunch.' And a few people, most notably [comic] Doug Benson, would never let us not be *The Fun Bunch*. When we'd show up anywhere, that's what we'd be called." Aukerman adds, with irony, "We just kept the name, so people would know who we are."

Scott Aukerman is from Los Angeles. Oddly enough, he left L.A. to study theater in a two-year program at an acting conservatory. "No real college courses," he admits with pride. "I was always attracted to comedy. Letterman was my hero all through high school. I never thought I would get into performing comedy, because what was really popular at the time was Jerry Seinfeld, Richard Lewis, people who did observational comedy. That kind of stuff just didn't really interest me. What I really found funny, I always felt that no one would ever find it funny. My sense of humor was too crazy and too offensive, so I never tried to do it. Instead, when I went to school, I became a writer, writing plays. I wrote a lot of serial comic plays — Mamet — kind of funny but also dramatic. Then, I wrote a straight-out comedy, like silly, silly comedy, and my friends said, 'Wow, this is this best thing you've ever done. It's you.' I started thinking, 'Well, what does my life have in store for me — Broadway?' I never wanted to do that. Why did I even go to that school? What the fuck am I doing? And I moved back to LA. I didn't have a car; I took the bus to the Olive Garden. I didn't know what to do." And then his friend B.J. Porter moved to town.

B.J. Porter
sometime performer - season 2, 3
writer/cast member - season 4

B.J. Porter grew up in Scotsdale, Arizona and had an early awareness of what he wanted to do. "I was specifically interested in comedy my whole life; I couldn't focus on much more. I knew eventually I wanted to move to Hollywood, but I didn't want to make the Hollywood commitment right away, so I moved to Orange County, which I thought would feel a little more like Hollywood. Well, it turns out Orange County could not be any less like Hollywood, and it couldn't be more like Scottsdale."

He wasted a couple of years in Orange County, doing theater at a junior college. In 1989, he met Scott Aukerman, who would become his writing partner, when they were both cast into a show. "Scott was clearly really funny, and he liked my work a lot. As usual for me in theater, I was not the most popular figure in a show. The director didn't like me that much. I was very combative all the time, a smart-ass. People really disliked me, and rightfully so. I knew it was time to move away from Orange County, because I went to three parties in three weeks, where, waiting for me, was someone who wanted to beat me up, for something I had said or done. Scott had already gone off to college, and he was one of only three people who liked me. So now it was down to two, not enough to back me up. So, I went to Hollywood. I had no plan whatsoever, I was just going to feel my way through it, and it took me a long time. I was 22. I didn't really do anything in show business for a long time, just trying to keep myself alive." Aukerman and Porter continued collaborating, even while living in separate cities.

Now both in Los Angeles, Scott and B.J. were officially aspiring writers/waiters at Chin Chin on Ventura. Around 1995, fortuity, in the shape of Meleva Barbula, stepped in. Meleva, an actress Scott met in Sacramento, was now in L.A. and was rooming with Karen Kilgariff. Meleva knew a lot of comedians in town, and, as Scott recalls, she encouraged him to perform at a show C.J. Arabia and Mary Lynn Rajskub hosted in the Belly Room, a small space at The Comedy Store. ("It frightened me more than anything. I didn't think anyone else would like my humor.") That same week, Scott met Bob Odenkirk. "I had no idea who Bob was," admits Scott. "He just said to me, 'Oh, you're a writer? What do you write?' He gave me a card for the show he and David were doing, *The Cross/Odenkirk Problem* — 'Yeah, you should come on by, if you want.' I took the card home, and B.J. knew David Cross from stand-up and thought he was really funny. So, we went to their show at the Upfront Theater, and it totally blew my mind."

That night also had a big impact on B.J. "Really, I could not have been less interested," he recalls. "I did think that David was a funny stand-up comic, but I never thought I'd ever see a comedy sketch again that would make me laugh, so I didn't really want to go. I don't know how I wound up going, but I do know I left my bells at home in a drawer. And, of course, it was hilarious. I sat right in front. It was amazing! Scott described it best — 'It's one of those things that you see, and it's great, and you know why it's great. It's not one of those things that just intimidates you, like 'I never want to do it. I have nothing to add.' It really inspired us."

They suddenly felt that people would "get" them and their unusual sensibility. "It made me call Meleva and say, 'Yeah, we want to do C.J. and Mary Lynn's show,'" remembers Scott. "But I was scared. We'd seen the show in the Belly Room, and it was Janeane Garofalo and David Cross, all these really funny people. But we did it, and it was huge. It was pretty cool. A whole bunch of people I really respected thought it was funny. Mary Lynn and C.J. asked us to do their show again. The second week, Bob was there — Bob was at the second thing we ever did! And he liked us. He said, 'Yeah, I'm doing this TV show, maybe you could be on it. I don't know what I'd have, but maybe you guys can do it.' He downplays his show — he wants to give you a helping hand without giving you too much hope."

Two months later, *Mr. Show* began taping the first season's episodes. Scott and B.J., of course, showed up for the taping. "We got in the regular person line for the audience, and somebody called us over to the VIP line. We got in first," Scott recalls enthusiastically. "Then, when they came out to start the show, Bob was waving at people, and he pointed at us. And I thought, 'Oh, my God, I just got here! This is fuckin' awesome!' I was in the audience for all the *Mr. Shows*, I couldn't believe it, just thought it was the funniest thing I'd ever seen."

Scott and B.J. were very interested in writing, and were aware of their amazing opportunity — registering on Bob and David's radar just as they were starting this new, fantastic show. But, as B.J. explains, they made a conscious choice not to be too aggressive: "We felt like we kind of got to know Bob and David, and we didn't want to be presumptuous and ask them for a job. We always thought if they wanted to hire us, they would've asked us. I feel like we did exactly the right thing — not turn them off, and not make them worried when they saw us, 'Oh, these guys are going to be bothering us about a job again.' More than anything, it was great to watch it, and study it, and learn. And we really valued the job when we got it. It made us really work hard."

In the subsequent seasons, Bob and David occasionally used B.J. and Scott as actors, always very small roles. Then finally, they were asked to submit sketches for the upcoming fourth season of *Mr. Show*. They submitted five sketches, three of which were actually used: '*Taint, Intervention,* and *Blind Girl*. "It was a difficult thing for them," David adds. "They came in with no experience, into a show that was already established. And there is, certainly among those other writers, a little bit of competition and jockeying for whose bits are going to get in, whose bits are going to be nurtured. And as a testament to their talent, they were able to stick through it."

Although Scott and B.J. had submitted as a team, they were hired separately and discouraged from writing together. "I think they anticipated some resistance about that," Scott recollects, "because they didn't know how we work together. We never write together. When we are working on something, we write alone, tag-team style." B.J. adds, "They felt like by breaking us up, they were putting us on a level field with everybody else. I think we both benefitted a lot."

B.J.:
"I make remarks that are very innocuous that people take very harshly. So I think I was very wary of saying something about a sketch that might hurt someone's feelings to a degree beyond professional. That was an obstacle. I had to get notes that I didn't take personally, and see the way it was presented, to learn how to give them."

Bill:
"B.J. had really good conventional scene ideas, which are really valuable to us. Really funny. And he was a good guy to work with. Even the scenes he wrote that didn't make it on, I liked."

B.J.:
"Because it's a job that you value so much, not being fired is such a high priority. Any other job I ever had, I had the luxury of never caring if I was fired. But *Mr. Show* was the one place I wanted to be. Not being fired was this inordinately high priority that was really an obstacle the first couple of months."

Mike Upchurch (right) with Brian Posehn and cigars at Third Season Wrap "Party."

Dino:
"Brent is a person who likes to convert things into money-making schemes. Anything he enjoys doing, he has to qualify it with, 'All right, how is this going to make me money?' He was born in Malibu. And if he was born in a coal mining town, he'd be a coal miner. He would not be a writer if he'd been born in Kansas. It's coming from a good work ethic. He was raised by four doctors. (His parents are both doctors, and they divorced and each married doctors.)"

Mike Upchurch
guest writer, season 3

"I had been writing sketches in notebooks since I was a teenager and watched every sketch show on TV. In grad school, I actually wrote a 100-page Master's Thesis on sketch comedy, which helped me put off the real world for three years. I chased down Sid Caesar and Al Franken and interviewed them, and I read a bunch of really boring literature. That was one of the hardest and stupidest things I ever did. What a dumb idea! I moved to L.A. in 1995. I had no sooner plunked down on my roommate's 800-pound couch when I saw a promo for *Mr. Show*. Apparently, the guy, who had the apartment before, hadn't cut off his cable, and I caught two episodes. I thought it was the coolest show I'd ever seen, and I amused myself with the notion that I might get a job there. Almost a year later, I bumped into Bob Odenkirk at a stand-up show in Los Feliz and discovered *Mr. Show* had just wrapped a second season. After some wrangling, I got Bob to look at some sketches. Bob was exceptionally cool, but said he didn't know if the show was being brought back. For the next few months, I came home from my crappy day job and worked on sketch ideas. Whenever I saw Bob or David at stand-up shows, I pitched ideas and generally acted like a big spaz, 'cause I'm not too good at playing it cool. One day there was a message on my machine telling me to meet the guys at a coffee shop in Hollywood called The Pig. Come to find out, I'd been hired. I contributed three premises to the third season — *The Devastator, Lie Detector,* and *Blowing Up the Moon* — as well as bits and pieces in all the episodes. I don't think I'll ever write on another show that allows such creative freedom and purity of ideas."

Jerry Collins
guest writer - season 4

"I met Bob and David a couple times during the heyday of L.A.'s 'alternative' comedy scene in the mid '90's. Their stuff was always really inspired. I also knew Jay Johnston through some mutual friends, plus Brian Posehn and I did a Semester-at-Sea together back in college. In '97, I sat next to Dino Stamatopoulos on a plane coming back from Burning Man — he let me use his neck pillow. Then, Bill Odenkirk and I met at IKEA fighting over a great rug that I still have! The funny part is I had never really written anything before *Mr. Show*, but I guess I knew the right people."

Eric Hoffman
guest writer - season 4

"I was a huge fan of the show before I was hired. It reminded me of watching *Monty Python* for the first time. I kept thinking, 'I wish this wasn't the very first show I was ever hired to write on.' Jay got me hired. We were college buddies and later worked together at the Annoyance Theatre in Chicago, where we honed our wig-work, comedy-jacket, and salty humor skills. I was also in a play Dino directed called *Trent*, about a guy who takes his newborn baby out for a stroll on the coldest day in Chicago history, and it accidentally freezes to death. It was billed as a 'light tragedy with music.' Later, in L.A., Jay got me into the *Mr. Show* tapings, and I hung around some, and eventually they used my 1990 Cadillac Fleetwood in a *Goodfellas* sketch. There was an opening in the fourth season for some new writers, so Jay passed along some of my comedy samples to Bob, and, eventually, I got a meeting with him. Bob said he liked *Bugged Drug Deal* [#408], but what would prevent him from, say, just taking the sketch and not hiring me at all? I told him the scene had a 'secret ending' I was withholding until I saw a contract."

Brent Forrester
contributing writer - season 3, 4

At the time of *Mr. Show*, Brent was a writer on *The Simpsons*. The two pieces that he contributed were co-written with Dino: *The Pre-Taped Call-In Show* (#309) and *Audition* (#404). "Those two sketches, I actually think are the best things I have ever written. They're the things that I feel the most like, 'That's a classic piece of comedy.' And I didn't even write them, I co-wrote them. There's no question that those two things are a result of collaboration. The collaborative essence of Forrester-Stamatopoulos is the rational mind (Forrester) and the irrational mind (Stamatopoulos). You can see these two scenes are mathematical, yet insane. They are nice pieces of comic architecture. That's why I'm so proud of them."

John Moffitt
director, live tapings - all seasons

John Moffit directed all episodes but one of *Mr. Show*. He was the live director: he directed each show as it was being performed live, in front of an audience. Directing live sketch comedy is a specialized skill; there are not many people who can do it. Moffitt got his start in the mid-70's, helming comedy series and specials starring icons such as Richard Pryor, Lily Tomlin, Dick Van Dyke. His resume is saturated with sketch/live comedy directing — probably more than anybody else working today — required viewing for students of comedy: *Not Necessarily The News* and *Fridays*.

Mr. Show was still in development when Bob and David were brought to Moffitt's attention. Bernie Brillstein (Bob's manager, executive producer of *Mr. Show*, and Moffitt's long-time manager) had a plan. He wanted the strongest possible support for Bob and David, rather than go low-end, to provide them with a really good start. "Early on, Bernie said, 'You've gotta see these guys,'" recalls Moffitt, "and I sat and watched the live show with Bernie. And he had great faith in Bob (and with his new collaboration with David). He said, 'This is going to be really great, why don't you get involved with them.' And I saw some great raw talent there, and I wanted to be a part of it."

"Directing live sketch comedy is incredibly difficult," acknowledges Bob. "It's unlike any other directing job. You have to know what angles to get, and where the jokes are in the scene, and how to play the moments. You have to call it live [call the camera shots as it's being taped], and be able to react to the rhythms of the scene as it changes in front of an audience from what it was in rehearsal with no audience — there's laughs, and people fuck up lines, and there's little things everywhere. So it's very active direction. It's very challenging. It's one of those things you have to do to know how to do it, and there aren't many opportunities to do it. So, we were so lucky to get a guy who'd done it and knew it really well. And on top of it, with all his experience and all the job offers he gets, John was willing to work his ass off. John went to every rehearsal, sat there, walked through the sketch with us. We'd do it over and over, as much as we wanted. Saturday morning, Sunday morning. And he's willing to just work, work, work. And he's great; he's a great asset to the show."

David realizes, in retrospect, "how big a favor that Moffitt did us (or Bernie)" by agreeing to take on their show. "For John, it was kind of thankless, in a way," admits David about his and Bob's awareness at the time of Moffitt's contribution. "You get Bob and I casually saying, 'Thanks, John. You did a great job,' and then we're off doing something else. He put so much time in there — all things that I had no appreciation for, basically, due to ignorance, and I've since learned exactly how much a guy like that does."

Tom Kenny, John Ennis and John Moffitt outside the studio.

Being British

Bob: "I wrote a piece called *British Toothpaste* for *SNL*. Lorne hated it. He was insulted by the depiction of Brits with bad teeth — 'I have British friends, and their teeth are fine." I wasn't trying to make a serious criticism of Britain. And, anyway, it's true. Lorne also thought the accents were horrible, crappy, and cheap. And they were. But, who cares? I like to do British voices, and I don't observe any boundaries — I do all different British accents together, an amalgam. I love doing it, and I love doing it poorly. I'm not trying to be British. I'm stealing a sensibility, an air that I perceive, being from the Midwest. But I'm not trying to insult them, and I'm not trying to show you what they're like in my stupid comedy sketches. It's about the character I'm creating; it's just an attribute of his. It's a manner of speech that carries with it all kinds of atmosphere that's hilarious."

Eban Schletter (music director):
"Troy had this way of making you scared shitless that you didn't want to blow it, but at the same time you really wanted to impress him. He's like one of those good professors, who knows how to make you work. You're scared, but you're inspired at the same time."

Troy Miller
producer - all seasons
director, video and film segments - season 1, 2, 3, some of season 4

As *Mr. Show* was graduating from stage show to TV production, Bob and David knew they wanted to partner with Troy Miller. They knew they needed a guy like Troy — someone with his resourcefulness — if they were to accomplish the improbable: producing such a complex show on a nearly non-existent budget. Troy was thrilled to be involved. "They wanted me to produce the show with them. It really was, 'no matter what,' for me," he explains. "No matter what the money was, what the schedule was, who was in it. What I saw in it — I remember reading the first scripts that they wrote — I was blown away. It was such a perfect fit with the things that I'd been trying to do. But not being a writer, I couldn't find any writers who were writing like that. I went to one of their live shows, which was them onstage doing live comedy, going into tape pieces played back. Which is something I'd wanted to do for years and had never gotten close — to be able to take advantage of what I can do as a single camera director, and what I know as a producer of sketch comedy, trying to combine those two in a show. So they had that, plus they had something that was funny."

The guys knew Troy from *The Ben Stiller Show*. He had directed a filmed piece, which that Bob wrote and was in called *Buildings and Women*. Also, they contributed a sketch to Troy's Disney pilot, *The Big News*. Troy recalls, "Bob and David were going around shooting little sketches for their show on a Betacam, out of their own pocket. Part of the way to get them to do something on my pilot was to let them have the tape, let them shoot something with my crew. They did this little scene for my show — which they used in their club show and ended up going in the later episodes of *Mr. Show — Earth Shoes*" [#409]."

Troy Miller began as an intern with John Moffitt, director of *Fridays*, the 1980's is ABC late-night sketch show. "The first five years of my life was working in TV for guys like Larry David and Larry Charles and Rich Hall and Michael Richards. Those guys were the ones who most impressed me. And John Moffitt. So, that level of broad performance comedy was always what I would strive to do."

He always knew he wanted to be a director, "but in those days, there were only thirteen channels, and you wanted to work wherever you could," he explains. "I worked my way up to a certain position, line producer — a producer that was primarily in charge of the money. And I became such a successful line producer that I was able to say, 'Okay, if you want me to produce, I'm going to direct.' And that's how I became a director."

With his own production company, Dakota Films, Troy quickly earned a reputation for getting things done on the cheap. "When HBO told Bob and David, 'We love the show, but we don't have a lot money,' what other company was going to be able to do it?" Troy asks earnestly. "I was able to raise my hand and go, 'Me, me, me!'"

"I've often said that Troy Miller was the third element of the puzzle to make it happen," tells Bob. "Production-wise, we did the show so, so cheap — that was the only way it was going to get on the air and prove itself. And there's nobody who could do it like Troy. Nobody. And with all his experience and talent, he's willing to go out there and pull a fifteen-hour day. Day after day after day. So that's what we needed. We needed a guy who could do everything for nothing, and do it well. The show looks good for how much we had. Without him, there'd be no show."

David remembers being impressed with Troy from the start. "Our first sense of what Troy could do came from *Ronnie Dobbs: The Movie* [#101]," David says. "We were blown away by that. We had no budget, and he just nailed it. It was in some alley, downtown, and he made it look great. There was a series of thrilling moments for us in the creation of the show, and that was one of them. That was our first big shoot with film. And we were thrilled when we saw it. It was another moment Bob and I were really happy — 'this is going to be good!'"

"And what I learned from them, one of the most valuable lessons ever," Troy adds, "is that you don't have to over-produce it. Other shows I did, we would spend so much time and effort in making it look so great, and it wasn't funny. 'We had all the cameras on all the people. Why wasn't it funny?' Because it wasn't funny. But with Bob and David, I didn't need cranes or dollies or anything. Ultimately, just point the camera at them, and, with their point of view, it would come across. So, I learned that the story, what they were saying, is first and foremost what the show was. And once the voice was right, it wasn't as important how I captured it. Unless it was written like *Coupon: The Movie*, written into the comedy itself, in the form."

Steve Welch
editor - all seasons

"Everybody is pretty involved in editing," says Steve Welch, *Mr. Show's* editor for all four seasons. "And there's not really a hierarchy. Everyone's ideas get entertained, all the writers have a say, and the directors, and Eban, whoever. Suggestions are always welcomed, whether they get used or not. Very collaborative. I take one or two passes at it by myself, and then I show it to Bob or David or whoever wrote the sketch, and we go over it. Then I take another few whacks at it from there. For however long it takes for everybody to be happy with it, I sit in the edit room and just hack away, and I usually have my door open, and people would come in and hang out on the couch, watch stuff and laugh. And everyone's so excited when the stuff first comes back. They all come running in, 'Let me see! Let me see!'"

Welch started in L.A. as a production assistant for Troy Miller. "I told Troy I knew how to edit," says Welch. "One night Troy was doing a project, and his editor had to leave, so I came in as kind of a last minute replacement and kind of stayed ever since."

Welch works on an Avid, which he describes as like using a word processor, but with pictures and sound. "You really have total freedom over how you order things. And you can do a lot of special effects stuff. Almost all the SFX stuff we did, we did over the Avid. But they're not conceptually difficult, they're just time-consuming."

Welch would familiarize himself with each episode long before it was shot — he read the scripts, he went to the read-through — all to get a general idea of what Bob and David were going for before he sat down with them in the editing room. "After a certain point, I'd worked with the guys long enough that I could pretty much guess what they wanted. But there were always some surprises."

Lying to Reporters

Jay: " One of the craziest things — you can hear them talking on the phone for an hour to some reporter — and saying, 'Yeah, I taught comedy at a university. I was a professor for a while. It was Shakespeare, comedy and movement. But mostly it was stage combat, but that's another thing. Bob got on the class, and he stood out because he had no pants on.' And it was fucking amazing! There are little lies in about three or four articles, and reporters would lie and say they'd seen the show, but obviously they hadn't."

Bob: "David and I both did it like crazy. The thing would be to find a reporter who bought our lies, most of them were from small papers, I'm not sure they exist."

David: "The cue for us to really cut loose was the reporter who clearly hasn't seen the show, or if they say something really dumb. One time a woman said, 'Now I've seen your show, and clearly there's a lot of improvisation.' So we run with it, 'Oh, yeah, off stage, we have a box of hats of glasses, we never know what we're going to do, we go back stage and we grab a hat. We're not allowed to see which hat we grab.' There was one woman who said, 'Now there's a rule in comedy, if it bends it's funny; if it breaks, it's not funny.' That's from a Woody Allen movie! See the thing is, I hate fucking talking about comedy, or the show, or comedy theory, or comedy aesthetics or any of that shit. I hate it. And Bob loves it. He could sit and talk about it for hours. I think he feels (correctly) that he's earned it. And that he has something to say about it. I feel no obligation to 'the fans' or some lame culture-chasing journalist when it comes to a dissertation on comedy theory. It bores me to read it, much less talk about it, because, dude, seriously, I'm totally into partying!"

Eban Schletter:
"My first year (Season 2): scared me to death. My second year (Season 3): worked me to death."

Eban Schletter
music director - season 2, 3, 4

"If *Mr. Show* is like *Monty Python*, then Eban Schletter is Terry Gilliam — the 'extra writer' on the show, major contributor," says Dino Stamatopoulos. Eban is the show's music director, responsible for big production pieces like *Jeepers Creepers, Fuzz: The Musical, Ewww Girl Video*, and *Philouza*, in addition to all the stuff in the background that you don't notice, but would notice if it wasn't there. Dino succinctly adds, "He gets the sensibility of the show."

Eban was not the first music director for *Mr. Show*; he didn't arrive until season 2. (Before that, Bob and David used Willie Etra, who they knew from his work with the Groundlings improv troupe.) But since then, Eban's amazing work on the show has garnered him an Emmy nomination for *Fuzz: The Musical* (#303) and a Cable Ace Award for *Jeepers Creepers* (#206).

His first exposure to *Mr. Show* was from a seat in the audience. During the first season, he went to the taping of *The Joke: The Musical* (#102). "I was blown away, honestly, just stunned," he enthuses. "I thought they were both talented guys, but I had no idea." After the taping, at the Cat & Fiddle pub and restaurant on Sunset Boulevard (the usual post-taping gathering spot), Eban nervously approached Bob. "He barely knew me," recalls Eban. "I was all flustered. I said, 'That was really one of the best things I've ever seen, it was every bit as good as *Monty Python*, it was so awesome.' And I went from that to never thinking about it. I never tried to get a job on that show, because I figured it was taken."

Although Eban holds a law degree, he only ever wanted a career in music. "The law school thing was a fear-based decision. I did that because my parents, as wonderful and supportive as they are on a hobby-level, definitely instilled in me the idea that you can't make a living doing music." Not surprisingly, as a musician in his late-20's, Eban was very broke.

His dire financial situation aside, things had been heating up for Eban in L.A. He was the guy all the comics asked to play accompanying music in their live shows, which he gladly did, but for no pay. "I could see my world change from the first couple of *Tantrum* shows [Laura Milligan's weekly installment at the experimental space, the Diamond Club]. I was there just to play a little opening music, and to play people on and off stage, and that's it. And the first person to use me in another way was Tom Kenny. He and Jill [Talley] were doing a show, and they had me underscore some scenes. And it worked. And more and more, people started utilizing me."

However, he was still broke, so much so that he actually accepted a job in Alaska — a job drumming for a cover band in a hotel, playing five sets a night. But fate, disguised as David Cross, intervened. As Eban was packing for Alaska ("How do you pack for Alaska?"), David called to talk him into staying in Hollywood to work on *Mr. Show*.

Bob and David had used Eban in a couple of live shows. One show was new material for *Mr. Show* — where they were working out scenes for their next possible season — and the other show, *Three Trips to Europe*, was thrown together for fun after Bob, David, and Bill Odenkirk had each recently traveled to Europe. "In the Europe show," Eban recounts, "one scene has some Americans going over to Europe with no sense of the history there. There was a big, crazy musical number with David singing this song — '*Europe is a country with many funny things...*' — talking about Europe from the American perspective that was retarded. I did that and the *Red Balloon* song for their live *Mr. Show* show. I guess they liked it, because it was a shock when David called me and said, 'We'd hoped to get you on the show.' There was one week of taking a risk; I was very scared. I dropped out of the job in Alaska, but they didn't know whether *Mr. Show* was going to be picked up for a second season."

The studio Eban worked in was a dark, stuffy garage. "If you went in there and turned off the light, you'd see light coming in from all sides through slats, with air coming through, with spiders everywhere," he describes. "So, I went to a garbage bin, and found all this carpet that some carpet company had thrown away, and hung up layers and layers of carpet. It was this spider-haven shack and really super hot. Very uncomfortable to be in." David, Bob, and other actors would visit this "studio" to lay down the vocal tracks for the show, but for most of the season, Eban would lock himself in for days at a time, emerging only when necessary. "The first year I worked on the show, I would show up just for the live tapings, haggard and tired. And I would make a beeline for the craft services table where the coffee was. I knew that no one knew who the hell I was, because I was never around — 'Who's that schleppy, weirdo guy who comes in every taping and takes coffee and we never see him again? Does he even work here, or is he some homeless guy?' No sleep, no shower, wearing the same clothes, jonesing on coffee."

Eban prefers to play all the instruments in an arrangement himself, and he uses live instruments whenever possible, "so it doesn't sound cheap." However, his equipment was limited and not that great, so it was a slow process. "I had to set up amplifiers and move mics around. Very old school." As he got paid for shows, he bought more equipment. "Right at the last minute, they told me there was this big piece, *Coupon: The Movie*, and it's got to sound like a big movie trailer. I'm biting my nails — I don't have something that's going to sound that good. I got an advance on that episode, so I could run out and buy this equipment that I needed to do that episode. And I had 48 hours to do the entire last episode [of the season, #206], which had *Coupon* and *Megaphone Crooners*. Sounds simple, but they shot that thing by singing to it with no click track and no music, and I had to put the music underneath it. I had to do two full passes; it was difficult to get that to match."

As a tribute to the group's live stage show roots, during the last two seasons, Eban scored several scenes live, as they were taped in front of an audience. "There were moments, like when Bob was singing in *Hail Satan* [#301], where they wanted to be able to riff certain things and have more freedom."

"Eban is amazing," says Bob. "He is able to realize any sound we ask him to create. And he's incredibly resourceful, knows all kinds of music and how it's constructed." David agrees, "Eban gets everything. I can hum something over his answering machine. I can't even articulate exactly what I want — 'I need some music and it's gotta be kinda that early-80's/mid-80's techno-y stuff when techno was just coming out but they were trying to make it like new wave....' I don't even know what that means, but, somehow, Eban would get so close in the first try." "And the great thing is," adds Bob, "he is able to copy sounds or styles without sounding like it's the same guy producing every one of them."

"*Mr. Show* was like a music school," says Eban, "because I had to learn all these new styles. That was my first real experience scoring stuff for television on a regular basis, and I got really spoiled. Because even though the schedule was a nightmare, when Bob and David give you notes, they have reasons for their notes. If you nail something first time out, they'll go, 'You nailed it, move on.' On many shows, you get notes from executive types, who just want to have notes. They want to feel like they're having an opinion, and they'll make one up if they don't have one."

Bob's Singing

Eban Schletter: "I've never worked with anyone who's like Bob musically. Most people, if you're going to be bad, you'd be consistently flat or consistently have a rhythm problem, etc. Bob would be all over the map. There'd be moments where you're thinking, 'You can't sing to save your life. What are you doing?' And then, in one section of the take, he'd nail it, and then you're like, 'Wait — where'd that come from?' And then, the next take, the rhythm's off, but the pitch would be good, or vice versa. Even if he gets off pitch, or melodically he's off, there's a really endearing quality to his voice. But really, it's not about how good the music is, it's how funny the scene is."

WRITING THE SHOW

The most commented-upon aspect of *Mr. Show* is the writing. While difficult to characterize, it is usually lauded as 'smart' and 'absurd' and 'irreverent' and 'silly.' *Mr. Show* episodes are always surprising. They are jammed full of ideas (especially in later seasons), and, as the L.A. Times pointed out, "hardly a moment of the show is left unfunny." The key is that Bob and David and the other writers on the show write things that they find funny. "We were writing the show for ourselves, and as it turns out, we were practically the only ones who watched it," says Bob.

When David and Bob brought *Mr. Show* to HBO, they pitched doing the show the way *Monty Python's Flying Circus* had operated: showing pre-taped pieces and live sketches to an audience, all flowing in the context of the show. The guys had to convince HBO that this was a valid production approach. Bob says he actually copied the page out of one of Howard Johnson's books about how *Python* did their show. "It was the page that tells you that they wrote all their scripts beforehand, and then they shot the films, and they did it front of a live audience. If you ever watched *Python* and watched how hard it bombed, then you know that it was shot in front of a live audience, because they certainly would have been more generous to themselves if they'd used the laugh track."

In rough estimation, to write and produce *Mr. Show*, it worked out to three weeks per episode. Bob outlines the process: "At the start of a season, it was two weeks with David and me. Then writers would join in and we would do about three more weeks of just writing. And then we'd start organizing the material: 'Here are some films we're gonna do, here's some live stuff.' We had a very simple, basic grasp of probably five live scenes at the end of five weeks and maybe six filmed pieces. We had lots more in the pipeline but we had things solid, done, for probably one or two shows. At that point, we're starting to make scripts of whole shows. It was another six weeks before the block of scripts were finished." The following two weeks went into shooting the video and film pieces, and another week of editing, graphics and music.

Bob: "*Mr. Show* was, certainly from a writers perspective, the best show to work for on TV. Which is to say, you have the most freedom. On other shows, there are so many rules and constraints about what you have to write to get anything on. And I'm proud that at *Mr. Show*, we'd go, 'What are the funniest ideas, and what's the funniest way to do them? That's how we'll do them.' We'll do *'Taint* as a film with all these film tricks, and we'll do *Shampoo* as a live scene, because those are the best ways to do those ideas. Whatever served the idea best. And that's a great thing for a writer to get to use any one of those venues for their sketch ideas, but it's also the most challenging."

David: "It's really annoying — the idea that we just sit around high, writing the show."

David: "When I first started doing this, I don't think I was a very good sketch writer. I think I had some cool ideas and I think I had an interesting point if view, but clinically, I wasn't a very good sketch writer. And if you're not, then you shouldn't be writing a show, much less being at the head of it. That is really something that was hard to do at first, and I solely credit Bob with just sort of teaching that aspect of it, and actually making it work."

David: "To this day, I still get kind of attached to ideas. On my own, I did seven versions of a sketch that isn't in the show. I had to finally let it go."

Bob: "That's the most amazing thing about us working together — David can admit, 'you're right,' after writing fifteen versions of this idea that's funny, but we can't make it work. That's the thing that's most amazing about us working together, and that I still can't explain. It's not because he thinks I'm a genius, or I think he is a genius, or a mastermind. (Although I do think he is evil incarnate). No matter what we write, we respect each other's doubts."

David: "The most blatant example of Bob's influence on me: work ethic. I never worked this hard. I was quicker to say, 'Let's only work a seven-hour day, because there's a concert I want to go to and I want to get all fucked up.' A shift in priorities. Also: writing and rewriting and rewriting. Constantly crafting and not getting so married to it. Before, I would have done just three or four rewrites, and then I would have convinced myself, 'Yeah, that's good.' But then I would have walked away knowing I could've done better, but I was just lazy."

The room. David, Brian, Dino, Bill, Paul, Jay, Mike Upchurch. Season 3.

David: "I think I changed Bob in the sense of expanding his idea, the possibilities in a sketch of the way things can turn, the way things end up."

Bob: "Something that David brought to my writing was this aspect of story-telling which you don't often see in live sketches – usually one premise or joke is played in various ways until it's all tuckered out, and then you finish it. But David influenced me in the way he works in interesting elements of story. It started from *T.J. O'Pootertoot's*, the scene that David wrote at *Stiller*, and going through many scenes at *Mr. Show*. There's a story being told. And the really interesting thing is, not just in filmed sketches like *Recruiters* (#205) or *Dream of a Lifetime* (#310), but we did it in live sketches too, like *Asshole at Party* (#101). It's almost like the scenes construct the joke, then go to another, separate place to end the scene."

Bill: "I love working with David. He's brilliantly hilarious. He's very accepting of trying other people's angles on things, and attitudes. I think he's less possessive of pieces. But that can go too far and his pieces can become a little kitchen-sinky."

Paul: "Bob's big strength, to me, was that he could write stupid people better than anybody. And his characters were all these fucking morons. Don Pratt, Philouza, they're just so dumb. Dumb, dumb people. He and I shared an affinity for that — just creating really stupid people."

David: "Most of the female actors on our show were not given a whole lot to do to showcase exactly how great they are. It's because we are a bunch of guys writing for each other, pretty much. But it would have been interesting if the show had continued, to see if we wrote sketches around women. We did try to hire a couple women as writers, and we tried to get Brian to have a sex change. But it didn't take." (Brian: "I'm growing pot tits.")

David: "At a certain point, around the middle of season three, the ideas were the most valuable thing. Not necessarily the finished sketch, because we all figured them out together, but the ideas. We needed lots of ideas. No show eats up ideas like that show does. Sometimes you'd have a great scene idea that's five minutes long and it gets reduced to 30 seconds. It gets reduced just to its essence."

The Room

Bob: "What *Python* did and what we did is this thing where you have 'The Room.' Now, the first season and a half, the room was just David and myself, but after that it was the entire writing staff. And any idea you came up with, it had to win that room over. There are no scenes that both David and I didn't agree on. Every scene on the show both of us said, 'Okay – that's good enough – let's make it.' And we've done the best we can with that and I believe in it. And every scene in the show had a majority of the writers saying, 'This is great.' Very few scenes were there people on the writing staff who did not like it and we just said, 'You're wrong.' *Everest* (#405) and *Fad 3* (#306) are examples. And what that gave us was

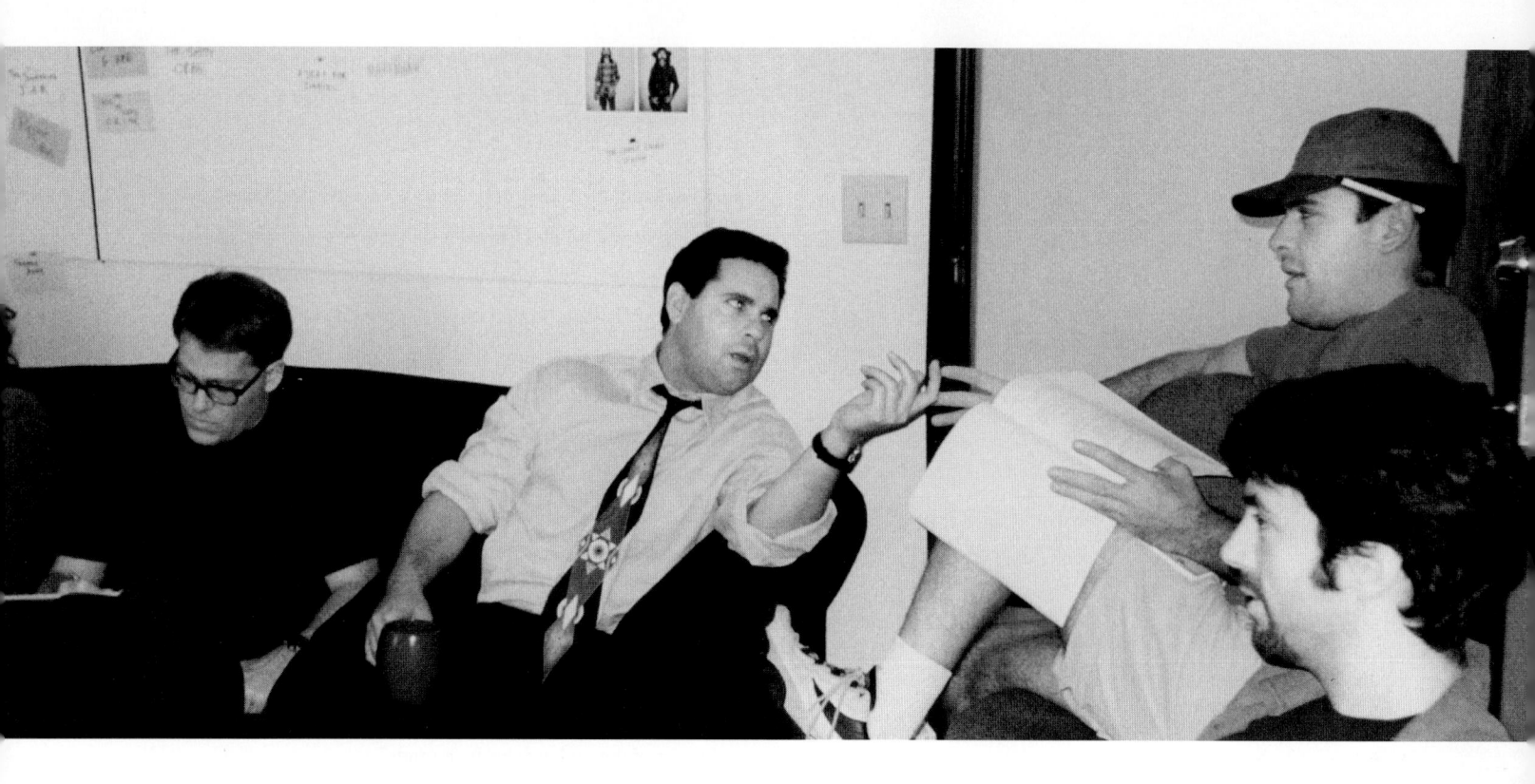

— the show had a 'head.' It had a sensibility. So even though the sketches are very different in every way, they feel like they belong together. And that was true of *Python*, although if you watch enough *Python*, you can see, 'Okay, that's a Palin-Jones idea, and that's a Cleese-Chapman idea. And that over there is an Eric Idle idea.' You can learn to spot these things if you watch enough of it. But in general you understood the tone of the show. And if you tuned it in, aside from the fact that it was pretty much the same guys, you would recognize it as the *Monty Python* show even though it was completely new every week."

Bob: "We started the same way every year when the others writers joined us — three weeks to a month of talking about ideas, and writing any idea you had, anything that was funny. And making it as long — whatever you wanted to make it."

David: "How much more enjoyable can a day be than sitting around with guys that make you laugh, that you respect, there's not a lot of pressure on yet, no production decisions, no interviews, none of that stuff. You're just kicking around ideas, and building on them. It's great!"

Bob: "And then it starts getting hard."

David: "We had a very strict rule in the beginning of the year: no more than 50 gay sketches. After like, three weeks, boom, we got 50 of them on the board."

Bill: "The magic was wrung out of that subject, though, at a certain point for everyone. A lot of scenes seem to gravitate towards some sort of comment on homosexuality."

Scott: "In the last season, the third week, you put three cards on the board which were 'Jesus, Gay, Hitler: no more of this in any scene.' It was crippling!"

B.J.: "I was, early on, reluctant to argue with Bob and David, not really realizing that that is my job: to fight against something that I don't think is funny. And it took me a few months to realize that that's what I was supposed to be doing."

Scott: "I like writing alone. That was my big fear when I came into *Mr. Show*, was I knew that was the way I like to do it, and I felt I wasn't quick enough to be in a room and sit there riffing something. I always felt I needed time to sit in front of a computer and think of a joke. So I was really afraid coming in. I didn't think I'd be good in the room, and I was afraid if I wasn't given the opportunity just to be by myself and write, that I wouldn't do a very good job. On the first day, Bob said, 'Hey, let's you and me write that sketch I thought of together.' And I thought, 'Oh, shit.' And I sat there, trying to pitch things. But it was good; it built up my confidence. The stuff we wrote later in the season when we were all in a room pitching it is better than the stuff we wrote separately."

David: "As Brian would be the first to admit, at least in the beginning, by far and away he had the worst habits of all the *Mr. Show* writers. Like falling asleep, and complaining. It was amazing. We'd be writing, and he'd be asleep on the couch. Asleep! And he'd say, 'Hey man, I write better at home, can I just go home and write this up?' — y'know, home with his leather couch pit group and his 60" TV with every PlayStation game you could ever imagine on it, and a pound of weed, and a swimming pool. The guy could sleep, let's be honest. And it's one of the reasons we hired him."

Eric Hoffman: "My first writers' meeting, we were discussing *Bugged Drug Deal*, an old sketch I had from Chicago. And everybody's arguing and yelling - and I can't even talk because I had, of course, over-romanticized the whole thing: 'I can't believe I'm here, it's just like working for Sid Caesar in the golden age of comedy, Bob and David are Sid, Jay's Carl Reiner, Paul is another Carl Reiner, I'm Larry Gelbart, or, no, maybe I'm 'Doc' Simon, Dino is Woody Allen, is it possible I could be a THIRD Carl Reiner? Etc., etc.' Insane. So everyone's trying to punch up the scene and getting nowhere and finally Bob looks at me and says, 'Well what do you think, Eric? This is your sketch. How do we fix it?' With the utmost respect and reverence I said, 'Whatever you guys think is great.' He looked at me like I'd asked him for an autograph. It was horrible. I would have almost preferred a Caesar-style reaction - with Bob first dangling me outside the window of an 18-story building, and then ripping a sink out of the wall with his bare hands."

The Pitch Meeting

Paul: "There are some ideas that didn't go anywhere, but we'd all talk about them for a little bit, see if we can make anything out of it. The most amazing thing about *Mr. Show* is, when you really thought you had something that was perfect for the show, 'This is perfect for Bob to do,' or, 'This would be a great David character,' you think they're going to love it, those would be the ideas that would be dismissed without conversation at all. 'No, I just don't see that.' And it would be so frustrating. We didn't have the luxury, like *SNL*, of bringing back characters. Not that that's a luxury; I'm sure all the writers on that show would say that is far from a luxury. But you didn't have that to fall back on, ever. It's not like, 'What's the *Van Hammersly* sketch going to be this week?' (Although I tried to bring him back.) You had to just come up with ideas, you couldn't even think of it in terms of *Mr. Show*. Because we would do really smart, heady shit, really satirical stuff, we would do just silly, ridiculous stuff, so you just had to operate on instinct."

Scott: "My experience: I was surprised by how supportive everyone was — we would say stuff, just say anything, and I remember David laughing a lot. I couldn't believe it. As the season progresses, you realize the stuff you said in the first two weeks would never make it into the show in the season."

David: "You heard my laughter, but you didn't see me rolling my eyes."

Paul: "The types of ideas I would try to tackle would be: any idea at all. Because I am the slowest writer, and I'm pretty good with beginnings, but I have trouble with middles and endings. I would start a sketch and

The writers (Paul, Jay, Bill, Dino) outside the studio; Scott helps Brian look at a centerfold; The writers (Brian, David, Dino, Paul) on a break. Photos courtesy Bill Odenkirk.

In the conference room at Dakota, Season 3. (Bill, David, Mike Upchurch, Paul, Bob, Brian, Dino, Jay)

I would keep writing just to keep writing, because I didn't know what to do with it. It would just go off, and I would look at it, and it didn't make sense. I had some good ideas, but I'm also not the most inspired guy in the world. So I dreaded pitch meetings, because I never had anything. I would have not even half-ideas. It might as well be: 'Two guys in a house, and let's see what happens.' The one thing I remember, we were always encouraged to come up with ideas that were really simple. Like a couple talking in a bar — something really simple to shoot and not that crazy. Because we had so much crazy shit, and so much crazy location shit. And I feel I tuned into that more than most. Most of the stuff that I wrote and got on the show was just that: a scene set in somebody's house — the one where David has to marry the whole family (*Our Secret Love,* #307), and *Hanged Man* (#304) all take place in a house. All my ideas took place in a house."

Scott: "You come into the season thinking you have a lot of really good ideas stored up. And in the space of a couple pitch meetings you realize they're not very good. I got a good education as to sketch writing in the first couple weeks. What makes a good sketch idea? Having something to say, having a point-of-view. A lot of my early sketch ideas were jokes for the sake of jokes. A lot of people think they could write a *Mr. Show* sketch and think they can be gross for the sake of being gross. As I watched the show, and as I realized, that those guys always have something to say when they're doing that. So I looked back at some of the stuff I pitched it the first couple of weeks, and I would never choose to pitch that now."

Paul: "I am the worst pitcher. I can't remember many of the pitches because they didn't go anywhere. You have your sheet of ideas, and you pitch them to the room. Everybody goes, 'Mmmm. Yeah...' And that's the end. I had many more ideas the second season, but the third season, I would go into a pitch meeting, and I would sit there, look a this piece of paper, a big white piece of paper that had three lines written on it at the top, and then all white. 'How about all the banks in the world decided to use gum instead of money?...Alright. I have another idea where a movie star thinks he is a gorilla... Alright.' I am just making these up right now, but these are even better than the ideas I actually pitched. I wish I was in the room right now! Get in a time machine!"

Nurturing The Bits, Pieces, Shit, & Stuff

David: "Bob is really generous about giving an idea a chance, unlike anybody I've ever worked with before. I think it stems from his negative experience at *SNL*. He's really good at nurturing ideas, but sometimes to a fault. It's one of these things where your gut was telling you — especially by season three — 'We're never going to use this scene, don't waste this guy's time.' But, a lot of times it worked. Immediately there'd be nothing there [in an idea someone pitched], and then some-

ON RECURRING CHARACTERS

Bob: "You have rules, and then you break them when you want to, and you do it for a good reason. Recurring characters would have made us more popular, and would have made the network happier, and sometimes I wish we'd done them. When I see recurring characters, sometimes I get a little thrill, but when you start belaboring it, when you're using time, and it doesn't fit and you're forcing this character in there, that really feels very self-conscious to me, and I question why that's happening. It feels like it's a self-indulgent, egomaniacal thing to do. 'Oh, I want to do this guy again!'

"It's just fucking boring that people repeat their crap, and just because it will get a laugh. And then you start getting laughs because people know stuff, not 'cause it's funny. People like to see things repeated; it's like how babies like things repeated. They like you to read the baby story over and over to them. Why? They're not getting anything new. Why do they like it more the second and third time than they liked it the first time? It's comforting. People watch TV for comfort. They watch TV to watch the same people do the same things, say the same things, react the same way to the same situations. But as an artist, it's incredibly boring and easy, and we just didn't want to do it. Plus, we had so many ideas.

"When we recur characters, they either service the sketch or they are entirely new extensions of that idea and what that character does in his world, and finding a new thing to do with it. But there was never an effort to use that character again. It only was when we were writing something, and someone would say, 'Why don't you do that one guy again here? He's perfect.' And if it fit perfectly, we'd do it. I do like the idea that their worlds intermingle sometimes, and you get to see Senator Tankerbell as a real senator, for example. But when we did it, it was usually pretty brief — almost like a callback to different episodes. If it ever got to the point where we started repeating something for the fourth time – 'The Senator Tankerbell Show,' and we just started spewing off these catch phrases — that's really distasteful to us. We were interested in the opposite of that. We did *Mr. Show* for ourselves. And as it turns out, we're the only people who saw it."

David: "It was a conscious decision we discussed early on [to not recur characters]. I think it mostly came out of our mutual distaste for what *SNL* did. A couple of times is okay if you can find a reason for it, or a different take on the character, but just to trot it out there to say the same lines so you can sell t-shirts and posters, or maybe make a mid-budgeted super-shitty movie is reprehensible, if not lazy. As much fun as it was to do some of those characters (I could do 'Ronnie Dobbs' forever or watch Bob as 'Droopy' and never get sick of it), our show is a better show for avoiding that easy and contemptible route."

how Bob would coax something else, or a little side part of what somebody had written, and he'd say, 'That's your scene.' But only after really talking about it, really talking it through. It was tough, because time was a luxury for us and sometimes it felt like we were spending a little too much time doing that."

Dino: "*Titannica* scene (#309) is one of the rawest, funniest scenes on the show. It's not incredibly intelligent, but it just provokes the most laughs. Originally Brian Posehn pitched it, because he's a heavy metal guy, and he also just likes pitching shit that is gonna gross people out. And his first script was the basic premise of the scene — where he listened to the song, and was a burn victim. But there was nothing funny about it. Like it didn't have a puppet body, it was just very realistic. And this is where *Mr. Show* is the antithesis of *SNL*, because if it was pitched there, they would just throw it away — but at *Mr. Show*, we usually take time to really focus on, 'Well, what *is* good about this scene? What *is* funny? What can we make out of this?' So we just all sat there. And I was ready to lay into this scene, I was ready to say: 'Are you crazy? There's nothing funny about it. It's not even funny in how far you're going. It's sophomoric. It's like you're laughing at someone who's deformed, and you're not saying anything intelligent about it.' I just thought there was no way of redeeming this scene. I even thought, I'm gonna shut up, and I'm gonna let everyone else attack it. And Bob said, 'Well, what if you really took it far, and this guy was this crazy puppet body…' And we all started riffing on what this body was gonna look like. And that's where the idea really was… I mean, for my money, it just came from Bob trying to make this thing work, and then that just set everyone off, thinking, 'Yeah, this is really hilarious.'"

The Scene That Got Away…Officer Ladyguts

Bob: "It's a shame how much time we spent trying to figure out a scene that we can use this Halloween costume. A lycra/spandex body suit with plastic parts. The Invisible Man - where you can see the organs of the body. At *Conan*, Jack Plotnick played *Slim Goodbody,* that Dino would write, where he would come out and his organs were outside his body, and he would sing to kids about organs, but he would also sing about how awful it was to have organs outside of his skin. So then, after Dino did *Goodbody* a couple times, he had to make a suit of a woman's body with a baby, and it was called *Ladyguts*. And she was going to come out and sing, and do a bit. But they never did it. It was a gross outfit, and no one thought it was funny. But the costume cost a lot of money, way out of our range. So Dino came up to us: 'We should write a scene about that.' So he had *Conan* send it out; they were willing to send it out, even though they paid for it. So we got a free gag suit."

David: "The only thing you had to add was a scene to it. Funny costume — scene not included."

Bob: "Numerous attempts were made to write the scene based on the idea of *Officer Ladyguts*. Seventeenth version: She was a police officer who had been in an accident, and her organs were on the outside of body now, and she went around to students, and she tried to teach them about safety, and they were grossed out by her organs. And then it became an army scene, like a citadel, where she was the only woman admitted, and it caused all kinds of problems, but not 'cause she's a woman. The joke was that she keeps trying to make it about the fact that she's a woman, and they're

Some "bills" become "laws." Ideas on cards on wall at Brian's desk.

telling her, 'No, it's because you're so gross.' Y'know what? Wasn't funny. Hours and hours and rewriting and rewriting."

David: "The thing is, we were told that the scene writes itself. So we sat there waiting."

Bob: "It was almost like a prank Dino played – 'What about *Ladyguts*? Honestly, there's gotta be something there.' You're skeptical: 'I don't know.' And after about three minutes, you start going, 'Yeah, it's a weird suit.' Dino just sits back and watches another four hours disappear into thin air. Also, keep in mind, the suit didn't fit anyone."

David: "All I had to do was lose another ten pounds, and I would have been able to fit into it."

Scott: "You guys would have dropped it, but the whole argument was, 'To get this suit, it would cost us so much money. We have to use it.'"

Frame Of Reference Argument

David: "Some of our most ridiculous arguments — and we still didn't learn from it, it still goes on — is all about frame of reference. And we're all guilty of it. If somebody mentioned an idea, I'll say: 'What are you talking about? Why is that funny?' And they'll explain, 'Remember when you were twelve years old and you got *Doopdidoos*?' And I'll go, 'What? I don't know what you're talking about.' And I never heard of *Doopdidoos*, but every one else in the room's heard of *Doopdidoos*, and they have this experience. And I'll say, 'Well, it's not funny to me.' And everyone's done it. Everyone's argued about a frame of reference that they're not privy to. And other people are in the room going, 'Oh! *Doopdidoos*! That'll be hilarious!'"

Bob: "You can't always just play to ignorance. It's a weird balance: everybody gets this, and one person doesn't get it, and therefore it's not well written. You kind of have to go by percentages. If you go around the room, and two people don't get it, you might have a problem."

Under The Gun Giddiness & Spite

Dino: "Jay made the great observation that the more work we had to do and the more up against the gun we were, the more we would sing. 'You have three hours to write the last show.' 'Da-da-da-da-dee-da-da-da-da-da-dooo!' We were losing our minds."

Paul: "One of the biggest on-going jokes was, 'Jay you're fired. Now you're rehired. Fired. Rehired.' And that went on forever, where I fucking hated it. The jokes would get to a point where it was just words after a while, and you would just hear people screaming from their office, 'Fired!' 'Rehired!' That is eventually what all our inside jokes would lead to; they would just devolve into just screaming words."

Bob: "When writing a scene, we'd talk about it in length, and we would go around in circles sometimes, and someone would pitch something that had already been suggested, and we see it as the solution. It wasn't overlooked the first time it was mentioned; it is just part of the process of seeing the best answer. One time, we had been working for an hour on this one thing, and someone pitched an idea we all liked. We asked Brian, who hadn't said anything yet what he thought of it. In a crabby voice, he said, 'I think it's great, since I'm the one who suggested it about an hour ago!' And then Jay, without missing a beat said, 'Oh. Sorry. I guess we couldn't hear you over the crinkling of your diaper.' We all laughed. It was such a pointedly funny remark. Brian took it like a man. Who'd been insulted. But even he couldn't deny it was fucking hilarious in spite of the fact that he also knew it was true."

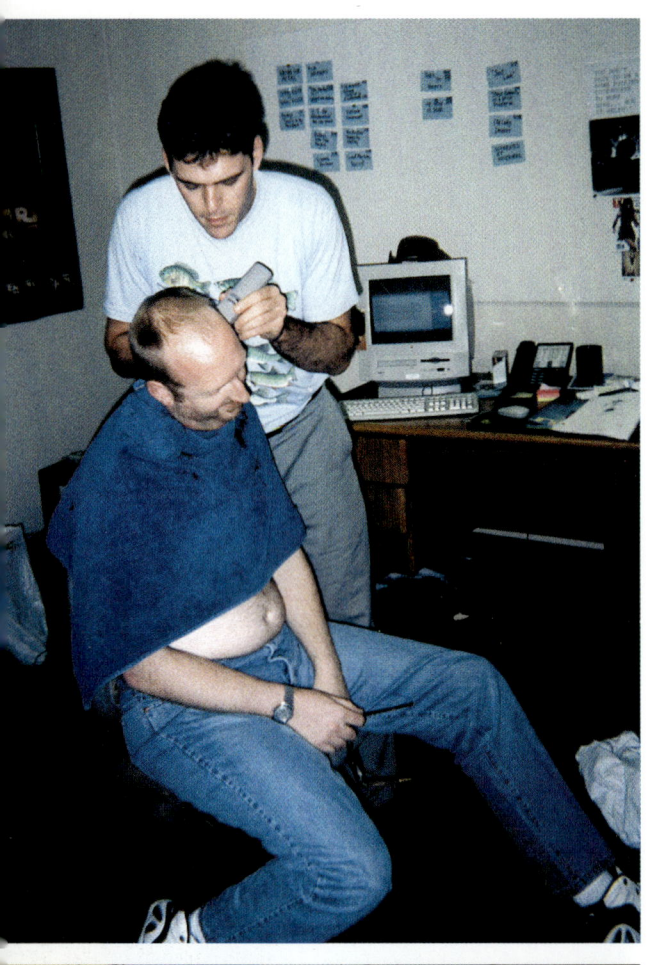

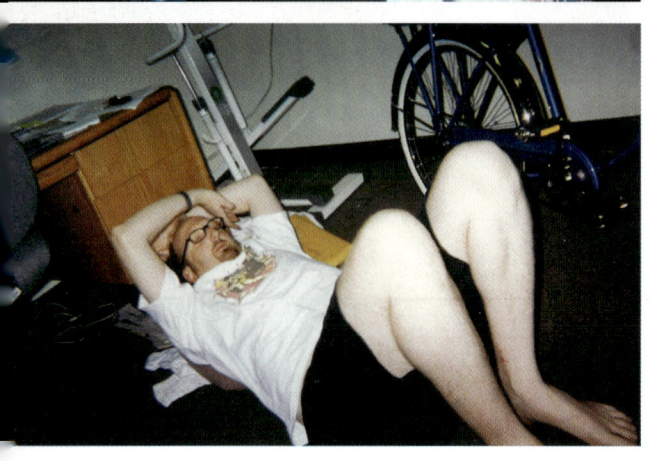

David: "I would put Brian in the group with Paul and myself, where our blood sugar was low, and we were closing in on the twelfth hour in that room and trying to come up with something, we were knocking our heads together and not coming up with anything. Man, we could turn vicious. We'd say funny — but really mean — shit to each other. 'Crinkling of your diaper' – that's as great an example of what it was like – you've got somebody complaining and then you've got somebody complaining about the complaining."

David: "Whereas sometimes I would make a sarcastic, yet unbelievably hilarious comment about somebody's sketch idea and try not to be too much of an asshole. Bob almost never did stuff like that. Which was decent of him."

David: "Dino was good about getting silly when it needed to be silly – taking the tension out of the room. It was frustrating – I was certainly aware of it – there were times when Bob was taking the mantle of being serious and getting shit done, and then we'd all be giggling about shit. And there were other times where I had to do the same exact thing because Bob and Dino were giggling about something and it would make me angry: 'Come on, guys, we gotta finish this!' And Dino was always good at helping you get silly again, just when you needed it."

Building Shows

David: "The *Ladyguts* costume was delivered third season. And the card was still up on the board when Scott got there. It's funny how some scenes hang out as long as they did, and actually got on. *God's Book on Tape* (#407) was from the third season. *Don Pratt* (#307) was really old. *Racist in the Year 3000* (#403) was written long, long ago; it was in the original Diamond Club show. The key is, it doesn't fit into the show. You try to force it in and you see that it doesn't work."

B.J.: "*Intervention* (#406), at one time or another, was supposed to be in every one of the first five shows, and was taken out. Looking back, I see they just do what is best as far as putting sketches together; I think they really do a good job of creating shows where sketches feel right with each other. It took me that long to figure out they had a plan, and they were actually trying to achieve something by the way in which they group sketches together. But at the time, I felt like they secretly hated the sketch for some reason, and I couldn't shake it. The fact that it had been put in every show, I thought they were trying to be nice to me."

Links

Bill: "The transitions between the scenes were carefully crafted to form a seamless flow of pure comedy or to provide a quick getaway from a bad sketch. Since many of our scenes involved TV shows or commercials, the initial ideas for these links would usually be that we either pull into or out of a TV screen and into the next scene. We

(top to bottom) Jay cutting Brian's hair; Bill brings his revisions to Bob; Brian sleeps in the writers' room.

(above) Hat #1 & Hat #2. (below) From bottom left: Steve Welch (editor), Bob, Scott, Dave: middle, Peter Giambalvo (coordinating producer), David, Bill; top, B.J.

tried to avoid this option as much as we could because it was too easy and boring. Hours of screwing-around time were wasted cooking up an alternative means of linking the scenes, only to find that Nature had decreed another 'television transition' be used. And who were we to go against Nature (except in our private lives)? For #310, using a video screen in the line-up as a transition from the news and into the VTV scene was one of the first ideas to be considered. Days of contemplation then led us back to where we had started."

Dino: "Links are a nightmare. 'Checkmate!' There were never links between scenes before *Python*, but *Python* guys had the luxury of using anything they thought of that was funny. *Mr Show* uses links that make their own scene, or at least make a seamless transition. Bob sometimes hated the show for that reason. We could be writing so many funny scenes instead of spending eight hours trying to link the opening to the first scene."

David: "We spent the whole day with another reporter in the writers' room just for *Bugged Drug Deal* (#408). And we eventually said, 'Fuck it, man, just pull into a commercial.' And you know what, no one cares. It didn't hamper anyone's enjoyment of that show. That link took at least four days."

Bob: "People always say, 'You didn't have to have endings to your scenes, that was great.' You're right. I guess we don't have to have endings, but we *have* them. Just look. There's a button line or moment to almost every sketch, and a good one. The only sketch I can think of where we don't have an ending is *Gay Son* (#204), where it is interrupted by Grass Valley Greg. It's not really a sketch at all: it's a premise that goes on for about two minutes, and then it's interrupted. Other than that, we made ourselves have endings."

THE PRODUCTION

© Photo by Adam Timrud

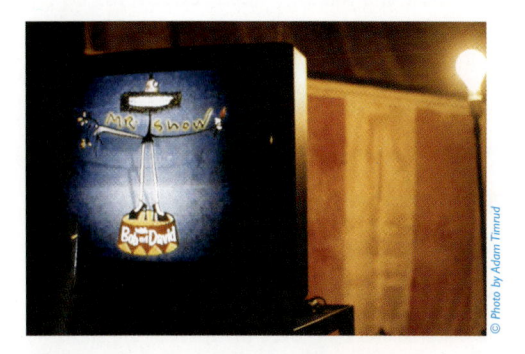

The Production Meeting

After about two months of just writing, with five scripts completed, the production meeting is called. All the departments get together with the directors, Bob, David, and the writers. Unlike other television productions, they are covering the production needs for the five scripts all at once, not just for one of them. The writers explain what it is they envisioned for each scene, and every department asks questions and takes notes.

Troy Miller: "In the production meeting, you go through the scripts scene by scene and discuss the stage direction for the most part (as opposed to the dialogue), because that'll tell you who the characters are and what's happening in the scene. And we discuss with department heads what it takes to put this together: tape or film, what the equipment is, who's responsible for what. Bob or David would pitch out what they see as the creative point of view, and then it may be the first time we are discussing it/arguing about it/agreeing about it what the creative point of view and how it was going to be shot."

Paula Elins (costume designer): "Everything in the scripts is broken down by producers: 'Okay, we're going to shoot all these scenes this first week.' And we'd go through, and every department would talk to Bob and David in one big meeting. And you just yell out, 'What does this character look like?' I ask about wardrobe and take notes. They give you an idea of what they need. They have a total trust in me. They'd say only, 'Y'know, a 70's school teacher.' And I say, 'Okay. I know.'"

Tonyia Verna (hair/make-up): "Whenever they have characters, I ask at the production meeting: 'How is that character going to talk?' I want to hear what he sounds like. They have an idea what they might want him to look like, but after I hear them, I get it, too."

Paula: "Troy is always trying to tell you not to spend money. Like the *Civil War* piece — we had a lot of people just wear jeans, instead of a whole uniform. Or, for this 20's thing, he tells me, 'Can't you just get brown pants and brown shirts?' Because everybody wore brown back then. It's really frustrating, because it feels we are not doing the best job. And he says it doesn't matter. A lot of times, he's right. He knows how he's going to shoot it. One time we argued because we needed a lot of monks at the last minute, and we didn't have any. And those outfits are $75 each. And he said, just get some red fabric, and drape it. And I was mad, because I didn't want to do it that way. And I did it, and he was right. It was a little photograph that they put in the newspaper, and you couldn't tell at all."

Questions, Queries, Queasts

The questions did not end after the production meeting. Oh! How David and Bob loathed the never-ending barrage of questions needing answers, and options needing approvals. It wore them out. They would often complain about this aspect of their job as executive producers, but rarely anything else. Nevertheless, they were aware that they'd brought it upon themselves because they were particular about every detail of the show. They chose to be involved, mostly because they wanted things the way the wanted them.

Bob: "That was our job as producers — answering the questions of, 'What does this look like?' 'What is the set?' 'What is the tone of the comedy?' 'What does this sign look like?' Every production question, every element in the frame that you see, had to be decided on and chosen to fit. And we were the people who made those choices in everything — in all the films and all the live stuff. And that's a lot of questions, because we have a lot of concepts on our shows, and we had a lot of locations and we had a lot of props and everything. That kind of work really does make you feel worn down. But that's the job."

Paula: "The great thing about them is they are really precise, and they know exactly what they want. They have vision. A lot of people don't know what they want, and want to see millions of choices. Bob and David like to see choices, but they kind of give you an area to work within."

Rehearsal for Law School *on a set just good enough for sketch comedy.*

THE SETS ON *MR. SHOW*

Bob: "One thing about the *Monty Python* sets was the walls would shake. Which is what we wanted. We asked for that. We said, 'We want things to be plain, we want walls to shake, we want it to be cheap.' We don't want it to be about the sets. We're not in an actual office, when we're in an office; we're doing a comedy sketch. I loved that about *Monty Python*. I feel a little differently about the films we made. We tried to make them real. Sometimes there's mood there. But the sketches should just be, 'Here's a comedy sketch.' There's an element of fun there. But the other side of the coin is that if your material isn't very good, and you don't rehearse it much, and you don't rewrite it, and you don't get to pick the best stuff, like we did, then you emphasize other things. You emphasize the costumes, the excellent sets, you have a guest star who's a musician who's acting, you have all these diversions that keep you from going: 'You know what, this sketch sucks.' We were trying to do a great comedy show, one where you would watch it over and over."

David: "Who gives a fuck about the sets? They should only serve the piece. Let's move on."

The Work Ethic

Paula: "We don't have the luxury of time at all. You kind of get into this mode where you're constantly going, and it's like a runner's high. You're really into it, and you can't stop, because if you do you just collapse. The schedule is really intense. You just don't even have the time to think about it."

Bob: "I always felt so ridiculously thankful to everybody for working so hard almost to the point of implying — 'What's wrong with you? Why are you working so hard on my thing? It's my and David's crazy idea, why do *you* care about it so much? Do you realize that you are not getting paid shit, and that you're having to work out here all day?' I was shocked and surprised and worried for people at their commitment to the project. And thankful, too. It was really unpleasant working conditions and long hours, and people did it because they loved the material and they loved the spirit of the show. I mean, you almost don't believe that – what people say: 'I want to do this because I think it's good work. Most the shows I work are just crap; I just do it for the money and it's unpleasant and I wish I wasn't there.' Just to find that many tech people and crew people who are interested in making good work, too, to the point where they would sacrifice so much just to be a part of something good, is really pretty cool."

Eban Schletter (music director): "The thing about Bob and David — they'll request things of you that, if it was anybody else on any other show, you'd be very angry because of the last-minute nature of it. Here's a perfect example — the "Weird Al" Yankovic parody (#404) — they got that idea the day of the taping. I had to get it there within two hours. And I was maybe going to get a nap in after working that hard. And at first I'm like, 'Dammit! Why did you…!' And then it's, 'Oh, that's *hilarious*! What a great idea!' And then you dive in and you do it. Because it's such a funny idea. And the little anger thing vanishes."

Paula: "I was panicking because they needed a giant tooth costume. And Bob and David would say 'Oh, y'know. A giant tooth costume,' like they're just floating around out there. It's something that most shows would just make. But it costs thousands of dollars, and we don't have that kind of money to do that, so you pool your resources, just hoping that someone happens to have one hanging around. But Tonyia, our makeup artist said, 'There's this woman down the street and she has this giant tooth in her front yard.' So we called her. It turns out she makes costumes. We rented it from her. She let us paint it gold. It was super easy, and it worked out perfectly, but it kind of ruins things for us because it set a precedent. Bob and David never flinched — 'you can get that.' It seems like we are always lucky in making things like that work out. You can't say, 'No.' Everybody feels that way because they believe in the show so much."

Troy: "I think within the crews and the staff, everybody ran around trying to do a great job. Everybody believed in the show so much, that I never had — and it's so unusual, I so appreciate it now — I never had anybody come to me and say, 'No, I can't do this,' or, 'No, you're not paying me enough money,' or, 'No, the hours are too long.' In all the shows I've supervised, I always had one or two people. On this show, I've never had a salary issue or a work issue. The reason that 90% of everybody who's in television got into television – it's for the quality of it. They want to make their mark. On *Mr. Show*, it became almost peer pressure — it's no whining, everybody's loving this, everyone's friends. Everybody contributed something, and they saw their contributions on the show. They also saw David and Bob and myself loading up the truck and running around, and trying to make things better, and not hiding out in a trailer. I think that added to it, too. I think in other shows, there's a definite segregation between cast/directors/producers and the crew people and staff. There was none of that on *Mr. Show*. I think that's because Bob and David and I tried to be fair."

Bob: "It was clear everybody was in this thing to make it work. People got part of that attitude and that energy from David and me — and for me it was my reaction against the attitude I found in other shows I'd worked on. Our attitude was, 'Look, whatever we have to do, we'll make it happen.' David and I would be happy to sit down and puzzle out how to make costumes and sets and locations work, instead of just dumping it in the locations guy's lap and going, 'I don't know, figure it out. Find a fucking castle.' We'd try really hard to work with people to solve these difficult technical questions that we couldn't afford to solve like a normal production."

Location Shoots

Location segments had to be shot and edited first, prior to the live studio performances. This allowed the pre-taped segments to be shown, in sequential order, to the live audience before and after the live sketches. With this system, audiences would get to experience the video segments in the context of the whole episode, with somewhat the same flow.

The pre-taped segments shot on location were produced more like a movie than a TV show – it was not shot chronologically. Rather, their method was to go around L.A. (and Simi Valley) for three weeks, shooting scenes at various locations for as many as five scripts at a time. They would shoot scenes out of order, often grabbing shots at a location for several different episodes.

Steve Welch explains the process from the editor's perspective: "For the first week, all that I'm getting is bits and pieces for all five episodes. So, I'm just putting in order what I can, but I don't really have enough to do completed pieces. It's not until the second week that I start to get into the real editing. What I tried to do is get the first two shows under control as much as possible, and then sort of piece away the three shows after that. And the schedule's not too bad, until the week before the first live taping, when everything starts to get crazy. Since we don't add any laughs in post, we want them to be as funny and finished as possible for the audience."

Most stories told about *Mr. Show* location shoots are 'low-budget' stories. How they overcame the limitations of the budget, what was inspired out of necessity due to the budget, etc. They stole locations (shooting without a permit from the city), and used crew and friends as

(top to bottom) David, Paul, Bob, Tom on location for "Fad 3" (© Adam Timrud Photography); David and Brian between shots in "Philouza" shoot, writing a scene for a different episode; Jay between "Mustardayonnaise" takes. (© Adam Timrud Photography); David climbing to rocky peak for "Jeepers Creepers."

extras in scenes. They shot a lot of things right there at the Dakota Films offices. They usually had only one person who did everyone's hair and make-up, Tonyia Verna. Troy even did some stunt work himself: he was the guy getting hit by a car in the NAMBLA *Ad Awards* scene (#203). What they shot looks pretty damned good, especially considering how many ideas were jammed into each sketch, their tight schedule, and that thing about the budget.

Troy: "There are things these comic nerds cite as being great choices and great ideas on the way things are shot, but they're almost always out of necessity. Because we couldn't afford a crane, we had a guy sit on the tailgate of a truck. Things like that, that we would come up with on locations, because we probably had 'plane noise' or something. That's a lot of it. I think with my low-budget, un-fearing ability, if they write something in an airport, we'll go to an airport and we'll shoot it. Instead of me saying 'no' first, my theory always was: 'Yes,' take a beat. I'll find a way, with a plan. And if we can't find a way, then I'll go back to them, and say, 'What about A, B or C.' I think for the most part, most producers in town are too lazy to figure out a way to do it. That's why we had a clandestine approach of stealing locations, no permits, shooting wherever we wanted to shoot, and just being smart about it. People are not as daring as we were — and they also have money. We got caught once in four years. We were shooting in Glendale — *The Devastator* (#310) — a testimonial in this guy's front yard, and the Glendale permit police came and shut us down. They said, 'if you keep shooting you'll go to jail.' Normally you need cops, permits, and pay for it. All that is, is to show the state that you have insurance, and we always had insurance. But you'll spend up to $2-3,000 on permits and locations fees for a shot of a reporter on a sidewalk. It's because we're an entertainment show, but if you're a news show or a magazine show, you don't have to pay any of those things. Our way also enabled us to do three or four different locations in one day, running around like crazy with Tonyia and her wigs, being able to do heavy prosthetics and wig work, when normally you have to have a crew of three or four people and tons of set up time and support. We just never had that."

Tom Sherren (producer, season 3, 4): "A lot of times we'd have four or five locations in one day. I remember once we had seven locations — we were in the Valley, we were at a house in Hancock Park, we were at the Vine American Party store, we were all over the place. We would jump around between episodes. Bob and David were really amazing because we could schedule a lot of things for a single location — we would get a suburban house, and we'd shoot things from five different shows. We'd shoot the living room, and we'd redress it, shoot the living room for a different episode, shoot a back porch. Like the first day of the fourth season, we were at a house all day and we had Hitlers, we had old people, we had girls, we had a donkey, we had monks. We spent all day at the house doing segments from five different episodes."

Bill: "The thing I most remember from all our location shooting was how on the fringe of everything in L.A. we were. It was always in a dirty, dusty area. Always hot, the hottest time of year. It was always dirty at the end of the day; you would wash, and grime would pour off of you. But those are the scenes we wrote, guys running around and rolling in dirt." (Dino: "I tried to pitch the clean scenes so many times.")

David: "We would always tell our location person that it's really important that this doesn't look like L.A. I think we did a good job, mostly. Troy is amazing in cheating locations. *Fad Three* (#306) — looks like streets in London. He just found a location downtown, a small area. In the background, there's even an entrance that looks like a tube station."

Tracey: "We have no money so we end up in Simi Valley for so much stuff, because it's cheaper and you can turn a high school into your own back lot. Which everybody hates but we have to do it, because of budget, and because it's so easy; they were happy to have you there. High schools in L.A. County would cost thousands of dollars, and it's days of trying to get it cleared. In Season 3, scripts were finishing the day before we had to shoot it. We'd be at one location, trying to find the next one before we can move. We'd get clearance on a high school one hour after we realized we needed it. You can't do that in L.A. city limits."

David: "Simi Valley (once home to Mark Furman) is just about the whitest place in California. It's got that bullshit Suburban veneer of being 'safe.' People who like it and choose to live there always say things like: 'It's nice. We've got things to do here. We've got sushi places and museums and things, too. Plus our Mexicans are super friendly.' Yeah, great. Some of that delicious food-court, mall sushi after perusing the exhibit at the Greater Simi Valley Horse Museum. Sounds rewarding. It's not even the suburbs! It's, like, a fucking hour and a half drive away from L.A., which is already culturally challenged. Oh, yeah, it's a fucking desert. But they've got a point; no negros."

Bob: "Simi Valley — it wasn't a very fun place to go to, it was hot, and it took forever to get there. Just a cultural-less, colorless suburb. But in a way it was great.

(left) David directing "Goodbye" segment; (right) Troy as "Gurgles" puppeteer at Druggachusettes shoot. Photos © Adam Timrud Photography

You go out there and nobody bothers you. We were able to cheat a lot of locations, and we got to do our show. People talk about it negatively, but it's just about how we had no money, and it's resentment."

Tonyia: "*Mr. Show* is like renegade film making. You have to pull shit out of your ass because they always come up with things that don't pertain to what they talked about in their production meeting. So you have to be well prepared from everything from blood to mustaches. They know I hate bald caps — whenever they're in them, they're in them for over twelve hours. You can't keep them on somebody's head for that long. They sweat and it's 105 degrees outside. They start puckering, and showing the line. It's the only thing that gets under my skin — whenever they have a character who needs one, they'll write it in the script: 'ha ha Tonyia!' because they know it makes me crazy. Whenever they hate it, I say to them: 'You wrote it! So suffer and eat this glue.'"

Tracey: "It's really satisfying to pull these things off last minute. And it's really appreciated. That's the thing on *Mr. Show* that's so good, is that everything is such a group effort. There's no other way that show would work. With the resources we have, and the amount of money. There's no other way."

Tom Sherren: "It was probably the hardest show I've ever worked on. If you have more money you can spend more time doing everything, and it's not as difficult. But, due to our budgetary constraints, we were always trying to pull deals on every location. We had to beg and plead and cajole The Palace (a club on Vine Street) into letting us shoot there for four hours for $1000 so we can do the *Electric Underwear* (#401), and then do David's Marilyn Monster character (#410), and then turn around and shoot all our writers as leather homosexuals in front of a green screen so we could composite a full audience for Wyckyd Sceptre's Fire Island concert (#403). We couldn't afford to fill The Palace and dress all these people, so we shot like fifteen guys — the writers and a few others like PA's and our coordinator, and we shot them in front of a green screen from the stage. And we just moved them back — so we got them close, and we got them further back, and we got them even further back. So we shot them in three perspectives on the side, three in the middle, and the three perspectives on the right hand side. Each time they were in a different configuration. And then we duplicated that in the Avid; we were able to size it down in composite so it looks like it's a whole crowd. It actually turned out pretty cool. That's typical of *Mr. Show,* that we would have really ambitious ideas, and no money to do it the way other shows would do it, so we would have to come up with a more creative way to get around it. And Bob and David were always great with that. They were always willing to hear some ideas or change things slightly to make things work."

Wendy Wilkins (talent coordinator): "We used crew as extras, constantly. In the *Popemobile Chase* (#104), it's me driving a cop car, and a PA driving as a security car, and another PA dressed up like the Pope."

What your mama doesn't know won't hurt her. ("Chip on Your Shoulder Club" ventures up mother's ass.) © Photo by Famous Mortimer.

EXTRAS
STRANGERS WHO AUDITION AND ARE CAST TO BE PART OF THE SCENE

Jay: "Probably one of the most enjoyable things for me to watch on the set with extras is knowing in my bones that they have no idea of what any level of the joke is. They're just doing their thing and they don't know what's going on at all."

David: "Occasionally, I got the feeling that extras had contempt for us because we were young, and just goofing around, and we had a camera crew, and a time slot and a network that would pay us to fuck around, as they saw it. And they're real actors and they've been doing this for a long time."

Bob: "I was always nervous around the extras. I wanted them to be done and go home. I just felt like we're never paying anyone enough to do this. They show up at the set at 6 A.M. to shoot at 2 P.M., and they're there all day. And then there's a few Nutter Butter bars, and some coffee, and three doughnuts. And nothing to do except stand around. I wish they were out of there. I wish there was a holding area that was really nice for them, and they can come do the scene and get the fuck out of my face. Because I just felt guilty, and I didn't want to meet all these strangers who want to act. I don't want to meet people who want to act."

David: "I've yet to meet an extra that wasn't at least partially nuts. They are quite often strange and deluded. But if you can eavesdrop on their crazy conversations and 'grand plans' you will be richly rewarded with stunning absurdities."

Jay: "My favorite extra ever was one of the 'Hitlers' (*Cloning Hitler*, #401) — the guy with the perm. He was a doctor, on his head shot it says, 'A funny guy.'"

David: "In *Shampoo*, the old woman behind me in that scene — years ago, when I was throwing my trash away, I found this video tape, and it was hand written on masking tape in green felt pen 'Audrey — actress.' I pulled it out, and I popped it in. It was really bad, something from cable access and some community theater. I had that kicking around for a long time; I could never throw it out. And all of a sudden, she shows up years later on the set of the show."

For the *Best Of Season 3* (to air before premier of Season 4), they did a mock 1970's news show. Dubbed-over news anchors from a 1970's local evening news program introduced the sketches on the *Best Of*. They couldn't get permission to use a real 1970's news program, so they built a dated-looking set and hired actors to read news copy.

Dino: "We were auditioning very straight people with straight newscast script that Bill wrote. All reading the copy with their great anchor voices, and they stopped when they flubbed a line. They didn't know we were going to dub them. We watched people for hours. Hundreds. The editorial part: 'Loss of park space is both real and frightening.' That line just got to me. I would try not to laugh, but I couldn't help myself. Part delirium. I couldn't stop laughing hysterically whenever the actors got to that part. I was laughing so hard, I had to leave the room. Got in trouble with the casting director."

Tracey: "They used my car a lot (red convertible). Pretty much whenever they decided they needed to see people in the car. Which wasn't always the greatest thing. I had to get it repainted when they decided to drop shattered glass on the hood (*Emergency Psychic Hotline*, #402). In the *Goodbye* sketch (#410), that went until 4 A.M., and I was really sick, and I couldn't get home some nights. But it saves money that way."

Jay: "I had a great deal of energy for getting out on location and understanding how to shoot these things. And that's something I always found impressive about Bob: he was very keen on his own idea of how things should be shot. He was very connected with that. And I think I learned one thing from him: have a choice. Choose to do it a certain way so you can look at it and decide if you want it or want something else. It's just like writing a scene — write it so you can rewrite it and make it good."

John Ennis: "They sometimes have three parts for me, and apart from the read-through, I wouldn't see anything that had to do with it, not one scene, until I would show up for work. I'd show up on, like, a Tuesday, in the middle of the valley at 6am, and they would say — 'That's your dress, that's your priest outfit and that's when you play the cop.' And I love that."

Wendy: "We're shooting a scene in the middle of Hollywood. And we have a trailer, but it's during *Ronnie Dobbs* (#101), and everyone constantly had to change, because we're shooting the eight places on Cahuenga Blvd. to create the different places Ronnie Dobbs gets arrested. And Bob starts changing on the street. And there's homeless people walking by, trying to steal food from craft services. And here's Bob in his underwear and socks, just talking to somebody, until Paula pulls out his wardrobe, and hands it to him. And that was a constant with Bob and David. No matter where they were, they just changed. They had no problem being nude. Ever."

Paula: "When David and Bob find themselves complaining, they catch themselves: 'Listen to me complaining. I have my own TV show, that's fully my own vision, and here I am complaining about the clothes and the schedule.'"

Location Segment Directors

Troy Miller directed the location shoots for Seasons 1, 2 and 3 (the exception being the *Recruiters* segment in #205, which was directed in Detroit by Tom Gianas, years before it was a TV show). Other directors, Peyton Reed, Valerie Faris, and Jonathan Dayton, came in during Season 4. Bob and David each directed a filmed piece for Season 4: Bob shot *'Taint* (#406), and David, *Goodbye* (#410).

Bob and David always knew what they wanted, creatively. A big part of the task for any of their collaborators was accepting that. Troy Miller's attitude is a good example: "I've always been a guy who works for writers. When my writers have a vision, I try to serve that vision. And that became a really good relationship, because they had such a strong mind in how they were writing."

"It was a very mixed blessing to direct our show," Bob confesses. "You got to work on some really cool, funny stuff that had unique looks throughout. But as a director of *Mr. Show*, you had a limited ability to influence the pieces, they were pretty well conceived and often times very visually conceived. So, at times, the job would be just working your ass off, trying to fit into the time and money constraints. Our directors were so good about it — with all their expertise, they were completely willing to listen to everything we had to say. Everything. The tenth hour of the day, the hundredth shot. We'd say, 'No, no, that's not what we want, we want this.' But it's why Jonathan and Valerie only did one session, why Peyton only did on session. Those were all creative people with their own ideas.

"To give our directors credit, in a piece like *Coupon the Movie* (#206), those images were written in, but, man, Troy was the one who put that together. And *Megaphones* (# 206). Troy made it with a super 8 camera, super 8 b&w. That was very creative. He realized that piece. Likewise, Peyton Reed directed *Monster Mash* with the TV mystery-reality show, *Probings* (#407) — there's a lot of visual jokes in there that we had in the script – but they were very well-realized and done with patience. And Jonathan Dayton and Valerie Faris shot the *Monk Academy* movie (#402), capturing the look, the early 80's summer movies. That was loaded with good stuff."

David on Jonathan and Valerie: "They were shooting a documentary of comedy in L.A. in the early 90's — a lot of following us around, going to shows, and we all had interview sessions with them. That's how we got to know them. Their video work is amazing (including Smashing Pumpkins' video for *Tonight, Tonight*, featuring Jill Talley and Tom Kenny)." David on Peyton Reed: "He was so much fun to work with. He never flips out. He is a bottomless well of energy and enthusiasm. Also, he has a complete lack of ego — that never comes into play when he's making a decision. Which is very refreshing. Peyton would handle every situation like a very calm friend. One of the most immediately likable people I've ever met."

(top to bottom) Directors Valerie Faris and Jonathan Dayton on set at pork-rind factory ("Prenatal Pageants"). © Adam Timrud Photography; Peyton Reed at Hollywood Forever Cemetery, on set for "Monster Mash" shoot. © Adam Timrud Photography; Brian Posehn and costume designer Paula Elins.

Audience at taping, Season 4. © Adam Timrud Photography.

Live Episode Tapings

Live tapings. Typically two a week. Two shows each night – one episode, taped live twice in front of two frothy-mouthed audiences. Usually 8 P.M. and 10 P.M. These tapings were a feast for the comedy-starved. New *Mr. Show* sketches!! The guys' directive was to keep these tapings moving along. It took only about an hour to tape the half-hour episode. It was not much different from watching it in a club. You were treated to live sketches that went into pre-taped scenes, then back to live, all flowing one into the next. Between the live scenes at a taping, when the cast members were backstage changing into their next character, you were probably watching the video or filmed segment. Someone good 'n' entertaining warmed up the audience before the show, and talked to the crowd during any down times — Paul F. Tompkins or Patton Oswalt, always someone fabulous to hang out with for the evening. Occasionally, for the longer breaks, they would run a film piece from a previous episode on the big screen.

During the first season, the shows were taped at Hollywood Moguls nightclub. Subsequent seasons were taped at an actual studio, which was made to look like Hollywood Moguls. Season 2 was taped at the KTLA lot (on the *America's Funniest Home Videos* stage). Seasons 3 and 4 were taped around the corner at Hollywood Center Studios, home of *The Keenan Ivory Wayans Show* (remember he had a talk show?) and MTV's *Lovelines*.

As anyone would tell you, the second show of the night was always the best. By the late show, the cast members were warmed up, and the kinks were worked out. Sometimes, scenes were re-worked a bit. Rarely were there any major re-writes, but there might be a small cut, or a decision to do something live in front of the audience, scrapping the pre-taped scene. Finesses that always made big differences in getting laughs. There was also, of course, the small matter of the pressure being off. By the second show of the night, they saw that their pieces worked and were well-received. Also, the first show has more time-constraints, since there is a new audience lining up outside the studio. While the second show went briskly, it was not pressurized to do so.

They rarely did pick-ups — where a scene or part of a scene that gets re-shot. John Moffitt, who directed all but one of the 30 live episode tapings, basically had just those two shots at it, with five cameras going. "Even though moving very quickly, he always made certain that his cameras were making all the right moves to service the jokes within a scene," says Troy.

David: "For me, that's the best part. I like performing live more than any other aspect of creating that whole show. The writing was fun sometimes, the filming was fun sometimes, and the editing was cool. But absolutely, performing it live was my favorite part. It always will be my favorite part of anything. Pretty much, starting at Season 2, that was our audience. And so they were pretty amenable to waiting [between scenes], of course when we stepped down, we would have Paul or Jay or Patton Oswalt or whoever was coming out, talking to people in between, and sometimes Bob and I would come out there. And it was great. It was like a big fun experience. It wasn't like a sitcom where everyone runs off to their dressing room behind set #4, the kitchen set. And they have some clown entertaining people giving away free shitty watches. It was really fun. The audience knew us. It was great going out and talking to people. It was a whole fun night."

Paula: "The live stuff was the most fun. It's so fast, we make quick changes, even though it doesn't need to be done that way, they try to do it in the space of an hour. They like to keep the pace up and the audience involved. Because they run the taped pieces in between, they do it like a live show, like *SNL*. When there's not enough time between scenes, we'll make break-away clothes you can rip off very quickly, that look normal from the outside, but inside it's held together with velcro, or you layer one costume under another. We *(top) Paul F. Tompkins, Season 4. Entertaining audience between scenes at live taping. © Adam Timrud Photography; (bottom) Backstage, readying to start live show, Season 4. © Adam Timrud Photography.*

are only dressing Bob and David because they are in every scene. Everybody else changes by themselves, and we don't even get to look at them sometimes. The changes are very quick and everybody's together, and there's a lot of energy from the audience. It builds; everyone reacts to what you've been working on previously. It's a really great feeling."

Tonyia: "Live shows — it's so much adrenaline. You have to be fast, and you have to be thorough. And they're either angry or happy and they're talking and they never sit down and they don't shut up. And sweat's flying everywhere. It's definitely run and gun. But it's definitely the most rewarding show ever, when you can pull that shit off."

John Moffitt (director): "David and Bob never wanted to augment the applause, or the laugh. So when we played back pre-taped scenes for the audience, we couldn't make camera moves. Everybody just had to freeze. And when the tape was over, we had to move fast."

David: "It was tenser for me on set [on location shoots], and Bob was more at ease there. Bob enjoyed the process of the pre-shoots more than I did. And the reverse was true for live stuff. I'm definitely better in front of a live audience than I am on the set. I always finish [location shoots] and think of a million things I could have done. At the live shows, to me, that was like, 'Ohh, that stuff's behind us, and now I get to have a little more fun here,' and I would enjoy that process more than Bob did."

Bob: "Live shows are really hard for me, because it's like having a guest over at the house: I want to make sure everything's okay, all the time. There are a lot of variables when you do a live show — especially when you have the audience packed in so close. And one of the things that was important to us was to keep the show going, to have the people in the audience experience the show somewhat like you would when you watch it on TV. But unlike most TV shows, we had less time to prepare, and we had two shows to do pretty much back to back. Most sitcoms that are taped live or filmed live, they struggle and wander through their evening and people in the audience have to sit there until 1 A.M. sometimes to watch one 20-minute episode. And our goal was to do this show for people in as real time as we could, so it was really nerve-wracking. Every delay was just way too annoying to me. The thing that was hard — there's a control center in the back of the room and I'm not sitting there because I'm getting in makeup and running around backstage, and I don't know what's going on. And I don't why we're delayed for two minutes, and I don't know how long we'll be delayed. Someone will just say, 'there's an audio problem.' We would hear that all the time. And I'm sure there were audio problems. But what is the fucking audio problem? What are they doing about it? There were so many times that I would do stuff, just myself, and with a pissed-off attitude, moving a set, moving a prop. I would get so mad over and over: don't move the sets during the scene! I did things that were totally unnecessary. I was right on the edge the whole time: 'How do we get this show done?' And I feel, to a great extent, that I was the only person asking themselves that question. And I know that is really unfair to everybody else. But it just felt that way. When you are really upset about something and trying to get something achieved, and you run into someone who's as nervous as you, or more nervous, you can suddenly relax a little, because you go, 'Oh, it'll be alright. Because if I miss something, this person'll catch it.' But David is just more easy-going than I am. And he's more about just letting things be and playing along with that."

(top) Between early and late shows, at taping for #306. Tom, Brian, Scott, Doug; (bottom left) Paul, Jerry, B.J., backstage before show #409. © Adam Timrud Photography; (bottom right) Brian Posehn's subtle commentary on another show taped on the at Hollywood Center Studios lot.

David: "That's how it's been since the very beginning, when it was a stage show. I think it is a lot easier to worry about everything than to kind of let go of stuff that you really don't have much control over and to be able to enjoy it. And I think that's reflected in the performance, for any performer. And I think at some point, that's the most important thing. It's harder for Bob than it is for me because he really relishes and is good at having control – as much control as possible. But at some point you just have to give it up a little bit and enjoy the performance. That's what it's about. There's a moment that I got to see Bob that nobody else ever got to see him. When we were both waiting in our respective off-stage wing area to come out for the introduction of the show. And I would have a glass of water or a beer or whatever, and I'm hanging out. I'm so fucking psyched. I'm pumped, I'm ready to go. I'm thinking about all my shit, I'm really loose and waiting to go on. And he would look like a big ball of nerves and energy. He would be checking this, and looking over there, 'Is that thing ready to go?' and, 'I hope that guy knows his fucking audio cue.' And I'm like, 'Come on. You've got like 90 seconds to just sit back and let it wash over you and enjoy it and check it out. Y'know, just have fun. This is the part where you have fun.' We would come backstage after the first thing and he'd have a million questions about it. And I'd say: 'It's fine, man. What are you talking about? Let's change for the next thing. C'mon, let's have fun. It's fine.' 'Yeah, no, no, no, I know, you're right.' I know it's difficult to let all that stuff go."

David: "But to Bob's credit, he was really great at observing things we needed to change between the first show and the second. 85% of his observations, when we changed something around between show 1 and 2, worked so phenomenally well. So obviously well. Like with *Swearing Preacher* (#306). We pre-taped the scene for the first show, showing it to the audience on video playback, then changed it around to have it performed live for the second show. It was one of those things where Bob saw it and he said, 'You know what, we got to do it live.'"

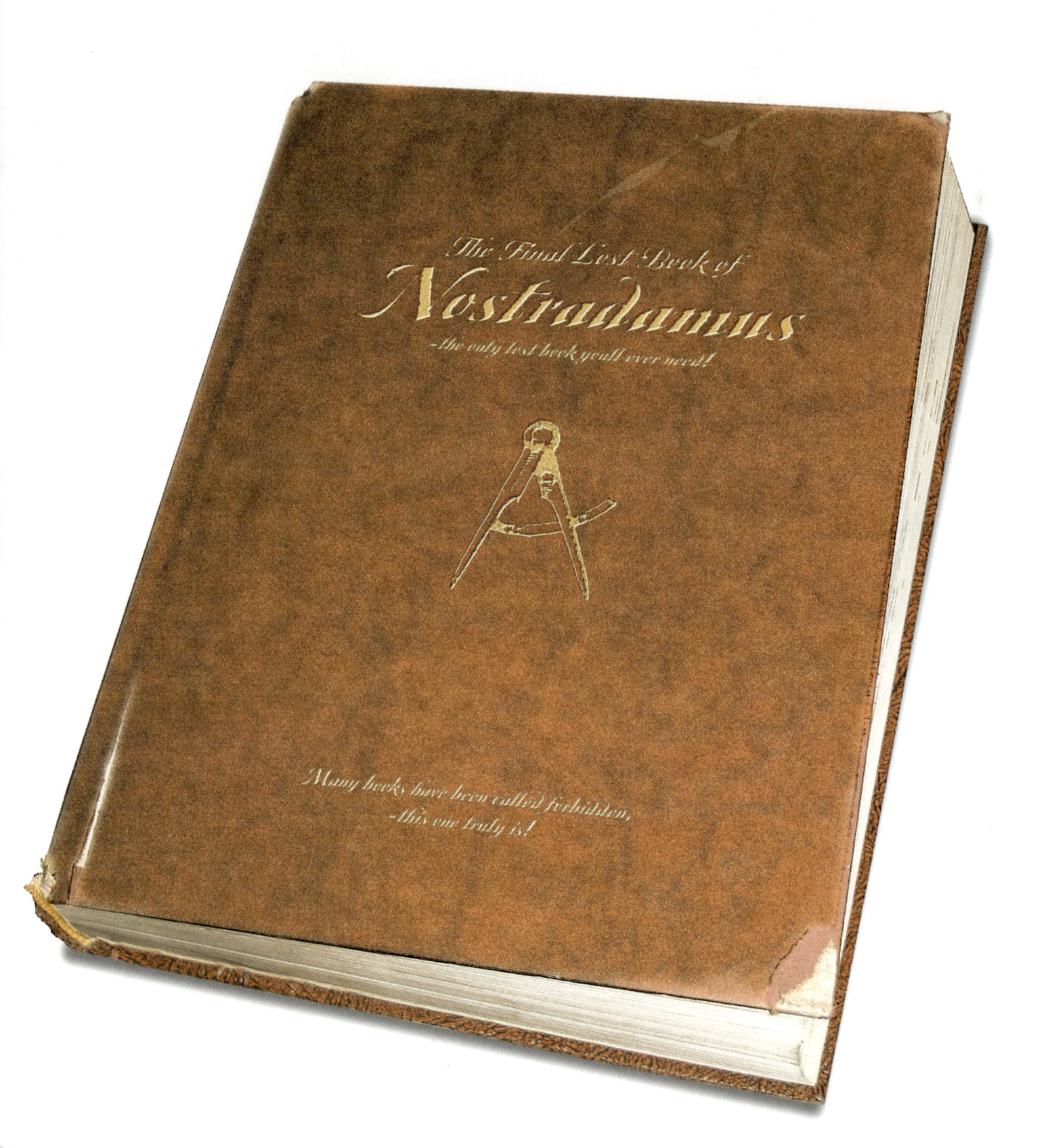

The Final Lost Book of
Nostradamus
—the only lost book you'll ever need!

Many books have been called forbidden,
—this one truly is!

EPISODE GUIDE

To any who happen upon this solemn tome, a warning and a wish;

Mayst thou leave unplayed the play-lets described herein! For when the last of these is performed, the darkness of the final days shall descend on this mortal world. Lest ye be the twain specified in the foretelling, cast this book aside!

For more info, read from quatrain 6, book 8 of my prognostications:

When the two dancing monkeys [1]
One with legs bare [2]
The other a screaming mani-ac [3]
Gather cloaks, false hair, forged noses, and pillowed stomachs,
Cavort and wail before gasping onlookers [4]
In the blackest hours [5]
These unseemly notions and besoiled language
Trumpeting the exploits of Gary of the Whiffles, [6]
False news-sooths [7], and an acid tinged child, [8]
All the happenstance and entwined balderdash contained herein,
And alight the eyes of the beast [9]
In one thousand and one hearths total [10]
So shall be the sign for the final days!

There, thats done. If you are the two described above, then make haste! This book describes a series of short, comically-tinged play-lets which you must bring to life forthwith. Commence! It is your destiny. Initiate humankinds brutal extinguishment!

Oh, and one more thing, just get out there and have fun.

Footnotes
1. Bob and David
2. David
3. Bob
4. Gasping, many of our viewers complained / bragged of being high when enjoying the show.
5. Our time slot.
6. Fartin' Gary
7. News satires
8. Titannica
9. T.V.
10. Our highest rating.

SEASON ONE
EPISODE GUIDE

Four Tight Little Masterpieces

It was now July of '95. Bob and David wrote the first four *Mr. Show* episodes on their own, with some additional material from an uncredited Bill Odenkirk (*Popemobile Chase*, #104). Bob and David regularly invited friends to the table-readings of their scripts. They valued the feedback from their like-minded peers, and they welcomed notes and discussion about what worked and what didn't. Brian Posehn was invited to a read-through of the first two scripts: "The script featured a few sketches I had seen already [in live stage shows], but also introduced brand new ideas. I was so impressed by the flow of the shows; they were tight little masterpieces. I don't think I had any notes for them; they were ready to shoot. I told all my friends that weren't lucky enough to be at the read-through that when they saw the show they were gonna get their asses kicked with humor. And they did — their asses are still hurting."

Of those first four episodes, Bob says in retrospect, "We were experimenting. Just having a lot of fun. *What To Think* (#102) has a lot of what soon would become common themes for us: The Government intrusion in the arts, lame performance artists or folk artists, a lot of religious stuff. Ha, ha! There's a taste of what's to come."

The cast for the first season was drawn from the cast of the live show they'd been developing and putting up over the prior two years. Jill Talley, John Ennis, Tom Kenny, and Mary Lynn Rajskub. Brian Posehn can be glimpsed in each of the first four episodes, and Jack Black makes memorable guest appearances. Janeane Garofalo appears for the first and only time. And if you look closely, you'll see Jenny McCarthy and Maynard Keenan in episode #101.

Hollywood Moguls

The first season was truly a rag-tag operation. They even knew it then. HBO ordered just four episodes (with a budget for only two), and, even more so than in subsequent years, the theme was to stretch a thin budget. It is (or will be someday) legendary what the production team on *Mr. Show* accomplished given this limitation. Luckily, Bob and David had producer/director Troy Miller, the master of making it work on any budget, and making it look good.

"A theory of ours especially in the first four episodes, was no matter who had to die to make the show, we would kill them," tells Troy. "We shot at a nightclub, it was hard. We didn't have enough time, enough money, or anything. But I think with Bob and David and me, it was that — no matter what we had to do to get the show done, no one was going to stand in our way."

The episodes were shot off of Hollywood Boulevard, in an obscure bar/night club called Hollywood Moguls, dressed up as a make-shift studio. There was a bar in the back of the room (as David points out in episode #103, during the *Third Wheel* scene, when he breaks character to complain about their cheap pseudo studio — "Isn't that why we're in this shitty city to begin with, because there are studios here?!"), and the stages were shoe-horned in. The director for the live sketches, John Moffitt, and his crew had to maneuver their equipment around tight niches in the audience, severely limiting the range of accessible shots.

Bill Odenkirk describes a few of the other downsides to shooting in this bar: "The dressing rooms were at the end of a hallway that was no more than two-feet wide. And the actual dressing room for the whole cast was a room about twice the size of your average house bathroom. You had to stand in one place to change, you could not move. On one show, I remember I had to keep pounding a beam on the wall during the show, to quiet the crickets because they were right near the stage. No air conditioning. We complained about it, but we couldn't get extra money. Until people from the network came down and noticed it was hot."

Giving HBO What They Wanted

Chris Albrecht of HBO had seen Bob and David's show at the Upfront Theater in Santa Monica, and he felt that *Mr. Show* would work best in a night club setting. "It was a good idea," says Troy Miller. "I told him, 'I can build a night club in a studio, and we can save a lot of money and have a lot more control.' And he said no. He really felt that's what it should be. To HBO, this was a deal breaker — we couldn't do it in a TV studio; it had to be a club. And, already, this had become kind of like a hobby show for Albrecht. A smaller, low-stakes thing. Luckily, we had Carolyn Strauss (at HBO) pushing for it. So we said, 'Okay, we'll do it in a night club.'"

John Moffitt explains the rationale behind HBO's edict: "I think initially they thought *Mr. Show* should have its own feeling — not a feeling that you're going into a television studio, but you're going into an environment. And a real club would be the only place for it. And so we were frantically trying to find something that would work."

Troy and his crew came up with Hollywood Moguls. They chose this club as their site because of its location (just blocks away from their offices in Hollywood) and because it was one they were able to afford — other options were too expensive or too big (where they couldn't spend the money to close them in). So by default, after looking everywhere, "The Moguls," Troy said, "we have to make it work."

Moffitt recalls the technical obstacles at this funky club: "It was such a bad neighborhood that when stuff was stored out back, homeless people would be sleeping on our set. And doing other things. And we looked at it; it was no place to do a show. We liked the look, but there's no way we can make set changes and do that kind of stuff there. Tom Buderwitz (production designer), Simon Miles (lighting designer), Troy and I really looked it over, trying to figure how to make that horrible space work. It was horrible in the sense of practicality. A whole wall had to come out, and then, at the show's expense, the deal was, it had to be replaced when we were finished. And Buderwitz and I came up with an idea — to have wagon stages and to have three stages. So we can make the set changes, rolling them around very tight quarters. This space was so cramped that it was a challenge. The bar, the stools. We all were moving chairs around frantically. It was just really the hardest things we've ever done, having to stage this show, and yet have the ability to do everything Bob and David wanted to do, which is to go from live to tape play back to live to film, use the audience. Another little detail: where are you gonna put the cameras? It was such a confined space. So it was like a final exam, to figure out where the hell to put the cameras. And it was the kind of a challenge that we all were proud of because we did make it work. It had a great feeling to it; it was really funky. In fact, Simon thought that we never did quite replicate the feeling (which they attempted to do when they moved to another, more practical space for the second season), because it was so real. Which we were all very proud of, as well. It was an audio nightmare the first year, yet everything worked. We had good people. It was a really good team. What we didn't want to do is ever say no to Bob and David."

Jill Talley characterizes their make-shift studio fondly: "As much as it was so awful, it was really great. It was just about the work. We all had a lot of fun; everyone was so committed to it. The place was so disgusting. You just had to laugh about it!"

Finding Your Audience

For the most part, the audiences for the first season were not fans. It's difficult to fill a studio audience for four episodes (120 seats to fill, two show tapings per night) when the show doesn't exist yet. There were a number of friends who came, plus insider fans who'd seen the earlier night club version of the show while it was being developed. But the rest of the audience was "bussed in." The majority of the seats were filled with people who not only didn't know Bob and David, but who probably would never watch the show otherwise. Bill Odenkirk remembers the struggle to fill the seats: "They got this audience wrangler to do the audiences for the first season. They were told to get college students. And the result was what looked like gangs, Latino couples. You just look out in the audience, and you think, 'They're not going to get any of this.'" Wendy Wilkins, the talent coordinator, recalls one night, before the early show when they were shy on audience: "It was completely bare. We sent the PA's out on Hollywood Boulevard; it was Friday night around 8 P.M. And the reports coming back were all about hookers and homeless they were able to wrangle. They ended up with four tourists who were German, who maybe understood a little bit of it." However, Bob admits, "Even though we got depressed every time we came out on stage and found a roomful of Hispanics on dates, they always got the show. Considering they are strangers who probably don't know comedy at all, they were all laughing. That's the great thing."

By the fourth show (the last of their first "season-ette"), everybody wanted to be at the taping. Word of mouth had spread, plus the realization that this may be the last taping the guys do — they couldn't fit everybody in. Brian Posehn, not yet a writer on the show, was in the audience for all of those first show tapings: "I didn't act in any of the live scenes during the first season, so I got to sit in the audiences with people who were seeing the stuff for the first time. The response to that first show was overwhelming, people lost their minds during scenes like *Asshole at Party, Change for Dollar,* and *Ronnie Dobbs* (#101). And I laughed my ass off right along with everybody else. I felt *Change...* was an instant classic, up there with scenes I loved from *SCTV* (my favorite), like *Half Wits*. I felt like Jill Talley was our Catherine O'Hara, Tom Kenny, our Joe Flaherty, and in keeping with the *SCTV* comparison, I'd like to be remembered as *Mr. Show*'s Tony Rosato."

The Center For Diseases

Research and Identification Division
Trailer 4, Jan's Trailer Park

December 3, 1998

Dear Mr. Show,

On behalf of the scientists and researchers here at The Center For Diseases, we would like to extend a thank you for the pioneering work Mr. Show has done in creating a viable new disease, I.D.S., or "Imminent Death Syndrome", (the psychologically devastating effects that the imminent death of one person has on the people around them). Especially, when the victims are artists, this syndrome compromises the honesty, integrity, and finally mental health, of those wishing to maintain the high spirits of people who are on the verge of death although they may not know it.

Recently, we submitted I.D.S. to the A.M.A. Board of Directors for certification and inclusion in the Medical Handbook. Sadly, it lost the vote to a fabulous new foot fungus (our work!), the Super-Flu (influenza 3.4) and the Super-Duper Flu (influenza mach-5). However, we believe I.D.S. has a great chance at the next panel, and we have even identified thousands of new victims, including: Whoopi Goldberg, Matt Damon, Ben Affleck, Jerry Lewis, Barry Sonnenfeld, and many more,

A word about our work. The twentieth century has seen the wholesale slaughter of diseases of all kinds, and even the extinction of a few. We are committed to reversing this trend, or at least leveling it off. We were based on the campus of Princeton University until 1956, when the university found out, and our work was funded by government grants until 1997, when the government found out. Now, working out of a trailer in South Florida, we carry on. Due to our limited resources, we rely on the efforts of private citizens such as yourselves. We also owe a debt of thanks to the Pentagon for its chemical weapons research. Together we can counteract the efforts of the do-goody-good Nobel ass-kissing toadies and bring new diseases to a hungry world.

Thanks,
The Center for Diseases

P.S. - "Entitilitis" and "Walter P. Francis' Syndrome" are two wonderful diseases we found while researching your program. However, research has yet to ascertain any symptoms for them. But we're working on it!

EPISODE 101 THE CRY OF A HUNGRY BABY

written by:	Bob Odenkirk, David Cross
locations segments director:	Troy Miller
live show director:	John Moffitt
cast:	David Cross, Bob Odenkirk, John Ennis, Tom Kenny, Jill Talley, Mary Lynn Rajskub
featuring:	Brian Anton, Greg Behrendt, Doug Benson, Ken Daly, Todd Glass, Adam Jones, Paul Kozlowski, Brian Posehn, Bill Odenkirk, Paul F. Tompkins
special appearances by:	Maynard Keenan and Tool, Jenny McCarthy, Conan O'Brien, Andy Richter

Entititus Cold Open (filmed)

Ronnie Dobbs (David), a long-haired, shirtless white trash gentleman, delivers a serious PSA from the National Entititus Foundation. "By the time you see this I will have passed," for he is afflicted with the mysterious disease. He urges viewers to take part in "Talk Backwards for One Day to Raise Awareness About Entititus" Day.

Mr. Show theme song and logo. Mary Lynn introduces.

Hitler Sings/Guys In Audience Open (live/video)

Bob and David greet the audience with, "Well, America, you asked for it. You told HBO. 'We want a sketch show hosted by two people we've never seen before." They ask the audience for sketch ideas. An ignorant loser, Ernie (a pre-taped Bob), offers a suggestion: "What if, for your show, you play different characters?" while his asshole friend, Gary (a pre-taped David), abuses him, tweaking and poking at him.

"Let's show them why HBO gave us this show." David performs "When Will I Be Special?" from his one-man musical, *Hitler Sings*, where he confuses Hitler with Anne Frank. Next, Bob names every state in 18 seconds. David explains that Bob "thinks there's only 5 states, [and] that one of them is named Chim Cham." Ernie in the audience interrupts with another lame suggestion. David loses it, and Ernie and Gary are kicked out of the studio.

Hit By Truck (video)

Walking down an alley, the banished Ernie and Gary lament on how fame has changed Bob and David. "They think they're Ronnie fuckin' Dobbs." Gary deserts Ernie to go with Jeep-driving friend Stevie (John). Left alone, the sad-sack Ernie wanders the night, whining about how everything's changed for the worse: his friends, the leaves on the trees, a caterpillar into a butterfly ("he thinks he's so big"). Finally, standing in the middle of an intersection, he laments the lights changing from red to…he's run over by oncoming truck.

Asshole At Party (live)

Stevie (John) and Gary (David) show up at a party at Geena and Lyn's (Jill and Tom), where Father Jim (Bob) is a guest. Gary immediately starts making annoying bets. No one ever agrees to the terms of his bets, yet he demands that they "pay up." He "wins" the bet that he can eat broken glass, and now everyone has to "be his slave." The group scoffs, but Father Jim has a ridiculous sense of ethics and insists that, since they never said no specifically, they have to serve Gary. Gary gets the priest to do various humiliating things, ultimately having him hold a banana in his ass cheeks. The truth comes out: the whole betting thing was a prank played on the oddball priest. They laugh and reveal that they secretly taped the incident and run off to watch it, leaving their victim to a monologue about his stupid "ethics" — "If I ask for a glass of water, and somebody hands me a glass full of sand, I turn it over, make a sand castle, and pretend I'm the king." He finds solace in the fact that his friends must surely feel worse than he does.

Watching VCR Link (video)

The other guests of the party are laughing at the video of Father Jim and the banana. From a stack of similar videos they select Convenience Store Security Cam 5.

Change For A Dollar (live)

At McGinty's 4-Day Market, a nameless businessman (Bob) requests change for a dollar. Although his uniform says Ed, Pete the clerk (David), after an eternity of rumination ("Hmmm, click-click-click-click-click"), decides to go ask his manager if it's okay. His manager (Bob) ponders…then calls his superior (David), who can't decide on his own and phones his boss who's golfing on vacation (Bob), "Dammit! It's too late to fly back!" He paces like crazy while he thinks and thinks, then calls the President of the United States (David) who says, "No." The reply is communicated all the way back down to Pete, who comes back out front to tell Bob the answer. Bob says O.K. and leaves.

Ronnie Dobbs (video/live)

Bob leaves the store and we learn that he was getting the change for a drunk. Not just any drunk, but a shirtless drunk named Ronnie Dobbs (David)! Ronnie hears his name called — it's Terry (Bob). He recognizes Ronnie, and so begins the reminiscing of the saga of a man who gets famous for getting arrested on the reality TV show, *Fuzz*.

Movie Ronnie/Movie Terry (John and Tom). The best worst acting.

Fuzz Theme Song:

> *Naughty Boys, Naughty Boys! Naughty Boys, Naughty Boys!*
> *You got ants in your pants, and bees in your bonnet.*
> *Doin' things you shouldn't, and doin' things you oughtn't.*
> *Naughtyyy!*

Ronnie is an energetic, immature troublemaker and liar. We watch Ronnie getting arrested in various scenarios, (including a domestic dispute with his woman (Mary Lynn) - "She's a professional Lieologist!" - and narcotics busts. Ronnie's spin-off show, *Ronnie Dobbs Gets Arrested*, becomes a big hit. Ronnie is a star. Then things go desperately wrong when Ronnie forgets what got him there.

(live) Terry confronts Ronnie at his mansion. He finds a bag of white powder, which Ronnie insists is his cocaine. "Bullshit! It's fucking baking soda!" Ronnie's been hanging out with health-obsessed Hollywooditextes, and his fans have noticed. Terry reads a letter from an 8-year old fan, "How come you're not so drunk anymore?" Ronnie cracks, complaining about the stress of fame. Ronnie kicks Terry out, leaving Terry at a loss as to how he was to "make more money off Ronnie." Then a stroke of luck — Ronnie dies. Terry triumphantly declares, "And I sold his life story to the movies."

Ronnie Dobbs Movie (film)

Natural Born Drunk: The Ronnie Dobbs Story. Movie Terry (Tom, who is dressed like the BeefEater man) finds Movie Ronnie (John, dressed like a hillbilly) in a dark alley with jug of moonshine. In an overly dramatic scene, Movie Ronnie, tells Movie Terry that he's dying of Entitilitus, finally dying in Terry's arms. Movie Terry cries anguished primal screams, "Ronnnnieeeeee!" into the night.

Incubation Pants Close (live)

On stage, Terry (Bob) gives the epilogue, but is cut short by David running on to tell him that his 30 minutes are up. Bob excitedly rips off the Terry beard and pulls a live baby chick out of his pants. "The pants worked!" Other cast members gather around to coo at the tiny bird.

Show Sponsor (video)

"O'Henderson's Incubation Pants. Dark, warm, with plenty of egg room. The pants that get you chicks." Credits roll over the newly-hatched chicks sitting on a pair of jeans.

Notes About Episode 101

Where'd title come from?

Bob: *"The phrase appears in a scene from the live show, that didn't make it to the final cut. In the first draft, the show was going to start with us [Bob and David] peeking out from behind a curtain at the audience. And we would see people and we would comment on them. At some point we hear something distracting and one of the lines was, 'Yeah, y'know, it's like the cry of a hungry baby; if you ignore it, eventually, it stops.'"*

Bob breaks record for standing on stage during a live taping.

The scene starts out live in Change for a Dollar. Bob (as customer) comes into the market, then waits while the clerk (David) goes to ask boss if he can make change. From there, while the live audience watches the pre-taped video of each superior calling for approval, Bob is left standing on stage waiting with his dollar until, finally, the clerk re-emerges with the answer ("No.").

Scene cut - montage of scene deemed not funny enough to show: Terry sells the 'Ronnie Dobbs Gets Arrested' show idea to Hollywood producer (Tom).

Special appearances: Maynard Keenan of Tool (Ronnie's busted friend in Fuzz sequence). Also, Tool is "Puscifer." Jenny McCarthy as Ronnie's Hollywood wife. She did have lines, but the scene was severely cut down. All cops and criminals on Fuzz cast are from group of friends. The French cop a production assistant who could speak French.

David: *"Asshole at Party was an idea for a sketch that I riffed with (writer/comedian) Louis C.K. one day. Bob and I wrote it. It's clear. It's one of those pieces that stand out as pure collaboration. It's got Bob jokes in there and my jokes in there. The whole thing just feels like that."*

David: *"Change for a Dollar is still one of my all-time favorites. When Bob and I were writing it, we were just jamming on this thing that just telescopes out, and how much fun it will be. It comes from a true story — we decided we wanted to get a caricature done for the program for our live show. So I called some guy that our friend recommended and told him what we needed. And I asked him how much it will be, and, I swear I am not exaggerating, I had to press my mute button on my phone I was laughing so fuckin' hard. The whole time he's doing it, I'm just sitting there going, 'I can't wait to call Bob. I can't wait to call Bob.' And he went on as long as we did in those scenes on the phone with this fuckin' bullshit clicky-clack, like trying to determine how much it would cost him, trying to calculate it: 'Well, there'd probably be a marker or two, and a piece of paper…' whatever his excuse was. And it was all for show. 'How many you want done? Two people?… two… two…clicky-click-click…when do you need them?… okay…hmmmhmmmm.' and so on. And then he said '$75.00,' and I said thanks, hung up and immediately called Bob."*

Wendy Wilkins (talent coordinator): *"Bob is a bit of a yeller. We all know it. The first time I saw him freak out, was the first day of shooting, first week, on a golf course in the middle of the valley, right next to an airport. Change for a Dollar. Each time they start, another airplane went over. So it gets to a point where Bob takes his club, and starts whacking it against the ground and throwing a fit. It was the only time he ever threw that kind of fit, but it was the very first thing, and we were worried about what was ahead."*

David: *"One time we shot in this Scientologist place. It was for Change for a Dollar, the oval office. It was some weird travel office, but it was a front for the Scientology organization. You get in and there's desks, but there's nobody there. It's all dusty. There's two guys in the back room, but in the front there's nobody. And there are rows and rows of books in all different languages, Scientology, books on buying and selling real estate, and the paths to success."*

Paul: *"I can be glimpsed briefly in episode #101, the first appearance of Ronnie Dobbs. I played one of the many policemen who arrest Ronnie. I was very excited because I'd seen the live shows Bob and David had done at the Upfront Theater in Santa Monica and loved them, so it was thrilling to be asked to participate in a sketch. I played the policeman rather poorly, I think. You can see, in the few seconds that I am on camera, that I am extremely awkward and ineffectual when Ronnie lunges at his wife. I thought it would be good to put my hand on the butt of my gun, as if I'm ready for trouble. But it just looks like I didn't know what to do."*

David: *"Incubation Pants is a great example of a bullshit little turn we took. But it's funny so who gives a shit. I certainly don't. I hope you don't."*

Some live scenes – (top) Asshole (David) winning bets; (bottom) an "Incubation Pants" hatchling.

Mr. Show #101   "The Cry Of A Hungry Baby"   9/13/95   28

                      ITEM #10   **
                    TERRY RECRUITS RONNIE SKETCH
                    (Terry(Bob), Ronnie(David),
                    Producer(T.Kenny),Cop(J.Ennis)

                          LIVE

LOC: PRODUCER'S OFFICE SET

TERRY HAS JUST FINISHED SHOWING THE TAPE TO A PRODUCER, TOM KENNY.

          PRODUCER (T.KENNY)

So, if I hear you correctly, you're suggesting that we "book" Ronnie for these shows?

          TERRY(BOB)

Nooo! Better than that. We give him his own program. Ronnie Dobbs gets arrested: in Vegas, in Houston, in Wherever.

          PRODUCER (T.KENNY)

Would he cooperate?

          TERRY(BOB)

That's the tip-tip-tipper of the chip-chip-cheree! I'm so glad you came to tea! (MAGICALLY PULLS A TEACUP FROM INSIDE HIS COAT) Ronwell?

DAVID ENTERS AS RONNIE, DRUNK.

          (MORE)

Mr. Show #101   "The Cry Of A Hungry Baby"   9/13/95   29

                    ITEM #9 (CONT'D)   ***
                    TERRY RECRUITS RONNIE SKETCH
                        LIVE

          PRODUCER (T.KENNY)

Ronnie, sit down. Ronnie, how would you like to have a low-rent apartment in every major city in this country? How would you like to drink for free everywhere you go? How would you like a whole closet full of shirts, that you could forget to wear [*wear*] every day?

          RONNIE(DAVID)

It's like a dream! What do I have to do?

          TERRY(BOB)

Go on with your life, just let us film it, right?

          RONNIE(DAVID)

Y'all gone put me in the movies?

          PRODUCER (T.KENNY)

That's not all. We're also going to give you, uh...five thou.. thou...eight hundr... hundr...twenty dollar bill of your own.

          RONNIE(DAVID)

Huh? What's a five thou.. thou...eight hundr... hundr...twenty dollar bill?

          TERRY(BOB)

It's special money, that only you can see!

          (MORE)

"Ronnie Dobbs" script pages — the scene the network deemed "Not funny enough for you."

Mr. Show #101   "The Cry Of A Hungry Baby"   9/13/95   30

                              ITEM #10 (CONT'D (2)
                              TERRY RECRUITS RONNIE SKETC[H]
                                     LIVE

              RONNIE(DAVID)

    Wow! It's like another dream! Where do
    I sign?

              PRODUCER (T.KENNY)

    Right here.

              RONNIE(DAVID)

    What name should I use?

              TERRY(BOB)

    Use your real name.

              RONNIE(DAVID)

    Huh?...Ohhh! Okay.

PAUSE.

              TERRY(BOB)

    Ronnie Dobbs.

              RONNIE(DAVID)

    Okay. When do I start?

              TERRY(BOB)

    Right now!

A COP, JOHN ENNIS, BURSTS IN AND CHASE RONNIE
OUT.

              RONNIE(DAVID)

    I didn't do nothin'.

(INTO: VTPB #10: THE RONNIE DOBBS SHOW)

2 WHAT TO THINK

written by:	Bob Odenkirk, David Cross
location segment director:	Troy Miller
live show director:	John Moffitt
cast:	David Cross, Bob Odenkirk, John Ennis, Tom Kenny, Mary Lynn Rajskub, Jill Talley
featuring:	Meleva Barbula, Jay Johnston, Paul Kozlowski, Bill Odenkirk, Brian Posehn, Ben Zook
special appearances by:	Jack Black, Janeane Garofalo

Arts Funding Cold Open (video)

Senator Howell Tankerbell (Bob) holds the floor at a subcommittee meeting. "The Arts Funding issue reminds me of the humorous story of the traveling salesman," where the farmer lets the salesman stay in his barn for the night. "But do me a favor," says the farmer. "Don't stick your willie into any of the three holes in the wall." But the salesman, like the government, "cain't help himself." He "sticks his willie" in the holes and it feels good, but the third hole hurts like hell and it won't let go. Turns out behind the first hole was the farmer's wife, behind the second his daughter, and behind the third hole was a milking machine that won't let go until it gets 50 gallons! Tankerbell's point being: "Gentlemen, I propose that this Arts Funding is like a milking machine, and, unless we shut it down, it's gonna rip our dicks right off!"

"Tonight's show is brought to you by The New U.S. Government. Improving the Arts by Severely Limiting Them."

Mr. Show theme song and logo. Mary Lynn introduces.

Tracking Collar Open (live)

Bob comes out on stage alone. Certain artists — including David — have been assigned senators to monitor them, and David has to wear a tracking collar. The collar emits a painful electric shock whenever he steps on a stage, unless his performance is approved by his senator. Bob ridicules David into trying a bit, and, despite the electroshock, David attempts to perform the duo's old baseball routine ("Peanuts and Cracker Jacks! Jesus, Bob, it hurts!"). Suddenly, Senator Tankerbell (Bob) pops up on the big screen. He disarms David's collar, but scolds him for not reporting this performance ahead of time.

Old Swerdlow (video)

Senator Tankerbell (Bob) appears via satellite from the Annual Folk Festival and Jelly Off, in Valdosta, Georgia, where he is monitoring the various folk arts performed there. The Senator orders a humble, Amish-looking fellow named Ole Swerdlow (David) to "make with the art." Ole describes his talent as "The Ozark Mountain Tradition of Song-storyin'." He sings as a rough-hewn wooden puppet jangles around on his knee:

Oh, Mr. Limber Legs went walking, down to old Miller's Creek.
And when he saw that big 'ol cow, he jumped back in the sink.
Oh, Limber Legs, where are you going to…?

The Senator is appalled, and abruptly halts this performance. He complains to David in the studio, "You see what I have to contend with? I got a naked puppet doin' a lewd and lascivious fandango on the lap of a full grown man!…It's like a pioneer porn shop!" He closes the whole thing down and laments, "I wish I could be everywhere that people are doin' art…To keep people from being titillated, or aroused, or in any way confused by the counter-culture…I wish, I wish, I wish.…"

Books For Seniors (video)

This is a story being read by Tom, from a great big story book about a "Magical Senator." "I think he's asleep," says wife Jill. Tom has been reading to a peacefully sleeping old man. It's a commercial for bedtime books for seniors, a series of oversized books featuring characters seniors love, like *Bible-ey the Bible and his Undersea Adventure*. This commercial is on…The What-To-Think Network.

Good News (live)

The tail end of a talk show called *Good News*. The host is a slow-talking, Southern-twanged TV preacher, Dr. Rudy Moore (Bob). He tells us that tomorrow's show will feature the return of guest Burton Quimm (David), the leader of 'Overcome,' an organization to help men and women renounce the sin of homosexuality. We're shown a clip from Burton's first appearance on *Good News* in 1982, "Part of the gay conspiracy is recruitment…Now I know I was just a confused heterosexual." Then we see a clip of Burton's slide back into temptation: home videos of a pile-on of gay men at a party. With each appearance on the show, Burton has reformed since once again being lured back into unabashed "homosinuality." "Now I have a wife. We're working on a family…." He shows a photo of himself stiffly posed with his 'beard' (a butch Janeane). "Now I just want to help others." Dr. Moore promotes, "Burton will tell us about the lapse he has planned for late August which should take him to Rio De Janeiro." And then it's…"stay tuned for *The Bible Machine*."

Jesus & Marshal (THE 13TH APOSTLE) (live)

A cheap documentary show about the Bible. The host, Don Olomite (John), tells of an unknown 13th Apostle, "Marshal." The Book of Marshal is titled *Power, Profit and Passion*; he's the world's first annoying, cliché-spewing, motivational speaker. Marshal (David) interrupts Jesus (Bob) in the middle of the much ballyhooed sermon-on-the-mount with the pitch, "What if I told you that the meek can inherit something a whole lot better than the earth?" When Jesus asks Marshal to hand out loaves and fish to the poor, Marshal offers the food at 12 drachmas apiece. Jesus scolds him, saying the food should be free. Marshal then sweetens his offer to include "an unleavened-bread leavenator!" At the tomb of Lazarus: "Lazarus, what if I told you that only losers die? The only thing preventing your resurrection is <u>you</u>!" Frustrated, the jelly-spined Jesus is forced to fire him. Left alone, Marshal asks for God's advice. God (voiced by Jack) urges Marshal to "leave everybody alone." Marshal sees yet another opportunity to sell his program; "God, ask yourself: Are you happy settling for omnipotence?"

Cut to plug for Marshal's book, *Power, Profit and Passion*.

Announcer: "Offer is limited to God and God-like deities...."

Announcements (live)

Bob is the Voiceover King is in a recording studio finishing the disclaimer for Marshal's book, "get all excited and speak in tongues." He is rattling off a list of crazy commercial tags for the studio producer (Tom): "Not to be confused with the disease 'cancer'" and, "Funtime Abortion clinics — we bring out the kid in ya!" The final one is a company slogan for Globo-Chem Corporation: "We own everything, so you don't have to."

Commercials Of The Future
(GLOBO-CHEM) (live/video)

A corporate conference room Globo-Chem CEO (John) and executives (Jill and Tom), listen to two hyper advertising execs (David and Bob) pitching an ad campaign which involves the extensive use of swear words. They show three commercials for a variety of Globo-Chem products, all loaded with inappropriate language ("and with prices going through the fucking roof...") The ads also feature a cute character, "Pit Pat," who waves and says, "I love you." The corporate types focus on the crude language, and the ad guys on "Pit Pat," the "magical, pan-sexual, non-threatening spokesthing." When the CEO dies from shock, it's revealed to be the true goal of the ad guys. Happy, everyone files out of the boardroom except David.

David breaks character: "Hello, I'm David Cross from television's *Mr. Show*." He explains the purpose of that scene was to attack Corporate America, which, in conjunction with the Government, suppresses information about the many uses of hemp.

Suddenly, Senator Tankerbell appears in the form of a magical, twinkling light flitting over the stage. He scolds David: "What the hell am I watching?...Why can't you do something with merit and family values?" David switches from self-righteous to confused victim: "It's this darn counterculture! It's got me all bugaboo!" Tankerbell understands, "It reminds me of a humorous story of a traveling salesman..." This gives David an idea.

"A House of Representatives Production, (performed at the Globo-Chem Center for the Performing Arts): *The Joke: The Musical*".

The Joke: The Musical (live)

An *Our Town*-type narrator (Bob) walks through the audience, introducing the tale of the traveling salesman (David) whose car broke down, leaving him without a place to stay. The salesman sings, *"I'm selling leather pants in the Ozarks. Where do I go now?"* He spots a farmhouse. The farmer (Jack) allows him to sleep in his barn, but he must follow a simple rule: "Don't stick your dick in these holes," referring to the three alluring holes in the barn wall. While sleeping on a hay pile, a demon temptress (Meleva) and the Devil (Jack, in leather pants) appear and try to get him to *"do it, do it, do it!"* The salesman fights temptation but loses, singing *"The kindly farmer said, 'No.' But I want to do it, so ...I think I'll stick my dick in these holes!"* He gets stuck in the third hole, and it's excruciatingly painful. The night passes, and in the morning the farmer is shocked. The salesman pleads, "What's in these holes?"

The farmer replies (singing):

> *You don't deserve an answer / but I'll give one anyway.*
> *Behind the first hole was my wife / That is where she stays.*
> *Behind the second hole was my daughter / Young and supple like a fawn.*
> *The third hole was a milking machine that doesn't quit,*
> *Until 50 gallons are withdrawn!!!*

The salesman then dies, singing a moving falsetto aria — *"Oh God, I'm dying. Knocking on heaven's door..."* — leading into a reprise of the childish "Knocking Song."

The "hated milk machine" (Bob) emerges. His delicate ballad morphs into a rousing rendition of "Auld Lang Syne." The entire cast, inexplicably dressed from a Dickens' novel, joins in, and it inexplicably begins to snow onstage. Senator Tankerbell appears as the twinkling light and congratulates everyone on doing such a great job: "It was funny, and it taught us all an important lesson about holes!"

Theme song and credits role over cast hugging in the falling snow.

Senator Tankerbell Tag (video)

Senator Tankerbell (Bob), comes out of a shitty motel bathroom humming the "Knocking Song." He approaches a messy bed with a reclined Mr. Limber Legs puppet. "There you go. Treat yourself," he says, tossing a crumpled twenty on the bed and giving the wooden doll a little kiss before he leaves.

Notes About Episode 102

Bob: "Again, we're experimenting with how thematic and intertwined the sketches can be. This one's amazing to me, so full of ideas, I can't believe it. It makes my head hurt to think about it. That's not praise, it's just amazement. It also does some things that even then I felt were easy and cheap. The CEO dying in Commercials of the Future was a bullshit turn in the scene. As time went by we got better at delivering whole scenes. What to Think has a lot of what soon would become common themes for us: the Government intrusion in the arts, the lame performance artist or folk artists, a lot of religious stuff. Ha ha. There's a taste of what's to come."

David: "I agree with Bob, there were some bullshit turns, but it's stuff we had done on stage, (the CEO dying, and then turning into the hemp thing) and you see our influences, before we really learned how to make it best for TV."

Paul F. Tompkins: "One of my all-time favorite characters and songs: Ole Swerdlow singing "Limber Legs". It's one of my favorite David performances. I always wished Ole Swerdlow would return somehow, but I could never think of a way to fit him into anything. This episode also has The Joke: The Musical, which is such an excellent and well-executed idea. This may sound strange, but I found Bob's milk machine to be absolutely adorable. I wanted to hug him. Also, this is the first of Bob's many wondrous singing performances."

Bill: "In Marshall I was Lazarus, and Tom Kenny was kneeling over me wearing a hood. And the whole time, he was contorting his face to try and make me laugh. He did when we were rehearsing, and I would laugh. But when we went to do the show, I was supposed to lay there like I was dead, like most of my roles, and I closed my eyes, and I imagined what Tom was up to, and I laughed."

Bob: "I'm glad we didn't repeat the tag lines announcer scene. It's a great simple template for a series of clever lines, and it could have become a staple of the show if we'd gone that way [recurring bits, characters; the way of success]. But fuck it, leave that to the rest of TV."

Bob: "Good News, about the constantly lapsing homosexual, is one of the smartest and funniest scenes we ever did, and it's stuff like that that makes me wish we'd had a bigger audience."

David: "Good News is another one of my favorite pieces. I remember coming into the office, and I had rented a copy of The Gay Conspiracy, a warning/educational tape some Christian group had put out. It was something both Bob and I gravitate towards — how religions suppress an independent way of thinking. And they had these guys giving testimonials, Christians who were ex-gay, who were so blatantly the stereotype of a gay guy. And we just started riffing on the sketch, and it was really fun. We shot the gay parties at the home of an unwitting family, who really didn't know what they were getting in for. Kind of a wealthy family, whose house we went back to a number of times."

Bob: "The musical was an idea I'd had for years. I don't care about musicals, but even I can't help but notice how thin the premises of many modern musicals have been. Also, I've always loved this randy, effort-full old salesman joke, and it's the perfect joke for a senator to tell when he's just hanging out with other senators. Or for eight year old boys. So get your favorite senator and your favorite eight year old boy in a room and show it."

Jack: "The Joke: The Musical. I did it with them at the Upfront Theater. And we did it in Aspen at the comedy festival. By the time we did it for the actual show, for the season, I had gained some weight and became very self-conscious. Usually I went shirtless in that thing, but for that one, I put on a little leather vest. I was embarrassed about my fat boobies, and so I don't think I did it quite as well 'cause I was little self-conscious about my body. I was a little shy at the taping."

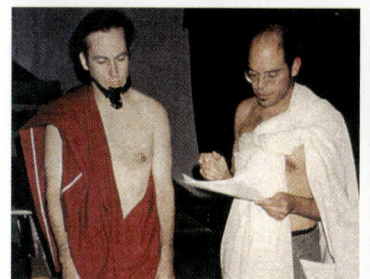

(top) Janeane Garofalo as David's "beard" in "Good News." Photo © Famous Mortimer; (center left) Sheets and electrical tape make the character. "The 13th Apostle" from Bob and David's live show; (center left) and the TV version; (bottom) Jack Black giving the salesman (David) the answer he doesn't deserve in "The Joke: The Musical."

David: "The end of the show has an inexplicable, nonsensical ending, but part of the attraction of that, and what's so engaging, is you don't have to explain it, it doesn't have to make sense. It's just steamrollering — piling crazy upon crazy. Bob's a milk machine, he's singing "Auld Lang Syne," and then people dressed as Dickens characters come out, and then it snows. And we acknowledge the audience, it's one of the first times we say 'hi' or 'bye' to the audience as a cast, and it feels like the end of a variety show."

FROM THE OFFICE OF
SENATOR HOWELL TANKERBELL
REFERENDUM NO. 2102

THE JOKE: THE MUSICAL
Music by Willie Etra
Directed by Famous Mortimer

APPROVED

An "Our Town" type Narrator (Bob) walks through the audience
"Oh. Hello. My, it's been a hot summer here in Gallagher's Corners. Good of you to all come down. Well let's see. It happened exactly one year ago today. Seems a salesman's car had broken down over by the creek, and he was lookin' for a place to spend the night. As the Narrator exits, The Salesman (David) enters. He bears a heavy briefcase in hand, and he's tired.

>   Where do I go now? My car has broken down.
>   I'm selling leather pants in the Ozarks. Where do I go now?

Suddenly, he spots a farmhouse. He rushes up to the door, and the music turns into the up-beat "Knocking Song":

>   This is the Knocking Song / I'm knocking on a door.
>   Knock-knock-knock, knock-knock-knock, knock forevermore
>   Knockety, knock, knock, knock . . .

The Farmer (Jack) opens the door, "Stop that infernal knocking song!
"Yes, Sir. I'm Sorry. My car broke down, might I spend the night?
"Yes, you can.

>   Step this way, right this way. See my house.
>   That's my house, but you shall not stay in my house.
>   You shall stay in the barn, the barn!
>   But adhere to this simple rule,
>   Don't stick your dick in these holes,
>   Don't stick your dick in these holes!
>   These holes three are not for thee!

The grateful Salesman agrees, and offers leather pants as payment.
The Farmer accepts: "Leather Pants? Well, I suppose I could give them to my gay son." The Farmer leaves and The Salesman settles to go to sleep.

"Well, that worked out quite nicely. What a kindly old farmer."
He lays down to sleep. "Goodnight, Moo Cow. Goodnight, Hay. Goodnight . . . Holes."

A tinkling note sustains, underneath comes a driving beat.
A Temptress (Maleva) dances out.

>   Do it, do it, do it! "Do it, do it, do it!
>   Do it, do it, do it! You know you want to do it!
>   C'mon Mr. Salesman, What do you say?

The Salesman fights the temptation with reason:
>   No way!!! He told me that I could not!
>   He told me that I should not!
>   What would the farmer say?
>   And what about the Moo-cow? And what about the Hay?

The Devil jumps out (Jack) — who is the Farmer, now evil, in leather pants:
>   Good God, man! You're weak!
>   You're a worm with no will.
>   Be bold son, no one's watching
>   Show some spine, have your fill!
>   What magic lies in wait for you?
>   What miracles in store?
>   Could heaven be on the other side?
>   Come on open the door!
>   Do it, do it, do it.
>   You know you want to do it!
>   Do it! Do it!!

more>

FROM THE OFFICE OF
SENATOR HOWELL TANKERBELL
REFERENDUM NO. 2102

APPROVED

PAGE 2

"Noooo!!!" screams The Salesman.

> I am just a simple man, I sell leather pants.
> But now I'm torn by my conscience. I sell leather pants.
> The kindly farmer says, 'No.'
> But I want to do it, so
> Should I stick my dick in these holes . . .?
> I think I'll stick my dick n these holes!

And The Salesman sticks his dick in the first hole. The Temptress and The Devil rejoice: "Yeah!" and get more and more excited as The Salesman samples each hole.

Devil:	Number one feels good!
Salesman:	Oh Yeah!
Temptress:	You finally feel alive!
Devil:	Go on, now, try number two!
Temptress:	That one makes you thrive!
Farmer:	Now it's time for number three!
Temptress	The best of the lot!
Devil:	With number three you'll make history!
Temptress:	C'mon, give it all you got!

The Salesman sticks his dick in the third hole! He is in obvious excruciating pain and he's stuck: "Oooooowwwww!!!" The Devil and The Temptress laugh then vanish, leaving The Salesman gasping for breath.

The rooster crows, signifying early morning.
The Farmer, no longer evil, re-enters "Oh, my God! I told you not to!"
The Salesman pleads: "What's in these holes? What's in these holes?"
The Farmer replies:

> You don't deserve an answer / but I'll give one anyway.
> Behind the first hole was my wife / that is where she stays.
> The second was my daughter / Young and supple like a fawn.
> The third hole was a milking machine that doesn't quit,
> 'Til 50 gallons are withdrawn!! Yeah! Withdrawn!!! Withdrawn!

The Salesman, deflated, falls off the Hole.

> Oh God, I'm dying. Knocking on heaven's door!

He finishes by reprising the up-beat Knocking Song and runs off stage.

Lights go down and a pin spot grabs the Milk Machine (Bob) who enters meekly.

> I'm the hated Milk Machine.
> Everybody hates me now,
> For doing what I'm told.
> He was trying to be bold.
> Why can't people keep their willies out of holes?
> Where do I go now?
> Where do I go now?
> This is the Knocking Song,
> In days of Auld Lang Syne

EPISODE 103
WE REGRET TO INFORM YOU

written by:	Bob Odenkirk, David Cross
location segment director:	Troy Miller
live show director:	John Moffitt
cast:	David Cross, Bob Odenkirk, John Ennis, Tom Kenny, Mary Lynn Rajskub, Jill Talley
featuring:	Greg Behrendt, Bill Odenkirk, Brian Posehn, Melissa Samuels, Sarah Silverman
special appearance by:	Kato Kaelin

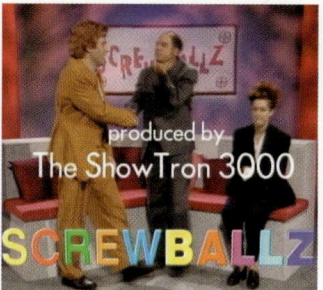

Mr. Show logo and theme song. Mary Lynn introduces.

Letters Open (DEAR GLOBO-CHEM/MAIL ORDER BRIDE) (live/video)

(live) The show opens on Bob and David sitting across from each other at little wooden desks. David is wearing a frilly blue dress. Bob is writing a letter: "Dear David Cross, My name is Bob Odenkirk. Although we have never met, I would like to do a TV show with you. Please respond. Signed, A Stranger." David reads the letter and is prompted to write a complaint letter to Globo-Chem: "I recently had an unpleasant experience with a package of Creamy Doodles…" David's non-response angers Bob, who writes a threatening letter ("…praying to God won't help. Signed, Your Killer.") When David reads this, he panics, and writes to Globo-Chem again. David frantically runs off stage to find a mail box.

(video) David runs down the street, still in the frilly dress. He gets to a mailbox, relieved, drops the letter in. He's suddenly picked up by two shady UPS guys (John and Tom), who stuff him into a huge cardboard box.

(live) Back on stage with Bob, the UPS guys deliver the box, announcing that it contains a "mail-order bride." "How ugly could she be?" Bob laughs. Out of the box pops a beautiful girl (Sarah, in a dress identical to David's). Now the show can start. "Welcome to *Mr. Show*, I'm Bob Odenkirk," says Bob. "And I'm David Cross," says Sarah.

Kissing Booth (live)

Bob and Sarah perform the *Kissing Booth Sketch*, where Sarah is the customer at Bob's kissing booth. David is backstage watching this, upset. Bob dares the patron to prove he's not a gay man by giving him a kiss: "A real man who's confident in his heterosexuality wouldn't let that bother him a bit. He'd French like there's no tomorrow." David shows up to stop the sketch. David realizes why Bob had a woman take his place: Bob is homophobic. David pleads, "Men can kiss, Bob…They even have a pill now that lets men make love to each other!" David pulls out a gay porno reel out of his pocket — "Here, watch this."

Gay Porn Titles Link (video)

Low-budget porno music plays over footage of a cruise ship out at sea — *A Pipefitter's Union*…Starring Billy, Kenneth and Charles (and the boys from 'The Motherlode Bar'). These opening credits are cut short by a disclaimer that the film has not been altered for television and "if anything, [the film] has been made *more* gay." The film is repeatedly interrupted with warnings about the film's re-editing and its resulting "gayness." Ultimately, the film is deemed possibly "too gay even for some gay people." Once more, the film is interrupted to announce that the film has been "re-re-edited for television," and it is now a scene about a couple on their honeymoon.

Third Wheel (live)

A couple (Jill and Bob) are honeymooning on a cruise ship. Wife is upset because Hubby (Bob) has invited along his best friend, Jerry (David), a really annoying, crude, regular guy ("I have to take a crap…hand me that *Hustler*"). The wife argues that he doesn't belong on the honeymoon, that "he's like a third wheel." Jerry sings from off stage: "*The Legend, The Legend. The Third Wheel Legend. Always in the way.*" The couple argues on, and Jerry soulfully reprises his song each time they utter, "Third Wheel," eventually building to a dancing gospel rendition with choir. Finally, Jerry gets the point and offers to leave. Hubby still argues for his friend's right to be there, after all 'honeymoon' is a nonsensical word, "for all we know, we're in Jerry's way!…Let's promise never to use the word 'honeymoon' ever again." Hubby announces to the audience, "The tyranny of the word 'honeymoon' is over!" As in a play, they all take a bow. Bob (dropping character) thanks the writer of the scene, Peter Cancatanktin.

Writer In Audience (live)

At a table in the audience sits the "writer" of that last piece, Peter (John). With him are his lover Ken (Tom) and Ken's friend Geri (Mary Lynn). Peter eagerly asks his friends for their opinion of the play-let. Ken is gushing, but Geri tactfully points out that it was a bit serious at the end with all the talk of tyranny. Peter explodes: "You don't get it, do you, Geri?…That scene was about you! Duh! You're the 'Third Wheel'!" Geri storms off, and Peter consoles a weeping Ken in his arms.

Sarah Silverman as David Cross, and David Cross.

Another televised warning:

"We apologize for the homosexual content of this last scene. We now join a fiercely heterosexual sketch already in progress."

Skrewballz (video)

Jim (Bob) is the host of *Screwballz* where guests pick one of three contestants from videotaped interviews, and "just go have some sex!" He welcomes back a couple to interview them on the sex they had. Beth (Melissa) and Fred (David, holding his throat to produce the Barry White voice), who just "finished up" — "Well, according to our judges, Fred did." Fred begins to explain how romantic he was, but Beth is distraught over having had empty sex with this stranger in front of judges. Host Jim asks Fred if he wants to have sex with Beth again. "I would love to." Beth turns it down. "Oh, well, Fred. You know what that means. We'll give you $20 to masturbate into a cup." Fred thinks that's great, and the dating show wraps up.

Video Complaints (live/video)

(live) Bob's back on stage, and admits that David's character in the last scene may have been offensive. He encourages viewers to send in any complaints on video. He shows some complaints already received.

(video) A series of angry complaints about the show's content, including a man in a "hug therapist" t-shirt (David), standing in his kitchen, getting so upset that he can't speak straight. "I have never, ever, ever, nerver, effervery, nevener…".

(live) Bob suggests people get their home video camera ready because there'll be plenty to object to in the next scene.

Borden Grote (film)

A reporter (Bob) takes a special bio-peek into the life of Borden Grote (David), America's most dedicated actor. Borden is a method actor: he experiences the things his characters must go through, to represent them in a truer fashion. He went to medical school for two years in preparation for his 15-sec cameo as a doctor in Mel Brooks's flop, *Badman Whatever*. For his latest challenge, a movie about a mental institution, Borden had the frontal lobe of his brain removed and replaced with bubble wrap "for realism's sake." As Bob tries to interview him, drooling, catatonic Borden can only respond with nonsensical babble. The mention of The Oscars™ hurls Borden into a fit until Billy T., his personal secretary (John), calms him with a shaking rattle. A day with Borden: Borden's chef, Fontaine (Brian), prepares spaghetti and jelly on white bread ("It's very textural."); Borden attempts a work-out on the treadmill with assistance from his personal trainer (Greg). Throughout the evening, celebrities stop by: Kato Kaelin, soul-singing sensation Larry Black (Bob), and hot college comic Blueberry Head (David), who entertains a room full of Hollywood hangers-on with his completely unfunny, on-the-spot props ("A paper cup hat for fruit!") While the partygoers are enjoying themselves by the pool, Larry Black hits on a cutie and tells her about his show that night — "At least I think it's tonight. I should probably write these things down."

Soul Singer (LARRY BLACK) (live)

Larry Black (Bob) introduced live on stage. Bob comes out and sings (poorly) a Barry White-ish sexy song: *"Tonight's the night, we'll make loooove! Tonight. No waiting, no hesitating…"* Larry catches what he's saying and gets concerned, crossing to a desk and checking his day-planner. "Damn, Baby, not tonight!" He apologizes and pencils in his Baby for tomorrow night, and gets back to singing (oh-so-poorly). The lyrics change to *"Tomorrow night,"* but he finds even that is booked up, and then the damn phone starts ringing. "I'm singing a song!" he shouts into the receiver. We see on the big screen it's Nikki in a commercial for….

Supermodel Hotline (video)

The "Supermodel Calling Service." Regular teenage schmo, Andre (David), sits at home. An announcer declares, "There are thousands of supermodels waiting to talk to you around the clock!" Andre says with excited disbelief, "Thousands?! Clock?!" Andre signs up for the service, and the calls from beautiful supermodels start coming in. Andre is thrilled, but the calls keep coming and coming, as promised. Soon annoyed, then terrified, he is forced to grab his backpack and run for safety. But every pay phone he passes rings with supermodels calling for him; hundreds of messages are on his machine. He cannot escape.

Film Festival Close (live)

Bob is on stage in a tux, presenting *Supermodel Horror Film* as a part of the *10th Annual My Film Festival*. He is interrupted by a shout from the audience, "Why won't you show my movie?!" It's David in a bad wig. Bob scolds this protesting artiste, telling him he should have followed "procedure," to which David shouts, "But I *don't want* to have sex with you!" He rips open his jacket to reveal a lone firecracker-size explosive taped to his chest — "SHOW MY MOVIE!!" Bob cracks, "Sh-sh-sh-show it!" On the big screen we see *Credits. A Film by David*

Spaghetti and jelly? No, jelly and spaghetti. Chef Fontaine (Brian) and Billy T. (John) assist actor Borden Grote (David), as earnest reporter (Bob) watches on.

Cross, backed with Fellini-esque music. Added in hand writing is "with no help from Bob Odenkirk." Bob reacts, "What the heck!?" He knocks the matches out of David's hand and socks him with a hard right. They tag-team fight with crazy wrestling characters as David's altered credits roll.

Notes About Episode 103

Bob: "A completely nonsensical opening. Not about a recognizable social or personal issue. We didn't do too many of these. But we were still finding the show. Gay, gay, gay. So many scenes with this subject matter. More on this later."

Bob: "*Third Wheel*, like the Spank trial (#104), or the end of Commercials of the Future (#102), are our own kind of free-form logic scenes. They all have premises that are played conventionally, until you can sense us grasping for direction, at which point the scene twists around the logic at the core of a character's argument. A character will launch into a tirade about his hurt feelings and argue for some new, inane way of viewing the entire scene that just happened. This, in itself, may then be twisted, until it becomes a meaningless game. It was fun and seemed cool at the time, but we learned that it was thin and kind of empty. Much harder to make a scene evolve in a genuine way, or come up with a strong closing riff."

Bob: "*Python* did lots of very funny 'TV Warnings' and 'Apologies for Content.' Since entertainment ethics is still an issue, perhaps more these days, we felt it was valid to do. But we made a real effort to avoid these kinds of ideas as the show went on. After all, we were on HBO and nobody complains about the content of their shows. At least they better not, if they don't want a boot up their ass. From me. My boot."

David: (Bob was the singing *Third Wheel* character in some of the live shows.) "We switched characters a lot when we were doing the stage show. Unless it was really obvious that one person should play a certain role, we would switch it off just for fairness' sake. It kept it fun."

David: "The dumbest thing about that show — and there were more of these things to come — when Bob and I wrote the credits up, which was part of the end, all the jokes were in the credits about Bob not helping. The only credit we weren't allowed to alter was the Writers Guild credit, because of the WGA's strict rules. We called them, and said, 'We're the writers. It's okay; we're talking about ourselves.' We were able to do it with every other credit, production credit, and cast credit, but they wouldn't let us do it."

EPISODE 104 — WHO LET YOU IN?

written by:	Bob Odenkirk, David Cross
location segment director:	Troy Miller
live show director:	John Moffitt
cast:	David Cross, Bob Odenkirk, John Ennis, Tom Kenny, Mary Lynn Rajskub, Jill Talley
featuring:	Jack Plotnick, Brian Posehn, Craig Anton
special appearance by:	Jack Black

Mr. Show *theme song, logo. Mary Lynn introduces.*

Watching Chase Of The Chaste Open (live)
Bob tries to start the show, only he can't get David to come out, his attention is glued to his portable TV. In fact, the audience members are also watching TV's and listening to radios. There's a big news story on and simply everyone is following it. Bob and David decide to skip the show and watch TV instead.

Popemobile Chase/News (video/live)
A special news report: *The Chase of the Chaste*. The Popemobile is being chased by police.

(live) News anchors (Jill and Tom) report that the Pope is the chief suspect in the death of Bishop Francios Pertaup (Brian), who was found "brutally excommunicated outside his door." The Pope's ring and staff were found at the scene, covered in blood.

(video) A glimpse of the scene shows police mishandling evidence. A conical hat left at the crime scene has not yet been confirmed as belonging to the Pope.

(live) Anchors interview a "Pope Expert," Tim McCracken (David), who's not a Catholic; he just, as his sweatshirt reads, loves the Pope. He rambles on about the little-known history of the Pope's strange hat, when the anchors cut his interview short to get back to the chase. They invite him to stick around. Tim can't decide where to sit — "Hello! Ding-dong!…Under the desk!" The annoyed reporters ask Tim to wait in the Expert Lounge.

Dudes Arguing Link (video)
Popemobile chase is being watched on a small handheld TV by three heavy metal dudes as they cruise around town. Two dudes (Bob and David) argue whether the chase is "classic" or "awesome." The third dude (Brian) insists that it's "core." The arguing escalates to "Fuck you's," and, finally, the first dude is pushed out of the still-moving truck into the gutter. Luckily, it's right in front of Nil's Guitar School, which is where he was headed. He gets up, brushes himself off, shakes angry fists at the speeding truck, and enters the shop.

Nil's Guitar Shop (live/video)
Inside a cheap guitar store, Larry (David), a young beginner arrives for a guitar lesson. He is as terrible as any first-timer, but Nils is taken aback — "Whoa, dude! You're incredible!" He doesn't believe this praise at first, but when Nils's friend Blackie (Tom) is equally impressed, Larry gets excited. After a brief phone call, Nils's attitude changes completely. He explains that Larry's mom had called earlier, telling them that Larry had only two weeks to live, but she just phoned back to say that Larry's test results were actually okay. Larry still wants his lesson; he suggests that he can learn. Nils explodes: "NO, YOU CAN'T! YOU SUCK AND YOU'RE WASTING MY TIME!"

Nils has another phone conversation and does a 180° on his attitude. He acts like Larry rules again, but Larry's on to them. Nils swears the whole dying thing was a prank. Nils answers the phone. "Chart mix up?" Larry tries to decipher his medical condition based on how great of a guitarist these two rockers say he is. "Do you still think I'm that great of a guitar player?" Nils carefully responds, "No. But you don't totally suck, so don't start celebrating." Nils invites him to play in Blackie's place for their big rock concert tonight. This cheers Larry and he runs off. After he is gone, Nils assures Blackie that Larry won't survive that long.

(video) Larry is playing horribly in front of a cheering crowd. "Larry's mother individually called all 3,000 screaming fans to go to the concert and spare Larry's feelings."

Imminent Death Syndrome (video)
The continuing story of Larry (David) as he confounds his doctor by not dying. He keeps getting dying wishes fulfilled and being overpraised by people who've gotten calls from his mother about his condition, including a Florida hospital which brings him on staff as a doctor. One of Larry's patients (Brian) inquires if Larry is still alive, then attests from his amputee's crutches that, "He's the best doctor ever." A journalist (David) interviews Larry's doctor (Bob) about IDS. IDS is when someone is "literally on the brink of death for 80-100 years." He adds that when the victim doesn't die, it puts loved ones in the "awkward position" of feeling cheated after putting so much effort into making

their dreams come true. The doctor lists over-praised people living with IDS, including: Juliette Lewis, Anne Rice, Stephen Hawkins ("brilliant man"), Quentin Tarantino (the actor, not the director). The phone rings; Larry has passed away. He excuses himself to go watch the trial.

Trial Of The Millennium (live/video)

(live) News anchors (Jill and Tom) report on the Pope's trial.

(video) Courtroom video footage of the Pope (Bob) demonstrating that the bloody papal ring is too small. Next, papal staff manufacturer, Derek Hummries (David), testifies that other than the Pope, he only sells that staff to Sigfried and Roy.

(live) The newscasters report next that for entertainment, the sequestered jury was brought to a coffee house to see hip performance artist Spank.

Spank (live)

Coffee Clutch host Arty (Bob) introduces performance artist Spank (David), who takes the stage with an American flag around his shoulders. He angrily rants an anti-American beatnik sermon. "America, you shit on us everyday! You shit on us?" He lays the flag on the floor. "I shit on you! Yeah!" He pulls down his shorts and squats over the flag. Nothing comes. Arty tries to help Spank by covering him up with a blanket. "Did you eat? You gotta have fiber, too." Spank, trying to whisper, says "I had that Newton." He shoos Arty away and regains his performance composure, set now on pissing on the flag ("Let it RAIN!"), to no avail, then tries puking. Nothing. Spank turns to the audience and vows, "I will not rest until this flag is shat upon…"

Expert Truck (video)

In a courtroom, Spank (David) explains that he is a taxpayer who makes a living shitting on things ("money, religious icons, what have you") and he demands the flag be put in jail for trampling all over his rights. He calls to the stand a leading flag expert. Bailiff (John) walks into the Experts Lounge, where various experts are waiting for work. As needed, the Flag Expert (Bob) is called from the list, along with Experts on Donkey Basketball and Prostitutes. A down-on-his-luck expert (Jack Black) humbly asks for work, so he can feed his hungry family. "I can be an expert on anything, if you just please give me the chance." A sympathetic bailiff: "Well, can you handle ten ways to please your man?" He gets the job. The Expert Truck with all four experts in back. The formerly-down-on-his-luck expert rides on the roof of the cab, wildly waving his hat.

The Expert Truck Song (sung by Craig Anton)

> The Expert Truck's comin', Comin' to your town!
> Comin' to your town! Well the E-truck keeps a rollin'
> Movin' them experts up and down!
> They drop off the Flag Expert in front of the courtroom.

He takes the witness stand, and testifies that Spank was rendered constipated by the colors in the flag, a theory he can *show* them if they "all take the magic pills he's provided." All in the courtroom take a pill, and it is evidenced on their faces that it's working.

Founding Fathers (live)

Benjamin Franklin (David), Lincoln (Tom), Jefferson (Bob), Washington (John), and Button Gwennet (Jack Plotnick) discuss how to design a flag so that "ye olde performance artist won't shit on it." All come back in a week and offer their suggestions. Franklin places a box of shit on the table. "Gentlemen, who would shit on a flag made of shit? It would be an empty gesture!" Lincoln tells him to put his poo box away — his design uses the colors red, white and blue in such a way that will cease all lower bodily functions. The rest gather around Lincoln's flag and try to poo upon it, but they cannot.

History Museum (video)

Inside a museum of history where a droopy guy (Bob) is vying for a job. "So that's how they decided what colors to make the flag. Because Lincoln helped. So do I get the job?" The museum guy (David), disgusted and disbelieving, tells him no. Droopy is full of attitude as he slumps off and air punches a painting on his way out. The museum worker answers the phone. "Imminent Death Syndrome?!" He rushes after Droopy. Droopy is now behind the museum desk. He answers the phone. "New exhibits?" He surveys his desk. "We've got some pens and pencils, and a telephone, and an information sign, and a television set…" He numbly hangs up the phone to watch the TV — It's the news anchors (Jill and Tom)….

Watching Murders Close (video/live)

Bob and David backstage, watching the same newscast and eating cereal. The anchors announce they are about to show "the gruesome footage of a double murder caught on tape in Los Angeles." The footage is of Bob and David, in the same clothes, sitting backstage, watching the news, when suddenly two masked men come from behind and choke them to death. "Classic," says David. "Awesome!" says Bob. They high-five. Credits roll as they enjoy their cereal (Pit-Pat-Os).

Like a GUITAR GOD! Bob and Tom as Nils and Blackie encourage Larry (David), a sufferer of IDS.

Notes About Episode 104

David: "This show is a pretty cool show, as far as how it flows, it's pretty neat. Although 'take this pill and I'll show you' is bullshit. Spank I did at the Diamond Club, just on my own. And that was inspired by this actress, Pam Siegel, who took pictures of a performance artist in New York. She showed me these pictures of a guy who was shitting on a flag, and that's all he did. That was his big statement. And I just thought that was so empty and silly and just a dumb red-necky thing to cheer on. Goody for him. He showed that flag."

David: "The Popemobile chase was Bill's idea [even though not yet a writer on the show]. We never sat down and said let's do something about the OJ Simpson thing."

David: "In rehearsal for Founding Fathers, Tom riffed the line, 'Gentleman, here we sit broken hearted...' That was a 'poo box.' I'll take credit for coming up with that term. I loved the ending; I love stuff that fucks with the reality of it and brings everything around in a neat clever way."

Paul: "One of my favorite things in this episode is Tom Kenny's weird character choice for Lincoln. It's so insane. Tom doing Lincoln like one of the Dead End Kids."

Bob: "The guitar lesson is one of my all time favorite scenes. It's such an interesting premise, that people are being nice to a guy who's dying, and so greatly silly — over-praising his terrible guitar playing. And then the back and forth starts with the phone calls. It's one of the reasons I'd like to do a Mr. Show live tour. It would be a really fun scene to do over and over."

David: "Bob's character, from the history museum, 'Droopy,' we just called him around the office, because he didn't have a name. I fuckin' love that character, makes me cry."

Bob: "'Droopy' is based on a person that I know from high school, and a couple of guys I grew up with would impersonate him, and that's how the character came up. He's just a guy who did a lot of drugs and drank a lot. He's really slow, and negative, and pissed off all the time. But I'm reluctant to talk about it — you see the characterization, you can see it's not a very complimentary thing. And I don't want to put him down because he's a nice guy."

SEASON TWO
EPISODE GUIDE

Season two of *Mr. Show* — six episodes. Everything grew. A little more money. They developed their writing staff. Larger cast of regular performers. A real studio. Audience filled with fans. It was a bigger episode order than the previous year, but not so many that the schedule was unbearable. In many ways, the second season was the most exciting of all.

Second Season Not An Obvious Thing

HBO hesitated in picking up the show for a second season. The show received critical acclaim — what HBO claims to value most. Their reviews from the first season were all very strong (including the *Village Voice*: "*Mr. Show* deserves its own channel.") David was "fully expecting" they would get to do more: "I never thought we were just doing the four shows. All we needed was luke warm critical success, and we were going to get to do it again." But Bob felt it was never an easy, obvious thing that they get to continue the show. "It was a really iffy proposition, as it was every year we did it. But especially the first two years, it was people going out on a limb for us. Carolyn Strauss and Chris Albrecht [from HBO] primarily."

John Moffitt, too, says he was eager for the pick-up: "We knew there was something really terrific going on there, and we wanted it to keep going. I always had a feeling that Carolyn was very much behind it, Chris wanted to be supportive, but the East Coast [the marketing department at HBO, which carries a lot of weight in the cable channel's programming decisions] didn't understand it. And so there's a battle."

It took a big nudge from Garry Shandling, then starring in HBO's prestigious, *The Larry Sanders Show* (in which Bob had a recurring role as 'Stevie Grant,' Larry Sanders's fast-talking agent) to persuade HBO to renew the series.

Brian Posehn recalls hearing the long-awaited news: "It was spring of '96 when Bob called and told me they had finally convinced HBO to let them do Season Two. I'll never understand how HBO could have even questioned picking up the show when they seemed to pick up dreck like *Arli$$* without a second thought."

From A Night Club To A Night Club Set

For the new season, they convinced HBO that the production problems far outweighed the creative positives of doing the show in a "real club environment." So they were able to move their stage from the Hollywood Moguls night club to an actual studio, a stage on the KTLA lot. Tom Buderwitz, who designed the sets for *Mr. Show*, created a "night club set" with three stages. "We had three performing areas; it always felt like a three-ring circus," says Troy. With this move came many welcomed improvements to the production. During the first season, the pacing at the Moguls was severely challenged by having to move everything around (set changes, move cameras, move audience members). "Once we got into the bigger space," explains Moffitt, "we had the facility of really being able to have set changes and a backstage kind of life that had things going on, with dressing rooms and all that. We were able to do the shows faster, more in real time. We reached a point where everything would move fast, the only thing we had to wait for were the makeup changes because Bob and David were in every single scene. The fastest we ever did a show, we broke 30 minutes. The timing was perfect — we had a play-

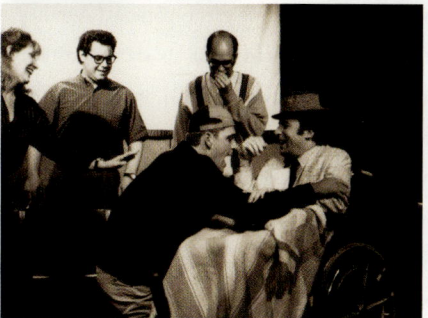

Trying out scenes before second season at the Upfront Theater in Santa Monica. Clockwise from top left: Bob in convincing bald cap, for "No Adults Allowed"; Jay doing what he does best; Grandpa coming out as gay (with Brett, Paul, Jay, David and Bob); Dino sings "Cracker Barrel" song. (photos: © Jenine deShazer, 1996)

back piece while they were changing, and when the playback piece was finished, they came out. It was like a live show."

Get The Writing Going

Bob and David started the writing session together alone, a few weeks before the other writers joined it (which is how they did it every year). Partly for budgetary reasons, but mostly to maintain that the show comes from them — ensuring a "show head." "We hadn't been writing together for weeks, so it was a chance for us to get together and think and focus ourselves and the show," explains Bob. "When the other writers came in, we've got a handle on the show, and at that point, a lot of sketches."

Joining as writers were Bill Odenkirk, Jay Johnston, and Paul F. Tompkins. A staff of three was all the budget would allow. David and Bob also planned to buy individual sketches from Brian Posehn and Dino Stamatopoulos (they tried to get Dino to join them, but he wanted to stay in NY). Half-way through the season, they brought Posehn on staff, after picking up three scenes from him and realizing it would be the about the same cost to hire him on. Dino came in for a few weeks to do *Jeepers Creepers*, an idea he had come up with at *The Ben Stiller Show*, and to collaborate on a few other things. Regarding bringing on Jay and Paul, David admits that it was seeing their sketch show, *The Skates*, and not a writing submission, that convinced him. "If I would have gotten writing samples from them, I don't know if I would have hired them.

Their show was the funniest sketch show I'd seen live. It was basically what Bob and I did with *Mr. Show* in presenting it to HBO. It doesn't translate on the page as well."

"It was great to have these new writers, to have a writing staff which we hadn't had," tells Bob. "It was really fun to get together with Jay and Bill and Paul and, later in the season, Brian and Dino, too. They were people with unique, clever ideas. From that group, came some great material." Although the whole writing staff contributed on all six shows, writing credit only went to Bob and David for #201 and #202. Bob explains: "We all wrote everything, and the other writers only got paid for four shows. That's all we had a budget for, and that's why their names are only on four of the shows. It was a Writers Guild thing. The guys came aboard and agreed to give us the credit. It is fucked up, and I thank them for it."

Another big addition for them in the second season was getting the amazingly talented Eban Schletter aboard as their musical director. It was a tall bill, writing the music for *Mr. Show*, with the gamut of genres and styles. Eban recalls his first meeting with producer Troy Miller: "He said 'Bob and Dave think you can do this, and I trust their opinion. But remember, this has to be able to go head to head with other shows that are completely professional — I know we don't have a lot of money, but you're going to have to perform on that standard.' I left that meeting feeling I have to prove myself. That season was like a blur, working hard all the time."

More Means Less

Jay and Paul (and, later, Brian) were also added as regular performers. For the other original cast members, Jill Talley, Tom Kenny and John Ennis, it meant sharing what little they had. Jill explains, "It is a little bit of a bummer when you see Jay and Paul walk in and get bigger parts their first season than I ever got. In the beginning, John and Tom and I did the parts that Bob and David couldn't do. Sometimes some juicy roles were thrown Tom's way and maybe John's way. But basically we knew what our function was and why we were there. We were happy to be part of a good show, and we were able to take what we got and make it our own. And maybe, we thought, by the second season, Bob and David might start to burn out and open it up a little more. And then cast members are added. So, for me, it was like, 'Wow, where were these big parts?' in the beginning."

John Ennis felt similarly at the time: "With all these other actors coming in, they were threats at first. 'Holy shit! Are they bringing these guys in because they're not happy with me anymore?' We'd do a read-through and it was my part, and then we'd come back, after re-writes, to rehearse it, and the part was someone else's. I'd never go up to David and Bob and say, 'Hey what about that part that was mine?' This is the process of doing a show; I know that now. But if you're in the show, and you get a two-minute bit, and it does not seem very big, you start to look at the script — 'That's the only thing I'm in for the whole show?' Then you realize that thing we filmed a month ago is also in the show. But that would freak me out. I wanted to be in everything."

Some good cameos: Ben Stiller is very funny as "Jimmy" the faux-accountant in *Bhopal* (#204); Julia Sweeney and Dave Foley appear together in fake sitcom *Second Wind* (#205); Jack Black and Maynard Keenan show up in the credits sequence of #206, and of course, Jack as *Jeepers Creepers*, with Jeanne Tripplehorn (#203).

Dino likes episodes with a variety of ideas: "Season two is my least favorite season. Themes too strong. Each scene about slackers — it got boring, things started bumping."

"We had our first office," recalls Bill. "It was just this tiny affair that had nothing to the outside. There was no door. We don't know how we got in it."

Flyers to Season 2 tapings.

INTERMISSION

THE FAILED MUSICAL MAGAZINE

NOV. 29 1996 $3

Jeepers Creepers SEMI-STAR!

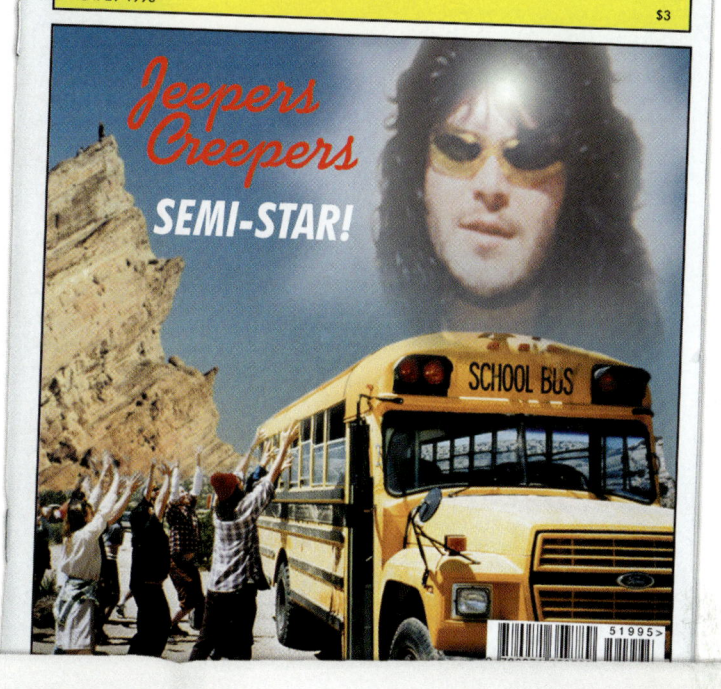

INTERMISSION

A SCHOOL BUS SCHREECHES TO A HALT IN THE DESERT, AND THE CAST POURS OUT AND UNLOADS THE PROPS FOR THEIR MUSICAL.   DAVID IS SITTING ATOP THE HIGHEST PEAK, IN JUDGEMENT.

Followers: The Who, The What, The When,
The Where, The Why, The Who
The Who, The What, The When,
The Where, The Why, The Who

Jeepers: Attention, please, if you have the time.
I'd like to blow your mind!
Always be good, except when you're bad.
Choose to be happy, except when you're sad.
Don't quote me on this. Don't hold me to that.

Follower: Is there a God?
Jeepers: Don't know for a fact.
Follower: Should we live a good life?
Jeepers: I guess it shall be.
Follower: Are you the Messiah?
Jeepers: Yes, I … No, I … But perhaps — could be!
David: Hey, Jeepers, over here! Check this shit out!

DAVID DOES AN INPIRATIONAL DANCE.
VIDEO GOLF SWING. JEEPERS IS UNINSPIRED.

David: Hey, Man, why can't you commit?
Stop walking the line!
The parents speak of kicking us out.
But you play video golf and get high all the time!
It's okay to get high sometimes.
But all the time, that's not fine!

HE UNPLUGS JEEPERS' VIDEO GAME

Jeepers: Nooooo! I was on the 18th hole!
David: Your people need some leadership
Jeepers: Cut me some slack. I can't make up my mind.
Get off my ass. I heard you all the first time.
I'll get to it eventually. Just leave me be.
I can moan and groan, but I'm still on my throne.
My throne is this stone. Who'll throw the first stone?

CLUNK. A BIG STONE HITS HIS HEAD, AND BOUNCES TO KNOCK OUT A FOLLOWER. EVERY ONE LOOK ACCUSITORILY AT JEANNE, THE THROWER BEING SHUNNED.

Jeanne: I don't know what to think of him.
Who is he? I just got here.
He told me to throw the stone.
Now I'm so alone. I'm going home.

PARENTS AT THE CREEPERS' HOME

Mother: What should we do about our boy Jeepers Creepers?
Father: He's not all that good, and he's not all that bad.
Mother: He won't mow the lawn and he won't get a job.
Father: Where does he get his money from?
It's driving us mad!!

DAVID ENTERS, RECOGNIZING AN OPPORTUNITY

David: Mr. and Mrs. Creepers, for 30 pieces of silver, Jeepers I can deliver. Check this shit out!

JEEPERS WAS AT THE FRIDGE,
DRINKING MILK OUT OF THE CONTAINER THE WHOLE TIME.

Jeepers: Stop dancing!!

DAVID STOPS DANCING. HE SEIZES THE CHANCE TO RUN OFF WITH THE SILVER.

Mother: Shut that refrigerator door!
Father: I'm not paying to cool the out-of-doors!

JEEPERS HAS NO RESPONSE.

Father: Well young man, no choice have I
but to sentence you to leave.

JEEPERS HEARS THIS AND SHRUGS. PUTS BACK THE MILK, AND GOES TO LEAVE.

Jeepers: Forgive them God. Or don't. It's entirely up to you.

FOLLOWERS DANCE AROUND IN WORSHIP, SINGING:

Followers: Jeepers Creepers, slacker guy.
Just walks away without saying 'Goodbye.'
Jeepers Creepers. Not so great.
A guy we'll never really love nor hate.

EPISODE 201 NOW, WHO WANTS ICE CREAM?

written by:	Bob Odenkirk, David Cross
location segment director:	Troy Miller
live show director:	John Moffitt
cast:	David Cross, Bob Odenkirk, John Ennis, Jay Johnston, Tom Kenny, Mary Lynn Rajskub, Jill Talley, Paul F. Tompkins
featuring:	Brian Posehn, Bill Odenkirk, Keith Ballard, Gabi Kozak

Cabin In Woods Cold Open (video)

"Tonight's *Mr. Show* is being broadcast from a cabin in the woods. It's our cabin. It's our property. Leave us alone."

Mr. Show *theme song and logo. Mary Lynn introduces.*

Sovereign Nation Open (live)

Bob and David enter, announce that *Mr. Show* is now a sovereign nation — no longer part of the "de facto corporate prostitute calling itself the United States" — and they are surrounded by FBI. Bob reassures the audience that they've stockpiled food and Bibles. David demonstrates the plaid shirt, hillbilly beard, and beer belly everyone must wear to go outside and talk to the "Jew-run media." Suddenly, a hysterical Jill bursts through the door dragging a wounded Tom. "They shot Tom! Tom was just shooting at them, and then they shot Tom! Why!?" David, enraged, pulls a wig onto his head and heads out to become….

Mountain Dougie Part 1 (video)

Mountain Dougie (David), outside a cabin in the back woods, stomping around, waving a rifle. He kicks over a "TV TAPING IN PROGRESS" sign and yells, "Get off my land!"

Peterson Family News (KPFN) (video/live)

A news report on the stand-off. Harmon Peterson from KPFN (Bob on pre-taped video) reports that nothing new has occurred in the 16-day "Mr. Show-down." Anchorman Brinks (David, live on stage) pesters Harmon for new information, finally asking for a "guesstimate." Harmon cracks — "I DON'T KNOW! MAYBE THIS TREE KNOWS!" Brinks's paranoia takes a personal turn. Harmon tells Brinks not to check back with him anymore, and it devolves into petty bickering. Brinks closes the news program with (video) footage of the miraculous Spitting Madonna statuette in Sao Paulo, Brazil.

Miracles Link (video)

Other miracles from around the world: the Pipe-smoking Apostle in Grover's Corners, Mexico; The Miraculous Money-Eating Madonna in Rome; The Miracle Cloth in Hollywood, CA ("As seen on TV").

Thrilling Miracles (video open/live)

(video) *Thrilling Miracles* infomercial, with hosts Pat Franks (David) and "resident homemaker" Nancy Gumphrey (Jill). They introduce delightful British pitchman Ernie (Bob). Today he's going to demonstrate the "Pantastic new 8-in-1 SUPERPAN." Pat excuses himself (to go take a crap), and Ernie's dark side emerges. He glares at Nancy — "Now it's just you, me, and the pan." Nancy tries to remain cheery, as he goes from charming to scary and back again without warning. Nancy finally drops her fake happy-face when Ernie burns her hand on a super hot Superpan and throws boiling milk on her face ("The Superpan is not magical. It *will* burn you"). Pat re-emerges. "I fell down the stairs," a scared Nancy explains of her injuries. Pat seems to know just what's happened. Pat intimidates and abuses a now-scared Ernie. ("Kiss the pan, kiss the pan" — kiss — "The pan kisses you!" — bonk!) Ernie bolts to the window, and he beckons Nancy to follow, "We've got to get away! Fly!" Ernie jumps out and finds that….

Ernie Flies (video)

He can fly! Ernie (Bob) flaps his arms in a cartoon sky. Nancy jumps out and falls to her death. "Oh, Nancy, only British people can fly!" A couple of cute kids flap into the picture, and they fly and sing with Ernie:

There's a world above, come fly with me!
A magical, fantastical, miractical, spectaticle! World!
If only you were British you could see!
A wonderful-tastic, incredible-astic world inside the clouds!

A gunshot! And Ernie falls from the sky.

Mountain Dougie Part 2 (video)

Mountain Dougie (David) has shot Ernie out of the sky and drags off his kill. Two FBI men (Tom and John) approach, he prepares for a fight, but they surrender to him — the Government is letting him have his own country. Mountain Dougie signs a paper, and, as they leave, he shouts a friendly "get off my land!"

Mountain Dougie tells about his life in his country, "Newfreeland." He makes money out of bark and stones to pay himself for the twigs and berries he collects. As the judge of his own court, he places his dog under house arrest. He hires a "lady form the city" (a flamboyantly gay

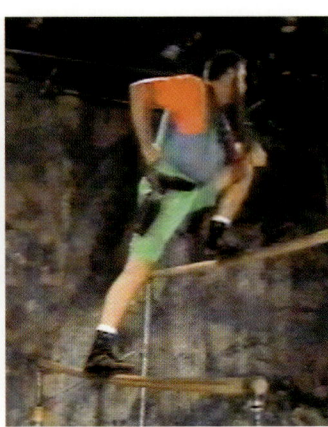

On set for F.F. Woodycooks crime re-dramatization.

Bob) to write a national anthem. It's a disco-beat composition with a fey "Pet Shop Boys" sound:

> GET OFF MY LAAAAND! GET OFF MY LAAAAND!
> We can find love! Love is on our land with a man in our hands!

But Mountain Dougie admits that it's lonely in his own personal country and sets off to visit…America. He's fascinated by its scenery, but mostly by the food available at the stores ("sizzling steaks and creamy cakes!") Mountain Dougie decides to emigrate to the U.S….

Shampoo (video/live)

(video) The U.S. Customs Office. The Official (Bob) behind the counter is confused when Mountain Dougie (David) says he's coming from Newfreeland, a country in Montana. Dougie tries to bribe him with all the tree-bark money he has. The official just plays along and allows him entry.

(live) Next in line at customs is a college student returning from Amsterdam (David). He informs his traveling buddy (John) that he's stashed some hash inside plastic baggies and stuffed them inside shampoo bottles. The Customs Official begins his questioning, being especially curious about his visit to Amsterdam. David tries to downplay it: "Oh! You mean Holland! Yeah, I was in Italy, and I shampooed up to Holland." David gets increasingly nervous, and can't stop himself from saying "shampoo." But the official doesn't seem to give a damn, and when he tells the red-faced, sputtering David he can pass through, all David can say is, "Shampoo!"

John steps up. When asked where in Europe he's been, John cooly replies, "I was in Italy, and I took a balloon up my ass to Spain." The official just waves him through, and a nervous John moves on. He notices his face on a "wanted" poster — HAVE YOU SEEN THIS MAN? — and rips it down as he hurries away, revealing another poster of a bare ass — HAVE YOU SEEN THIS MAN'S ASS?

F.F. Woodycooks (live/video)

The nasal, shlurpy lisp of F.F. Woodycooks (Bob) announces, "Have you seen this man's ass?…It's wanted for smuggling over 20 million pounds of narcotics into America…" Woodycooks, a red-headed, handlebar-mustached oddball, hosts this crimestopping show, *Take Back The Streets*. Tonight, he's going to "shake the Crimestick" (a tree branch with a jingle bell on the end) at "two kookoo-birds who thought they could get past a trained private security agent." He narrarates a "dramatization" of a crime wherein two cliché criminals (Jay and Paul) fight a "street smart" security guard (David). Woodycooks puts a heroic spin on even the lamest actions of the guard. F.F. explains, "By screaming loudly and often, and playing the 'nap' card, the guard had torn their plan into two pieces — bad and worse." He jingles the stick. "You said it, Crimestick, those two were a couple of Ding-a-lings!" He then reveals, "That wily guard and I shared a name…ME! Now, who wants ice cream?" We discover our host serving up at an ice cream parlour.

"F.F. Woodycooks Ice Cream Parlour Precincts are the official ice cream suppliers of the first annual INDEPENDENT NATIONS GAMES"

Independent Nations Games (live)

Two sportscasters (Bob and Tom) and recent emigre, Mountain Dougie (David), comment on Olympic games held by all the "independent nations" in the U.S. A gaggle of bearded, beer-bellied, mountain men engage in competitions like "The Commonlaw Wife Swap," "Threatening," and the "400-meter Food Hoard." The games are in progress: Hank Dobson (Jay), of Hank Dobson's Mini-Mart and Country, does a bad routine on the uneven parallel bars as the credits roll.

Old Man In House Tag (video)

The FBI, armed and ready, are crawling all over a quaint home. "Stand-off, Day 4," with a picture of a sweet, smiling old man. The report informs, "Four days ago, this man entered his home and has yet to come out." On the playback of a recorded telephone conversation, the FBI asks the old man what is going on in the house. "Yes, I'm watching TV." The FBI requests he cooperates so that "the whole ordeal can end peacefully and everyone can just go home." "I am home…Hey, I'm on television. Goodbye."

On set for F.F. Woodycooks crime re-dramatization.

Notes About Episode 201

Bob: *"This is definitely one of the best shows we ever wrote. It's silly, relevant, irrelevant and silly, all at the same time. God bless us for doing it."*

David: *"The first show in every season, always in retrospect feels like the first show. It feels like the place we left off from last season, as far as ideas and how it's evolving."*

David: *"Bob as the gay, flamboyant musical guy in the Mountain Dougie sketch, the 'lady from the city,' who helped him write a song. That's one of those pieces — there's a handful of them — that I wish at some point we could put out a video of the entirety of those shoots, because Bob doing that song, in full length is really funny, and it never stops being funny. And it gets funnier and funnier. It makes me wish we didn't have to edit it down for pacing's sake."*

Bob: *"Shampoo is a scene David and I wrote for the live stage shows which helped us to get the TV show. It's a great scene, with a solid punch line, John's "Balloon up my ass." It reminds me of Monty Python sketches, like Marriage License. It has a classic feel to it, but, of course, it's about drugs, so that makes it practically futuristic on American TV."*

David: *"The Shampoo sketch was inspired by something that I thought was actually happening when I was in a half-dream state. I had been in Amsterdam, and I had gotten very, very fucked up, and I had to leave very early to get back to New York. I was actually sitting in my hotel room, I just had to sit there, and kill time for 45 minutes. And I have my peacoat on, and my suitcase and backpack are packed, and the next thing I know, I open my eyes and it's like an hour later. The water's running in the faucet. And I just fell asleep sitting up, I wasn't even lying down. And I looked at the clock — 'Oh, fuck!' And I did the panicky, 'I'm never gonna make it! I gotta try! No, fuck it.' All fucked up. And, basically, got to the airport and had to scam my way onto other airlines because I didn't have any money either. So I ended up flying to Manchester, and then to Boston to New York. By the time I landed in Boston, I'd been up for close to two days. Hadn't had any sleep. I put this hash I bought in my shampoo bottle. And on the plane, I was so overtired, that I shut my eyes, and I would instantly start dreaming. Very vividly. These guys with drug-sniffing dogs - squirted the shampoo bottle, out comes my hash. And then that became a funny sketch — really fun, classic sketch comedy. Bob and I had a blast writing that one."*

Jay: *"The scene we worked on that day [when Paul and Jay came in for their first meeting with Bob and David, which actually turned into their first day of work] was what ended up being the F.F. Woodycooks crime scene. It was something I did at the Annoyance Theater in The Bean Can Tour. It came from this idea of trying to overpower a security guard. The whole scene that played out in the reenactment was the scene, and then Bob came up with the context — F.F. Woodycooks."*

Paul: *"I was fascinated with this guy J.J. Bittenbinder, who was an ex-cop from Chicago who gave lectures on how people could defend themselves. He had a TV show called Tough Target. Everyone else had seen him, too, and we all agreed that he was insane. We laughed extremely hard writing this sketch — we all loved doing the Woodycooks voice and thinking up his ridiculous catchphrases. On location, when Jay and I played the two crooks who assault David, Jay and I thought it would be funny if, when we're arrested and put in the squad car, we did that thing that bad extras do where they have a pretend conversation, but both of them are 'talking' at the same time. Well, we did it, and the joke's on us 'cause you can't see us at all."*

Bob: *"The part in Woodycooks where the guard gets hit over and over was something we wanted, but almost didn't get on tape because to actually shoot it felt incredibly boring and stupid. I had to insist that they just hold the camera steady and repeatedly punch David in the face. Even then I wish it went on longer."*

Bob: *"Using my grandfather's photograph for the old man at the end was a terrible mistake. We were pressed for time, and I didn't think anyone in my family would ever see it. Anyway, the FBI are the buffoons of the piece. But it actually upset people a lot. Of course, I never asked my grandfather if I could use his picture, he'd recently passed away. But he was a sweet, generous, lovely person, and what I did was wrong. And if you ever see his ghost, don't for a second think that he was ever in a house that was surrounded by jumpy FBI agents. It never happened."*

EPISODE 202 — A TALKING JUNKIE?

written by:	Bob Odenkirk, David Cross
location segment director:	Troy Miller
live show director:	John Moffitt
cast:	David Cross, Bob Odenkirk, John Ennis, Jay Johnston, Tom Kenny, Mary Lynn Rajskub, Jill Talley, Paul F. Tompkins
featuring:	Bill Odenkirk, Johari Johnson

Mr. Show theme song and logo. Mary Lynn introduces.

David Acts English, Rap Open (live)

David comes out wearing a bowler hat and monocle, speaking in an English accent and using nonsense phrases like, "Indeed! Let's get this wallypopper abrighting!" Bob and the rest of the cast (Tom, Jill, John) confront him about his outlandish put-on persona. David feigns innocence, then admits it might be left over from his visit to England "a few whiffens past." That's it, the cast can't take anymore. David drops the charade, saying he just felt excluded, since everyone else has a special affectation: Jill has a parrot, Tom has lice, John gets high all the time, and Bob raps. ("Well, that's me, man. I'm from the street.") Having gotten no sympathy, David brings up the one friend he has left. Jill snaps, "How many times have I told you there's no such thing as a talking junkie!" Bob scoffs and heads off to do a concert "here on planet earth." He puts on his "street" clothes and gold tooth, gets behind a pair of turntables, and begins "fuckin' shit up old school."

> Snappin' back wit' y'all's punk-ass bitch!
> Ain't no party like a Mr. Show Party, 'cause a Mr. Show Party don't stop!
> HEY! HO! HEY! HO!

David mopes off stage and into….

Talking Junkie (b&w video)

An alley, where a Junkie (Bob) is half-passed out. David whines to his buddy, the Junkie, that all he wanted was personality and, surprise, the Junkie talks! (An effect like any talking animal in an old TV show, he looks like he's chewing peanut butter and his voice is dubbed.) The Talking Junkie suggests that David try heroin — "Worked for me!" David is unsure, but after a time passage cut we see them both nodding in the alley and hear David's dubbed voice — "This was a bad idea." It wraps up with a laugh track, sitcom titles, and a theme song: "Everyone knows a junkie squawks, and everyone knows a junkie walks. But have you seen a junkie talk? The amazing Mr. Junkie." This show is being watched….

New Son (live)

Ty McGinty (David), sitting in a living room, flipping channels and drinking beer, while a young couple, Dad (Bob) and Mom (Jill), sit nearby cooing and videotaping him. Their friends Todd (Tom) and Sarah (Mary Lynn) arrive to see the new baby. Mom and Dad point to Ty, "Isn't he precious?" Todd points out that Ty is their age. Mom gets defensive and emotionally explains she told the foster home that she had no preferences, just "someone that wanted to be loved." Ty is clearly taking full advantage of the situation. The visiting couple try to play along, but Ty responds with crude college reminisces and then lasciviously comes on to Todd's wife ("Why don't I clear off a little space for you to sit down," indicating his mouth). The friends are repulsed and leave. Dad tries to reach out, but Ty is only insulting. Dad confides to Mom that "this guy's a real asshole," and he wants to send him back. Ty suddenly acts hurt, reeling off rote hurt-kid phrases, "I didn't ask to be born." On his way out the door, Ty gets defensive: "I've been adopted 43 times. And 42 times, okay, that was my bad. But not this time. You fucked this one up. I tried, you didn't." He grabs a beer and leaves forever.

Red Balloon (video)

Outside, Ty (David) mopes with his beer as a jaunty tune begins:

> When you're feelin' low and things have gone astray,
> Remember, my friend, that help is on the way!

A magical, floating Red Balloon bumps into Ty and cheers him up. He follows it on an adventure around the city, chattering to it while the song continues:

> Red Balloon is here, to take your hand and steer.
> Red Balloon will help you fly away!
> Red Balloon has a tale to tell, of candy, fun, and golden bells.
> Red Balloon will push you down a well.
> Red Balloon will send you straight to hell!
> You've got to follow your Balloon! You've got to follow your Balloon!
> Red Balloon will lead you on, Red Balloon will make you strong.
> You've got to follow your Balloon! You've got to follow your Balloon!

The happily bouncing Red Balloon leads Ty into a liquor store where he comes out with a brown bag of booze, hooks him up with a street craps game, takes him to a skanky strip club, and finally leads him into a neighborhood porn shop.

Damn. TTOMO's video "Ewww, Girl, Eww."

Mom & Pop Porn Shop (live)

Proprietors, Mom and Pop Applesway (Jill and Bob) welcome Ty and his balloon. Pop yells at his son Jimmy (David) for not restocking the giant black dildos. Jimmy acts put-upon, and Pop gives him a bonk on the head with the faux-cock. ("Stupid Dildos," Jimmy complains. "Don't blame the dildos," says Pop.) A Mr. Tink (Tom) enters — he's after them to sell their shop for re-zoning; they refuse. Mother is appalled when she discovers an X-rated CD-ROM in Jimmy's backpack. She believes the old-fashioned way —magazines — are better. Jimmy rejects all old-style porn. Pop can't stand this impudence, "That 'stupid' *All-Anal Action* paid for that new mountain bike of yours!" This tragic family spat culminates with the appearance of the Ghost of Pop's Great-, Great-, Great-grandfather (Paul on Jay's shoulders), who thunders, "Who speaks ill of pornography!?" The Ghost reminds Pop of the scorn he faced when he first introduced dirty videotapes — and "now look, an entire wall of hard-core gay anal sex." The family has renewed faith in porno. After a moment, the Ghost asks for quarters for the booth. Mr. Tink emerges from a booth and says the Ghost's sermon moved him to help them keep their shop. They thank him profusely and bid him goodbye. He hesitates, then asks for more quarters. With life back to normal, Pop is annoyed by the loud racket from the neighbors upstairs. He bangs on the ceiling — "There are people trying to masturbate down here!"

Ewww Girl Video (film)

The camera pans up from Pop's broom, into the neighbor's shitty apartment, ending on a distraught, pretty, young black girl. She is crying and hammering a noose into the ceiling — "I got no reason to live." A magical "whoosh!" and flash of light, and Three Times One Minus One, a two-man R&B/soul group, appears! Pooty T. (David) waves his flashy cane and the world becomes alive with color, the apartment is beautiful, and our girl is in flimsy peach lingerie. (The noose remains). Pooty T. sings their new soul hit "Ewww, Girl, Eww." Wolfgang (Bob) chimes in with the occasional "Damn."

Video Soul (live/film)

(live) Host Brent B. (John) in his best white-boy gangsta-speak welcomes us to WPCBCN (Logo: White People Co-opting the Black Culture Network). His guests in the studio are Three Times One Minus One. ("TTOMO") — Pooty T. (David) is busy sucking on a candy cane, so his partner (Bob) does the talking — his name is Wolfgang Amadeus Thelonius Von Funkenmeister the XIX 3/4. They explain that their influences are "all kinds of white performers who have been influenced by black entertainers." They bitch about Pooty T.'s bogus jaywalking arrests. Wolfgang remarks, "My man, Pooty T., is from the street. He has to be able to cross the street." Pooty adds righteously, "I ain't got no flying shoes." Before the show ends, Wolfgang wants to say one more thing. He looks directly into the camera — "It's like...I'm sayin'...y'know?"

(film) One more clip of video — which ends with a landlord (Tom) showing the suicide girl's apartment to TTOMO, re-hanging noose — "hope that doesn't bother you." All Wolfgang can say is, "Damn."

Rap! The Musical (video)

Commercial for Sir Lloyd Wilson Webber's *Rap! The Musical*, a musical about rap music that "contains no rap." Excerpts are shown: "(Just) Give Me a Big Booming Bass!" sung by a straw-hatted, seersuckered David. "I'm Going on a Driveby," by Cockney chimney sweeper Tom. Alone in a wheelchair, Mary Lynn sings the melancholy tune, "I'm In a Gang of One." Bob does a number in a giant gold tooth costume, *"I'm an old gold tooth and I'll tell ya the truth, I live in the mouth of my Homey!"*

"...And now, we return to the third annual Homage Awards. Honoring excellence in the field of borrowing black culture!"

Homage Awards (live)

'Nilla Ice (Jay) announces the award for the Most Soulful Single Performed by a White Duo. The winner is TTOMO for "Ewww, Girl, Ewww." Wolfgang gives a shout out to his black brothers: "Keep pumping out the rhymes, so we can keep re-pumping them." TTOMO takes us out with their award-winning hit as credits roll.

Creepy Peeping Videos Tag (video)

After the HBO logo — a promo for HBO's *Creepy Peeping Videos 4*. A "reality" home-video show which showcases unsuspecting people in private moments. They captured an abusive nanny "Auntie Helen" (John in a babushka) and her charge, Ty (David). She gives him good smackings for offenses like taking a french fry off her plate: "Those are my fries! Now you don't get anything!" Later, with her cigarette, she pops Ty's special Red Balloon, and when he cries, she knocks him down. "HBO. We're naughty," teases the voiceover.

Notes About Episode 202

David: "Bob sings the Red Balloon song — when Bob gets to singin' and puts his mind to it, don't get in his way. He'll fuckin' steam roll ya. You gotta let the man sing."

Bob: "People seemed to love Red Balloon. We heard Pearl Jam was even singing it around their rehearsals."

David: "The funniest take in maybe four years of Mr. Show is Jay turning to the balloon, when they're playing craps, in that dumb-ass 70's 'fro wig. That's one of those perfect little moments that kill me."

David: "An idea that [comedian and friend] David Earl Waterman had come up with, this all-American family runs this porn shop. I called him to ask if we could use it because it would work perfect for this thing, and he was very cool about it. He had written this rough version that we had done a couple of times [in Cross Comedy]. The whole thing was completely re-written. It was always such a great idea. Seemingly, the thing lacking was a ghost."

Bob: "Mom and Pop Porn Shop was really fun to do. Acting all quaint and homey about those porn items is a riot. Jill and I had to improvise while David was offstage changing from Ty to the kid, Jimmy. We knew it would be cut out, so we got real crude. She picked up a latex vagina with gross fake hair on it, squeezed it like air was coming out of it, and said, 'Look, Father, a pussy fart.' I tried not to laugh but failed, and added, 'That's called a "queef," Mother.' The Maker himself surely cracked a smile."

Paul: "To play the porno shop ghost, I had to get on Jay's shoulders. This came out of a discussion as to who should play the ghost. Someone said Paul, someone else said Jay, and then I think it was me who said, "How about me on Jay's shoulders?" Ha ha ha ha. This arrangement made both Jay and I a little irritable at times, but it was worth it. Poor Jay. I remember when we were taping the second show that night, right before I was about to get on Jay's shoulders, I said to him, "Once this sketch is over, we'll never have to do this again." He smiled like I told him the braces were coming off his legs tomorrow."

Bob: "I don't think the Talking Junkie looks right because I used big false teeth for it. That sketch came out of a meeting with an executive who told me how much he liked my work, and he wanted me to write a movie for Frances The Talking Mule — which is weird, because if you like my work, why would you want me to write that? That's not remotely what I do. And the Talking Junkie came from talking about The Talking Mule and how stupid it was."

Paul: "I loved playing the drunk who sees the Talking Junkie — that character was always one of my favorite comedy references, the barfly who sees something crazy and then throws his bottle of booze away."

Bob: "Three Times One Minus One was a big hit. Especially among rappers. We heard that Dr. Dre saw it and played the tape for all of his friends. That's fucked up, huh?"

Ghost opens minds and borrows quarters at "Mom and Pop Porn Shop."

David: "Eeew Girl Video. Great idea. Thank you very much, I take credit for it. Great excuse to do that kind of bullshit — we'd riff around that dumb ass stuff. Bob came up with the name for that, Three Times One Minus One. 'I ain't got no flying shoes' was something I riffed in rehearsal. Initially, I wasn't going to say anything. The joke was I do all the singing in the videos, all Bob says is 'Damn,' but when we're interviewed, he's the one who does all the talking and I don't say anything."

Brian: "To my detriment, I do get really married to certain things because I know that world so much. Bill and I got into a big fight over Three Times One Minus One, which wasn't even our scene. They were doing the song, and the idea was just one of the characters sang and the other one doesn't say anything. And Bill fought me really hard saying, 'No, the pure joke is that David just sings, and the other says nothing.' And I thought the pure joke was that's all that guy does. And there are guys like that where their only job is to say 'bitch' in the middle of the song, or the fifth rapper in a rap group that just says 'come on, party people,' and that's his job, and he's done. I took offense that Bill was fighting me so hard, because I know the music. My knowledge eventually was worth something. Things would get heated occasionally, but we would never stay mad at each other, at least it didn't feel like it. 'Dude you don't know this fuckin' music, so just take my word for it.'"

Bob: "Creepy Peeping Videos was our critique of HBO's late night programming which, at the time, had a cheap salacious voyeuristic strain running through it."

Paula Elins (Costume Designer): "The gold tooth costume (Rap! The Musical) we rented from a woman who makes costumes out of her house. It was actually sitting out in her front yard. The day we went to shoot it, Bob went to put it on, and I hadn't cleaned out the inside. I painted the whole thing gold, and I think I stuck a broom up there. But he gets in there, and it's already a horrible, uncomfortable thing, and there were spiders in there. And he freaked out. He was so mad at me."

episode 203: THE BIGGEST FAILURE IN BROADWAY HISTORY

written by:	Bob Odenkirk, David Cross, Jay Johnston, Bill Odenkirk, Dino Stamatopoulos, Paul F. Tompkins
location segment director:	Troy Miller
live show director:	John Moffitt
cast:	David Cross, Bob Odenkirk, John Ennis, Jay Johnston, Tom Kenny, Brian Posehn, Mary Lynn Rajskub, Jill Talley, Paul F. Tompkins
featuring:	Dave "Gruber" Allen, Danny Cebalos, Warren Hutcherson, Laura Milligan, Ali MacLean, Suli McCullough, Bill Odenkirk, Brett Paesel
special appearances by:	Jack Black, Jeanne Tripplehorn

Mr. Show song and logo. Mary Lynn introduces.

Beating Hippie Open (live)

Bob sits alone onstage waiting, alternately annoyed and worried, for David, who traipses in "late," brushing snow off his coat. Bob blames David's lack of respect on being from a different generation — Bob came of age in the *mid*-70's, while David was shaped by the *late*-70's. David argues that Bob's generation ruined everything for his generation — "We're still cleaning up *your* mess!" A hippie cameraman (Gruber) tries to get them to "chill," and they discover they have something in common, a mutual hatred of hippies. They beat him up and are a rejuvenated duo — "I think we have a show to get to!" They run Batman-style. As the image of the ailing hippie spins behind them, we find ourselves watching....

No Adults Allowed (live/video)

(live) Bald, bearded Dr. Ken Thurmond (Bob) with "old fogey" friends, Katherine and Lionel Winslow (Brett, John) speak about how, as parents, it's difficult to talk to teens, since teens only listen to other teens. They introduce a show where, they claim, "terrific teens get to talk to you young people out there…So say goodbye to us, because for the next half of an hour, it's 'No Adults Allowed.'"

(video) A "wacky" show open features the same three adults dressed up like teens, doing "teen things" — "I'm Kenny, and I'm 14. I like to play those damn video games!"

(live) In the show itself, the three imposter teens hang out and chat about things that are "cool," but they can't help sounding like pissed-off adults. When they introduce the "Learnabout" segment, the real teen who is supposed to appear misses his cue. "Kenny" breaks his teen charade and explodes, "CRAIG, GODDAMMIT! GET IN HERE!!" The adults storm over to the green room, Ken muttering all the way.

No Slackers (live/video)

(live) The three adults (Bob, Brett, John) march into a rec room and find Craig and his friends lollygagging about. This is all seen by the parents in "TV-druggy-vision," all wavey and shit. Ken sees Craig (David) playing video golf and pulls the plug ("Awww, I was on the 18th hole!"), ranting about how they're all slackers. Craig blames just this kind of prejudice for keeping today's teens from becoming productive members of society. He takes the adults on a first-hand tour of discrimination against so-called slackers.

(video) They are shown a sign in a window — "HELP WANTED. SLACKERS NEED NOT APPLY." There are separate public drinking fountains for slackers. Two slackers (Brian, Mary Lynn) at a coffee house are hosed down by police.

New KKK (video)

Marjoe Crawley (Warren), a black man and Grand Wizard of the KKK, is interviewed about his views on slackers. "Don't dislike 'em. Just don't want 'em," he says with a smile, proposing they all be confined to Seattle. When asked about how a black man could be involved with the KKK, he answers, "This is the new KKK." He shows a promotional video with white and black KKK members in robes, frolicking about to a catchy campaign song:

Hey check us out! Have you seen us lately? We're the New Ku Klux Klan! And we're 100% hate-free! We're back to stay and we're here to play! Fishing! Cookin'! Badminton! Stamps! The New KKK, we're gonna have a fazooool!

This commercial is being shown at....

Ad Awards (live/video)

(live) "The New KKK" campaign is a nominee for "Most Improved Image" at the Awards for Advertising American Ads (AAAA). The next nominee is a campaign for the North American Man-Boy Love Association, titled, "NAMBLA: We're Not Killers." It gets no applause. In the ad (video), we see a creepy guy (Brian) driving slowly in a van, cut to photo of Jeffrey Dahmer who NAMBLA proudly declares was "never a member." A group of men cavort at a picnic, all with black bars covering their eyes as they laugh and shout, "NAMBLA! We're not killers! Hooray!"

(live) Awards Host (Paul) is disgusted by the whole thing. "The Awardy" goes to the team behind the NAMBLA campaign! Kermit (Bob) and Steve (David) each run to the podium, amidst boos and hisses, and hastily renounce their participation in the project. However, Trevor (John) excitedly takes the podium: "Whoo! We did it! Oh, man, this has been a labor of love." The audience becomes violent and starts throwing things at Trevor, who runs for his life.

Mob Chase Link (video)

With his Awardy clutched tightly, Trevor (John) runs out of the auditorium, trying to escape the angry, torch-brandishing mob. ("Monster! Monster!" cries a torch bearing man [Jay]). Trevor runs into the darkened street and tries to flag down an oncoming police car.

Drunk Cops (video)

Two intoxicated police officers (David and Bob) comment in slur to the cameraman in their back seat that this is a typical quiet night, as they obliviously run over a frantic Trevor (John). "I hit a bump." It's a reality TV show: *Drunk Cops: Hammered in Detroit*. On the front lawn of a drunken white trash couple (Jill and Jay), the drunk cops try to settle the domestic dispute, but a tussle almost breaks out — between the policemen — until one cop sobs to the other, "Think for two seconds and wonder why you want to fight!" As they weep and hug, the drunk perp (Jay) tiptoes to the police car and drives it away. Barely. This whole show is being watched….

Iguana (live)

By Nathan (David), in his bachelor apartment. He hurls a beer can at his pet iguana (Bob in green unitard) for blocking the TV ("Stupid iguana"). Two friends (Mary Lynn and John) stop by. Nathan shows off his pet iguana, Sulu, bragging about the lizard. ("See how smart he is? I've only had him a couple of days, but I know he already loves me.") The iguana is simply terrified and darts off. Nathan tries to control the mad iguana, finally resorting to the "Bad Sulu" paddle. Nathan boasts about his soon-to-be new exotic pet, an albino boy. When Sulu knocks over the bong water, Nathan loses it. He grabs a nearby book and beats Sulu to death. He instantly feels sorry for himself — "Oh, God…Who am I without a lizard?" Just then his albino boy (Bill) arrives to remedy his dearth of personality. We see the funeral for the iguana.

Pet Funeral Link (video)

"RIP SULU 1996-1996" is on the tiny headstone. A preacher (Tom) sermonizes in length about all of Nathan's beloved exotic pets. A mourner (Brian) whispers to his friend "Jeepers Creepers, get to the point!" The priest sharply tells him never to use the Lord's name in vain. He holds up his Bible, *The Book Of Jeepers Creepers*, and tells us all the tale of…

Jeepers Creepers (film)

A school bus screeches to a halt in the desert, and a bunch of actor/hippies rush out and party to rock'n'roll "Broadway" style. They are setting up to perform the story of *Jeepers Creepers Semi-Star*. David sits alone atop a mountain watching the group. A very indecisive Messiah, Jeepers Creepers (Jack), sings that he can't commit to anything. "Are you the Messiah?" "Yes, I …No, I …But, perhaps. Could beeeeee." David tries to inspire him. Jeepers ignores him and plays video golf. David unplugs his video game. Jeepers cries out in anguish, "Nooooooo! I was on the 18th hole!" David scolds Jeepers for getting high all the time. Jeepers tells him and all of his followers to get off his back and stop judging him. "Who'll throw the first stone?" he wails. A rock knocks him in the head. The shocked followers turn to see that it was a woman (Jeanne). She sings her explanation: she just got there, heard someone tell her to throw a stone, and did it. Shunned, she leaves.

Mr. and Mrs. Creepers (Bob and Jill) discuss what to do about their lazy, indecisive son. For 30 pieces of silver, David offers to deliver Jeepers to them. It turns out Jeepers was at the fridge drinking milk from the container the whole time. His parents have had enough of his lazy, irresponsible ways and kick him out. He shrugs. "Forgive them God, or don't. It's entirely up to you." The Followers join in on a big dance finale.

Jeepers Creepers, slacker guy. Just walks away without saying goodbye.
Jeepers Creepers. Not so great. A guy you'll never really love nor hate.

Hippie Pie Close (live)

Bob and David are onstage reading from *The Big Book Of Broadway Failures* to the cast, assembled at their feet. *Jeepers Creepers Semi-Star* was the biggest failure in Broadway history. Brett brings out a giant "hippie pie" for the cast. "I got the braid!" John yells with excitement. Credits roll over everyone digging in.

Hippie Pie Tag (video)

An overstuffed Bob and David are alone onstage feeling nauseous. They did a bad thing, Bob moans; "Tonight's show offended every racist, Christian, exotic pet-loving, NAMBLA card-carrying, alcoholic cop in America." David groans, "I ated too much pie." The film goes to black and white, *Little Rascals*-type music plays, and a black border closes in on their cute li'l heads.

Notes About Episode 203

Bob: "Although I love almost every idea in this show, it's one of my least favorite shows. I feel like everything could have been done better. No Adults Allowed would be much better with actual old actors trying to portray teenagers, and Iguana shouldn't be on TV at all, only live on stage. And who likes to see me in a leotard? Not me, I can assure you."

David: "One of my least favorite shows. It's got funny ideas, but the stuff that kills it, really kills it."

David: "No Adults Allowed — it took forever to write, and it was really tough. It was one of the pieces that went through several different revisions and formats. It was perhaps less about the logic of it than crossing the line of what is our reality, and what is the reality of the sketch. Do we not play teenagers? Do we just get real teens to do this? We're in our 30's. And there's only so much you're going to get out of me wearing a wig. It was really difficult."

Bob: "The bald caps are always bad, but the worst day of all, was the full day in a full bald cap for No Adults Allowed, on the hottest day. Holes would pop in the plastic. And if you pressed on it, you felt the water moving around."

David: "Some of my favorite little things about the episode — in the beginning of the show, I come in and there's fake snow on my jacket. It's just those little things that make Mr. Show Mr. Show. It's just one of those little things I loved in it. Drunk Cops has some of my favorite bad acting in it. Watching those guys overact as drunks is really funny to me. I don't mean to be insulting, but Bob and Jay and Jill all doing the classic Red Skelton, slurring, Box Car Willie-type of drunk makes me laugh."

Tom Sherren (producer): "In Drunk Cops, when they needed somebody to be hit by the police car, they couldn't afford a stuntman, so Troy did it himself. He's the guy who bounces off the window on the police car."

Dino: "The initial idea for Jeepers Creepers I wrote for Stiller about a Messiah who didn't have a point of view. But Bob, David, and Eban just took it and wrote it. I feel adding the slacker angle took away from him simply being a bad Messiah."

Bob: "No doubt about it, Jeepers Creepers was one of the most massive undertakings we ever took under. The production elements were overwhelming for a small, cheap show. The pre-recorded music, the number of actors, and the whole thing had to be shot in one day far out in the desert. It's a tribute to the resourcefulness, speed, and talent of Troy Miller, our director and producer, that we were able to do it so well. It was maybe the most talked-about piece of that season. People loved it. However, I agree with Dino that we mucked it up by injecting the 'slacker' dimension in it. Sorry."

Paul: "Jeepers Creepers we shot on location at Vasquez Rocks, out in the desert. That is where Captain Kirk battled the Gorn in the original Star Trek. History. We all got there at 6:30 A.M., and were given a little talk about the location, which included a warning about snakes. 'Snakes' was the only word that ran through my head all day."

David: "Jeepers — that was a 16-hour day in the desert. That was tough. That was starting to head out at 4 A.M. so we could have as much light as possible. You can see at the end of the piece that the sun was going down. When we filmed that, I was in really good shape. I'm not anymore. I went running to the top of that rock — I got about a third of the way and had to stop, because it was crazy steep — and got up there. And as I started running down, I almost slipped. Had I slipped, that would've been it. I would've tumbled, I wouldn't have been able to stop myself."

Jack: "I remember I was jealous of David's role. He got to do that crazy devil dance. Hilarious."

David: "The Jeepers '18th hole' callback from No Adults Allowed — that's something we put in later, as we had the show. He had to be doing something in the rec room when the adults come in. Let's have him playing video golf. To me that's a sprinkle of a theme; that's not a heavy theme. The two pieces were totally separate, they were written in different years, there was a lot of separation between the two of them, and then you put them in the same show, and it feels like that there's this theme. But I never got the sense it was too heavy."

(top left) Paul F. Tompkins, Tracy Katsky, Mary Lynn Rajskub and Jeanne Tripplehorn working on the "choreography" for Jeepers Creepers' followers. (top right) John and David hopping off the musical tour bus (bottom) Paul F. Tompkins, Jack Black and Jeanne Tripplehorn at "Jeepers" shoot in the desert.

Eban Schletter (Music Director): "I was sick, and I had a very short period of time to do (the music for the film) Jeepers Creepers, four days researching it. Which is a luxury when you look at the rest of the stuff. I listened to Jesus Christ Super Star, the cast album about fifteen times. I'm not a big fan of Andrew Lloyd Webber stuff; I figured this would be a great opportunity to skewer him — 'Fuck that guy. This shit, who cares.' But when I listened to that over and over — the cast album, the one with the brown cover, not from the film — I was like, 'Man, this is great! This is why this guy's famous.' So I started from a point of actually loving that musical. I walked around and let it sink in, and, man, the people are singing their asses off. Yeah, it's dated, but it's really amazing. For Jeepers, they based their lyrics on the actual songs, but they knew it couldn't be the same, and judging by what it's about, I figured it's gotta have the grunge thing. In the meantime, I was getting really sick with a throat infection. It got to the point where I'm drumming in my little shack of a studio. It's boiling in there, it's a sweatbox. Bob and David came in there: 'How the hell are you working like this?' I kept thinking I was Alec Guiness in Bridge Over the River Kwai, I'd walk out covered with sweat."

Sarah: "Jeepers Creepers. I remember Tracy Katsky [roommate] and I wanted to get out of it real bad — 'Oh God. The whole day in the desert.' We were thinking what excuse could we give. And we even tried, and they were like, 'You guys! Come on!' And it was one of the most fun days ever of my life. Everyone was wearing SPF45 sunscreen, and everyone was having so much fun. It was like 30 friends. And the thing about Mr. Show — you never get bored, you never sit around. It was just bam-bam-bam. And it was so much fun."

Jack: "We were out in the desert and it went like lightning. David, at the end, gave me a strange note. He said at the end I should just look into the camera, wait a beat — just be myself and then walk off. Be myself?! I didn't know what to do. I just sort of looked into the camera and did something with my upper lip. And the next day I thought of much better things I could've done there. So I am waiting for the remake of Jeepers Creepers. Just to put that ending in."

EPISODE 204

IF YOU'RE GOING TO WRITE A COMEDY SCENE, YOU'RE GOING TO HAVE SOME RAT FECES IN THERE

written by: Bob Odenkirk, David Cross, Jay Johnston, Bill Odenkirk, Brian Posehn, Paul F. Tompkins

location segment director: Troy Miller

live show director: John Moffitt

cast: David Cross, Bob Odenkirk, John Ennis, Jay Johnston, Tom Kenny, Brian Posehn, Mary Lynn Rajskub, Jill Talley, Paul F. Tompkins

featuring: Laura Milligan, Theresa Mulligan, Bill Odenkirk, Ryan Cusino, Dusty Neilson

special appearances by: Ben Stiller

Cold Open: "Tonight's show is brought to you by the GV Corporation." Grass Valley Greg (David) pops through the GV logo. "Where ideas can hang out…and do whatever!"

Mr. Show *song and logo. Mary Lynn introduces.*

Mr. Show Corporation Open (live)
Mr. Show is now a publicly owned company, and David and Bob take questions from stockholders. Various business types ask about downsizing and exceeding the FDA allowance of human hair and insect parts in the jokes. "We can't be 100%," David coolly replies. "If you're going to write a comedy scene, you're going to have some rat feces in there." A guerilla TV news reporter (John) wants to know who writes the show, insinuating "illegal hiring practices." Bob and David are evasive, and he makes a break for the backstage door marked "NO ADMITTANCE". His shoulder-bag cam captures the action.

Child Labor Writers' Room (video/live)
(video) The Reporter (John) and his camera storm the hall backstage, checking every room, until he finds, "hidden from view, in this dank, squalid back room…an army of children sitting in their own filth, writing comedy." A Middle Eastern Man (Paul) rants in "Arabic" and whips the bedraggled children. One hungry-eyed child looks up — this is Bhopal (David). Bob runs in and wrestles the Reporter out of there.

(live) The Reporter shows his video report at the *Hard Scoop* desk. The anchor (Tom) thanks him for the story, then adds, "Better luck next time." Off the Reporter's confused reaction we cut to a commercial for….

Van Hammersly (video)
"Worldwide Billiards Champion" Van Hammersly is hawking videotapes that teach and entertain through billiards. In his first tape, *I Ought To Be In Pictures*, he recounts the Golden Age of Hollywood ("Just pick out a few balls and say hello to the stars!"). He names the balls after movie stars, then tells a "story" while shooting them around the table wildly. In other videos, he choreographs the 1974 Kentucky Derby and The Great Bus Disaster of 1939. Another Hammersly tape qualifies the viewer for a GED, with subjects such as Math, Science, and American History ("And that's when Lincoln said…[he corner-pockets one] don't dis my homies!" Clap, snap, voila).

Gay Son (live)
Conservative parents (John and Jill) are watching the billiards ad on TV. Their teenage son, Tommy (Bob), runs in upset, carrying a poster with his face and the words, "WE LOVE OUR GAY SON" on it. His parents admit they put the posters up all over town. "You're gay, son," announces Father. "I feel like a great weight has been lifted." When Tommy shouts that not only is he not gay, but they've ruined his life, his father threatens him: "NO GAY SON OF MINE IS NOT GAY! YOU BETTER GET GAY, OR I'LL MAKE YOU GAY!" He calls in "one of the best," the hot-panted, scabby-kneed Rodrigo (Brian). "Gay him up!" Mother commands. As Rodrigo sashays toward a horrified Tommy….

Major Stockholder Interrupts Link (live)
Ponytailed Grass Valley Greg (David) rides onstage on a recumbent bicycle with an overly chipper attitude, he congratulates everyone on a great scene about a gay coming out. Bob (now out of character) growls that he's missed the point, plus the scene isn't over. Greg begs to differ, "Everything is possible if you imagineer it!" he chirps. Bob apologetically explains to the audience that GVG is the principle stockholder *of Mr. Show*. GVG pulls rank and calls for a Tofutti break. "I'm the boss, Robert, and the boss says work is play! Tofutti break today!" he annoyingly sing-songs, and begins spooning out Tofutti to annoyed cast members.

Grass Valley Greg (video)
A documentary on Greg Sniper, or Grass Valley Greg (David), the multi-billion dollar genius/New Age nerd who invented the "delete" button. We learn about his passions for health food and goats. At his corporate headquarters, he has a large staff who develop new mistakes ("Or, as I like to call 'em, 'opportunity-stakes'!"). Greg is constantly breaking up their work day with dumb events like "Tofutti breaks" and puppet shows. One employee (Brian) gets on Greg's bad side when he ditches his cup of Tofutti, and he is sent to work at Nanadu, Greg's "special"

goat farm. Inside his mansion, Greg lets the goats run rampant. "All these goats are retarded." His accountant (Bob) comes in bearing bad financial news, but Greg won't hear it — "I'm not talking clouds on a sunny day!" — and he runs off to play. To camera, the accountant frustratingly recounts GVG's catastrophic investments which have rendered him broke. (Invested in a tofu falafel-substitute; hired Canada to sing *Happy Birthday*; spent millions on a campaign to legalize the tomato.) The accountant rants that GVG treats his goats like royalty: "Goats are stupid, mean, and hard-headed animals…that's why they're called nature's president."

Downsizing (live)

Businessman Mr. Twilt (Bob) consults a portrait of the goat, "What should I do, Mr. President?… Yes, thank you!" Mr. Twilt then carries on the following one-sided meeting with Mr. Flain (David) — see if you can follow this: he gives Flain a $20,000/year raise and a company car, then informs him the company is downsizing and can't afford him anymore. He hands Flain a written recommendation to find new employment. After some blithering small talk, Twilt says he heard Flain was available, and he can get him $12,000/year. He takes the recommendation he just gave Flain and reads, "Mr. Twilt, huh? Great. I'll just give myself a call." He has a pleasant one-sided phone conversation that ends with "I'll see ya Tuesday," congratulates Flain on getting the job, then warns him of rumors of "own-day izing-say." The phone rings, and it's for Flain; Twilt's been fired. Twilt throws a fit and storms off, "You put in one week and look what they do to you!" Flain excitedly takes the seat behind his ex-boss's desk and begins undressing. Flain figures out how to answer the buzzing intercom and is told he's fired. He suddenly senses his nakedness and covers up in shame.

Big Boss Link (video)

"That ought to boost profits," says big boss (Tom) about firing his last corporate executive, Flain. Sitting alone at a vacant conference table, his satisfaction turns to apocalyptic fright: "Am I the only one left? Is there no other human on the planet but I?!" He screams into the void until his secretary (Jill) comes in to see if he's all right. His sanity returns. He thanks her and fires her. The boss now has a new problem: who will run the company? He makes a call.

Bhopal/Newsreel (video)

A newsreel, which opens with Bhopal on covers of business magazines, reports that, due to downsizing, white collar workers are being replaced by child laborers. Filthy, undernourished Bhopal (David) is shown featured on covers of magazines such as *Power* and *Fortuned*. An economist (Ben) punches up figures showing the corporate savings from hiring foreign child labor. "I mean, I'm no economist," he chuckles, "but that is a load of dough!" Offscreen someone calls, "Jimmy!" Busted, he runs off.

A wartime-style newsreel shows Bhopal playing golf with white collar executives. The newsreel segues into a clip of Senator Tankerbell (Bob) on Capitol Hill who proposes selling off useless landmarks, parks and states to relieve the nation's debt — New Mexico, the Grand Canyon ("just sittin' out there, collectin' dust"), and, lastly, San Francisco ("Depraved! Festooned with criminality and depravity!") He starts the bidding….

New San Francisco (live)

(live) The Chairman of Globo-Chem's theme park division (Bob) announces plans for the new family-friendly San Francisco, which they bought and turned into a park. "When you see the new San Francisco, you'll say 'San Fran-tastic.'" A "typical family" mimes along to pre-taped dialogue in this industrial presentation. The daughter (Mary Lynn) persuades her parents (Jill and Tom) into checking out the *New* San Francisco. A backdrop of a cartoon city San Fran comes down, amid ooohs and aahhs. "Look, it's a hippie!" Groovy Gravy, a tie-dyed-shirted character with a big foam hippie head appears. The Spokesman reassures them that the old hippies have been replaced with "the kind that the whole family can enjoy." Groovy sings a jaunty song about the rides in Hippieland. Then the family visits "Bachelorland." ("We got rid of the dirt, but kept the pansies.") Big foam-headed leather-boys dance and sing about Dad getting a good work out and Mom going antique-ing. Then it's time to visit "New Chinatown." "Talk about your alien cultures," says the Spokesman, as silver aliens waddle down a U.F.O.'s ramp and sing ("*Meep meep, moop, moop! Have some hot and sour soup!*") to the family's wonderment. The big dance finale is interrupted by Grass Valley Greg (David)! He rides up on his recumbent bike to congratulate the cast. Bob, dropping character, is livid and screams at Greg, whose quivering lower lip makes Bob feel guilty. He offers the fallen billionaire five dollars to clean up the studio mess. Credits roll over GVG cleaning up the studio.

GVG Cleans (video)

Grass Valley Greg (David) is sweeping up the stage of a now empty studio. He sweeps the spotlight into a tiny beam, which he scoops into his hand. He removes his hat (and attached ponytail) and pops the captured light into his cap, places it back on his head, and grins.

Bhopal Tag (video)

The image of grinning GVG from the previous scene is a cartoon think-bubble over the head of hard working Bhopal (David) in the studio's squalid "Writers' Room." He hands the new script page to the Middle Eastern man with a whip (Paul), who hands it to Bob. Bob hates this ending: "I'm not in this! No!" The angry Arab taskmaster whips Bhopal.

(from left to right) "Gay him up!" Rodrigo (Brian) is enlisted to help their gay son find his way; Majority stockholder Grass Valley Greg (David) interrupts the scene; Tofutti-break insolence.

Notes On Episode 204

Bob: "This is probably the best show we ever did concerning a recurring theme. The appearance and reappearance of Grass Valley Greg and Bhopal really impress me now. Also, it's one of the funniest shows we ever did. Later we got away from the running ideas, the recurring themes, because we felt they were alienating. Like if you tuned in halfway through the show you wouldn't like it much. If the show had been a big success this wouldn't have been a problem, but since we were continually pushing ourselves to reach out to viewers, we went in a different direction."

Paul: "I got to play a guy who whips kids in the 'writers' room.' There are two significant things here: first, it was my first time using the Mr. Show 'Standard Foreigner' accent that I think all of us used at one point or another. Second, as the scene ends, I scream 'Al Wazir!' at the camera. Al Wazir is the name of a chicken restaurant in Hollywood that we ordered lunch from practically every day, and it had become sort of an all-purpose exclamation around the office. The name would pop up again."

David: "God bless it, we finally got Van Hammersly in there. It took a while, but we did it. That was one of those sketches that was floating around. We had filmed it for the stage show. There's a lot of stuff, unfortunately — Ronnie Dobbs footage, Van Hammersly — that we shot for the stage show where all the tapes were in my car, and my car was stolen. So we don't have access to some of that original footage. I think that's one of those ones that the original version was even funnier than the later one. Just performance-wise. Because it was so shoddily shot, it was ridiculous. We had shot it at the [coffee house/pool room] Bourgeois Pig on Franklin Ave. They let us in there for an hour, no sound control or anything."

Bob: "Fans talk about the Gay Son scene like it was a whole scene. We needed a scene for Grass Valley Greg to interrupt, and we'd been trying to figure out this premise and it just never went anywhere, so we had him interrupt it."

Paul: "I loved the Grass Valley Greg character because it was so retarded. It came out of a hat David found that had a ponytail attached to it. He started doing this voice around the office, then Hollywood magic took over, and Voila! A sketch is born. The image of David on that recumbent bike made me so happy because it was funny, but at the same time you wanted to throttle the idiot. We had a tough time coming up with the name of the tofu-based treat that GVG makes his employees eat; all the ones we thought up were actual products. Finally, we called Tofutti, who freely let us use their name and gave us a ton of free Tofutti products. You know what? The stuff wasn't half bad."

Bob: "Grass Valley Greg is a great character. All the writers invented him, and all of them have ideas in his story, but you gotta admit David in that hat with the pony tail attached is funny with almost nothing else to back it up."

David: "Grass Valley Greg was a fun sketch. He was a fun character to do. And that's something we could all relate to. We've all seen that kind of guy — the intellectual, poet/nerdy center of whatever respective towns you come from. In my case, Cambridge in Boston. There were guys who rode recumbent bikes, and they had those big ponytails and goofy beards — they were fucking annoying. Bob came up with the term 'funboarding,' still one of my favorite, most succinct snapshots of American linguistics. 'Funboarding.' I don't know what it means, but it certainly conjures up all you need to know. The goats peed on me. I'm not that comfortable with animals. And I think they sensed I didn't like them, and they were really fucking with me, and one peed on me. Maybe for calling it retarded. The appearance of Boz Scaggs — I mean, c'mon. There's a real Boz Scaggs, and this is what he's reduced to. I wonder if he knows. And I don't know what that voice was that Bob was doing. I don't know if you've ever heard Boz Scaggs talk."

Bob: "We actually had goats walking around in this person's house that we rented for shooting. People are so dumb to let us shoot in their houses. I also love the 'all these goats are retarded' notion because it just adds insult to injury to the poor dead souls trapped in such ignorant beasts."

Bob: "New San Francisco was quite a challenging notion, with all the pre-taped music and all the costumes. But it's something any show can do if you've got people willing to work their asses off. We did."

David: "New San Francisco was crazy. Mary Lynn cracks me up in that. The end of the show is cool because it has two endings. That's one of the few shows that actually has an ending that makes sense and then the telescoping of that ending — where it's being written."

Paul: "I loved the New San Francisco bit so much, that I was bummed out that I was the only person not in it. Tom, Jill, and Mary Lynn are hilarious in this."

EPISODE **205** OPERATION HELL ON EARTH

written by:	David Cross, Bob Odenkirk, Jay Johnston, Bill Odenkirk, Brian Posehn, Paul F. Tompkins
recruiters segment director:	Tom Gianas
location segment director:	Troy Miller
live show director:	John Moffitt
cast:	David Cross, Bob Odenkirk, John Ennis, Jay Johnston, Tom Kenny, Mary Lynn Rajskub, Jill Talley, Paul F. Tompkins
featuring:	Scott Aukerman, Ken Daly, Jerry C. Minor, Theresa Mulligan, Bill Odenkirk, Patton Oswald, B.J. Porter, Angela Shelton, Dino Stamatopoulos, Wayne Wilderson, Matt Cather, Kim Givens, Tim Pryor, Jessica Reeves, Richard Singleton
special appearances by:	Dave Foley, Julia Sweeney

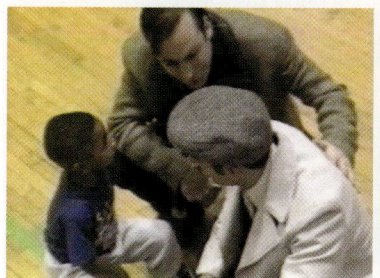

Mr. Show theme song. Mary Lynn introduces.

Young Superstar Open (live)
Bob and David bring out their darling daughter, "Superstar," a red-headed ball of energy in a pink tu-tu and tap shoes. The guys each flashback to their terrible childhoods. David's memory is of being unwanted by his fur coat-wearing 1920's archetype Dad. Bob's is of being tormented by his gambling-obsessed parents who cajole him into making losing bets. The guys make Superstar tap dance for the audience. They swear to Superstar she'll never know childhood pain, "As long as you *keep tapping*!" The terrified little dancer taps like a maniac, and we flash forward to....

Old Folks' Home (video)
Bitter, broken old Superstar (Jill in tattered tu-tu) remembering the above incident, blaming her miserable life on such abuse. "Dicklickers!" she calls her two dads, a very elderly Bob and David, whom she now pushes around in a two-seater wheelchair at the Steamy Acres Retirement Home. "They're the reason I'm like this, because I was deprived shitless!"

Deprivation (video)
At the Carlington Developmental School, a quiet man (Tom) complains that his parents gave him love and affection, and, as a result, he's an accountant. He wants better for his daughter. The school is teaching him how to deprive his daughter of just the right things so she can become a doctor, an astronaut, "even the President." The father yanks away the girl's toy, and she cries. Abraham Lincoln (Bob) testifies that the deprivations of his childhood are what got his face on a penny. That, "plus my father touched my butthole." Issac Newton (Paul) and Albert Einstein (Dino) also credit their genius to their fathers touching their respective buttholes. Footage of Hitler, with the fact: "Hitler reveals to a stunned nation that no one had ever touched his butthole."

Hate Group (live)
A picture of Hitler is on the wall of a community meeting room where a small hate group meets. Their leader, Ken (David), rallies the crew, made up of the tenants in his building, including a Jew (Jill), a black (Wayne), a gay (Tom), and Rajhit, a Middle Eastern man (Bob). Ken is stridently pushing his plan for "Operation Hell on Earth," the enforced separation of the races in America. He outlines his goal using a map of the U.S. partitioned into nine areas: "New York City will become 'Little Israel.' The Jews will love that." He asks Mrs. Shapiro if that's okay. Everyone is very nice and supportive, and Ken alternates between bombast and gentle accommodation. His plan is to begin with a bomb exploding in a van on a busy city block, but so far, no one in the group is doing their part to acquire the bomb parts or to rent the van. This infuriates Rajhit, Ken's biggest cheerleader, and he goes off on them: "This is Ken's one thing…the victory of the white race! Let's make it happen!" But as they discuss the plan further, everyone is concerned about the noise, debris, and danger of a bomb. "Operation Hell On Earth" devolves into blasting a Billy Ocean song from a van in the desert. Ken just gives up. But Rajhit is determined to go through with it for Ken's sake. We see footage of the lonely van and hear the "Caribbean Queen" blaring from speakers….

News Family Anchors (live)
Anchorman (Tom) is reporting on "Operation Hell on Earth" — "The world held hostage, day one," concluding with a somber, "You've got to wonder how much of this we can all take." He then turns to address his co-anchors, "Glen? Terry?" (Jill and Bob), who nod. He continues addressing co-anchors as the camera widens to reveal a motley crew assembled at this super-long news desk — "Burton?, Famous Mortimer?, Deltoid from the Planet Humonculus?" — there are 16 in all. He breaks his "news"; "Your mother and I are getting a divorce." All are sad, and the news continues…

Giving the bad news at the anchordesk. 1. Tom; 2. Glen; 3. Terry; 4. Rod; 5. Bill; 6. Superstar; 7. Burton; 8. Famous Mortimer; 9. I.P. Freely; 10. Bobo; 11. Sleepy; 12. Charlene; 13. Freddy; 14. Tex Mex; 15. Deltoid from the Planet Homonculus; 16. The American Dream; 17. Heywood Jablome.

Recruiters (video)

Carter Blanchard (David), a recruiter for the college basketball team at LaFonte University, is watching the news from a bar stool. This is a documentary on him and his competitor, Ty Keenan (Bob), a pasty faced sad-sack who recruits for the smaller Indiana Basin Silt College. They are both chasing younger and younger potential players. Right now both have their eye on a 5-year-old named Will Hawkins, and each one pitches their respective college to the parents. "Have you declared a major yet?" Ty boasts about Indiana Basin Silt's degrees to become a fireman, policeman, cowboy, or astronaut. Carter brings the family gifts, a LaFonte vest and slippers, and some potato soup. The father (Jerry) signs his boy to a 14-year holding deal with LaFonte. Meanwhile, Ty pursues even younger prospects including a six-month-old. The pressure is too much, and Ty confesses to Carter that he's been thinking of quitting and even of "running away…from my grandmother's house." He breaks down. Carter can only sigh, "That's what this job does to you." Six months later, little Will's father gets a notice that his son has been dropped from LaFonte, and that a "representative will be stopping by to pick up the potato soup." The father reprimands Will for being a ball hog, sitting around eating chocolate, getting fat. "You coulda' been something." This sad scene becomes a memory of….

Blame-A-Thon Link (live)

A grown-up Will Hawkins (Wayne) explains that his father's criticisms drove him to become the top producer of little chocolate basketballs. He emotionally brags, "Fuck you, Dad! I blame you for my success!" His testimonial is all part of the annual *Blame-A-Thon*. The host, grown-up Superstar (Jill), urges people to call in their blames — "our phone operators are standing by with their thumbs up their asses, waiting for you to call." She introduces the telethon's entertainment….

Fartin' Gary (live/video)

(live) Fartin' Gary (David), a nervous but earnest "fartist," gives us renditions of famous people cutting the cheese. He launches into a long, fart-punctuated story called "Give Peace a Chance." His tale is interrupted by a fellow in the audience, Rudy (Bob), who is farting louder than he is, upstaging him. Rudy apologizes profusely as he was loving Gary's act. Gary is too steamed at being trumped by this amateur and storms off stage.

(video) Outside the studio, Gary sadly toots as he walks past his poster (THE ONLY "FARTIST" IN THE WORLD). This poster is replaced by one bearing the image of Rudy, the audience member, with the slogan, "FARTIN' RUDY…THE NEW CLOWN PRINCE OF FARTISTRY."

Second Wind (video)

In fact, Rudy is so great that he gets his own sitcom called *Second Wind* with a lovable lighthearted theme over the opening credits:

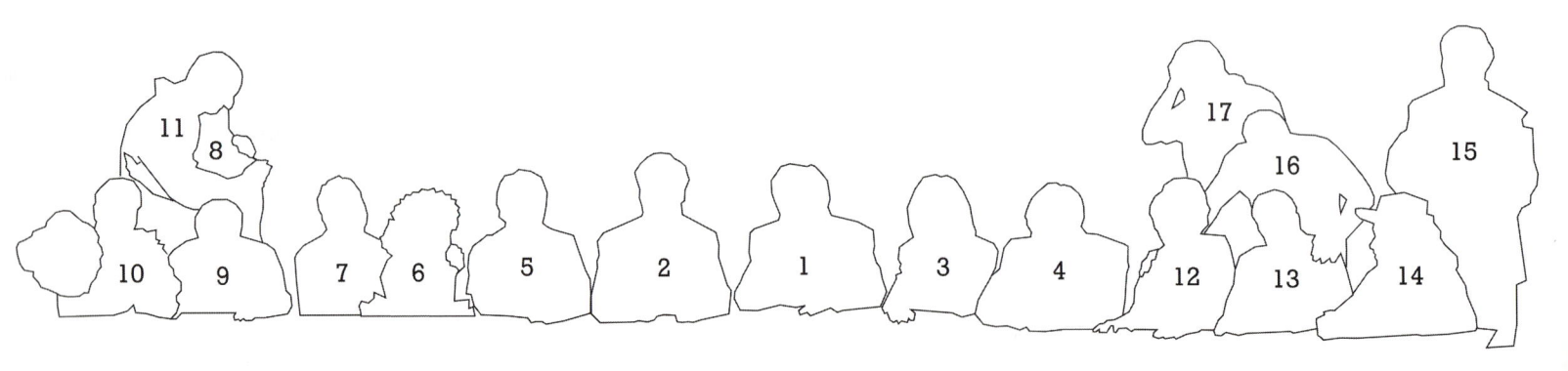

*If at first you don't succeed, don't despair
'Cause all you need is a second wind, and it's blowin' in
with a second chance for love!*

The episode opens with Rudy using farts to assist his son, Carlisle, with his book report ("pfffffft…in 1812!"). Neighbor Vaunice (Julia) enters, frantic because her husband's boss is coming over and they're in a fix. They want the boss to think they ate his wife's three-bean salad which they actually tossed out. "You've got to do an impression of my husband farting!" Rudy saves the day — the boss (Dave) is impressed by all the gas, and Todd (David) gets his promotion.

Older Superstar Close (live)

Little Superstar is enjoying *Second Wind*. Bob and David scold her, saying "that kind of garbage is what's ruining the youth of America…you should be watching *our* show." She reminds her two dads that they don't get cable. Bob and David make her tap for talking back. Old Superstar (Jill) suddenly beams onto the stage (a la *Star Trek*). She has a laser gun and turns the tables, forcing her abusive daddies to tap. Credits roll over Old and Little Superstar making the whole cast tap.

Notes About Episode 205

Bob: "It was cool to address the issue of artists and other intense personalities using their childhood traumas to goad them to their achievements. It's the kind of current social issue that was smart fodder for our silliness. To me it's the way in which Mr. Show is reflective of its time."

Bob: "The Little Superstar girl, our 'daughter' was so fun and funny. We had some great kids on our show, especially this girl and the little boy in show #409. Always fun to have these kids. But it was a little uncomfortable swearing around them, although mostly the parents didn't seem to care."

Bob: "One reason we aren't doing the show anymore is because we inevitably write scenes where David or I are very old (Steamy Acres Retirement Home), or bald, or in some way that demands we coat our heads with liquid latex in the middle of the flame-hot sunlight of Los Angeles. Fuck that shit. If you like Mr. Show so much, and you need to see more, then you go stick your head in rubber and sweat like a goofball."

David: "The Recruiters piece was one of those things that we shot before we had a TV show. We flew to Detroit so that we would have the right look, it wouldn't look like we were in L.A. And Jerry Minor (an actor in Detroit at the time) was brilliant in that. We had a story worked out, but we improvised a lot of the scenes. When Bob and I are in the diner, the idea that he's quitting the business was the only thing that we really knew we were going to do there. When he runs out of the restaurant, you can hear me laughing. That's why the shot switches to him outside because I was cracking up. And when Bob was trying to recruit the crying baby, that was all improvised."

Bob: "The Recruiters piece was based on seeing the great documentary *Hoop Dreams*, and I love the way it looks and the characters in it. David and I shot it in Detroit over Christmas the previous year, before we had a deal to do any shows. Tom Gianas directed it, and it's a great piece. It was one of those pieces that was able to elicit a sigh of sympathy from the audience [when Ty gives up and sits in the street, crying and eating oyster crackers from a little plastic bag]. The 'Awwww' response is something few comedy shows have honestly achieved. Somebody make up an award to give us, please."

Jerry: "Before Mr. Show was a TV show, Bob and David, who I just met, asked me to be in this scene, Recruiters they were shooting in Detroit. It was really vague. They

David as "Fartin' Gary," the guys' tribute to international sensation, "Mr. Methane."

said, 'We may be doing this TV show, we're doing this show in Los Angeles, and this piece might be a part of it, we'll let you know.' I knew what they wanted in the sketch, but I had no idea what they were talking about. They tried to explain to me how some sketches were going to be live and some on tape. I didn't understand that either. 'So you're going to tape it? And you're going to perform on stage?' I taped the sketch, and I had a really good time. They let me improvise a lot because it was a really loose script. I saw the finished result of the sketch, which I got. But it was still a part of the live shows they were doing, so I still didn't see how it fit into a whole show. And then I saw Mr. Show on HBO a year later. 'Oh, that's how they do it!'"

David: "Recruiters was one of the first pieces where I learned first hand about the effect and manipulation of editing. We had initially made a 12-minute version for the stage. It followed this story where my character was successful, and Bob's wasn't, and we kept trying to out-do each other. But when we were using it in the TV show, we had to get it down to about five minutes. This whole other story started to evolve when we took these other scenes out. It's really human, and I really like it. You actually watch the development of a character in a five-minute little film."

David: "When we came up with Fartin' Gary, we were at the Montreal Comedy Festival. We were crashed in our hotel room, and we were just giggling like fucking school girls, we were laughing so hard. And we wanted to do it because one of the acts at the festival was a guy who farted. Mr. Methane, he was from France. He farted Happy Birthday, he farted candles out, hahahaha. And he was the hit of the festival. It was depressing. You go to the festival with something to say, you want to make a point, you've worked on this stuff, it's important to you, and the biggest hit of the festival is a guy who farts. So Bob and I came up with idea of a guy who does impressions, and he's just very earnest. He's got this whole, 'Gee, shucks, I love to entertain' kind of quality. And we performed it at Montreal. It was hilarious. I remember laughing so hard that I was tearing up and my sides hurt."

EPISODE 206
THE VELVETEEN TOUCH OF A DANDY FOP

written by:	Bob Odenkirk, David Cross, Jay Johnston, Bill Odenkirk, Dino Stamatopoulos, Paul F. Tompkins
location segment director:	Troy Miller
live show director:	John Moffitt
cast:	David Cross, Bob Odenkirk, John Ennis, Jay Johnston, Tom Kenny, Mary Lynn Rajskub, Jill Talley, Paul F. Tompkins
featuring:	Bill Odenkirk, Brian Posehn, Sheryl Bartel, Lisa Boyle, Floyd H. Dodd, Sarah Kalen, James McDonald, Tina New, Robbie Weinstein
special appearances by:	Jack Black, Maynard Keenan

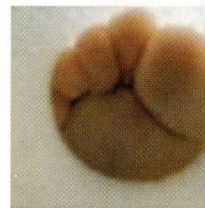

Mr. Show theme song and logo. Mary Lynn introduces.

Charity/Blind Gary Open (live/video)

(live) Bob jogs onstage in full running gear; he's in the middle of his annual 10-day run for people with Entitilitus. David shares with us his charity work for "David's Kids," some cute ragamuffins in the audience. Bob points out that they are David's illegitimate children. But David glosses over this, bragging about his work with "David's Girls," three buxom models, and his work with "David," (David himself in the audience, wearing a "David's David" t-shirt). Bob brags that he reads a daily comic strip to a blind man….

(live with video) Blind Gary (David), an extremely busy blind businessman, interrupts his day to take Bob's call. He humors Bob, who lamely describes a crappy *Calvin and Hobbes* strip. Impatient, Blind Gary laughs before the end, cutting Bob off — "On behalf of blind people everywhere, thanks. Okay, really gotta run." Attempting to speak directly to camera, Gary explains that handicapped people help others to fill their empty lives with meaning by allowing them to perform such works. From telethons to small, anonymous gestures….

Subway (live)

On a subway, a man on crutches (David) says, "You're welcome," to a biker guy (Jay) who dropped a few coins in his cup. Linda and Todd (Jill and Tom) enter. They are a couple having some sort of lovers' spat. The kooky passengers, (an old woman [John], a biker [Jay], a gay guy [Jack], a Japanese man [Paul]), overhear their argument and give Todd unsolicited advice, beginning with, "Ask her to marry you!" When Linda shoots him down, the group continues goading: "Hit her!" "Kiss her!" "Grab her ass!" Linda is disgusted at his behavior and exits. Todd is discouraged. The old woman tells him to "punch the wall!" Suddenly, the situation transforms. Dr. Sammy (David) appears in the foreground (actually in the live audience). He is a "PsychoActualist," who explains that within all of us are four distinct voices: an impatient Old Lady, backed up by a Biker, a Gay Guy who "takes it personal and makes it personal," and a Japanese Man who "utters nonsensical advice that only our Biker can translate." He plugs his speaking engagement at the Holiday Spot. Then a Dr. Randy Terry (Bob) appears in front of Dr. Sammy. He introduces himself as the author of *The Five Voices*. The fifth voice being Dr. Sammy, the "False Doctor," the "voice to avoid." The two doctors argue over who exists in whose mind and fight over mental control of the four crazy subway passengers. This situation, in turn, plays out like a pro wrestling match, with the announcer bellowing, "Six voices fight until there's only one left!…only one left!"

Donut Shop (video)

The voices above echo inside the bleeding ear of a droopy, slovenly oaf (Bob), as he tries to decide on a final donut for his dozen. The clerk (Mary Lynn) is tiring of his thickheaded indecisiveness. After an excruciatingly long time, he picks one, then, flinging wrinkled bills, orders her to "keep the change." He sits down with his odd friend, David, who refuses to eat a donut because he doesn't eat food that has "approval of the masses." He hates all things popular or modern. He proudly announces that he doesn't own a television — "notice how I didn't say TV, because TV is a nickname, and nicknames are for friends, and television is no friend of mine." He finally rails against the clarity of CD's and reveals a turn-of-the-century Victrola. He puts on a record and we hear the first strains of….

Megaphone Crooners (video/super 8 film)

1920's sensation Dickie Crickets (Bob), as remembered by Vaughn Peesler (Tom) in a documentary about "megaphone crooning". The industrial age is in full swing, and Dickie sings songs extolling inventions — "Automobile," "Aeroplane," and "Elevator" (*"Elevator! My baby loves the elevator! Loves to ride the elevator! Ride it up and down!"*). Every song has the same melody and his singing is more like yelling, but the people loved it. Then Kid Jersey (David) comes along. He had a hit with "Penicillin" and was beloved for his trademark phrase, "Thank you!" Dickie fought back with "Time Machine," but quickly learned that audi-

(left) Bob at The Union (nightclub on Sunset Blvd.), doing a stand-up bit about megaphone singers. (photo: © Jenine deShazer, 1996)
(right) Dickie Crickets and his trusty megaphone. © Photo by Famous Mortimer

ences didn't want to hear about things that hadn't been invented yet, only real inventions. The two crooners join up for a *Monsters of Megaphone Tour* — along with a man from the patent office — inventing new things and singing about them. But things go wrong when Kid Jersey is arrested after inventing (and singing about) a "Counterfeit Money Machine." The modern-day Vaughn then complains about the crappy Hollywood movies that pass as entertainment today, films like....

Greenlight Gang (MOVIE EXECS) (live)

Coupon: The Movie. Six Hollywood studio execs try to figure out why their film was such a huge flop since it was based on the #1 coupon in America. The boss (John) demands to know who "greenlighted" the picture. Each exec uses insider lingo to squeak by and pass the buck, "I farmed it out...It already had a 'thumbs up'...not my thumb." The pressure rises until one exec (David) cracks, stands up and, with demon eyes, screams "Nooooo!" He blames the American public for falsely leading them to believe that they liked that coupon. This notion leads to a lawsuit.

Coupon: The Trial (video)

A montage of the court case: *Coupon: The Movie* vs. The People of the United States. Done with extreme close-ups and crazy lighting (because they couldn't afford a real courtroom). Everyone in the country testifies as to why they didn't see the movie. The movie moguls win their case and the judge orders everyone in America to see the movie. ("Who wants to go Friday?")

Coupon: The Movie (film)

Amazingly dramatic blockbuster movie trailer for *Coupon: The Movie*. Huge scissors menacingly cutting in slo-mo, ominous music, serious voiceover ("In a world filled with desire…"), overhead shot through ceiling fan of housewives chatting, a shot from inside a sock! All used to tell the following story: a suburban mom uses a coupon to buy a pair of tube socks. An irrelevant subplot features a car driving off a cliff. "This is the movie all of America must see." "Warm…and mandatory."

Credits Testimonials Close (live)

People leaving a theatre offer enthusiastic testimonials about *Coupon*: "The woman totally used a coupon to buy the socks!" (Mary Lynn). "Try wet and wild 'Coupon: The Movie: The Ride,'" urges the announcer. "I'm wetter than I've ever been, and I'm from Canada!" yells an excited young man (Bob). More testimonials about a new movie, *Mr. Show: The Credits*. Credits roll as audiences rave.

Notes About Episode 206

Brian: "*Subway* was all making fun of film cliché. A guy and his girlfriend are dealing with this personal stuff and these cliché characters, like an old lady or a Chinese guy would say, 'Marry her!' 'KISS HER!' And then David came up with the four voices."

Bob: "The thing I like least about *Mr. Show* sketches are things like *Subway*. It's such a tortured logic puzzle. There's a simple scene at the core of it, with the corny characters telling this guy what to do, but then it becomes all these over-worked explanations for itself (with the psychologists). It's no fun. But, if it's any consolation,

Some Warhol-esque characters emerge to muse on the credits (Mary Lynn, Bob, Brian)

these types of scenes were a lot more work in the writing than simple, well-told, good ones."

Paul: *"I'm very proud of the stuff I wrote for the character David plays in the Donut Shop scene, and was thrilled that he ended up looking just how I pictured him, thanks to David and Tonyia Verna [hair/make-up]. The idea for the character came to me when I saw a guy give a little talk before a screening of* Lawrence of Arabia, *in which he said how great it was to see this movie on the big screen, as it was meant to be seen. Then a guy in the audience yelled out, "Death to video!" Idiot. VCR's are great. There was a wonderfully stupid mini-argument inspired by these two characters. I called them 'The Two Best Friends,' but Bob insisted that they weren't best friends they just knew each other. There's nothing like arguing over fake things."*

Paul: *"The Megaphone sketch was my idea to do, but hardly my sketch. I had seen Bob talk about megaphone singers on a stand-up stage one night, and thought, there could be a sketch there. I wrote a few drafts, but ultimately Bob and David really wrote it. I think that all the names in there are mine, but that's about it. Oh, and the phrase 'Monsters of Megaphone.' People always say they love this sketch, and then I say, 'I wrote it.' And then they are so impressed that I have to tell them, 'Not really.'"*

Bob: *"Megaphone Crooners was one of our fans' favorites of the season. Troy Miller did a great job getting the look. It was shot on Super-8 film. We shot it at a high school theatre, and the movie theatre is the Vista in Hollywood/Silverlake. I think one of the reasons people like it so much is that there is a sweetness to the story and, especially, in Tom Kenny's performance. He is really gentle and wistful in his narration. What can I say, there wasn't a dry eye in the house. People are saps."*

Paul: *"I love* Coupon: The Movie. *I was thrilled to be included in the trial montage and to be able to say, 'It was a baby!' Another longtime comedy reference of mine, in tandem with, 'Can't you keep that chicken quiet?' Hawkeye says both in the final episode of* M*A*S*H. *I did this thing with Mary Lynn where I'd ask her what her characters names were if they didn't have names in the script or were just there as extras. Her name for the character in Coupon was Pat Lemontime. Her name later turned up in the 'Special Thanks' section of the credits."*

SEASON THREE
EPISODE GUIDE

"Season 2 was a good solid season, and I certainly hoped we would get more shows after it," says Bob. "I wasn't sure we were — but then, I thought people were going to shut us down every time we did the show."

They did get another season, and at times, it was a case of, "be careful what you wish for." Season 3 was different from the previous two; it was their first ten-show order from HBO. And it wasn't long before they realized how tough the schedule was going to be. David recalls the strain of that timetable: "That was really where I started questioning how much I wanted to do this. After it was over, Bob and I said to Carolyn Strauss [HBO], 'We're not working this way again. We need more money [to allow for a longer schedule].'"

On the upside, Bob and David had finally won over Dino Stamatopoulos; he joined them as an executive producer. Line producer, Tom Sherren, also came on board, someone very capable who they immediately trusted — a huge boon to production. But even with the extra producers, the workload was incredibly challenging.

Creatively, they had a head start. Paul F. Tompkins comments, "Coming into the third season, we all had a much more concrete idea of what *Mr. Show* was and where everything went." And Troy Millers adds, "When Season 3 came along, what Bob and David did was take it to the next level, of really trying some things, sketches we had never seen before. But they did it the right way. It was never, 'Okay now we're going to just skate.' They never went back to the archives to bring back characters to make their jobs easier."

By the second five-show cycle, they were playing catch-up. Scripts were finishing the day before they had to shoot. Toward the end of the season, writers were trying to finish a script even as the live show was being rehearsed. Bill recounts: "We wrote the end of the Anne Frank scene and some transition. It was Dino and I, because a lot of people were on the set. We were running out of time, we were running out of material, we had to put shows together, we were under pressure. It was crazy. At one point, we broke up into two groups, Bob and David and Dino and Brian were in one room, Paul, Jay and Mike and I were in another room, under the gun, working on two shows."

Flyer for Season 3 audience tapings.

MAKE $80 A WEEK OR MORE!

That's right, **you** heard us. You should make at least $80 a week to get by in our modern world.

LIVE TAPINGS OF HBO'S
"MR. SHOW"
with bob & david

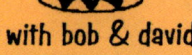

EARTHQUAKE TIPS
1. Shake along with it.
2. Take a scented bath.
3. Get out of your house and loot.
4. Say good-bye to your dog.

Taping Dates (@ 8:00pm & 10:00pm):
Aug. 26 (Tuesday)
Aug. 29 (Friday)
Sep. 6 (Saturday)
Sep. 9 (Tuesday)
Sep 13 (Saturday)

CALL 213.860.8031 FOR INFO

Flyer for Season 3 audience tapings.

Eban Schletter, the show's music director, provides us with a glimpse. "Season 3 — here's how crazy it was for absolutely everybody — the last two episodes, I went five days with no sleep. Tons of coffee and Verves. There's no choice. It takes time to write music, get it to them, get their notes on it, go back make changes, get to rehearsal, record it. At this point it's day 3, already the world was surreal — they were shooting #309, and I had stuff for #310 that had to be approved also. So I go to the set with a Walkman, instead of them coming to my studio. Dave is in wardrobe getting dressed for rehearsal for one sketch, while he's talking to Dino about a link that they have to rewrite, and I put the Walkman on him. He takes a minute to listen to it and give his notes on that music. Then I go to Bob. Bob is dressed up as the attorney guy, rehearsing *Don Pratt*, while I'm giving him music for another sketch, and while Bill is offside talking to him about a link for the next episode. Bob and David are in separate places, doing three things at once. They're having to listen to people like me, and they're supposed to still be writing. They haven't finished writing episode #310 yet. And they're still trying to be creative and come up with ideas, while they're dressed up like another character, acting like that character, and getting ready for an audience that night. That's totally insane."

"I remember being up on a roof, with a Hi-8 camera, shooting stuff for the show that we were rolling that night [for an audience]," recalls Troy. Tracey Krasno, production manager, remembers, "We'd be at one location, trying to find the next one before we can move. We'd get clearance on a high school one hour after we realized we needed it." "At one location, we thought we had a permit, but we didn't give enough notice," recalls Wendy Wilkins, talent coordinator. "We went to shoot anyway. In no more than ten minutes, there are neighborhood representatives there, they told us to shut down. And Tom Sherren went over and stalled while we tried to get as much as possible.

We would sit two P.A.'s at the end of the street with walkies, and they would signal when cops were coming, so they'd stop shooting, or we'd hide."

"But I've worked a lot harder on shows that were a lot less good," Troy adds in summation. "I've always had this ability to take a step away from it, and not scream about it, and just make sure that we were doing things the best way that we could. If there was a better way that we could spend our money or our time, then I would always push for that."

David shares a not-so-pretty example of the desperate toll taken by the middle of the second run, the exact apex of production craziness: "Paul is like me in that we can be really argumentative when we get cranky. But this argument had nothing to do with what we were arguing about. Nada. We were doing camera blocking for *Our Secret Love* (#307) — the show was to tape the next day. At one point in the scene, there's a place where Bob gets the phone and goes into the kitchen. And I don't know how this came up, but Paul and I had an argument that started out cordially, and then became vicious, and really just stupid and cutting about whether the phone was cordless or not. Absolutely ridiculous thing to be arguing about. Paul had his reasons, initially, and I had my reason, initially, and then it very quickly became not about that. And in retrospect, we both see it for what it was, two very frustrated people — not necessarily frustrated with each other, but we happened to be the closest people in proximity to each other. And we were insulting each other, and, at one point I just pulled rank — which is something I never did — and just said, 'Look, I'm the boss. It's going to be cordless (or not cordless, whichever one it was).' And he left. And I'm sitting in one of those chairs out in the audience, and Dino comes over, and I keep going off on Paul, 'That motherfucker, man! What the fuck is his problem?'…all this stuff. I'm just going off, and I see Paul through the doors about five minutes later, he's coming toward me from across the lot. He makes a beeline toward me, and it gets kind of quiet. He sits down in a chair next to me. And he doesn't look at me, he just looks straight ahead, and he says, 'Just so you know, your mic is on.' And I don't think I ever felt worse in my life. It's the kind of thing that if I was animated, I would have shrunk to the size of a pea, and my voice would have gone extremely high, and I would've run around going, 'yip-yip-yip!' But we made up, we apologized at the Cat & Fiddle. He was very cool about it. I can think back on several times when I was just a baby. I'd say with the exception of one or two people, everybody would react immaturely at some point. That was everybody's problem. It would manifest itself differently, but the problem was, 'I'm not getting my way, and I'm tired, and I've been here for five weeks straight, without a break. So, fuck you guys.' And then just sarcastic comments. It was tough. We all were babies. Except for Dino. And very rarely Jay. But everyone else."

Other shifts that year included: witnessing Jill Talley grow and grow until she takes maternity leave. Her only appearance in the second half of the season is in the pre-filmed *Philouza*, #308. Mary Lynn Rajskub does not return in the third season. Karen Kilgariff and Brett Paesel segue in. "Guest" writers were brought in this season — Mike Stoyanov for the first few episodes and Mike Upchurch for all ten. Some cameos worth mentioning: Jon Stewart (who is oddly uncredited in #302) plays himself, and — my favorite — Jonathan Katz as the animated Dr. Katz, bewildered at fake therapist patient Kedsie Matthews (#308).

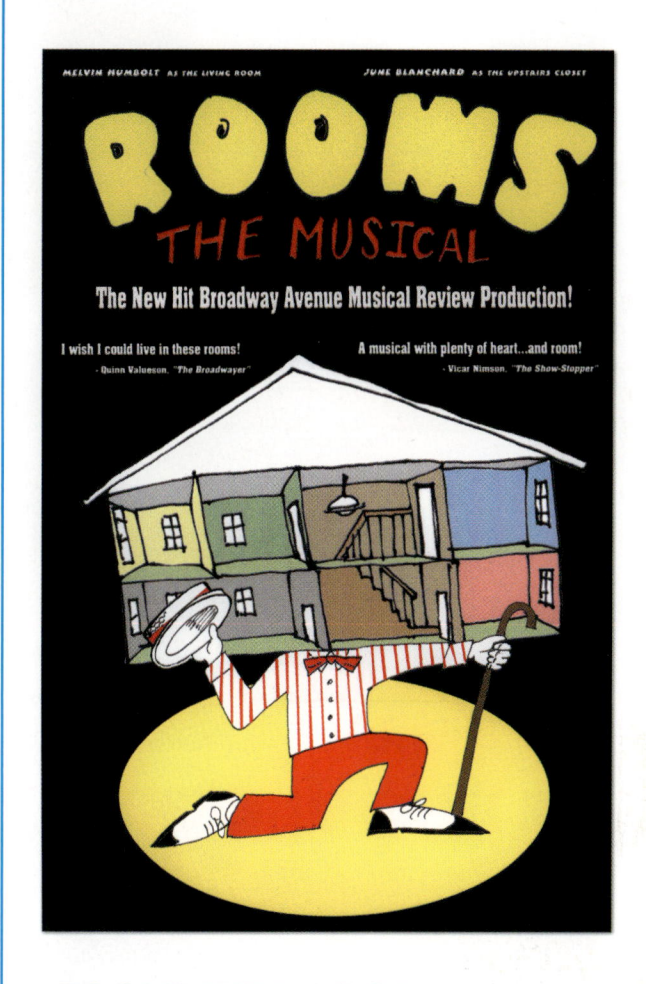

ROOMS THE MUSICAL

Bill Odenkirk: *Rooms — The Musical* was a fanciful notion which came to us and refused to leave. The initial concept was that it was a lavish Broadway show in which the various rooms of a house sang songs about what was like being a room. As far as I know, this idea was never realized beyond the poster which Heather Miller and I made. I think the poster is hanging in the background of a scene somewhere. It's unfortunate, because this is one musical I would go see."

EPISODE 301 HEAVEN'S CHIMNEY

written by:	David Cross, Bob Odenkirk, Jay Johnston, Bill Odenkirk, Dino Stamatopoulos, Paul F. Tompkins, Mike Upchurch
location segment director:	Troy Miller
live show director:	John Moffitt
cast:	David Cross, Bob Odenkirk, John Ennis, Jay Johnston, Tom Kenny, Karen Kilgariff, Brett Paesel, Brian Posehn, Jill Talley, Paul F. Tompkins
featuring:	Theresa Mulligan, James White

Mr. Show theme song and logo. Medieval Wizard (Tom) introduces.

Heaven's Chimney Open (live)

From the stage David speaks to Bob as "The Bob" on the big screen. The Bob, in shimmering robes, appears alongside ever-ascending images of himself and greets everyone with a hearty, nonsensical, "Terra Delu!" Mr. Show has become some kind of religious cult. David checks that everyone has their bags packed, for this is the day that we're all going up "Heaven's Chimney." Jay and John grab David, violently abducting him. The Bob nervously has some cronies pass out poisoned S'mores to the audience, so they all may pass through Heaven's Chimney and meet "the Grandfather in the Sky." The camera pans up to….

Deprogramming (video)

In a storage room, Jay and John are deprogramming David, who robotically recites dogma and praises The Bob. Tom, dressed like a priest, comes to help the delirious David, who recognizes him — "Tom Kenny! You're from Mr. Show! I'm a big fan!" Tom calmly tries to set him straight. He tells David that The Bob is a lie, and that there is no "Heaven's Chimney," no "Razzleberry Waterfall." However, there are Pearly Gates, St. Peter, and his Big Book of Names for heaven's guest list.

Heaven Tour (video)

David and a priest (Tom) fly by in a magic cartoon car as the priest explains what he can expect to see in heaven. Cherub angels on clouds play trumpets. David waves at his dead pets. Jesus swoops by and high-fives David with a "Chim-chim-cheree!" Tom introduces more of heaven's attractions: Buddha, Muhammad, "and who knows? Maybe even Shaquille O'Neal…"

Crazy Religious Beliefs (live/video)

"…Who knows who's going to show up on this edition of Crazy Religious Beliefs! "Grinning hosts, Clark Richardson (Bob) and Manny Edwards (David), come out on a cheesy TV-clips-show set, and introduce video clips of various religious practices, which they then ridicule. In the first clip, a Hasidic rabbi (David) dryly explains why Jews don't eat pork, then a zany cartoon pig "pushes" him offscreen. Co-host Clark laughs, "Somebody tell these people about refrigeration!" The final clip is of a woman praying in her kitchen (Karen): "Dear God, please don't let my guests suspect that I'm going to serve them a coffee substitute tonight."

Watch Us Have Sex (live)

A living room, where Pam (Karen), her husband Larry (David), and their guests, Chuck and Mary (Bob and Brett), relax with coffee after dinner. Larry reveals they invited their best friends over to ask an important favor: you see, they've been trying to have a baby and — Chuck interjects with a magnanimous offer, "Of course, you can have some of my sperm." No, Larry has plenty of sperm. What they want is for their friends to watch them have sex because that's their kink — in fact, it's the only way they can do it. "It'll only take a minute," Pam promises, "and then we'll have some pie." Mary finally agrees to help them; she offers to stand there and watch them have sex if she can be naked as she watches. So everybody's happy except for Chuck, who wants to go make some sperm. Chuck confesses that he likes to "masturbate in a small room while people are waiting for pie to cool." Everyone is understanding, and they all get busy with their respective chores.

Blatant Sexual Symbolism Montage Link (video)

Porn music accompanies random and extremely suggestive footage: a train goes into a tunnel; a pile driver; a hotdog with two walnuts at its base poking at an open clam; a roller coaster riding back and forth which becomes….

The Devastator (video)

A commercial for the world's most terrifying roller coaster, "The Devastator." It features "a heart-stopping 200-mph, 15-story drop! Spine-cracking 90° turns! And…two whole minutes under water!" Two idiot brothers (Bob and David) stand in line for the ride high-fiving.

Breaking news: "Devastation in the park — Day 97." Trey Brackish (Tom) reports from the scene, "where this roller coaster continues taking the lives of innocent people." Red Cross volunteer (John) says the casualties are mounting. "We're losing people to heart failure, spinal injuries, even drowning." One of the brothers from the commercial (Bob), now in a neck brace and an "I survived the Devastator" T-shirt, lost his brother and can't comprehend what happened. Local residents load up their van and evacuate — "How are you supposed to protect yourself from this kind of thing?"

The news report breaks for a commercial for: Thrill World's The Devastator.

News report resumes: an engineering expert (Paul) says he's working on the problem and that he only hopes that the carnage "will let up soon after midnight, as it's done for the past 96 days…" The news broadcast concludes with a video montage of the day's tragedy and a fey folk song by Livingston Brewster, *Thank You for the Ride*, on Opportunist Records.

> *Said Goodbye to a friend today / He was off to find some fun.*
> *And when he came back, he never came back / because his life was done.*
> *I don't know why so many people died?*
> *But I bet if they could talk to God they'd say*
> *Thank you for the ride, God. Thank you for the ride.*
> *Thank you for the ride, God. Thanks you for the ever-lovin' ride.*
> *Got a ride from God, did you hear? / Got a ride from the G-man today.*
> *He picked me up and all I could say was thank you for the ride.*

Directions (live)

Two guys (Bob and David) are listening to this song in their car. David turns off the radio and, his voice quavering with emotion, drops the news on Bob that he's got cancer. "Oh, fuck, Goddammit! I can't believe it!" Bob passionately screams. David tells him hopefully it can be treated, and Bob reassures him that he's upset because his turn signal's broken again. "But, oh, fuck, Goddammit, I can't believe about your cancer, too." David continues laying out the emotional news, at the same time interrupting himself with directions for where they're headed. Bob stews about the various hardships in his life: his wife nagging him about bringing home a magazine he keeps leaving at work, and now his best friend has cancer. David nods sympathetically. "And now you have it, too!" Bob adds, feeling sorry for himself. When David laments that he only has a few months to live, Bob's mood brightens, "Hey, all right! We're here!" The guys cheer, then scream, as they proceed to get in an accident.

Educational Film Festival Link (video/live)

The preceding scene, a drivers' ed. film titled *Driven to Destruction*, was an entry in the 12th Annual Educational Film Festival. The schoolmaster host (Tom) introduces *The Limits of Science*, the oldest educational film in the world, discovered in an archaeological dig near Stonehenge.

Medieval Science Film (video)

A scratchy, warbly, science film with narrator, reminiscent of the type shown to primary school kids. It's set in "present day" London where the broom, the wheelbarrow, and the donkey are glorified as modern conveniences. "Questions, questions, questions. Modern minds can come up with three questions." Peasant Pete's (David) head is full up, so he goes to see a "real scientist," the blacksmith (Bob). The blacksmith suggests they go see a wizard (Tom), who explains that we need leeches to "suck out the sick inside of you that witches put there." Other myths are dispelled such as the benefits of rubbing a hunchback's hunch, although, "it might make the hunchback (Brian) feel better…science marches on." How does a scientist know what's true? "Well, all facts begin as dreams dreamt by a wizard…" And, if the king is satisfied, then, "it becomes an old wives' tale, and science is once more advanced!"

Hail Satan (live)

Southern-style televangelists Bobby C. and Kimberly (Tom and Jill) are disgusted by this "educational film" that's being shown to children — "Where are the films about our Lord?" Their Lord being Satan. This is the "Hail Satan Network." Their first guest is Montcrief Lanier (Bob in a very fat suit). Montcrief lowers his hugeness into a chair and sweet-talks Kimberly — "You are just the mother of all whores!" He brings out a "special friend," little Kevin (David), a boy in a wheelchair who appears incapacitated. Montcrief asks Kevin what the doctor told him. "He said I was lazy." Kevin, Montcrief explains, "is a shining example of the beautiful sin of sloth." Kevin nods off during his brief interview, but we learn that this tough little boy keeps busy — "…I sleep, I eat, I take a bath, and watch pornographies." Everyone is so moved by Kevin's plight. Bobby C. brings down the house with his tent-revival speech on how Kevin will be built a dream house "with 1,000 TV's!" And a bathroom in bed, "so you don't have to get up at all!" Montcrief warbles through a song for Kevin and for the cloven one, as the credits roll.

Cartoon Cold Tag (video)

Animated: A little angel and devil argue about religion on the shoulders of a little girl (Little Lulu).

Medieval scientific film reel. (left) Tom as a wizard helping to discover new scientific facts; (top middle) Paul in king hat with friend; (bottom middle) David as "Peasant Pete"; (right) Brian as pleased hunchback. Photos © Adam Timrud Photography.

Notes About Episode 301

Bob: *"I believe this is the last heavily themed show we did. By the time we got to the point of rehearsing the live part, I felt like we'd made a big mistake with too many pieces about religion. But now that I look at it, it's not so bad, in that all of the pieces are funny, and our point (that all religions are equally silly) is a good one that doesn't ever come across as harsh, just true."*

David: *"In Heaven's Chimney, 'Razzleberry Waterfall,' the word 'razzleberry' is from the animated Mr. Magoo Christmas Carol special. Everybody has songs, and the Tiny Tim character, when they sing about the meal they're going to have, he pipes up on a little voice, 'and razzleberry dressing!' And even when I was a kid I thought that was pretty queer."*

Bob: *"The Medieval Science Film is good because Troy Miller is good. Otherwise, the notion is funny and fun to riff, but it's kind of easy. It's good to have a slam on science in the middle of a show slamming religion, sort of balances things."*

David: *"The Medieval Science Film, where we shot that out in the valley somewhere, I actually, years later, saw that set being used in a porn film that I was jerking off to."*

Bob: *"The Directions scene is a weak one. It lacks logic — why doesn't the guy just pull over? The joke shifts from moment to moment. It's basically just inappropriate behavior, but without a core. Students of comedy do not watch this scene; it will not help you learn how to write. It will hurt you. But I really enjoyed the hokeyness of the fake car set in front of the big screen, with a film of road behind us. Old fashioned, simple, tasteful, courtesy of Tom Buderwitz, our set designer, who made anything we asked for happen."*

David: *"Directions — That scene didn't quite work. That was something I had done in Cross Comedy. It came from an idea I was riffing with Jonathan Groff one day. He was giving me a ride home from a gig, and he was in the middle of this intense story about trying to break up with his girlfriend of eight years, and he had to give me directions. Sometimes sketches just work better when it's two guys sitting on a chair in a little theater somewhere, instead of on TV."*

Paul: *"Bill wrote* Watch Us Have Sex, *a great scene. (Originally titled,* Oh Say, Will You See?, *but Bob hated 'funny' titles for sketches and wouldn't let us use them anymore. Tyrant.) What was weird about this sketch was that the first time we all read it, it got a lukewarm response from all of us. Then about a month or so went by, and we read it again. But now, we all found it hilarious! Bill hadn't rewritten it at all. I don't know what happened the first time, but it went in the show. Really good performances by everybody."*

Tracey Krasno (production manager): *"There was this one woman who, for whatever reason, always came to tapings of the show. She was very obviously not a comedy fan, and you could tell she had no business being there. And she's semi-uncomfortable through this whole show, but she's sticking it out. And they get to Hail Satan, and she literally had the fear of God on her face, and she leaps up out of her seat and runs out the door. She goes outside and starts babbling all this religious stuff. She just flipped. It was spectacular."*

Bob: *"Hail Satan is a great laugh. It's such a performance piece, not like most Mr. Show pieces which are too think-y. A simple idea, and all about execution. David is so damn funny as the slothful child, and there's nothing more fun than being a fat, lying Southern preacher. Now I know why those dicks do it!"*

David: *"Something I don't think people know, the character, 'Kevin' in Hail Satan, that was based on Kevin's House, this feature on the PTL Club, and it was a big scam. Supposedly, there was this little 'kid' in a wheelchair. And they would solicit money from their parishes to build this house for Kevin. But it turned out — and it didn't really take a lot of investigation — Kevin really wasn't a 9-year-old boy. He was this 30-year-old guy. He just had a disease that made him look small, and they passed him off as a little boy to take people's money."*

Bob: *"I just saw that little cartoon tag at the end, and I thought, 'Who put this on our show?' I can't tell you where it came from or why. I remember standing in the offices at Dakota watching it, thinking, 'This will be great, yeah.' But who's idea it was, what we were thinking, I have no idea. I don't know how that happened. It's the weirdest thing to me."*

David: *"I love that little cartoon tag. I was a fan of those things that popped up after the credits. We didn't have an ending for that show. I think I came up with it. I just love it — this idea of getting this cartoon and doing the voiceover to it."*

EPISODE 302 A WHITE MAN SET THEM FREE

written by:	Bob Odenkirk, David Cross, Jay Johnston, Bill Odenkirk, Dino Stamatopoulos, Mike Stoyanov, Paul F. Tompkins, Mike Upchurch
location segment director:	Troy Miller
live show director:	John Moffitt
cast:	John Ennis, Jay Johnston, Tom Kenny, Karen Kilgariff, Theresa Mulligan, Brett Paesel, Jill Talley, Paul F. Tompkins
featuring:	Laura Kightlinger, Eban Schletter, Bill Odenkirk, Billy Daydodge
special appearance by:	Jon Stewart

Mr. Show theme song and logo. Last American Indian introduces.

Viewer Hate Mail/Cracker Barrel Open (live)

Bob and David are excited to read all the new hate mail that the show receives. But, sadly, the hate mail bag is empty. To solve this, Bob grabs a guitar, and they run over to the "Cracker Barrel," a stage where the "Rainbow Gang" (a black guy and an Asian guy dressed like hayseeds) are sitting on haystacks. There is a short josh with fake banter, followed by an awkward shift into serious topics and songs — songs from an insulting, elitist, insensitive, politically incorrect perspective. To their "African American brother," they sing "*You're Welcome*" for granting them freedom. To the "red man," who didn't give up his land without a long, bloody fight, they sing "*We Forgive You*." The last song just insults midgets. "That ought to do it!" they agree and walk fast out of the studio to check….

Bob And David Go To Mail Box (video)

Their rural-road mailbox (marked "MR. S-OW"). They're certain those songs would do the trick — "We're going to be swimming in hate!" But they've only received one letter, and it appears to be a raving fan writing about how much he loves Bob and David, *especially* the songs. It's signed with X's and O's and a smiley face. The boys are let down.

Sarcasmo (video)

In the home of the "fan," Sharwood Lish (David), we see him pen the letter to Bob and David. It turns out he's not a fan at all; he's just incredibly sarcastic, even when writing letters. He can't figure out why he's received a shipment of a cereal he hates — "I wrote them an angry letter saying there's *nothing* I'd love more than *tons* of your cereal!" A crying woman (Jill) knocks at his door, in the rain, gushing with joy at receiving his letter: "You're right, we *are* perfect for each other! And I hope *you* never die in a horrible car wreck either!" Sharwood's sarcasm has gone unnoticed again, and he slams the door in her face — "Learn how to read!"

Marriage-Con And Boat Show (video)

An announcer speaks to the drenched, broken-hearted Jill: "Ladies? Has this happened too often to you? Then come to the Tri-state Globo Dome for the Marriage-Con and Boat Show '97!" The Marriage-Con promises "you *will* be married," and it features scheduled speakers like African tribal marriage arrangers and Dr. Ayatollah Khoella (David), author of *The Rules*. And, of course, plenty of boats. "You have no excuse for not being married, or owning a boat!"

Map Link (video)

A cheaply-done map showing "Dome Mile." ("Over a mile of Domes!") Tri-state Globo Dome is "right behind the Biosphere! And remember don't bother the scientists at the Biosphere!"

Biosphere (live)

Inside the Biosphere, all the scientists are looking forward to celebrating their first New Year's Eve together at midnight. Lyle (David), the nerdy animal behaviorist, is dateless and lonely. He asks out Dr. Hubley (Karen) and is rejected. Alone, he turns to the cartoon animals that live in the Biosphere tree, Mr. Peeps, Chipper, and Timothy the bison. The bird and squirrel tweet and chirp encouragement. After Lyle is rejected by all the other women in the Biosphere, he sings a mournful tune, "*Oh, the birds have other birds, and the bees have other bees, but I don't have another one of me….*" His Step-Fairy Godmother (Laura) appears and grants his wish to not be alone tonight. She waves her wand, and a herd of animated animals converge on Lyle in an aggressive sexual manner. "Whoa, this is so wrong, yet so right!"

We cut to months later and Lyle proudly holds a baby freak, who resembles him and all the other animals.

Humanimal/Ice Cream Flavors Link (live)

"Humanimal Cracker Crunch," a new flavor of Benjamin Gerard Associates Ice Cream. This is a commercial for Howard Benjamin (David) and Frank Gerard's (Bob) office-themed ice cream parlours. "We started our ice cream company with one theory: there's money to be made in ice cream." Their latest promotional flavor, in celebration of the last living American Indian — "Last Indian Doodlesnicker."

The Last Indian (video)

A documentary about 103-year-old Ben Proudfeather, the last surviving American Indian. The narrator informs us that the 63-acres of Indian-owned land left is all that remains after acts such as the "Great Deal of 1789" and "Bargain of the Century" of 1846. Government agents (Tom and David) watch over Ben like vultures — "We're not waiting for him to die, we're here to watch a man live." A Historian (Bob) reads from the chief's blurry memoirs, *"There was something about snakes, the Indians danced, I seem to recall a man in a hat, I think that movie was called* Billy Jack." Chief Proudfeather, feeling obligated to continue his genealogy, places an ad in the personals: "Single, straight last Native American Indian seeks any female for fun and procreation…no fatties." "He'll be dead soon, and that'll be that," waxes the narrator. "Believe me, man, I know; I've been there…".

Vietnam Helicopter Link (video)

The voiceover continues in a rage: "That Indian ain't got nothing on me. I fucking saw God, Jack, and I laughed in his fucking face!" A helicopter passes overhead, full-on war sound effects and typical Vietnam-movie music bring us to….

Army Scene (live)

Two American soldiers in the brush in Vietnam. They stay low, trying to maneuver their way through sniper territory, when Joe (Bob) gets shot. Dave (David) says he's not going to leave Joe behind. Joe is immediately sarcastic — "No shit What do you want, a fuckin' medal?!" Joe seems gripped by the certainty that Dave *is* planning to ditch him, ("this is about those goddamn peaches!") no matter what Dave says. Joe gets rude in his paranoia; Dave returns the insult, "I'm just saying that I'll be more careful than, y'know, *you* were." Then Dave gets shot, and Joe can only laugh in derision, "Hahaha!" Dave's had it: "You are a dying asshole. There's no way I'm gonna stay here and die next to you!" "Neither am I!" Both scream in pain as they try to move away from each other.

Night Talk With The Senate Subcommittee (video)

The previous scene was a clip from the movie *Hell in a Handbasket*, shown on the awkward late-night talk show: *Night Talk with the Senate Subcommittee*. Held in a Senate hearing room with four senators as the "hosts" and a shitty, flashy, house band riffing in the corner. The first guest is Jon Stewart. Other guests scheduled include hot college prop comic, Blueberry Head (David). "This is for when y'all want to pass gas!" (a toilet seat with a rearview mirror). Senator Tankerbell (Bob) gives it to the band's front man (Jay) by stumbling through a scathing remark about his flashy outfit — "Somewhere in this great country of ours, there's an El Camino with its seat cover missing." The popular desk-piece *The Senate Sub-babies* (senators "in character" with bonnets and rattles) makes a return appearance. After this promotional announcement we return to….

All-Star Salute To The Last Indian (live)

A star-studded network extravaganza for the Last Indian, who sits alone on a stool in the center of the stage while the idiotic brouhaha happens around him. *Entertainment Junction* hosts, Liza (Jill) and Ed (Paul), reflect on the wonderful acts who've paid homage to the Indian, including "college favorite," Blueberry Head. They introduce the next act: "Le Balloon Sportif" — two guys (Bob and David) in black hooded-unitards, orange-painted faces, and huge orange balloons, first marching about to industrial factory noises, then dancing indiscriminately to happy music, all the while trying to keep many orange balloons afloat. Credits roll over this display.

Last Indian Cold Tag (video)

After the big event, Proudfeather sits alone on stage reflecting on the evening. ("Burt Reynolds still looks good!" and "Don Rickles's barbs stung like thorns of a blackberry bush, but its fruit was sweet upon my lips.") "Ciao for now, darlings!" he concludes. He finishes his drink, crushes the paper cup, and drops it on the floor. It falls at the janitor's feet. The camera pans up, and the janitor (Jay) sheds a tear.

Notes About Episode 302

Bob: "The Last Indian *is a strong piece, well-executed. Billy Daydodge was great and a very nice man. He's an actual Indian, of course. He had a great sense of humor about it. The rest of the show I'm not such a fan of. Dino's insulting songs are solid, but the crap we hung around it about 'hate-mail' is too involved and not fun. The two scenes* Biosphere *and* Army *are strugglers from the old school of sweat. Writing is hard. The guy in* Army *is just an asshole out of the clear blue.* Biosphere *has a good premise (can't get a date in the Biosphere), but the whole talking to animals thing is just an absurdist out that is fun, but easy. Although not easy to produce. A lot of work went into trying to be funny here. As time went by, I became more enamored of good, strong, scenes that could be played out without ditching logic, or adding an absurd new element. We always had a few of them, but the third season is the weakest. The fourth is probably the strongest."*

Bob: "The Cracker Barrel. *Did you ever see the great Elia Kazan-directed movie* A Face In The Crowd? *That's what this scene is based on. Dino wrote these unconscionable melodies."*

Dino: "Originally I pitched this idea [Cracker Barrel] at *Conan O'Brien, later to SNL, and then at* Dana Carvey [the short-lived ABC sketch show] — *two folk singers, who were very conservative, trying to get by on the liberal bandwagon. At SNL, I wasn't on staff, but I was friends with Janeane Garofalo at the time, and she said I should write some sketches for the show. I brought in this scene for Michael McKean to do with the host. It was the last scene read at the readthrough (where each week, the scenes are chosen). McKean didn't know the songs. So I had to be*

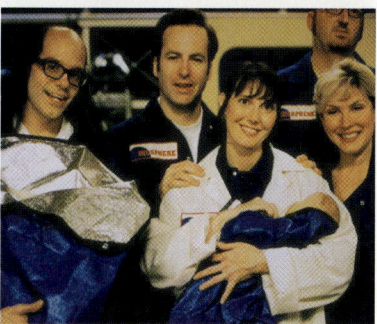

(top) Dave and Bob eagerly check for hate mail. © Adam Timrud Photography.
(bottom left) Troy Miller on set with Billy Daydodge, the "Last Indian." © Adam Timrud Photography.
(bottom right) Please don't bother the scientists in the Biosphere (David, Bob, Jill, Brian, Brett).
© Photo by Famous Mortimer.

dragged in that room to sing three songs. No one knew me. I was sweating. I bombed. No one laughed or even smiled. Janeane told me McKean was sorry. He knew the songs, he doesn't know why he didn't sing it."

David: "The extras — the Cracker Barrel guys — they did not like the show. They didn't get the show, they didn't like sitting there having to listen as we sang these songs. Especially the black guy. He didn't like me at all. I had to make eye contact with him quite a bit. He didn't seem to get it, or know what he was doing there; he didn't know why people were laughing at him, didn't know why he was sitting on a bail of hay while this white guy is singing a song about black people — 'You're welcome for your freedom.' He just didn't get it, and it was quite uncomfortable."

David: "The Biosphere sketch is something we had done in Cross Comedy, my sketch group in Boston. It clearly works better when you have a six-dollar production budget, and people are allowing you quite a bit of leeway."

Bob: "The Army Scene, about one soldier getting shot and then being a dick about it, has a strong Jay Johnston voice to it. In fact, if I were to do it again, I would have Jay play the part I played. He would have been hilarious in it, instead of me just being serviceable."

Paul: "I came up with the idea for the cold tag — the Last Indian throwing the paper cup on the ground, and the white janitor crying. I remember how excited we all got about it; we were in agreement that it seemed perfect. I wanted so badly to play the janitor, but I was already cast as the host in the previous scene. The laugh from the studio audience was most gratifying."

COMMENTS FROM BOB ABOUT SEASON 3

"Season 3 was where we really figured out how to make a great show. After the first episode, Heaven's Chimney, that had many scenes all related to one theme, religion, we realized a great show was one that didn't stick to one subject, but moved around all over the map. One of our best shows is 309, with the desperately dry humor of 'Happy Janitor' (Local World News) and Pre-Taped Call-In Show juxtaposed with broad physical stuff like Titannica and the crude beauty of Blowjob.

We also did some of our most challenging production scenes. Druggachusettes is amazing looking. Credit Troy Miller and the designers of that set for making this insanity a reality. The Return of the Curse of the Creature's Ghost was a fairly extensive piece, with wardrobe and hair and another great film look from Troy. Fad Three is amazing, The Bob Lamonta Story, Evil Genius Telethon, The Great Philouza, and even some small live scenes like Night Talk with the Senate Subcommittee showcase how strong our production crew had become. Everybody was up to speed and accomplished an amazing amount this season.

Also, in the third season, David and I, and the writers, utilized the cast well. Tom Kenny is hilarious as the cruddy college hack-comic Kedsie Matthews, everyone shines in Fuzz — The Musical, Brian Posehn rocked singing Titannica's lilting melody, Try Again.

Many fans believe the third season is our strongest. I love the third season, but for me the fourth is the strongest. Somehow, despite having mostly the same writing staff going into their third year, the fourth season had simpler, clearer comic premises and it's far more relatable. I wish the New York HBO bigwigs had recognized that. But they never paid that close attention to us, and of course that was also what allowed Mr. Show to happen in the first place."

EPISODE 303
PEANUT BUTTER, EGGS, AND RICE

written by:	David Cross, Bob Odenkirk, Jay Johnston, Bill Odenkirk, Brian Posehn, Dino Stamatopoulos, Mike Stoyanov, Paul F. Tompkins, Mike Upchurch
location segment director:	Troy Miller
live show director:	John Moffitt
cast:	David Cross, Bob Odenkirk, Jay Johnston, Brett Paesel, Brian Posehn, Jill Talley, Paul F. Tompkins
featuring:	Greg Behrendt, Danny Cebalos, Ken Daly, Bill Odenkirk, Eban Schletter, Kristy Dowler, Matt Howlick, Dave Lafa, Jimmy Orestis, Shannyn Sossamon
special appearance by:	Maynard Keenan

Very Special Episode Cold Open (video)

Bob (in shorts, glasses and T-shirt) and David (in a suit) sit onstage to make a special announcement about tonight's *Mr. Show*. It's a Very Special Episode, and they encourage everyone to "watch it with somebody that you care about." They add that you should count everyone if you're reporting to a TV-ratings service.

Mr. Show *theme song and logo. Giant Chicken (Bill) introduces.*

David Comes Out As Bald Open (live)

The whole cast (Brian, Jill, John) joins Bob and David onstage. They're all wearing "brave choice feel-good" ribbons in support of David and his very special announcement. "Get ready for the highest-rated minute of *Mr. Show* ever!" chimes Bob. David humbly launches into it: "Hi, I'm David Cross. I play the beloved character of David Cross on TV's *Mr. Show*. As you all know, the character I play is bald…" Then David drops the bomb — "I, David Cross, me, not the character, am bald." He removes a bald cap to reveal his true, natural, bald head. The cast members offer various degrees of support, and Bob and David excitedly run off to check with the Ratings Man.

Ratings Man Song/Map Link (video)

(video) A miniature *Mr. Show* van makes its way across a cartoon map, headed north. It passes various sights — Mt. Rushmore, The World's Largest Indoor Ladder (in Saskatchetario) — and ends its journey at the North Pole. A crudely drawn log cabin sets the scene.

Santa's Workshop (live)

The guys rush into the workshop of the jolly Ratings Man — and discover that he is also Santa Claus. The Ratings Man/Santa (John) tells them their ratings are up this year because "you've been very good." He explains that he checks what people watch on TV while he's checking to see who's naughty or nice, because "the Santa job pays shit." Bob innocently suggests that he quit the Santa gig. Santa laughs a little too loud at this suggestion, then urgently whispers that there is a guy with a gun in his closet who has forced him to play Santa for the last 500 years. He begs Bob and David for help. Pretending to leave, the guys hide. The Bad Guy (Jay) comes out and holds his gun on the fat man, prodding, "Now just keep being Santa, see, and never die, see, or you'll get it!" Bob and David spring out and throw a net on the bad guy, and Santa escapes. The bad guy reprimands them: "You idiots, have you any idea what you've done?!" A storybook-style tale tells of the sorrow that follows because there was no Christmas. "It 'twas a terrible, terrible winter…" This becomes….

Tatiana (HERMAPHRODITE WEATHERGIRL) Link (video)

A local weather report given by an accuweather-hermaphrodite, Tatiana (David in drag). "Mother Nature is full of surprises," he/she adds. Which becomes the lead line to….

Cock Ring Warehouse (video)

"…this year the winter storms have left us overstocked and up to our necks in cock rings." In an ad for "Cock Ring Warehouse," a bored announcer touts the largest selection of new and used cock rings, including "Old Ironsides" and "Pheasant Under Glass." "Any Cock'll doo!" crows the warehouse mascot, a man in a sad, worn-out chicken outfit. "Dust off your old cock rings," and they will pass them on to needy families. The Cock Ring Chicken is shown going door-to-door making a collection.

Marriage Announcement (live)

Pete (Bob) donates a few cock rings to the cause and returns to his living room where his best friends (David, John, Jay, Paul) are gathered to hear his big announcement — "Kate and I are getting married." His friends offer exclamations of surprise, (No fucking way!). Then, in an inexplicable instant, their hubbub becomes a violent melee, and they start beating the shit out of their buddy. David comes to his senses and yells at everyone to stop. Pete is astounded. At the next mention of it, the guys again beat the crap out of him. Pete orders them to leave, but they ask Pete to announce it again to "see if we react the same way." He reluctantly does, and they just barely restrain themselves. They toast with champagne to celebrate their self-control, and Pete tosses another "Kate and I are getting married." Just before they jump him, the cops (Greg & Brian) arrive, responding to a call on domestic disturbance.

Fuzz: The Musical (live/video)

(live) The cops enter the apartment, followed by a cameraman, British Terry Twillstein (Bob), who is taping their arrest for the reality-TV show *Fuzz*. Terry, who made Ronnie Dobbs a household name, explains that he intends to make a musical out of this TV show, and that he will use the "actual cops and actual criminals for actuality's sake."

(film) In a recording studio, Terry greets the officers (Ken & John), followed by a pregnant, trailer-trashy Tammy Dobbs (Jill), and finally Ronnie Dobbs (David), the most arrested man on *Fuzz*. Ronnie and Tammy have a nasty exchange — "Who've you been fuckin'? Travis?" But Terry jumps in, "Save this tension, we're going to use it to *sing!*"

First, in the sound booth, the Cops record their theme, "Looking for Trouble"

> We wear the hat, we wear the gun, we wear the shield, but not for fun.
> We're looking for trouble!
> Looking and driving and looking for trouble.
> Looking and driving and looking for trouble.

Tammy then sings; "911 (Wife's Theme)", a song that captures "the essence of abuse in a jolly jingle":

> Hello, 911, it's me again! Ronnie is beating me again!
> I got you on speed dial, wish you'd call me once in awhile.
> 911, it's me again.

Ronnie does a star turn for, "How High The Mountain (Ronnie's Theme)":

> Cop: "Come on, sir, you're obviously intoxicated."
> Ronnie: "You're obviously intoxicated!"
> Cop: "Okay, that's it, let's go."
> Ronnie: "You, that's it, let's go!"
> Both Cops: "You're under arrest!"
> Ronnie: "You're under arrest! Naaaaaaahh!"
> I thought that my home was my castle, with no one scrutinizing me.
> No pigs, no lyin' bitch, no hassle. Y'all are brutalizing me.
> Can't a man not drink his beer in silence?
> Can't a man not crudely lie and scream?
> Can't a man not control his bitch with violence?
> Y'all are brutalizing me.
> Y'all are brutalizing meeeeeee!

Terry is moved by this: "That one'll do." "Well, what the hell," Ronnie smiles, "let's go have us a champagne jam!"
In Terry's jaunty melody, *I Am A Camera*, he portrays "the silent observer":

> I am a camera, a camera am I…

Ronnie is getting frustrated listening to Terry sing. Ronnie barges into the recording booth, irate — "You're shittin' in my mouth and callin' it a sundae!" The rest of the group clears out of the studio and stands by as the sounds of domestic abuse filter out of the room. Other cops (Jay & Paul), who are patrolling the neighborhood (and being taped for *Fuzz*), get the call to go to the studio. When they arrive, they bust in to find Terry crying, with a cut on his forehead, and Ronnie swinging a cymbal stand. Terry covers for Ronnie like an abused wife. "Oh, this? I just fell down." He further rationalizes….

Terry Gets An Award/Fly By Awards Link (video)

"…It's because he loved me so much that he'd gotten violent." Terry's giving an acceptance speech for the Tony award he won for *Fuzz: The Musical*. The image of the Tony is followed by a slew of other awards ending with "The Dewey."

The Dewey Awards (live)

The Dewey is an award given to actors who have made the brave choice of portraying characters who are mentally challenged. It's named after Cyrus Dewey, a silent film actor, who did just that in every damn film he ever made. The host (Paul) announces the nominees, whom we see alongside their "special" characters from cornily-titled films, such as *A Bridge Too Long* and *The Mountain Too High*. Filmmaker/star of *Why Me? The Bob Lamonta Story* (David), walks onstage in a jogging suit, crosses to a wheelchair, and sits in it. He explains his film is his life story — the hardships he endured being raised by parents who were mentally disabled.

Bob Lamonta (film)

Arcadia, Indiana, 1976. In the school cafeteria a young Bob Lamonta (David) suffers the teasing of his classmates about his crazy brown-bag sandwich. "I think this one is, uh, peanut butter, eggs…and dice." His thermos is filled with spoons. All the kids laugh. "Dammit! I hate my parents!" Embarrassed, he runs out of the cafeteria, and runs and runs. This is young Bob Lamonta's whole life — running away from school to avoid embarrassment, and running back to school to prevent more embarrassment from his unpredictable parents. Meanwhile, Bob's parents are leaving his younger brother at home wearing winter clothes and a pot on his head, with a lunch of beer and frozen peas. Bob is expelled from school, and all his parents can do is jump around and shout, "I want to be expelled, too!" But Bob's self-pity disappears when the spirit of his father rises out of his body to explain to his sorrowful son how proud he and his wife are of him. He adds, "Whenever I say, 'My shoes hurt,' imagine I'm saying, 'I love you.'" Bob Lamonta uses his running experience to become a three-time Olympic Gold medalist. His parents make their way to him as he stands on the winners' podium, celebrating and shouting, "My shoes hurt!" Bob understands the true meaning of this now and responds "My shoes hurt, too, Dad. My shoes hurt, too." The film is dedicated "IN MEMORY OF BOB LAMONTA 1963-1987."

Handing Out Awards Close (live)

Back onstage Bob Lamonta swears this was a true story…except for a few dramatic choices. He's still alive, his parents weren't retarded, and he never ran in the Olympics. The awards show host (Paul) opens the envelope that has all of the nominees' names in it. "It's open! Come on up here and get your awards. You're all winners!" A mob of "brave" actors rush the stage and grab their Deweys as the credits roll.

Notes About Episode 303

Bob: "This episode has some very thin premises…the Ratings Man, but some super-powerful scenes, too. Again, with David doing the very special episode opening, and the closing piece being Bob Lamonta, and 'very special acting' roles, this is bookended by a theme. Not a good idea. I'm amazed at how many ideas, and how much tough production went into this episode. When people want to know why we don't do more Mr. Show, I would say watch this episode. The time and effort it takes to produce just the film The Bob Lamonta Story is tremendous for any crew. This show has two immense pieces like it in one episode. I'm sweating just thinking about it. There's a reason most TV shows feature the same characters doing the same things in the same places every week. It's not just because TV is about familiarity and soothing people's eyeballs. It's because this kind of shit is hard."

John: *"For Ratings Man, onstage I had the Santa wig with those guys on my lap. When David jumped into my lap, his arm or something hit the needles in my wig, and it went into my head, about 1/8 inch, the knitting needle. I literally could not think, I just went up on my line for one second, because I had this needle in my head. So I just leaned back, pulled the needle out of my scalp — and I could feel the blood trickle — and then went on with the scene. It was just one of those weird things. We were on live, with cameras, this was in front of an audience. It was the first show of the night, so we still had another show to get it right."*

Bill: *"It was a really hard episode. And we didn't know what to do with the David Comes Out As Bald open into Cock Ring Warehouse. We were working so late. We just had to bring in everybody to say we don't know how to work this transition. We don't know what to do for it. And then, slowly, we figured they knew they were going to get the ratings (Ellen-episode kind of thing), but that was kind of boring. We didn't want them to just get a sheet of paper. And then we thought they should take a trip to get the ratings. It was Dino's idea that Santa Claus is the Ratings Man, he also keeps track of ratings for television. And that idea I just fell in love with. One of my favorite all-time opens of any show is that. It ended up with this whole other scene in Santa's Workshop, and Bob and David acting like excited children."*

Bill: *"I remember a long, long argument about Santa Claus and this guy who had kept him hostage — what was the sequence of events, how could he do that. People legitimately arguing about Santa Claus and this guy — whom we just conjured up — forcing him to play Santa Claus. And people arguing about this endlessly. Finally, I think it started to dawn on people — that none of this matters! It's a funny idea. It works, let's just write the scene. It's not like the audience got diverted from the scene. They thought it was an important thing to elucidate, this relationship with Santa and the guy with a gun in the closet. It was torture. It was late, we were hungry and tired. But at the same time, I loved that piece. I thought it was so funny."*

Dino: *"These were crazy ideas not based on reality. We couldn't fit it into the realm of the world. They are fantasy characters and we try to make it have sense."*

Bob: *"We invited the NY Times guy, who was writing a big article about us, to sit in on a writing session that week. And the day he came, we had a full-day discussion of whether Santa Claus was a myth or a legend, and if he was real, and if a guy had a gun on him, would he continue being Santa Claus? All day, we couldn't get out

Ronnie Dobbs: "Can't a man not drink his beer in silence?"

Clockwise from lower right: Marriage announcement incites violence, as well it should (© Adam Timrud Photography); Jill Talley and Tammy Dobbs both expecting; The real Cyrus Dewey (© photo by Famous Mortimer); Bob Lamonta (David) receives a touching message from his not-normal Dad.

of it. It was just a convoluted logic of a scene argument. Everyone was getting really mad at each other."

Jay: "Everybody was switching sides the whole day. 'Okay, you've convinced me of that, now there's four people against it.'"

Bob: "Let's talk about something else — look, Santa Claus wouldn't...."

David: "It's so absurd to be saying, as adults, 'Look, Santa Claus wouldn't act that way...' And that was the reporter's day of Mr. Show writing."

Bob: "Luckily, his article was so bad, it had nothing to do with anything."

Bob: "The Ratings Man shit is just that — shit. And it took forever to argue the logic of 'Santa having a gun trained on him, would that work?' etc.... An insane argument that went on for two days."

David: "The whole thing had this Möbius strip, circular logic to it where we ended up contradicting ourselves. It was really stupid and not productive. It was one of those things where you look back, and you go, 'God, I wish I had those six hours back.'"

David: "As Tatiana, I don't look so much like a hermaphrodite as I do a cross-dresser. Also, that I look like my little sister, which is really disturbing. When I see that, I'm like, 'Jesus Christ, that's Julie.' It's gross."

Bob: "Cock Ring Warehouse is Bill's. Three miles of cock rings. That's a lot, depending on how they are stacked."

David: "I had a couple sketch ideas that I dreamed (the other was Date with the Queen, #407). I was in a dream state, this was right after Bob had told me he was getting married. And then I had a dream, I dreamed it was a sketch, about a guy, I think it was Bob playing this guy who tells his friends he just got engaged, and I don't know why but their reaction was to beat him up."

Paul: "In Ronnie Dobbs, I played a criminal running from the cops, which would have been part of the opening montage of the fictitious Fuzz show. I was chased around the parking lot by Bill Odenkirk and Todd Glass, a comedian from my hometown of Philadelphia. Todd's one of these guys who's really into cops. He goes on ride-alongs and all that. 'Todd showed up at the set with his own cop uniform!' Right before we go, Todd says to me, with this really serious face "I'm really gonna try to catch you" I laughed a little and said, "Well, I'm really gonna try to run away." So Troy calls "Action!" and I start running as fast as I can and snaking away until finally Todd gets a hold of my shirt. I try to get away, and the shirt rips off my back. I elude them once or twice more, and then Todd gets a hold of my wrist and swings me around. My other wrist hits the walkie-talkie on Bill's belt — hits it really hard — and then Todd throws me into a pile of garbage that's sitting there in the lot. Not prop garbage, but Hefty bags of real garbage. As I hit the bags, this huge cloud of white dust flies up, which I am now convinced was asbestos. Todd still has one of my wrists and my other arm is pinned under me. Todd is cuffing my one wrist, tightly, and yelling at me to give him my other hand. Finally, I shout weakly through the garbage bag my face is resting on "I'm lyin' on it" Cut. When I get up, my shirt is in tatters, and I have little cuts and bruises all over my torso. I don't think Todd ever apologized. Asshole."

Paul: "Bob Lamonta is one of my favorite sketches. I know that some people may find it offensive, and that eventually it will be unthinkable to even laugh at it, but, man, for some reason that retard stuff always makes me laugh. I'm terribly sorry. One of the things I liked the most was the little kid with the pot on his head who gives that really strange line reading of, 'They gave me some beer and some frozen peas.' His voice is really gravelly, and he sounds like Nick Nolte or something."

Bob: *"It's hard to write a comic piece about mentally handicapped adults, but I think we did it. We made it very clear that it was about a genuine phenomenon. I believe something like the last seven of nine Oscars for best actor went to people who portrayed mentally slow, handicapped or sickly characters. It's a good point — the easy way to garner respect is to choose subject matter which doesn't have to earn sympathy/value, it's just endowed with it."*

David: *"John Ennis' performance, as the principal in Bob Lamonta, it was so subtle and one of the things that makes John so great — he treated the retarded parents as adults and as children at the same time. I don't think many other comic actors would have had gotten that balance just right. He just plays it so perfectly. You couldn't ask for it to be better."*

Paul: *"I handed out the awards at the end of the show, and the extra playing the trophy girl at the end thought she'd be 'funny', when we taped the second show, and would start to hand them to me and then pull them back. Hilarious."*

Cyrus Dewey Awards

Nominees / Winners

"The Crack'd Mirror"
"Goin' Crackers"
"A Bridge Too Long"
"The Mountain Too High"
"Why Me? – The Bob Lamonta Story"

Cyrus Dewey Awards

Honorable Mentions / Winners

"A Clown in my Head"
"The Littlest Hero"
"Moe's Challenge"
"A Teaspoonful of Miracles"
"Don't Chew the Pennies"
"Joey's Story"
"Tommy's Story"
"God Dropped Me"
"The Boy from the Planet Special"

EPISODE 304 OH, YOU MEN

written by:	Bob Odenkirk, David Cross, Jay Johnston, Bill Odenkirk, Brian Posehn, Dino Stamatopoulos, Mike Stoyanov, Paul F. Tompkins, Mike Upchurch
location segment director:	Troy Miller
live show director:	John Moffitt
cast:	David Cross, Bob Odenkirk, John Ennis, Jay Johnston, Tom Kenny, Karen Kilgariff, Brett Paesel, Brian Posehn, Jill Talley, Paul F. Tompkins
featuring:	Ashlie Chan, Stacie Chan, Laura Milligan, Bill Odenkirk, Eban Schletter, Jonahtan Fowler, Sam Sarpong, Shannyn Sossamon, Stanley Ullman
special appearance by:	Sean Michael Howard

Lie Detector sketch freeze-framed ending that concludes the official "Lost Episode." © Adam Timrud Photography.

Mr. Show *theme song and logo. Cutie sisters Stacie and Ashlie introduce.*

Banana/Mayor Of Television Open (live)

Bob spies a banana that seems to have been left accidentally on the stage floor. The guys goof with it, laughing, "Who wants a banana?!" Next, the Mayor of TV (John) comes out and cuts the ribbon to ceremonialize their official "Lost Episode." After it has been taped, the tape will be given to a uniformed official (Brian) who will "escort and then lose" it, so that the people of the future can find it and remember a time when audiences were "brought to the verge of laughter." Bob and David then mention that if you don't want to wait until the future to enjoy them, you can contact their agent, Candy Addams, at "Entertainment 4 Every 1."

Entertainment 4 Every 1 (video)

Candy Addams (Jill), a middle-aged, small-time agent, offers Bob and David's services for any gig, "but be warned — they are satirical!" She then gives us a glimpse of the other acts she represents (who *don't* use "the 'F-word'"), including Choo-Choo The Hurkey-Jerky Dancer (Jay), "Champion" The Drinker (Paul), and ventriloquist Wally P. Doyle (Tom) and Pedro.

Ventriloquists (video)

News documentary: Gruesome footage of the bloody scene where Wally P. Doyle and his piney-pal were both were gunned down at a children's birthday party in New York. It's part of an ongoing feud between ventriloquists on opposite coasts, an echo of the feud between rap artists at the time. A discussion-panel talk show, *Night Watch,* brings face-to-face the ventriloquists, rappers and dummies from the two coasts. The rappers want nothing to do with the variety acts. ("Look, I don't need you defending me, you Howdy Doody-looking Motherfucker!") A peace summit is held; the dummies meet behind closed doors to hash things out. By Day 36, no progress has been made.

People Watching TV/TV Guide Link (video)

The public turns to TV for entertainment to substitute for the void of ventriloquism. A young couple (Jill & Bob) read TV Guide to plan for the night.

The Hanged Man (live)

The young couple's doorbell rings, and Mark (Bob) freaks out when he spies who is at the door. He immediately confesses to his wife, Gina (Jill), that "before I met you, I committed a murder!" He quickly explains that he hanged a man for stealing his newspapers, but somehow he got down. He expects his wife to support him in trying to smooth everything over with this stranger from his past. In walks Mickey (David), with a severe rope burn on his neck. He includes the words "murder" or "newspaper" with every utterance. Mickey works Mark's guilt, manipulating him like crazy, until Gina explodes. She orders him out of their house. Scorned, Mickey leaves, threatening to report the attempted hanging to the police, when a newspaper falls out of his sleeve. In a flash of fury, Mark and Gina finish off the job, strangling Mickey. Then, they pick up the evidence, only to realize the stolen paper is not theirs. Instead, it belongs to Mickey's grandmother, who may have given it to him, but they prefer to believe he stole it.

DeLongpre Dannon Show (live)

"Does your husband keep killing the same man over and over again? Then call to be a guest on the *DeLongpre Dannon Show!*" Today's guests confront deadbeat dads-to-be. Chris (Bob) is a guy who "thinks he's a pregnant teen whose 'boyfriend' wants him to have an abortion, but 'boyfriend' (Shawn) is just a guy he works with at tire store." Chris rants at Todd, "You don't have to love this baby, but it's gonna love you!" They get advice from a convenience-mart worker, who thinks he's a Psychiatric Expert (David), who also thinks that he is an irate audience member. (Fake girl: "You oughtta be able to have your imaginary baby.") A brief, typical interchange ends in swaggering finger-snapping, and we cut to the show's sponsor....

Sticky Pads (video)

"Ol' Fisherman's Sticky Pads." A medical supplies commercial targeting kids who are doctors or buyers for large hospitals. Multi-ethnic cartoon kids pop in and sing, *"They're gooey, they're sticky, doctors use 'em when you're sicky!"* "They got two uses!" announce adorable, giggling Asian twins. Now, also for lie detectors.

Lie Detector (live)

A man (Bob) is about to undergo a lie detector test administered by Paul and David while associates Brian and Jay listen in. Bob is nervous at first, as Paul asks questions about drug use and stealing from employers. Bob truthfully answers yes to every question, and the guys can't help but be impressed with the level of his escapades. He's had an incredible, wild life, doing heroin and crack, stealing from his job at NASA (just some pens and some space plans). The guys are all thrilled and impressed and get into the questioning, firing off ridiculously specific questions about derailing trains with his penis, skinny dipping with someone named "Michelle Goodwyn" (David's 7th-grade crush), etc. Bob always answers yes and, according to the machine, he's never lying. Finally, Paul congratulates him on passing the test and welcomes him aboard at Shoe Court Shoe Store. "Well, I love shoes!" states Bob, setting off the lie detector. All the actors mug shamelessly, and we freeze-frame.

Television TV Link (video)

Fake credits speed over the water-colored frozen frame with *SNL*-type closing music. "You've been watching the 'Lost Episode' of *Mr. Show*. Stayed tuned for *Time Caplet*." On the vintage rerun channel, Tee-Vee TV.

Time Caplet (live)

Early-70's children's show producers, Sam (Bob) and Criminy Craffft (David), come out of the time caplet to introduce their lost episode. They are two ex-hippies who made a kids TV program in the 70's, filled with obvious drug references that got them canceled. ("Hey man, we were holding a mirror up to society.")

Druggachusettes (film)

The lost episode of *Druggachusettes* opens with warning deeming it a "children's program...not suitable for children." A bright and happy Saturday morning show where Billy, a teen with pageboy haircut and Davy Jones' accent (David), skips dreamily down a hill, gets hit in the head by a talking pot pipe ("Gurgles," voiced by Jay), and magically enters the "Altered State of Druggachusettes." In this episode, his strangely paranoid puppet friends and Jonesy (Bob) are too afraid to order a pizza over the telephone. They take the joint-shaped "canni-bus" to use the phone at Professor Ellis D. Traills' (Tom) house. The professor freaks out and rips off his suffocating clothes. A hairy and tie-dyed man (John) coolly escorts him to the bad-trip tent, then turns to camera and gives the episode's moral: "Only take what you can handle, and always know your dealer." Spinning spiral cut to everyone enjoying pizza, which Mayor O.D. McCrack of Druggachusettes (Paul) declares as "Awesome!"

Lose The Lost Episode Close (live)

Onstage, Bob and David press a button and eject the now completed 'Lost Episode' tape of *Mr. Show*. Each cast member says an emotional farewell to it. ("Remember when there was only one set of footprints? That's when I was carrying you!" sobs Paul.) Bob and David tell the tape that they hope it will be better appreciated by the people of the future—"These people were assholes." Credits roll as they give the tape to the uniformed official (Brian), and instruct him to "lose it." A few steps outside the studio door, the official looks around, then throws the tape high in the air.

EPISODE 304

The Altered States of "Druggachusettes." (Clockwise from top left) David as Billy with talking pal "Gurgles"; Dino and production assistant Pacha operating the Pot Brownies; Jonesy whispering paranoia to ecto-brained Professor Ellis D. Traills (Tom); previous page: Bob as Jonesy. photos © Adam Timrud Photography.

Monkey/Outer Space Cold Tag (video)

The chucked tape is recovered in the future by the Earth-probe of super-advanced apes in their space vehicle. The space monkey-men (Bob and David) put the artifact in their VCR. They watch as Bob and David come out on stage, and go nuts when Bob dangles the banana, "Who wants a banana?!" The End?

Notes About Episode 304

David: "Jay doing 'Choo Choo The Hurkey Jerky Dancer' — there's only one thing funnier than watching Jay in that short clip, and that's watching the uncut tape footage of Jay doing that for a full minute. It's really surreal. It's so weird and stupid and dumb. I wish we could play it all."

Paul: "Oh, You Men, the title of #304, was one of the few touches of mine left in Ventriloquists. That sketch went through many, many rewrites. Originally, it was about East and West Coast lounge singers having a war, but that was deemed too "possible," so it became ventriloquists. The names of the characters are still mine, and they were almost all people I knew in Philadelphia. Vince Dantona was a real ventriloquist, changed to "Vince Daytona." In our sketch, his dummy's name was "Fitzpatrick," as in "Vince Daytona and his buddy Fitzpatrick," a reference to my good friend, Buddy Fitzpatrick. That's how clever I am. My friend Frank Barnett's name is in there, too. I also came up with the names of the rappers, Killer B. Killed and Professor Murder. Bob thought "Professor Murder" was too cartoony, but I loved it. And I noticed it turned up in the following season, so I guess it wasn't so awful, eh, Bob? I also loved Karen Kilgariff's performance in this as the drunken Gloria Doyle, wife of Wally P. Doyle (an all-purpose name I've used many times). It was exactly as I pictured it."

Paul: "I wrote The Hanged Man sketch, which consisted of a slightly amusing idea and little else. It got less and less funny to me the more we read it and rehearsed it, and, when I see it now, I'm amazed it's on the show. One thing about it — Bob reading the TV Guide at the top of the scene. You see, the previous year, we taped on the same stage as America's Funniest Home Videos and found a list of the five finalists of a random episode, one of them being 'Baby Loves Head Rub.' This phrase continued to haunt me. And I was obsessed with the fact that TV Guide would actually give you a description of what was on AFHV. The blurbs would always be really strange and kind of surreal, and I'd just walk around saying them out loud: 'A man taunts goat. A bird thinks it's a dog. A dog wears a toupee....'"

Paul: "The first appearance of the two little Korean girls, Ashlie and Stacie Chan — or 'Stashley' — the two most adorable girls in the world. They were so lovable and smart and well-behaved and sweet that I wanted to smash them with a hammer and grind them into a powder and mix them with water and drink them. Some of the staff think that Sticky Pads was a weak link, but not me. There've been worse."

Bob: "Sticky Pads, which is one of the most absurd, effort-full links we ever sweated out, is somehow worth it."

David: "Lie Detector was one of those sketches I wasn't really that crazy about, and everybody else was. But it turned out to be really good. Brian fucked up while we were taping the show, and, if you look, you can see me laughing. Brian said it out of order, 'what about crack?' He was supposed to ask about heroin first. Bob just played it off perfectly. And you can see me break a little bit and laugh. Which is not rare for me."

Tracey Krasno (production manager): "There was a big question as to whether or not to do the Time Caplet scene. HBO was afraid that Sid and Marty Krofft might sue. But we decided it was worth the chance, it was so funny. Sid and Marty called after the show — they loved it. They wanted copies."

Bob: "In fact, what we should have been warned is that they're nuts. And that they would waste our time with phone calls. He called me again in the fourth season, and he wanted me to do a 'Sigmund the Sea Monster' movie, or something. And then I told him: 'I gotta be honest with you, I don't really know your stuff very well.' I watched H.R. Pufnstuf, but Land of the Lost (Inside the Actor, # 409) — I didn't even help with that, because I never saw that show. I just told him I couldn't make that movie, because I don't know that stuff or care about it. I think he was hurt."

Dino: "Viewers sometimes assume the weirder sketches were written on drugs. Druggachusettes — of course, by it's very nature — looks druggy. While a couple were, this sketch was not. I had wanted to do a Sid and Marty Krofft bit on Letterman where a

(above) Jay Hurkey-Jerkying. Available for parties.
(below) "I ain't no 'Professor Pickles'!" Bringing the feuding coasts face to face in Ventriloquists.

child enters a strange, trippy land and meets whimsical versions of Late Show's characters. When I brought it up to Jay at Mr. Show, I was looking for another angle to parody the strange, psychedelic drugged-out world of Sid and Marty's. Then, he had the beautifully simple idea of really being really blatant about the drugs, even talking about them. I thought of the name Druggachusettes and we wrote it from there."

David: "I love that Paul decided to do his one line as mayor of Drugachusettes as James Mason. Did anyone catch that? No? Then fuck you."

Bob: "I have to comment on the last reaction of the show, where the little business with the banana is reincorporated and has meaning. Up to that point that was the biggest reaction I've ever heard from an audience anywhere. It was a sudden, crashing wave of appreciative group-awareness. It was like someone tickled them, put ice down their back, and kicked them all in the balls at the same time."

EPISODE 305
FLAT-TOP TONY AND THE PURPLE CANOES

written by: Bob Odenkirk, David Cross, Jay Johnston, Bill Odenkirk, Dino Stamatopoulos, Mike Stoyanov, Paul F. Tompkins, Mike Upchurch

location segment director: Troy Miller

live show director: John Moffitt

cast: Bob Odenkirk, David Cross, John Ennis, Jay Johnston, Karen Kilgariff, Tom Kenny, Brett Paesel, Jill Talley, Paul F. Tompkins

featuring: Kevin Seccia, Sarah Silverman, Janette Andrade, Kristy Dowler, Kennedy Kabasares, Tina New, Kimberly Quigley, Shannyn Sossamon, Robin Van Sharner

Mr. Show Morning Graphic Cold Open (video)

A cheery *Mr. Show* logo. "Today's *Mr. Show* was filmed in the middle of the day when all the men were at work." Bright, upbeat version of theme song and logo. A "Miss Thing" introduces: "Good morning ladies! It's time for Bob and David!"

Womyn's Solidarity Collective Open (live)

Bob and David sit at a table and sip from coffee mugs as though hosts of a daytime talk show. The Womyn's Solidarity Collective is in the audience. Today's show's condescending topics, including a visit from "Dr. Goodsex" ("He's gonna show you how to make your hubby climax faster so he can get on with his busy day."), have the Womyn hissing and spitting. When the guys take their shirts off and dance, the Womyn run them off the stage in an angry mob. Bob and David are oblivious to the anger ("they want to touch the merchandise!"), and run out of the studio laughing…

Black & White Film (HARD DAY'S NIGHT) (B&W film)

In B&W, to a Beatles-esque tune ("*Yeah, Yeah, Yeah!*"), an amused Bob and David run for their lives outside the studio as a gang of pissed off Womyn are out for chauvinistic blood. The boys are having a blast, wearing creative disguises (gay leathers leaning outside "Futtbuckers" bar) and finding crazy hiding places (in a "porn booth"), as the mad and frustrated Womyn run by, chasing, chasing. Bob and David have a gas 'levitating' around an open park, when Bob is shot down by a brick hurled at his head. The mob descends upon injured Bob, and David floats away, up the hill. A music video super appears: "*Got a Good Thing Going*" by the Beetletown Players.

VTV (SMOOSH, NORMA JEAN MONSTER) (live/video)

(live) "You're watching *Video Round-up* on VTV." "Just like you're told to," say Clive (Bob) and Ian (David) Shropshire — the boys from Smoosh, British pop sensations. VJ Alan (John) is trying to get them to talk about their new album, *Space-age Supersuit*, or *anything*. They are not much of an interview, bored with everything and thick with attitude.

(video) Promo break: Spend Spring Break on the moon with Smoosh! One lucky viewer will be featured in the new Smoosh video and then "shot in the back of the head, execution style! Enter Today!"

(live) VJ Alan struggles — Ian only answers questions with a disinterested "Dunno," and Clive just makes sarcastic remarks. Widen to reveal there is a therapist (Jill) in the interview session. She coaches VJ Alan on how to express his frustration in communication with the Shropshire boys. Their time is up, and Ian seems optimistic ("Hey, Alan, we're gonna make this happen").

Break Thru Weekend (video)

Next up on VTV is VJ Chrysalis (Sarah) with guests maudlin goth band Norma Jean Monster — Norma Jean (David) and Adolph Hepburn (Bob). The therapist (Jill) prompts them to tell about the "Break Thru Weekend" they all spent together working out their problems. All three giddily narrate the slides taken of them at the camp with Dave, their "trust guide" (Jay), doing organized trust-building exercises, laughing a lot, and putting on a show with straw hats and canes at the "spirit quest bonfire." "I don't know who those guys are," Norma Jean says of the young adults hiking in the last slide….

Young People & Companions (live/video)

Local news anchor (Bob) with a breaking story about "two young people and their companions," who are missing after a hike in the Angeles National Forest. Reporters speak to the fiancée (Karen) of one of the young people, and the parents of one of the companions (Brett and Jay). ("We're praying for our boy…We also pray for the two young people…and, of course, the other companion.") Community reaction is split — some residents feel the companions are responsible, while others see the problem being with "the young people of today." Reporter Dane Atkinson (David) is on the scene and confirms the recovery of two of the hikers: one young person and one companion.

Newscast Bloopers Link (video)

Some bloopers from the night's newscast. The reporters and the grieving relatives "flub" their "lines" and crack up when they lose composure.

From another news segment, an animal specialist (Bob) has an embarrassing moment with a rare "feathered" cat ("It's totally natural"). And, finally, a snippy reply from a local businessman (David) "the only 'young people' I'm concerned with are the ones that wear Wee Time Toddler Wear. Capiche?"

Fashion Forecast (live)

The curt businessman is Alexis (David). Inside the Wee Time conference room, he and his cronies, Stephan (Paul) and Toddy (Tom), pitch their design concepts for kiddie wear to the Ohio buyer (John). All their ideas are inspired by their dark apocalyptic visions the night before ("I see genitals bleeding of their own accord. The sea will boil…." "Little navy outfits! Classic! Nautical theme!"). The buyer walks. Suddenly, Nostradamus (Bob) appears in a cloud of smoke. He is enraged that the men have squandered the vision of the future he has given them. He chose them to see the future, because they "are all cut from the same cloth." Toddy protests he's not gay, and Nostrodamus is confused — "I can usually tell." He reads from the personal ad that caught his attention, and Alexis fesses up. Nostradamus whispers a private prediction.

Fashion Documentary (video)

An *Unzipped*-styled documentary follows fashion guru Alexis and his "500-year-old ever-present pal," Nostradamus. The special pair good-naturedly bicker with each other. Nostradamus is obsessed with The Beast and impending doom ("The Apocalypse is here; it's on its way"), while Alexis is a self-absorbed flibbertigibbet ("Extra cheese, if you please! I'm on my knees!"). Each segment is titled. In *Welcome to the Bunker*, we see Alexis at his hectic design studio. He bleeds his future-seeing pal for fashion trends, then kicks him out for being a doomsday downer. *Victory in Paris: 1997* catches Alexis celebrating with his team after a successful show, while a pouty Nostradamus sulks in the background. *These Modern Socks* finds Nostradamus undressing a drunk Alexis for bed, while weeping at the thought of "losing him in the Great New York Earthquake of 2003." A narrator epilogues that the "best possible bosom buddies" both perished in the great New York quake of 2003.

Constant Chum High Link (video)

In honor of their accomplishments, Nostradamus and His Constant Chum High School was built, teaching children about the can-do spirit.

Indomitable Spirit (live)

Live at a NHCCHS assembly, Principlal Rudolph (Jill) orders students to be tolerant of their "special" musical guests, Indomitable Spirit. "They're a little different from you and me…you have to try a little harder not to let them make you uncomfortable." I.S. (David, John, Jay, Sarah) is an "inspirational" band, in that the members are all severely handicapped (The drummer and guitarist have no arms, the flautist is just a head, and Fran is a woman). *"You can do anything, just look us — playing rock'n'roll, and riding the small buuus!"* At the end of their song, they reveal that they're all perfectly normal, physically. They just wanted to send a message of hope. Ex-bandmate, Tommy (Bob), crashes their show. Tommy was fired, he says, because he lost his arm. Terry, the leader (David), insists it was because he was a terrible drummer, who just happened to lose his arm. They argue in a circle, which doesn't end even when an emergency apocalypse alarm sounds.

Apocalypse Drill (video)

Credits roll as Principal Rudolph (Jill) files the students out of the building to kneel and place their textbooks over their heads. ("Now your genitals will bleed of their own accord…so be prepared for that. And I don't want to find anyone chewing gum.") Terry (David) and Tommy (Bob) argue until the fire storm consumes them all.

Smoosh On Moon Cold Tag (video)

From the vantage point of the moon, Ian and Clive Shropshire (David and Bob), are unimpressed as they watch the Earth explode. "Stupid consumers. Everybody blowing up together, like good little sheep."

Notes About Episode 305

David: *"When I took my shirt off in the opening — that was after I got horrifically dumped by Mary Lynn, and it was devastating, and I lost all that weight. You can see how disturbingly Holocaust-camp I looked. That's really unappealing. It's just skin and bones. Man, I was skinny."*

Dino: *"The premise of this [Black & White Film] is one of my favorite Bob ideas. 'Futtbuckers' is one of my favorite Brian Posehn jokes. But I don't think I ever got dime one from ASCAP for writing the words to this song. I wrote ALL OF THEM! Of course, Eban had the easy job of finding a melody for them."*

Bob: *"Smoosh is based on Oasis, but also on Radiohead and a thousand other bands that get interviewed on MTV and act like complete jerks, ignoring the interviewer, muttering reluctant non-answers to perfectly decent questions. The only rock star entitled to act that way is John Lydon, the original. Everybody else should get with the program."*

Dino: *"Brent Forrester and I were camping in Malibu Canyon and dropped some acid. We started wandering around and got a little lost. We started musing about what the newspaper blurbs would say the next day about the two lost campers. Brent assumed that we would be referred to as 'two young people lost in Malibu,' but I was feeling pretty out of shape and not that young. I suggested 'one young person and his companion,' preferring to be referred to with a more ambiguous description. Giggling in acidy madness, we found these terms curious and played with them all night. A few years later, I remembered the scenario and pitched it to* *(clockwise from bottom right): Smoosh (© Photo by Famous Mortimer); Young people and their companions on a hike (© Photo by Famous Mortimer); Brian reasons with a fatigued Alexis (David); The guy who's just a head; Armlessness does not deter this drummer's enthusiasm; David and Bob between takes in "Hard Days Night" parody. (© Adam Timrud Photography); Chrysalis (Sarah) and Goth rockers Norma Jean Monster with trust guide Jay at their enormously successful break-thru weekend (© photo by Famous Mortimer).*

Bob, sort of sheepishly. To my surprise, he got it immediately, and I called up Brent and we wrote it out. I remember thinking before it was performed that it was bound to bomb. There wasn't really any clear motive in the premise. It was just a random decision on the part of the newscasters. But the scene did pretty well, and, afterwards, friends raved about how clever it was and how it really pointed out how the media loved to label things. Maybe Brent was conscious of that, but I wasn't. To me, it was the one really high joke I was ever a part of."

Bob: "Fashion Forecast, Tom Kenny is the funniest fey gay guy ever. I wish he actually was gay, so he would walk around in that character all the time and I could just laugh at his tics and twinkles."

Brian: "Fashion Forecast, the documentary, I wrote by myself. I based it on that Unzipped thing [Isaac Mizrahi documentary], which I hated, and I think I was the only person on staff who'd seen it before we did that piece. It just came to me one day when I was driving. I just sort of flashed on the idea of this gay designer getting his ideas from Nostradamus, his 500-year-old lover. Dino and Bob came up with the idea of this guy having these visions, for the Fashion Forecast part."

David: "There was a long fight about whether to keep the smile Bob gives in Fashion Documentary after I walk off camera, and I yelled to him, 'More cheese if you please! I'm on my knees!' I just improvised that line, and you can see Bob smile. And he was adamant. It was everybody against him, but he didn't want to keep the smile in. He wanted to cut away before the smile. It's such a great little smile. It looks like Nostradamus is in love."

Paul: "The argument at the end that continues into the cold tag is the kind of thing I love: a character who is sheer stupidity. I love, when someone just doesn't get something."

EPISODE 306 PLEASE DON'T KILL ME

written by:	David Cross, Bob Odenkirk, Jay Johnston, Bill Odenkirk, Brian Posehn, Dino Stamatopoulos, Paul F. Tompkins, Mike Upchurch
location segment director:	Troy Miller
live show director:	John Moffitt
cast:	David Cross, Bob Odenkirk, John Ennis, Jay Johnston, Tom Kenny, Karen Kilgariff, Brett Paesel, Brian Posehn, Paul F. Tompkins
featuring:	Scott Aukerman, Doug Benson, Vahe Manoukian, Laura Milligan, Theresa Mulligan, Bill Odenkirk, B.J. Porter, Kevin Seccia, Sarah Silverman, Eban Schletter, Scott Selmer, Dino Stamatopoulos, Wendy Wilkins, Jimmy Orestis, Sam Sarpong, Eliza Watts

Mr. Show *theme song and logo. Mustardayonnaise Lincoln (Jay) introduces, "Hello Sexies! It's Bob and David!"*

Swearing Jar Open (live)

Every time a cast member curses, they must drop a nickel into the "swearing jar." The money goes to a non-profit organization, "Swears for Cares," dedicated to raising money through swearing. The guys hope they'll make "a little *fucking* difference," David says and plinks another coin in the jar.

TV Ministry Link (video)

Bob and David are raising money one nickel at a time as part of the *Mr. Show* TV Ministry Family Group. And now it's time for *Swear to God, with Reverend Winton Dupree.*

Swearing Preacher (live)

Televangelist Reverend Winton Dupree (Bob) preaches God's good word in his passionate and unorthodox sermon: "What is up Satan's ass?! All he wants to do is fuck us up, the dicklicker!" He inspires the congregation and ends his sermon with a call out — "Can I get a 'fuckin' A?'"

Rolling In It/Ferrari Poster Link (video)

David basks in a literal tubful of swear-jar nickels to a carefree whistler's tune. The image becomes a bad poster with the caption, "Rollin' In It!" Other tacky posters featuring a naked David follow — "Grin 'n' Bear It!" and "Being Poor Sucks!"

Landlords (live)

The last poster is among John's stuff as he unpacks at his new apartment. His effusive new Armenian landlord, Shamul (David), pays him a visit — "Don't think of me as landlord; think of me as neighbor." John's former landlord, Victor (Bob), shows up. He is hurt that John moved and tries to win back his old tenant. Shamul overhears and confronts them. A passionate argument ensues. John uses tough love to set Victor straight — "I'M NOT MOVING BACK," — and it works. The web of betrayal tangles further with Anwar (Paul), the former tenant of this apartment ("Only two days ago I move out, and already apartment filled? Whore!"). Shamul wants to explain. "I spit on your explanation!" seethes Anwar. "I spit on your spit!" Shamul insults back. They continue one-upping each other until all three men are dancing and "chanting" insults, friends again.

Victor & Dylan (video)

A dejected Victor (Bob) mopes back to his apartment building, and he sadly removes from the wall the picture of John and himself. He asks his persnickety tenant, Dylan (David), if his air conditioner is working, and gets treated to a speech on the evils of such devices ("It's a needless perversion of an already-perfected system, i.e. the fan.") Dylan is too intense for even the love-starved landlord. ("Rock 'n' roll is the most criminal of garbages!") For him, "the only pure pop group that ever existed was The Fad Three."

Fad Three (b&w super 8 film/video)

A B&W Beatles-esque documentary. In 1962, talent manager Brian Blemming (Tom) "discovers" three jolly, shaggy-haired, photogenic young men — Northern English charmers Roy Crossway (Bob), Val Thompson (Jay), and Neville "Larry" Smithson (David) — and together they would be known as "The Fad Three." Knowing a gravy train when he sees one, Blemming releases professional snaps taken of the lads. The first photograph is a huge hit, and the girls of London (Karen, Sarah, Laura) go wild ("They're so new! And so cute!"). For their first public appearance, the boys come out, pose stiffly, wave awkwardly, then bow — before a sold-out screaming mob of fans. At a press conference, Larry's randy statement, "Well, we've been photographed more than Jesus Christ," ignites no controversy, and the boys are shocked. The Fad Three experiment artistically, releasing *Overexposure* (or *The Blank Photo*), which doesn't sell. This disappointment, among others (such as Larry's suicide), causes the group to disband. Val, now working as a stock boy at a Norwich Quick-Mart, is willing to do a reunion photo, "but only under any circumstances." Other surviving member, Roy, now lends his "ex-celebrity" status to worthy charities and political causes.

Hunger Strike (live)

At a press conference, Roy Crossway (Bob) introduces an extremely weak Panzik-Pujiran (David), who is making his first public appearance since he began his hunger strike. For 23 days, Panzik has had nothing but water, protesting the oppression of his people. His plea today is about basic human rights, but he is incredibly distracted by his hunger and can't stop talking about food. ("I want the world to know that I am so hungry.")

Panzik's hunger strike is sponsored by Stenson's condiments, including Mayostard. "With over a thousand food products, there's over a thousand reasons not to go hungry."

Panzik tries to eat the superimposed sponsor's logo.

Mayostard/Mustardayonnaise (video)

Commercial for Stenson's Mayostard, a time-saving condiment that combines mustard and mayonnaise in one yellow and white striped jar. "It cuts sandwich-making time in half!" A suburban mom (Brett) easily fools her kids with delicious sandwiches — "Mmmm Mom, you used separate jars of mustard and mayonnaise!".

Commercial for competing brand Vaunnie's Mustardayonnaise, which combines the same two condiments to save time. Prisoners, or "two-jar slaves," are liberated by yellow and white stripe top-hatted Lincoln (Jay) with a machine gun — "Let's get the hell outta here!"

With every purchase, Vaunnie's will donate 20¢ to the *Dr. X Save the Earth Telethon*.

Evil Genius Telethon (video)

Evil madman, Dr. X (Bob), launched into orbit a doomsday laser that can destroy the planet at the touch of a button. "If the people of the earth will pay me $30 million once a year, I will be so kind as to not disintegrate them." The benevolent evil genius hosts a Labor Day weekend telethon ("I am wiped out, I've been up for 20 hours. But I'm doing it for *you*."), with "C-level celebrities and a wacky sidekick, Johnny (Tom). Cutie poster child Paul Peters politely begs, "Please don't kill me." "Awww. You see, this is why I do this! For the kids!" Via satellite from Chicago, king of the put-downs, Dick Rondell (David) entertains and offends Dr. X, who "cannot stand racial intolerance." He destroys Chicago, and, in a fit, sets the counter to 60 seconds to blow up the rest of the world. He climbs into his special "Escape Pod," when David and "Bob" (Bill as Bob) show up with one of their swearing jars full of money, and stiffly announce their contribution "on behalf of all the *Mr. Shows with Bob and Davids* around the world." But their donation still brings us 5¢ short of the $30 million goal, says Dr. X. "Sorry, you're all up shits' creek." They make him pay up for swearing, and the earth is saved for another year. Exhausted, Dr. X sobs with joy through his closing number, "*The Laserbeam of Love*", as we see moments from past *Doomsday Telethons*, and credits roll.

Mustmayostardayonnaise Cold Tag (video)

Commercial for Mundees brand (combines the other two in an ultimate time-saving spread): A typical suburban dad (Bob), who misses out on his daughter's (Theresa) entire life, because "he's always spreading Mayostard and Mustardayonnaise…and time." "Daddy, I'm dying," says his daughter, now older than he is.

"Grin 'n' Bear it!" (It's so true!) (© photo by Famous Mortimer).

Notes About Episode 306

Paul: *"This episode is unofficially known as the 'Accent Show.' Almost every sketch had almost all of us doing accents."*

Paul: *"At the end of the Landlords sketch, Bob, as Victor, walks away sadly, as David, John and I dance around in the background. We did a number of takes. We had to jump around in a circle chanting, 'I piss on your spit, I shit on your piss, I fart on your shit, I laugh at your fart, we are friends again!' When it was over, I was so dizzy, I almost passed out."*

Bob: *"David's character is his old landlord, and my character is my old landlord. My landlord never had anything to do and would hang around too much. And he was very sulky when I was packing up to move. David's old landlord, Shamul, actually said the line to him, 'You can do anything you want here, you can fuck pussy anywhere, I don't care.'"*

David: *"I had been looking for an apartment all day by driving around, looking for the 'For Lease' signs. I saw that place and I walked up, and that guy was like a shadowy figure in the window. And I walked in, because the door was open. 'Hello?' 'Yes! Hello, my friend!' A huge, barrel-chested, like out of central casting, guy. Swarthy, hairy. It was as if I walked through a portal into Istanbul and I was trying to buy a carpet. Within sixty seconds, I had the place. I wasn't even aware of it, but that's what was happening. 'Yes, my friend. Look around. It's beautiful, no!' It was a duplex, split down the middle, and his family lived on the other side. And every question I had — 'Look my friend. You do whatever you want here. You want to have a party? I leave.' (Which he did, by the way. Greg [Behrent, David's roommate] and I would have these huge blow-out killer parties. And he would put his whole family in the car and go out to the Grandma's house or something out in the valley and spend the night there.) But the one thing we couldn't do, he said, 'You can do anything, my friend. Anything. You can fuck pussy, I don't care. You can kill somebody, okay. BUT DON'T SELL DRUGS! Don't bring that shit in my house!' He was the best landlord I ever had."*

Paul: *"Fad Three is Bill's piece that I argued against including in the show. I thought that the Beatles had been done to death, and we shouldn't use it. I was wrong. It's a really funny piece with great performances, and it was a new take on a seemingly played-out subject. John Ennis in particular is hilarious as the outraged 'establishment.'"*

David: *"Ennis as the English jibber-jabber guy in Fad Three, we would play that in the editing room 15 times in a row. We

EPISODE 306

kept playing it. We were all giggling — that indecipherable 'afhaafafafha.' That made us laugh so hard."

David: "Troy had to go shoot something else, and he asked us to grab a camera and pick up a couple shots for Fad Three. It was just me and a cameraman and Jay. And we set up a shot and just had Jay eating his lunch, which you see in the piece, and it's funny, but I just let it roll and I never called cut. And it's fucking great. It really is like four minutes of Jay sadly eating that limp, shitty, hot, moist, nasty old sandwich and a cup of juice that a child would get in kindergarten."

David: 'Hunger Strike was a monster for me to perform. I was not fucking getting it. I wanted somebody else to play the part. I just wasn't saying it right, getting the joke. And Dino, Bob and Jay were coaching me through it. I think I may have done it right the very first time I did it, but I could not capture it. I was lost. I felt like I lost one of my senses."

Jay: "The character I had to play in the Mustardayonnaise sketch was none other than our eightieth president, Abraham Lincoln. I was wearing a bright yellow tuxedo and a striped yellow and white top hat. Later that day, we were to shoot the 'Mediocrity' guy in the Philouza sketch. After I dressed in the tux, our wardrobe gal (the best), Paula Elins, told me to be careful because it was extremely tough to find this yellow tux and they lucked out getting one big enough to tailor for me. So, heeding her advice, I promptly decided to practice riding the bicycle that I was to pilot later that day in the Philouza sketch. It was one of those old-timey bikes with the huge wheel in the front and the tiny wheel in the back. Real turn-of-the-century, waxed moustache kind of shit. It was scary and awesome, until I tried to turn and the handlebars instantly detached from the wheel. I plowed straight into a curb and flew over the handlebars into a bush. Somehow I was fine, but the tux had some delightful grass and mud stains on the knees and arms. But Paula, the consummate pro, promptly cleaned it and said nothing, which was far worse than a scolding."

Jay: "The shot we needed for the Mustardayonnaise piece was the group of convicts from the 'sauce prison' or whatever that was. A place where people go when they commit crimes against things you put on bread. The convicts were to carry me on their shoulders and set me down at a table in front of the camera. As a side note, occasionally I get an idea in my head that I must explore until someone in charge says, 'What in the fuck are you doing?' And on this particular day, in this particular situation, I was told we were shooting it for slow motion. So, if the entire shot would be in slo-mo, I considered it funny if I pumped my arms extra hard and fast with no emotion, because they would move faster than everything else when it was slowed down. Well, during the five or six times we did the shot to get it right, absolutely no one said a fucking thing about it. And, as it turned out, they did not slow it down. It wasn't shot for slow motion, and I don't think people should say stuff like that when they are wrong. The shot plays in normal speed, and my fast-pumping arms are not terribly obvious perhaps, but it makes Dino laugh. I think he has remarked that it is one of his favorite performances. In summation, some shots that you think will be slowed won't and others that you don't think will be, will. (See Philouza and the busted old-timey bike story, #308)."

David: "My only major contribution to the Evil Genius Telethon — I was lobbying that there's a voice, when he detonates the laser beam. Because all those movies, whenever a bomb is going to go off and they have a thirty seconds, it's always a very polite English woman's voice. There's no reason for it in the sketch, at all. It's just something I wanted to do. I made up the word 'explosionation' and said [in a refined English woman's voice]: 'Ten seconds to explosionation.' It's not that funny, but I like it. It's a nice little touch. It allows people to realize that I've seen movies."

Bob: "This marks [editor] Steve Welch's first joke on the show: for the cold tag commercial for Mustmayostardaonnaise, Steve threw in a warning: 'Mayostard expires before Mustardayonnaise.'"

(left from top to bottom) "Swearing Preacher" performed live in the second show taping of the night. © Adam Timrud Photography; Two of the Fad 3 (Bob, Jay). © Adam Timrud Photography; Evil Genius Dr. X and sidekick Johnny. © Adam Timrud Photography.

EPISODE 307
GOIN' ON A HOLIDAY

written by:	David Cross, Bob Odenkirk, Jay Johnston, Bill Odenkirk, Dino Stamatopoulos, Paul F. Tompkins, Mike Upchurch
location segment director:	Troy Miller
live show director:	John Moffitt
cast:	Bob Odenkirk, David Cross, John Ennis, Jay Johnston, Tom Kenny, Karen Kilgariff, Brett Paesel, Paul F. Tompkins
featuring:	Ashlie Chan, Theresa Mulligan, B.J. Porter, Sarah Silverman, Michael Hagen, Jack Manning, Norma Michaels, Angie Miller, Anne Miller, Louis Rappaport, Fortunato Rubin, Scott Selmer, Rebecca Smith

Mr. Show theme song and logo. Obnoxious Italian guy (John) introduces: "You toucha my car, I breaka you face! It's Bob and David!"

Elderly Open (live)
David and Bob point out their families in the audience. (David admits he received all the recessive genes from his flawlessly beautiful family.) David is aghast to find that Bob's Grampa Timmy is "elderly." He deduces, with horror, that Bob has elderly in his blood ("It's in your blood. You're 1/4 old.") He propagandizes about the "coming age war," and Bob is sucked in; he no longer trusts his Grampa. Grampa Timmy assures his grandson that the elderly are feeble and harmless, then gives Bob ice cream money, and asks, "Would a world run by old people be such a bad thing?"

Age War (video)
Grampa Timmy imagines such a world…people are more polite, bowls of hard candy on every corner, an 8-miles-per-hour speed limit, and their dark side of intolerance toward slackers (who sleep in on Saturdays past 6:30) revealed — "testicular electrocution would be administered to all those who get into monkeyshines." A young man (Jay) is strapped in and screams in pain from testicular electrocution….

Bills, Bills, Bills! Link (video)
A still of Jay's tortured scream is an ad for "Tooter's Ice Pops," the ice cream you'll scream for. The channel flips to commercial with another screaming man (John) as the announcer yells, "Bills! Bills! Bills!"

Our Secret Love (live)
A couple at home (Brett & Bob) are watching TV. Each of them fields a frantic call from their secret lover and attempts to be covert, although it's obvious to both that the other is withholding something. When Lee (David) shows up, both are flustered and shout, "I told you never to come here!" They are astonished and relieved that they are both cheating with the same guy. Their daughter (Theresa) and her date (Jay) come home. "Lee!" they both shout with surprise. ("You know Lee?") Two more on the list. Nanna comes downstairs and is struck by the sight of her clandestine lover, Lee, as is sweet Grandpa Gerald. Lee gathers them together to break the news that he is dumping them for another family — "It's funny, you'd like them. They're actually a lot like you." Just then, the twin daughters burst in and announce that they're pregnant. Lee does the honorable thing ("gulp") and marries the twins…and the whole family.

Marriage Photo Link (video)
Various snapshots of the ridiculous wedding with everyone in the family in a snow-white wedding gown except for the uncomfortable tuxedoed groom, Lee. Chocolatey fingers carelessly flip through the photos.

Photo Shop (video)
Droopy the clerk (Bob), dripping with attitude, eats his messy chocolate bar while looking at photos behind the counter at a dingy drugstore. He ignores his only customer, Air Force Colonel (David), who wants to pick up his NASA photos. The Colonel is horrified to discover that Droopy looked through his "space pictures," and that they have "chocolate fingerprints on them!" ("What kind of film did you use?") He refuses to pay and walks off in a snit. (Droopy: "Touché!")

Blowing Up The Moon (video)
Photos of the chocolatey-smudged Mars probe are included in a special news report: NASA plans to blow up the moon. (During a full moon, to make sure they "get it all.") "Blowing Up the Moon" fever sweeps the country. Families plan picnics for the explosion date, kids are excited, and patriotic country singer C.S. Lewis Jr. strikes gold with his ass-kickin' hit, *Blew Moon*:

> Look out, moon, America's gonna get ya.
> You're gonna go kaboom, was nice to have met ya.
> 'Cause you don't mess around, with God's America!

As a publicity stunt, Gallileo, the great-grandmonkey of Ulysses — the first monkey to travel in space — will push the explosive rocket's launch button. Through sign language, the monkey asks the scientists (Bob and David), "Why are you blowing up the moon?" The country turns against the wet-blanket monkey for ruining their fun. C.S. Lewis Jr. puts out a protest song, "*Big Dumb Ape*." NASA solves the problem by replacing the offending monkey with Mr. Wiggles, a circus monkey that does tricks and doesn't know sign language. "He'll do the job, no questions asked."

Spunk (live)

Through the window of an executive boardroom, the moon explodes spectacularly, but the big boss (Bob) doesn't care. He's too busy chewing out his underlings on their poor work performance. One of the junior executives (John) stands up to him — "how about instead of you sitting on your big fat ass, and bitching like a spoiled brat, you actually chip in and help!" He gets a promotion for his spunk. Another employee (David) attempts to jump on the constructive criticism bandwagon and gets fired for it. Other guys (Paul & Tom) come to David's defense and get promotions. Unable to insult his way into his boss's good graces, David gets even more and more fired. He storms, jobless, out of the room, and flips a bird to the camera. "This is bullshit!" he yells.

Don Pratt (live)

"Have you been fired, mistreated or injured on the job?" asks Don Pratt (Bob), in his low-budget commercial. Then call him, not for legal advice, but just to hang out, "I want to help you with *anything*. We can rent a video, clean out a backroom, or act out the lyrics to popular songs on the radio." Through sweetly-bemused "client" testimonials, we learn the three "Pratt Promises": (1) He is not a lawyer; (2) "Positively no sex"; (3) "You don't have to ask me to leave. I get the message." He urges viewers to call, then stares expectantly at the phone. An announcer adds, "if his mother answers, hang up quickly."

SMC/Streakers (live/film)

(live) Back to the *Seventies' Movie Classics* program. In tonight's showcase of the work of director Famous Mortimer, host Kennard Finneran (David) shows clips from the 1976 relic, the quintessential film about the heyday of streaking, *Bare Ambition*, which follows the life of streaker Jimmy Montello.

(film) A naked Jimmy (Bob) sneaks home late at night, fresh from a triumphant streak. His immigrant, pepper-making Pappa (John) is enraged by his streaking, as is his Italian-muttering Grandmama (Jay). Jimmy's lack of respect gets him a smack in the face. He rebelliously runs off. ("I ain't gonna spend my life stinkin' of peppah!") At the local streaker bar, trouble finds Jimmy when his streaker nemesis, Coco Robbins (David), summons him to the back alley. Coco's muscle (Jay) beats the crap out of Jimmy as a warning to not streak on Coco's turf. A sobbing Jimmy is forced to put on his clothes at knifepoint.

(live) Host Finneran sums up the movie — Jimmy and Coco buddy up after losing out in the first Olympic streaking competition to a man from Kenya who is "more comfortable with his nudity than they are."

Streak Dome '97 (live/film)

(live) *SMC* host Finneran (David) shows a clip from Mortimer's sequel, shot over the following weekend. Set in the director's vision of the future, *StreakDome '97* follows champion streakers, Jimmy and Coco (Bob & David). "The film opened in 1978 in a thousand theaters, and you are the first people to see it."

(film) Naked Jimmy and Coco, a little older and grayer, run their streaker-supply corporation from their 1976-version of a state-of-the-art office. Suddenly, the door bursts open, and three elderly men in futuristic uniforms hold them at laser-gunpoint. The boys raise up their hands (with Coco's hand shielding us from an NC-17 rating). They inarticulately read some proclamation and disintegrate Jimmy into a pile of dust.

(live) Kennard explains how director Mortimer had a prediction/paranoia that the elderly would take over the world.

Elderly Taking Over Link (video)

David is startled out of character as Grampa Timmy and two uniformed elderly guards bust onto the set with a beaten-up Bob. ("David, listen to them! They mean business!") The old really have taken over, and they shut down the show for not complying with the new law that states, "All TV must be nice, for the nice people." They sentence the guys to testicular electrocution.

Goin' On A Holiday (live)

The "improved" show ends with the cast dressed in pastel seniors' active wear and singing the very sleepy tune, "*Goin' on a Holiday*." The credits roll as the *Lawrence Welk* bubbles float, and elderly guards keep watch.

Notes About Episode 307

Bob: "The whole elderly takeover is something that will be happening in the next fifteen years. Mark my words. It'll be worse than what we predicted, old people wanting to see Lawrence Welk shit. It'll be old people wanting to watch Madonna videos and Friends reruns."

Paul: "If you look closely at the photos, you can see that everyone's eyes (especially David's) are red as hell. The photos were taken outside in the middle of summer and everyone had to stand there in these bridal gowns and stare DIRECTLY INTO THE SUN."

Bob: "Photo Shop once again features the character we all refer to as 'Droopy.' Much beloved, this little scamp is once again hanging around, disinterestedly slowing the whole world down."

David: "*Blowing Up the Moon* is a very typical, perfect Mr. Show-type scene. The initial idea was Mike Upchurch's and then we all ran it through the Mr. Show mills. It's got everything. It's goofy, it's fun, it's funny. It makes a nice, perfectly subtle point about America's ego and willful ignorance and celebration of nothing. And touches on all this pop culture. It's great. Really, a perfect scene."

Brian: "The original version of Spunk — I had written a draft that I found really funny, and I liked the whole thing. The ending became a Lord of the Flies thing, where these guys were actually trapped in this conference room for some reason or another, like an earthquake. And they were stuck inside the room, and you don't *(left) "Touché!" Bob's popular character, simply called "Droopy" because he was never given a name. (top right) The elderly take over! "Streakdome '97" features some good bad-movie acting, albeit unintentional. (bottom right) "Our Secret Love" philanderer Lee (David) does the honorable thing. © Photo by Famous Mortimer*

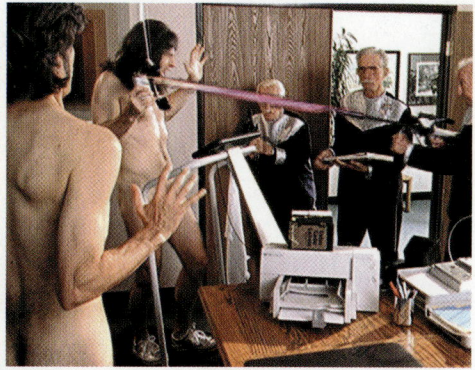

know that in the beginning of the scene, but you find out later that they've just been doing this piece of business, even though they were stuck in there for five days. And then it winds up that they've all taken weird sides, and they've killed the fat guy, Piggy, and they flipped the desk over on them. It was really dark and fucked up. And they loved the beginning of the scene, and Bob said right away, 'No that's not your scene; this is. Keep it in this reality base.' So I did a draft of that, taking their notes, and that was pretty much the piece. David leaving the room and flipping off the camera, someone else thought of that later, because it was a link."

David: "When I leave the room and I flip off the camera at the end of Spunk: 'This is bullshit!' That's one of those things, it perplexes me, for some reason people love this — too much. It's like the stupid dance I did in Jeepers Creepers, people thought these things were hilarious. And they're not. They're merely mildly amusing. And I know because I sent them to a lab in Palo Alto, and the results came back 'mildly amusing.'"

Paula Elins (costume designer): "A lot of people would ask to clear the unnecessary people from the set for a nude scene. When we shot Streakers, they couldn't care less. What they finally came up with — we tried nude G-strings, and Bob and David wanted it to look as real as possible — so we took these nude G-strings, and we cut the whole back off, so it was just sort of like a patch just the size of their front. And then they taped it with double-stick tape over the parts — by themselves — that was one thing I didn't do. David walked to the location in his G-string. Broad daylight. 'Don't you want a robe?' 'No. I'm just walking down the block.' For that scene, I forgot a full costume. We were shooting until 2 A.M.. It was a 70's costume for Jay. I ran to the stage (where the live shows are taped), and I grabbed whatever I could that was as close to it as possible. And it was a pair of pants that were David's size. Jay is 6' 6", and he squeezed in them, and did not complain."

David: "One thing that is really subtle, but I really like, in Streakers, is with my dumb little decision that every time they cut back to the live guy, Kennard Finneran, I always start the walk from the back. I'm just patting myself on the back, but I just like little things like that."

Paul: "I had a little back story for my character in Streakers. I tried to express that my character was secretly in love with Sarah's character and, so, a little jealous of her clear attraction to Bob's character, the champion streaker. I think it shows in the two lines I have. There are no small parts."

Bob: "We had trouble with the elderly extras — their vocal cadence sometimes would be weird and their emphasis. And it was also a lot of time difficult to correct them. Many of them are not really actors; the ones we got were extras who were willing to act. And they're old, on top of it. 'What? What did you say? You can't tell what he's saying, he runs the whole sentence together.'"

Jay: "'Goin' on a Holiday. Terribly catchy motherfucker. We sang it around the office, seemingly all the time, for a period until some other catchy tune replaced it. The standby tune was a song that Paul and Brian came up with — 'Petey Peterman.' I think it was about the man Petey Peterman, and how he goes about doing some stuff, and at one point his pet parrot communicates with the dead. That's all I remember. Perhaps it doesn't sound very catchy, but, neither did Happy Birthday when I was first told of that song."

EPISODE 308 BUSH IS A PUSSY

written by:	Bob Odenkirk, David Cross, Jay Johnston, Bill Odenkirk, Brian Posehn, Dino Stamatopoulos, Paul F. Tompkins, Mike Upchurch
location segment director:	Troy Miller
live show director:	John Moffitt
cast:	Bob Odenkirk, David Cross, John Ennis, Jay Johnston, Tom Kenny, Karen Kilgariff, Jill Talley, Paul F. Tompkins, Brett Paesel
featuring:	Ashlie Chan, Stacie Chan, Theresa Mulligan, Bill Odenkirk, Dino Stamatopoulos, Louis Rappaport
special appearance by:	Jonathan Katz

original artwork by Tom Snyder Productions

Kedzie Backstage Cold Open (video)

Before the show begins, David is backstage in a wheelchair with two broken legs. Bob and an HBO suit (John) try to convince him to use the understudy, Kedzie (Tom), instead of canceling the show. "I can do this. I'm so ready!" assures Kedzie. David reluctantly agrees. Bob says, "Great!" and rushes out to do some errands.

Announcer to the live audience: "Tonight, the part of Bob Odenkirk will be played by Kedzie Matthews, winner of the San Diego Red Owl Rye Laff-Quest and College Comic of the Year, Southwest Region, 1992."

Mr. Show theme song and logo. Drum Major (Bill) introduces "that new-fangled Bob and David."

Kedzie Takes Over Open (live/video)

(live) David wheels onstage with Kedzie (Tom), who introduces himself as Bob, and right away he's off the script with his hacky stand-up. (regarding his Hawaiian shirt: "I know what you're thinking — Did Steve McGarrett and Don Ho have a baby?") The audience loves it, and a charmed David goes with it— "riff, man, riff!" Kedzie goes into the audience to improvise. They *love* him.

(video) While out shopping, Bob catches Kedzie on the cashier's tiny TV — he's killing. Bob freaks out, "What the fuck!" and tears down Hollywood Boulevard, with his shopping cart, back to the studio.

(live) Kedzie is "riffing" relentlessly. Bob demands to know what's going on. "This guy's hilarious!" says David. "Everyone loves him!" David then fires Bob and himself; Kedzie is just *that good*. He brings Kedzie back out to "free associate," and….

(video) Bob and David argue backstage. Bob thinks Kedzie sucks, and David points out that Kedzie makes more money than he does. Bob considers this point.

Worthington's Law Link (video)

An announcer explains David's logic — The Worthington Law. "A person that makes more money than you is better than you and, therefore, beyond criticism." The law is used to gauge the value of human worth.

Value Magazine (video)

The editor of *Value Magazine*, Carl Espick (David), pitches the mag, which ranks the 500 best people in the history of the world, according to Worthington's Law. ("Who's better than Van Gogh? Almost everybody! He made nothing!")

Ranking Monkey Link (live)

Order *Value Magazine*, and receive the little gold "Ranking Monkey." "He can tell you where you rank. Just press his head and learn your worth as a person." A businessman (Bob) does, and the monkey says "eeeep eeep" and gives him his financial global ranking.

Siamese Twins (live/video)

(live) The businessman, Ted (Bob), gets a surprise visit from his ex-Siamese twin brother, Ned (David). Ned (leaning to the left) has returned to persuade Ted (who leans to the right) to get reattached, calling their six-month separation "an experiment." Ted's not interested; he's thriving on his own. Ned tries using nostalgia, bringing out their old four-legged jeans and reminiscing about the old days. Ted remembers differently: "No! I worked! You sat on my ass and did nothing!" Ted is, however, thinking of getting re-attached — to a guy in marketing. The marketing guy (Tom) comes in with some news of his own. He got attached to another guy at the office (Paul). The brothers will be together again.

(video) Coming out of the anesthesia, Ted gets the bad news from his doctor (John): although the re-attachment was a success, Ned didn't make it. Is Ted screams in horror, as a lifeless Ned is revealed attached to his hip.

Bad News Breakers (video)

The doctor (John), upset at having to break bad news, turns to the camera, a la a cheap commercial, "There's got to be a better way." The solution: "Bad News Breakers," two adorable little Asian sisters who, in unison, will sing-song the bad news for you. ("You'll never walk again!") The girls charm at hospitals and hostage standoffs; they break the news to the families of plane crash victims — "There were nooooo survivors!" The Bad News Breakers deliver a message to Mafia kingpin, Don Correli (Bob) — "Vito Benvetucci sleeps with the fishes!"

Mafia Mathematicians (live)

The mob wiseguys (David, John, Paul, Jay) argue amongst themselves about what is the biggest number. Squeaky-voiced Pauly (David) maintains that 24 is the highest number: "You got 10, then ya got 10 more, and then it's like, what's this? Four more!" The boss (Bob) can stand very little of the inane counting before he snaps and settles it with "24 is the highest number, and that's it. Let it go!" The guys respectfully comply, but can't help notice when the boss pays $30 for the cannolis, or when he threatens them with his .45 for not shutting up. It turns ugly when Danny (Paul), Franky (John), and Jimmy (Jay) get shot for discovering 46 and 49. Pauly saves his hide by quickly agreeing that 24 is the highest number. Pleased, the Don sends him on a mission to "make sure the world knows that 24 is the highest number."

24 Is The Highest Number/Marching Band Link (video)

Armed Mafia gunmen menacingly lurk during the following testimonials: an old man announces his age as 24; a Nazi (David) — "To say we killed 24 Jews is an exaggeration;" a stadium's attendance — "24...another sold-out crowd!" A marching band performs across the playing field....

Philouza (film)

The story of tortured marching band composer Sallini (David), who is limited by his burden — mediocrity. Constantly taunted by the image of Death/Mediocrity (Jay), he labors over a new melody, "for in two days, Hilford Hansen, the eleventy-twelfth President of the United States, was to hold a marching band competition." The bane to his existence is John Baptiste Philouza (Bob), a simple-minded genius who effortlessly composes marching band masterpieces. When Philouza decides "to apply himself" and enter the contest, the desperate and scheming Sallini tempts him to leave his work and go out with the town floozy. As soon as Philouza leaves with his nickel, Sallini spills ink all over the genius' composition sheets. On competition day, Sallini's two-note composition (titled "The Messiah's Passion Fanfare #4 For Tubas and Flutes") receives lukewarm applause. Philouza shows up in the nick of time and improvises a piece, which the band quickly picks up. It's brilliant. Sallini concedes to Philouza, when the President (John) interrupts to give the prize to Sallini, because "brilliance upsets people, makes them feel inferior. Better that they should make do with Mr. Sallini's blustery hoopla."

Mediocrity Close (live)

Back onstage, Mediocrity (Jay), lectures Bob, the wheelchaired David, and stand-in stand-up Kedzie on the lesson of Sallini: "So, you see, fellas, what happens when you choose mediocrity over originality...." Bob gets it — "So, that's why Kedzie became so popular, huh?" "No, no, no!" Mediocrity cries out. "It's because *he's* hilarious!" Credits role as Kedzie runs riffing into the audience, to everyone's delight (except Bob's).

Dr. Katz Cold Tag (video)

Kedzie is a guest comic on the animated Comedy Central show, *Dr. Katz*. He's on the therapist's couch, but it is obvious that he is using material from his act, not even trying to disguise it as conversation ("Cats are weird. Where are the cat owners?"). "Who are you talking to, Kedzie?" asks a confused Dr. Katz, who can't seem to open a dialogue with this hacky patient.

Notes About Episode 308

David: "Bush is a Pussy. How prescient of us."

Bob: "Kedzie Matthews is not a real comic. Do not try booking him for your college. He will not show up."

David: "The Worthington's Law idea, that a person who makes more money than you is better than you, is something that's always bothered me. It's a retort people say, and it's without any merit or logic. It's usually said if one is complaining, 'Jay Leno is such a...' with all these legitimate reasons, about all the grand injustice in the world, and then the person says, 'Makes more money than you.'"

Dino: "The two little Korean girls Stacie and Ashlie are great. We needed a kid for a link between two scenes (DeLongpre Dannon and Lie Detector, #304), we had to audition a kid to say, 'It has more than one use! It has two uses!' The little Asian girl did great. Next kid was the same girl. After she read, we said, 'You did good — both times.' 'That was my sister.' So we hired both girls. We used them to tease people around the office: 'Jay, you're fired!' 'Your wife's cheating on you.' A new bit. Running around giving bad news to people, Bad News Breakers. (And we used the sisters in Season 4's last five shows.) The girls are not twins. (Actually, the one who's two years younger is now bigger)."

Bob: "*Mafia Mathematicians* would have worked if we'd filmed it and given it a heavy dramatic atmosphere as a backdrop to the inanity. Done live it sticks out badly as a scene that would fit much better on Sesame Street."

David: "*Mafia Mathematicians*, never one of my favorite sketches. Talk about suspending disbelief. It's just about the most illogical argument you can ever make — an adult doesn't know that there's a greater number than 24. I never really cared for that bit too much. And I think subconsciously it's why I played it so broad. That character is almost like an animated character. You'd see him in one of those 1970's Disney films, that voice would be applied to the cockroach or a rat or something."

Paul: "I am very proud of my death-acting in Mafia Mathematicians. Also, Vito Benvetucci is a variation on my maternal grandfather's name, Vito Benvenuto. We were told by the legal people that we couldn't use the name Vito Benvenuto because I guess there are a few Vito Benvenutos out there, who might accidentally see Mr. Show and sue it. 'Benvenuto' means 'welcome.' Isn't that nicer than 'Benvetucci,' which is made up and might mean something bad in Narnia or someplace? (Coincidentally, Narnia is where the legal people live.)"

Bob: "When Dino and I wrote Philouza, people loved it, thought we were geniuses.

(top left) Not even the Levi's made for two can persuade ex-Siamese twin to re-conjoin; (bottom left) Jay as "Mediocrity" and Bill on location for Philouza. © Adam Timrud Photography. (right) The bad news is somehow not so bad. Link to Mafia Mathematicians. © Adam Timrud Photography.

I mean it was so funny and so clean, only one or two changes were made. But we did something wrong, because when you watch it, it's not as funny. It was disappointing, although it seems to work better on TV than it did for the audience. The best part of it is Jay as 'Mediocrity.' The concept, his portrayal, is Mr. Show touching the hem of Monty Python."

David: "Philouza doesn't seem to fit on our show. It really stands out as being from some other show, and that show was made by drunk English matrons. It's similar to Goodbye (#410), in a way, although I like both pieces a lot. But those two pieces always stick out to me."

Eban Schletter (music director): "I think it was challenging for both me and Bob, because he wanted to be able to riff stuff and have me score the marching band pieces off of Philouza's humming. So it was a technical problem of having to synch stuff. The biggest nightmare for someone like me is this: you shoot a piece with someone singing but with no music behind it, they're naturally going to change their pitch and maybe even, their rhythm. That piece put me behind and led up to my not sleeping for five days to catch up."

David: "The thing that hurt the most, of all that kind of crazy shit we did where you end up taking a beating — especially doing Ronnie Dobbs, I would cut myself, and have bruises, and get hit. But the thing that hurt more than anything was in Philouza, where I fell from the ceiling. The way we shot it was I fall onto the mats, and, obviously, you cut out before you see the mats, and then you cut to a close-up of me falling to the ground. For the fall to the ground, I had to fall from out of frame, and I had to do it a bunch of times. Try falling from a ladder straight down and breaking your fall, so your face doesn't smash into the ground. That hurt for a week."

Jay: "When we were shooting the Philouza sketch, we traveled out to a suburb of L.A., Monrovia. It was a quaint little town with old houses and suburban people walking around. The house itself was odd in that it had old toilets and old stuff that really was from the old-timey days. I much prefer 'old' things that merely look old or are painted to look old. You can get them at the store. And when you have them at home people will look at the 'old' lamp or 'old' house-key holder or 'old' wall clock and say things along the lines of, 'Wow.' And, 'Nice.' And, they'll start sentences with phrases like, 'Where did…' and, 'This is…' which will really make you feel good inside. Anyway, back to Philouza being shot at that fucking dump. To save money, we would often double, triple or even quadruple sets when we went out on location. If we shot at a school we could make one room into a doctor's office, another into a store and another into a school room (the easiest), etc. On the Philouza set, we were to shoot the Mustardayonnaise sketch (Dino's hilarious condiment lampoon) and probably something else but I can't remember [The Return of the Curse of the Creature's Ghost].

Jay: "When we shot the scene for Philouza with me on the old-timey bike, the steering was so shot from my crash [Jay crashed the bike while practicing on it] that we couldn't fix it. Someone had to push the bike hard, and I would just roll across the yard, looking to the side, waving. It was terrifying because I couldn't look forward towards the tree I was heading for. In the end, Steve Welch, our editor, slowed the shot to make it last longer, which worked great. Made it even creepier."

EPISODE 309
THE RETURN OF THE CURSE OF THE CREATURE'S GHOST

written by:	David Cross, Bob Odenkirk, Jay Johnston, Bill Odenkirk, Dino Stamatopoulos, Paul F. Tompkins, Mike Upchurch
location segment director:	Troy Miller
live show director:	John Moffitt
cast:	John Ennis, Jay Johnston, Tom Kenny, Karen Kilgariff, Brett Paesel, Brian Posehn, Paul F. Tompkins
featuring:	Sarah Silverman, Theresa Mulligan

Mr. Show theme song and logo. Beefeater Guy (John) introduces.

Moe Phelps Open (live/video)
Tonight's special episode is a "tribute" to Bob and David's inspirations, including their high school guidance counselor, Moe Phelps (Bob), who joins them live via satellite. They thank him for his helpful advice about acting: "All acting is, is jumping up and down, and yelling and screaming a lot." The guys are proud to tell their teacher that they have their own show. His infuriating, belittling reply is, "Well, maybe it will lead to something." Bob and David can't get it through to him that it already did — they're on TV. "Maybe you can keep it as a hobby." Bob and David jump up and down, screaming in frustration. This impresses Mr. Phelps — "Boys, that's some of the finest acting I have ever seen." The nighttime janitor (David) arrives in his office, and Phelps says goodnight.

Happy Janitor (video)
Gus Kryzinski, high school nighttime janitor/"community treasure" (David), is the focus of a human-interest segment of the local news. Gus peppers his nightly work routine with delightful "comedy bits" that no one is aware of. "There's a lot of sadness in the world, and a lot of kids, too. I'm just trying to do my part." He does what he can to lighten the mood: soft shoe dancing while mopping, unenthusiastically popping out of bin full of basket balls, Groucho nose and glasses while fixing plumbing).

Local World News (live/video)
The previous segment was a news report on *Local World News*, "local news from around the world." Anchorman, Brant Waterman (Bob), reports with gravity on such stories as the "Button Man" in Ontario, who has over 30,000 buttons in his collection. "The feeling in the street is that this is far from over," says field reporter Jazz Witherspoon (David). Breaking news — a local boy is making good as we speak. "Singing" "News" Reporter Carl Bellflower (Jay) reports from outside a top law firm, where young Daniel Smith (David) is being considered for an important job. Carl spots him, calls at him, and then turns away quickly, leaving Daniel confused.

Blowjob (live)
Daniel (David) arrives to his interview at a prestigious law firm, all the partners present (Bob, John, Tom). They butter him up with compliments and a huge offer, then tell him, "Dan, we would like you to give us a blowjob." Daniel's smile drops. He can't believe his ears. Needless to say, he is insulted and reminds them that he was first in his law class at Harvard. "Well, it should be a very good blowjob, then," says the senior partner (Bob). Daniel stands up to them, and he promises to oppose them in court at every opportunity "and win, too!" They are charmed at his naiveté at not knowing how the judicial system works. ("Court cases are decided by a series of blowjobs.")

Blowjobs Link (video)
"…In fact, our whole civilization is built on blowjobs." Medicine: a doctor (Paul) telling his patient (Brian), "Surely you don't believe that people get well through treatment with medicine or surgery, do you?" Religion: a priest (Jay) wises up a parishioner in confession. Prostitution: "You don't really believe that I'd just give you a blowjob in exchange for money, do you?" scowls a hooker (Sarah) at a headbanger (Bob). His friends walk up….

Titannica (live)
The three friends are the speed metal group "Titannica" (Bob, Brian, John). They're visiting their biggest li'l fan, Adam (David), who's in the hospital. They feel somewhat obligated because Adam tried suicide by jumping into a vat of acid, right after he listened to their new song, "Try Suicide." Tucked in his hospital bed, Adam is ecstatic at the sight of his favorite band. He's thrilled by the gifts they brought, including a backstage pass for their tour and a concert T-shirt, which, with awkward enthusiasm, they tell him to put on. They pull down his sheets and recoil in horror; Adam's body looks like a wet cigar, his shriveled limbs flapping. ("The acid came right up to my chin. The doctors said I should be dead, huh?") Adam cheers about how popular he will be with the other kids: "Especially when they see me hanging out with you guys backstage at every show in every city!!" The band realizes having him around will damper their tour. They fix the problem by recording a follow-up tune….

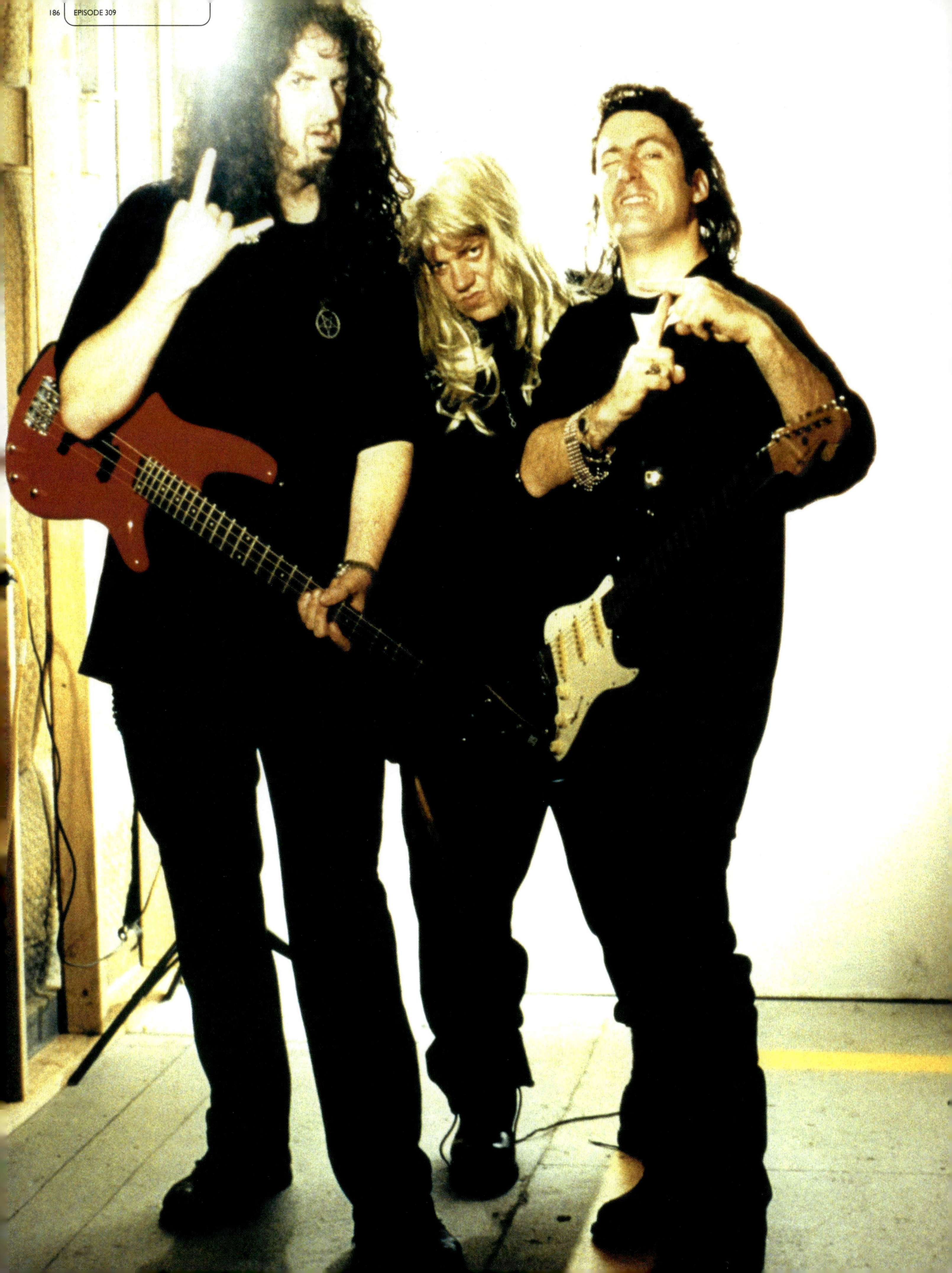

(left) Bob as Moe Phelps, Bob and David's mentor; (right) The real Moe Phelps at the University of Georgia.

Music Video Link (video)

Titannica's new rock video: "Try Again (Adam's Song)" — *"Try, try, try again. Head first this time, dive right in!"* "In memory of Adam Jimmy. You finally made it! Now make God rock!"

Pre-Taped Call-In Show (live/video)

The influence of rock lyrics will be the topic in two weeks on the Pre-Taped Call-In Show. Haggard-looking talk show host, Ken Doral (David), says tonight's topic is "The Elderly." He explains, "we tape all our shows a week in advance…so if you're watching me talk about the elderly, DON'T call to talk about it. It's too late." As he gets calls about "Pet Care" — last week's topic, but airing now — he can't contain his frustration. Why can't the audience grasp the simple concept that when you call into his talk show, don't call about the program that's airing now ("Pet Care"), have questions about the topic that he's taping today ("The Elderly"), which airs next week! Ever the host, he continues to take calls — "obviously your elderly grandmother is the problem because *that's* what this week's show is about!" When the confused caller argues back with, "But I'm watching the show right now…" Ken loses it. He grabs a TV. It's tuned to his currently-airing "Pet Care" show, with a dog as his guest. On it, we see Ken blowing his top: "For the love of God! Stop calling about racism! We did that a week ago! Look, here!" He grabs a TV to illustrate, and so on. In the glimpses of the earlier week's pre-taped shows, the audience is confused, but his patience and his hair are not as thin. The program was on the Convoluted Network. Next, already in progress….

The Return Of The Curse Of The Creature's Ghost (b&w film)

Stereotypical characters from 1940's mystery noir films (Bob, David, Theresa, Tom, John, Paul), are stuck in a mansion during a storm. They are trying to figure out what it is they are supposed to be afraid of — The curse? The creature? "The ghost has returned with the creature's curse." "So the creature put a curse on the ghost?"

Chip On Your Shoulder Club (live)

The T-shirt of the film is worn by a high schooler (Brian), one of the bored teens (Jay, Sarah, Karen, David) meeting for the "Chip On Your Shoulder Club," an extracurricular club for kids who "aren't interested in anything." Their enthusiastic teacher (Bob) tries hard to get the apathetic kids to vote on this year's field trip. He takes their suggestions ("Nowhere" "Brraap!" "How about up your mother's ass?"), which he validates by adding them to the list. He adds his own suggestion, the Henry Ford Museum, which he sells hard. But no takers. ("Sounds gay to me.") They are down to the last choice, "up his mother's ass." In an effort to take the kids seriously, he takes them there….

Up Your Mother's Ass (video)

In a photo montage, we see the kids meet the teacher's mother, and, hard hats and all, the group climbs up into her

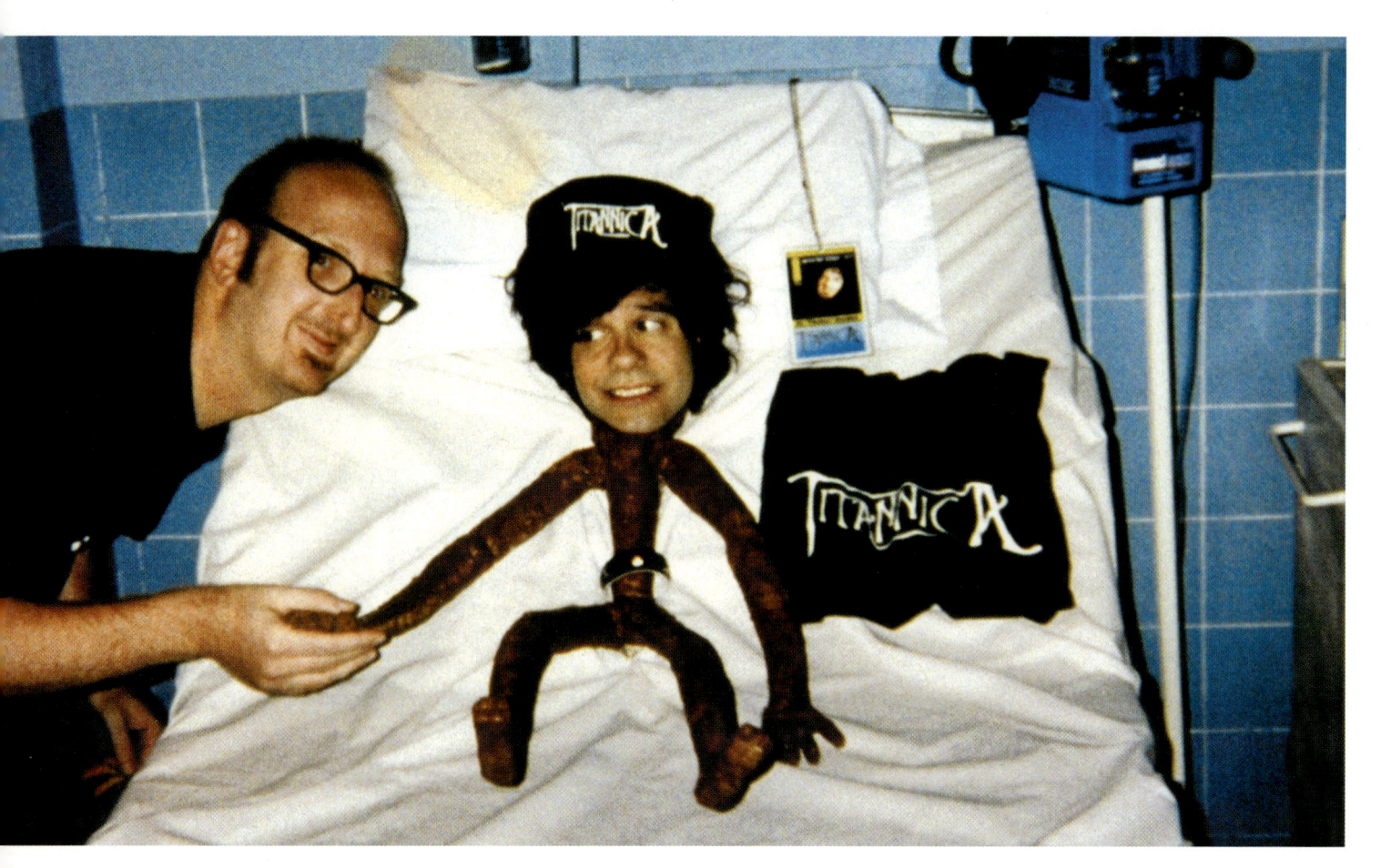

Brian visits Titannica fan in the ICU burn victims' ward.

ass. They explore the wonderful world of art and culture that is contained there. Hijinks and touching moments are underscored by a *To Sir, With Love*-type ballad (sung by David):

> Dear Mr. Teacher, you crawled up inside my head
> and I can't remember everything you said.
> You taught me so much, but a lot of it was geometry.
> Remember that time when that bee flew in.
> Oooh, teacher. Shake it now, teacher, now shake it, shake it.
> Shake it up now, teacher, shake it.
> (becoming disco) Shake you boody now. Shake it. C'mon
>   now shake it uuuup!
> Out on the dance floor, you're the king of dance floor!
> You're gonna be a disco star! Light the night on fire!
> Burn that disco ghost, yeah! C'mon and burn that disco
>   ghost down,
> Burn that disco ghost to the ground, Mr. Teacher! Phelps!

Moe Phelps' Play Close (live)

David wraps up the song, and the episode is dedicated to Mr. Phelps (Bob), who joins the cast onstage. "Maybe someday you'll get to sing that on a TV show," Mr. Phelps says, still not getting it. Mr. Phelps maintains that acting is easy — "you get up there onstage and you go nuts." He puts on a "king's hat" and demonstrates his technique — stomping, yelling, waving his arms. "I'm the king! I'm mad! I want the news from my kingdom!" He invites the cast to join in, and the demonstration deteriorates into a chaotic sword fight. Credits role over this tomfoolery.

Notes About Episode 309

David: "I was in high school, and I wanted to go to University of Georgia where all my friends were going. I had the GPA and the SAT scores, but I couldn't get in. So I call this counselor at the university and he says, 'Come up to Athens and meet with me.' So I get in my car and drive an hour and forty minutes to Athens from Atlanta. And I get there, and there's this guy named Moe Phelps, who's the absolute, typical, Southern, George Wallace type of guy. He had that kind of polyester, short sleeve shirt, big, bad, fat tie. He's the Dean of Admissions for UGA. So I go and talk with him. And he said, 'What would you like to major in?' And I said, 'I think I'd like to major in theater.' And he said, 'Theater? What is that but just gettin' up on stage, and jumpin' up and down and yellin' a lot.' The Dean of Admissions said that. Bob's never even met this guy, and he nailed him."

David: "At the very end of Local World News, where Jay calls my name before I go into Blowjob, and then he looks away — we came up with that right before we shot it. That was some little take we came up with on set."

Bob: "In the Blow Job scene, I was the kid sitting there, and David was the guy saying, 'We want you to give us a blow job.' And nobody backed me up on this, but I felt like it didn't work. When we were rehearsing it, I just said, 'This doesn't work. It just doesn't have the weight that it needs to have.' David just doesn't have the elderly energy (although he can play a really old man). It didn't seem to work for me, but that was my opinion. And I took everybody aside and said, 'I want to take that role, and David take this one.' And David was cool, because he could have gotten nervous and thought I was being a dick 'cause the role wasn't as funny, but that's not how I felt at all. I thought that role was a great role, the guy sitting there, reacting. But I just didn't think it worked at all. And he went along with it."

Brian: *"I had the idea about a metal band that writes a pro-suicide song. They have to visit a young fan who botched his suicide. And, of course, the band are insensitive dip-shits. It had been inspired by Ozzy's problems with his song 'Suicide Solution' and those two Judas Priest fans who misheard Rob Halford's message on 'Better By You, Better By Me' (like all Judas Priest songs, it's really about gay sex). Also, there was a special on MTV about Metallica visiting this burn victim kid, and it just seemed kind of awkward. This kid loved Metallica so much, and they appreciated him being a fan, but they were also kind of put off by his hideousness. Originally, in Titannica, the kid was burned from head to toe, and he had a magazine in front of him when they came in. And Bob came up with the idea that his face not be burned, and that he has this little, shriveled puppet body, and so that was their reveal. My original idea is still intact, where they convince the kid to finish the job by writing another song. I have more of a stomach for really hideous things, so I didn't think it was that horrible at first, but was easily convinced once I thought how the puppet thing would look. I remember the first taping; the reveal of David's 'wet cigar' body got one of the biggest reactions I witnessed during our run. I still have the puppet body; someday I'm gonna make a killing on E-bay. And when I get that eight dollar check, I'm buying so much candy."*

Paul: *"Dino wrote some really funny, silly shit. He and Brent Forrester wrote my favorite sketch — the Pre-Taped Call-In Show. An idiot who's got this show, who's set it up all wrong, and he's going crazy, because other idiots are calling in and they don't get it. And it all folds in on itself, and it gets all fucked up. That's exactly the kind of stuff that I love. Before we shot it, everyday people thought they saw flaws in the logic. I think he and Brent had to storyboard it. They had to break it down and figure out how it was going to work. And we tried to find flaws in the logic, but it was flawless."*

Brent: *"Pre-Taped Call-In Show was an idea that I had on The Ben Stiller Show, and I did not know if it was any good. I went into Dino's office, and asked, 'Is there anything funny about a pre-taped call-in show?' and we tried to figure out what it would mean. And, as we started graphing it out, it seemed much more complex and funny to us than we'd originally believed."*

Paula Elins (costume designer): *"They didn't tell me until the last second that John was going to play the woman in The Creature's Ghost. Not only is it hard to make him a woman, because he's a big guy, but it was a period thing. 'Oh, you can't just get a dress for him?' It was one of those situations where I got lucky. I went to a costume house, and they happened to have a whole section of dresses in his size, which is totally rare, because everything from that period is a lot smaller, because people were a lot smaller. Toniya, our makeup/hair person who is always crazed and has the best attitude, I remember she actually cried that day because it was so stressful, everything went wrong. The trailer wasn't ready, and they were yelling for everyone to be ready. They couldn't unlock the door to the makeup room. One of those really awful, everything-goes-wrong kind of days."*

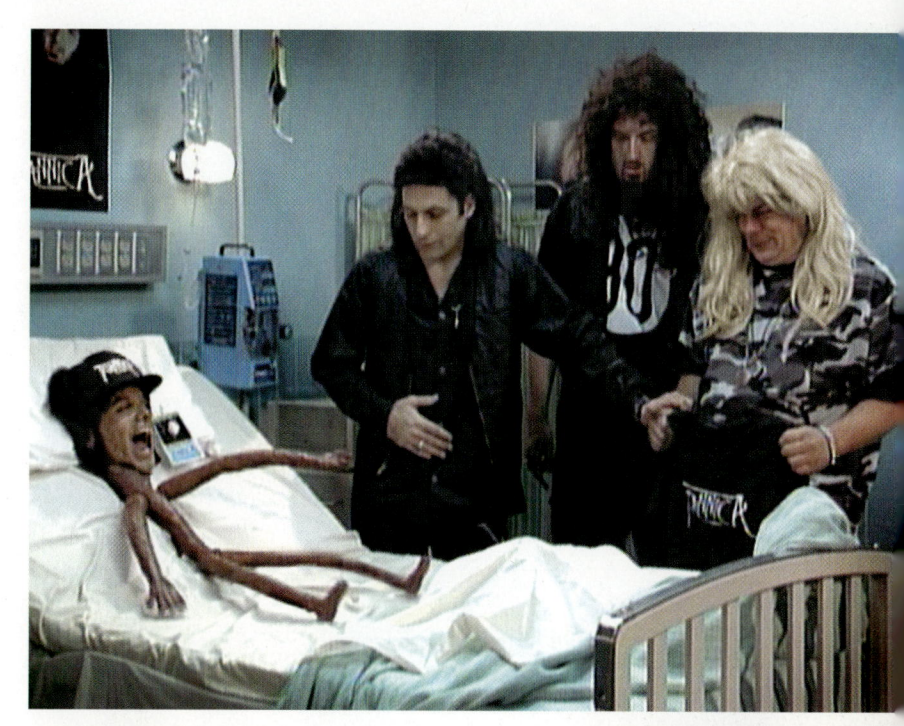

(above) A lucky little guy! David with "wet cigar" puppet body; (below) Chip on Your Shoulder Club's field trip. © Photo by Famous Mortimer

Brian: *"The idea for Chip on Your Shoulder Club came from Bob and I sitting around the writing room, everybody was on a break. And we were just goofing around about something, and I started acting like a jackass teenager, and he would say stuff to me in kind of an authoritative way, and I would answer it like, 'That's gay,' and 'That's dumb.' And then he started sounding like a teacher. And then we were talking — what if all the kids in the class were like that? What if it was a club, they chose to be in this afterschool club, but they don't want to be there. It's a retarded idea. And we were just laughing, 'Is this a scene?' And it turns out it was."*

Dino: *"Actors don't know — auditioning actors only see their part, not the whole show. The old woman who was hired to be the mom — to crawl up her ass — she didn't know. She had no idea we crawled up her ass."*

Tracey Krasno (production manager): *"The old woman who played the mother in Up Your Mother's Ass was coming to be in the audience for the taping of that episode, and I was the one who had to figure out how to tell her. But she confused dates and showed up on the wrong week."*

EPISODE 310
IT'S A NO-BRAINER

written by: Bob Odenkirk, David Cross, Jay Johnston, Bill Odenkirk, Brian Posehn, Dino Stamatopoulos, Paul F. Tompkins, Mike Upchurch

location segment director: Troy Miller

live show director: John Moffitt

cast: David Cross, Bob Odenkirk, John Ennis, Jay Johnston, Tom Kenny, Karen Kilgariff, Brett Paesel, Paul F. Tompkins

featuring: Loretta Fox, Theresa Mulligan, Vahe Manoukian, Sarah Silverman, Catherine Carmichael, Collette Jackson, Brandon Marriott, Jimmy Orestis

Li'l Devil Knee Socks Cold Open (video)

Logo with scrawny devil: "Tonight's *Mr. Show* is brought to you by Puny Devil Knee-high socks."

Mr. Show theme song and logo. Buddhist Monk (Vahe) introduces.

Protesters Open (live/pretape)

Bob and David try to introduce the show but are interrupted by a couple of modern-day hippie protesters in the audience (Bob and David) — holding picket signs and chanting, "*Mr. Show* unfair!" "Let Bob and David speak!" Confused, Bob and David point out that they are, and the protesters celebrate their victory. The protesters are on to their next cause — "Kick us out!" — and are promptly strong-armed to the door by a security guard (Paul).

Protesters (video)

The protesters (Bob and David) are outside the studio, pleased with their successful protest. Their Dylan-esque, underdog-victory theme (acoustic guitar with harmonica) plays. Their lame picket signs and annoying chants ("Give us a hotdog, we demand! Or close down this hotdog stand!") are effective. They are America's most successful protesters, irritating people into giving in and giving them a free car, free sex, and high-ranking jobs at a multi-national oil conglomerate. When a crowd of protesters gather to picket their oil company ("No more oil!"), they protest the protesters, who quickly give up. A reporter (Paul) covers the oil protest story live and warns that "even the most benign incident could touch off a full-scale riot." Then, he turns and hurls a rock at the back of a cop's head (John). A full-scale riot breaks out.

On The Spot News (video/live)

The reporter (Paul) now reports live from the riot. "As usual, Channel 6 news cameras are first on the scene," he smiles.

(video) "Channel 6 On the Spot News. We Make the News."

Field reporter (Bob) fans the flames of a fledgling brush fire and reports on a breaking story about a blaze in the forest. He is shot, and his story is interrupted by another breaking story — of a reporter shot down in the forest, covered by a fellow Channel 6 news reporter (Theresa), holding a smoking gun. Other breaking news: a rooftop sniper (Jay) in action. The sniper turns to report: "The terror began only a few moments ago. Channel 6 is here, once again, on the spot."

Lineup Room/VTV Link (video)

On the Spot News is on one of several monitors in a police lineup. The witness (Brett) identifies the program — "That's the show that killed my husband." A guard slaps cuffs on the fingered monitor and tells the other TV's they are free to go. One of the "innocent" TV's plays a station ID — "VTV: We get away with murder!"

Culture Hunt (video)

Culture Hunt, VTV's *Road Rules*-type show, has five American college idiots (Bob, Dave, Karen, Sarah, John) locate beanbags in the most historic landmarks throughout Europe. This week, in Amsterdam....

Frankly Anne (live)

The group must ferret out the beanbag at the house where Anne Frank's family hid. Chut (David) and Dilly (Bob) stay behind the tour to search in the attic hideaway. Their minds limited by their shallow lives, they liken Anne's hardships to their petty woes. ("Can you imagine being holed up in my apartment for two years? Now that would suck donkey dicks!") But Chut can't help being affected by the realities of Anne Frank's life ("What kind of God would make a world..."), and Dilly has to re-focus him on the beanbag ("...where a bean bag was so hard to find?") They're recharged, and they find it, and they get busted by the tour guide.

Europe Maps Link (video)

The *Culture Hunt* boys present a map they drew of their European trip. It's an outline of the U.S. split into 4 sections: "We saw France, Berlin and Europe, and England." A 1950's anti-Communist propaganda film with its map of Europe: a huge mother-Russia whose dark color bleeds over into other countries.

Jack Webber (video/live)

(b&w video) 50's right-wing Communist watchdog Jack Webber (Bob) warns America that within every fifth young boy is a "Commie dwarf," fulfilling the Marxist agenda. "Here's a simple test to see if your child is really a costumed dwarf — Hit him in the head with a hammer."

Calendar Link (video)

Snippets of folks enjoying the calendar at home, in the office, and, if your office is in your home....

Dream Of A Lifetime (video)

In a documentary, Lamar Kath (Bob) and his associate Geoff Cunniff (David) rip off a calendar page and celebrate their first day of their new organization, "Dream of a Lifetime," which grants wishes to terminally ill children. They hard-sell their organization to distraught parents. ("How about Michael Jackson, *today*! Yeah, that's right! Think Make a Wish could do that? No.") Over-promising, then trying to deliver, Lamar sneaks a little boy in at the stadium's service entrance to meet Shaquille O'Neal. When their promises fall flat, they have furious parents to deal with. Next, a little dying boy wants to see snow for the first time. Their plan of grating ice cubes is foiled (the landlord has turned off their water), so they get creative and freeze some cola. The boy's and his mother's excitement turns to disgust as they view the makeshift winter wonderland — twigs and Christmas ornaments stuck into a pile of brown slush. From jail, Lamar reveals that his partner Geoff is keeping the business going, with a few amendments. Now they take children with minor ailments to do things they "wouldn't mind doing." Footage of Geoff and a little boy getting a massage.

Massage Cream Commercial (video)

"Eight years of life got you tense?" starts a commercial. "Then, try Crazy Devil Kiddie Massage Cream!" to alleviate everyday aches and pains children can suffer from playing. It helps "all the major play points!" A zany devil cartoon decorates the jar. "Just look for the crazy devil with the googily eyes!"

Anders' Press Conference/Sloppy Close (live)

Satanic priest Anders Laevant (Bob) holds a press conference to put an end to the bumbling, cartoonish portrayal of his Lord and Master, the Devil. ("No other religious group has to put up with this!") His partner in the cause, Archbishop Trusdale (David), is also for an end to the "dumbing-down" of the Devil's image. It's hard to fear (or praise) a dopey Devil. The Catholic and the Satanist's familiar banter reveals them to be a little more than fellow activists — "Yes! I go to Anders' house for bar-b-ques and tossabouts."

To remind everyone that the battle between good and evil still exists, they're touring the country with their "fun-raisers," a Nickelodeon-inspired food fight/obstacle course. Credits roll, as the slicker-wearing friends send food flying everywhere.

Fishing Cold Tag (video)

Sweet ending on Anders and the Archbishop fishin' by a crick. The Satanist cracks wise that the only things biting today are the mosquitoes. "You get me every time with that one!" chuckles the Catholic, and they enjoy the lazy summer day and their friendship.

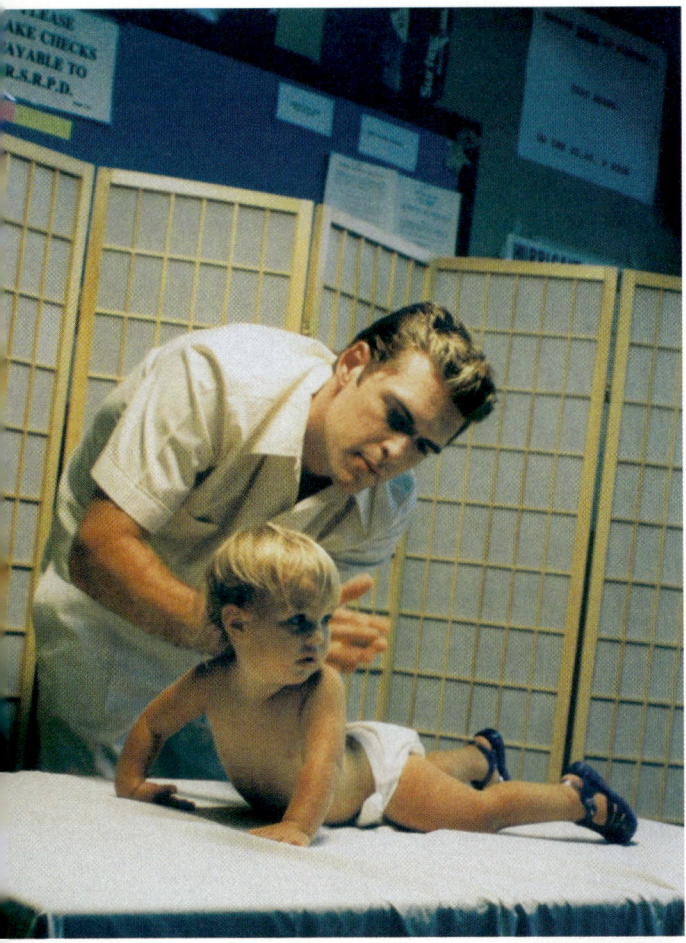

(above) Jay works out a baby's kinks; (below) Miller on location with Bob and David's "Protesters." © Adam Timrud Photography.

(live) A modern-day Jack Webber is remorseful and tries to repair the damage done by his early propaganda films with his new program, *Take It Back, Jack*. He admits that his theories were extreme — "just because a child is defiant, doesn't mean they want to overthrow the government." His short films also warned of the frigidity of women (*The Eagle vs. The Skirt* — "The women of America are out to bring this country to its knees, one man at a time! Case closed!") After spending an eight-year "week" at the Dalai Lama's mountain retreat, Webber found inner peace. Able to laugh at his old paranoia, he's made a humorous page-a-day calendar book, "Jack Webber's 365 Wrong Predictions."

(left and top right) Bob on a "Culture Hunt," both © Adam Timrud Photography; (middle right) David Cross and Mark Rivers in Amsterdam, where David was inspired by his own initial shallow response at the Anne Frank house; (bottom right) Flyer for the Bob-David-Bill live show, "Three Trips to Europe," from which came "Shampoo," and "Frankly Anne."

Notes About Episode 310

Bob: "Totally running out of steam. There are some good scene ideas here, but this show should have been shot."

David: 'The title, we called this show It's a No-Brainer just to fuck with Brian. We would do this thing, usually I would do it, because Bob didn't give a shit about it. I would get a script, and I would pick out 15 weird lines, where taken out of context would make a good title. We had a bunch of them for this episode, and he protested 'No-Brainer.' 'No! I fucking hate that phrase!' And it was almost immediate, everybody in the room said, 'Okay, It's a No-Brainer.'"

Bob: "A lot of college students touring Europe are really insensitive and oblivious to the history around them, and they might as well be on spring break. David, Bill, and I had that year taken three separate trips to Europe. We encountered a lot of college students there, and mostly they were idiots."

Bill: "As with many of the live scenes we did on this show, we tried Frankly Anne out in front of an audience in a local theater. It was met with cautious inspection. Despite this, we still believed in it. Part of the solution to fixing it involved trimming out the beat wherein the ghost of Anne Frank rails at the two boys. Did it work? You be the judge. But I think we all learned something from this experience: Lose the ghost of the deceased girl, who everyone in the world loves, and you might have a serviceable scene."

David: "I think everyone has something they can point to where the sketch started veering in a different direction than they had initially intended. And they lost the arguments, and they feel, 'Fuck, I wish I would have stuck to my guns and gotten my way, because I think it would have been better.' For me, it was Frankly Anne. It was inspired by my trip to Amsterdam, and I went to the Anne Frank house. I walked into the attic room, which I saw in plays, read about, read her diary, and was very familiar with. And my initial reaction, without consciously thinking about it, was, 'Oh, wow. This is bigger than I thought. This isn't so bad.' And then I was floored by my reaction, by how insensitive and ignorant that was. You see a lot of dumb American ex-hippies, college students, frat guys hanging around Amsterdam — 'Hey man, you can get high!' So I wanted to keep it insensitive, never have the characters be remorseful. And Bob felt like it was a little too harsh. He was afraid of being too offensive. For me, that was the point. It should be offensive. We're not saying she deserves this ridicule. We're making a comment based on a character, that people are like this and this is how stupid and ignorant some Americans are. It's one of the things that's always bothered me. I wish I didn't lose that argument. I think it could have been a much stronger, funny piece."

David: "Dream of a Lifetime was an idea I had that I always had kicking around. And Bob always liked it, but it took a little time to get around to it, which was true of a lot of our ideas. I like that piece even more than other people do. It really is one of my favorite pieces. It's such a great execution of a good Mr. Show idea. Bob will talk about the humanity the show has, which I completely agree with. It separated our show form a lot of other shows. And that's a perfect example."

Dino: "Bill and I wrote the Massage Cream Commercial. I think the initial image, to me, was a huge, muscle-bound masseur massaging a tiny baby. Unfortunately, it ended up being just Jay giving a three-year old a rubdown. Nothing against Jay or the three-year old, but it just wasn't enough of a contrast for me. Yes, to me, Jay has the body of a five-year-old."

SEASON FOUR
EPISODE GUIDE

After a grueling third season, Season 4 was a little more relaxed. "There was just this freshness to it that we didn't have in Season 3," David says. "We were able to delegate responsibility, which was imperative, and we brought in new writers. We knew we had much more time to do the shows. We weren't shooting a show before we even had a script done."

Season Four's Fantastic Newness

Jay Johnston and Bill Odenkirk moved up to new roles as producers. Scott Aukerman and B.J. Porter were added to the staff both as writers and as performers. Guest writers sharing the season were Jerry Collins and Eric Hoffman. Jill Talley returned, and Tom Kenny departed. Tom's animation voiceover schedule became such that he simply could not commit to the season. Becky Thyre, Jerry Minor, and Scott Adsit were also added as new regular performers. Brian left halfway through the season, and, while Paul opted not to return as a writer, he happily remained in the cast. Troy took a directing job on a feature (*Jack Frost*), but worked the fourth season as a producer. With Troy gone, Peyton Reed, Jonathan Dayton, and Valerie Faris became the location-segment directors. Many strong cameo appearances: Michael McKean (#401), Chris Rock as himself (#407), and Brian Doyle Murray and Jon Cryer in the *Monk Academy* movie (#402). Jeff Goldblum narrates the postcard in *Civil War Re-enactments* (#408). And, take a good look: that's Vince Vaughn chasing the herd of sheep (#402).

Four Years Is Four Years

As always, they were made to wait a long time for the fourth season pick-up from HBO. But, this time around, the wait was the most trying. At that point, they felt they'd proven themselves — they had done a great job for three seasons, and they were nominated for Emmys for writing. Then, right before the season was set to premiere, HBO changed *Mr. Show*'s time slot. "People ask us why we stopped doing the show, and that's one of the reasons. Moving us to Mondays at midnight killed the spirit of the staff, and certainly mine and David's. And I know there were fans at HBO certainly Carolyn Strauss and Chris Albrecht. But the time slot just killed us. So, we said no to a fifth season."

Flyer for Season 4 audience tapings.

$25,000 REWARD!

I recently received a $25,000 reward and then lost it. Embarrassing, huh? This money belongs to me and, if found, I hope you will return it all. It was last seen at Hollywood Center Studios, where you can go to see tapings of...

Mr. Show
with Bob and David

Choose A Time: 8 pm or 10 pm

Taping Dates

Nov. 3	Tuesday
Nov. 7	Saturday
Nov. 12	Thursday
Nov. 17	Tuesday
Nov. 21	Saturday

Information & Reservations:
(323) 860-KILL (5455)

Hey, and check out out website at:
www.mrshow.com

Flyer for Season 4 audience taping.

"I was initially not as upset as Bob was regarding the change to Monday nights," admits David. "The thing is, I just knew I didn't want to do it again. And I felt really awful, very guilty about it. I kept questioning if this was the right thing to do. But the last reason you should do something is out of obligation. Bob and I differ quite a bit in our personalities. First of all, he's way more driven than I am — thank God, or that show wouldn't have happened like that. I had to go up to his level, which is pretty intense. And, I think, into our fourth year of it, it just wasn't enjoyable. Bob and I were fighting a lot more and not communicating very well. There was a lot of mean-spiritedness in the writers' room that I completely was a part of, but I was very conscious of it. I don't think anybody else was. And it would take very little for me to jump right in there and start joking along with everybody else. I was becoming mean-spirited, and I was not having fun. And — I don't know what it is about my personality — I can't stick with something for a long time. I wanted to do other things. I wanted to move out of Los Angeles. So, I had been questioning whether I wanted to do another season. I think I would have ultimately not done it, and I would have felt really terrible about it. But then, when the time slot change happened, Bob felt the same way, but for different reasons."

Carolyn Strauss saw the true value of the series for HBO: "Every year it had been the same. It's not like it was through the roof, ratings-wise. But it has a very solid fan base, and some nice critical notices, Emmy nominations. And, underneath it all, we really felt there was something very valuable in this. While it may not get huge audience, this was what HBO was about: taking chances, doing provocative and innovative work. And, to me, *Mr. Show* and Bob and David really embodied that."

"No one ever got wealthy from doing this show," Bernie Brillstein adds, in summation. "Everyone was quite underpaid. But they honed their art, they had a chance to perform under the toughest of circumstances, and they pulled it off. And everyone has done good from it one way or another. It's really interesting, but when you do good, good comes out of it. There's a lot to be said for that. Four years is four years."

Commemorative poster for Season 4 premiere party. Original artwork courtesy Peter Bagge.

EPISODE 401 — LIFE IS PRECIOUS AND GOD AND THE BIBLE

written by:	Bob Odenkirk, David Cross, Scott Aukerman, Jerry Collins, Jay Johnston, Bill Odenkirk, B.J. Porter, Brian Posehn, Dino Stamatopoulos
location segment director:	Valerie Faris, Jonathan Dayton
live show director:	John Moffitt
cast:	David Cross, Bob Odenkirk, Scott Aukerman, John Ennis, Jay Johnston, Karen Kilgariff, Jerry Minor, B.J. Porter, Brian Posehn, Jill Talley
featuring:	Suli McCullough, Bill Odenkirk, Dino Stamatopoulos
special appearance by:	Michael McKean

Mr. Show *theme song and logo. Law Professor (Michael) introduces.*

Medical Marijuana (live)

David's feel-goody ramblings tip off Bob that he's high. "Medical marijuana," David defends. His prescription is "for stress related to working with Bob Odenkirk." Bob has the same stress. However, David is out of "medicine," so the two go to David's pharmacist.

Pharmacy (video)

The pharmacist invites them to "hang out" while the prescription is being refilled. David unenthusiastically agrees, and the guys are taken to the back room, where others, young and old, are sitting around, waiting or playing video games (Brian). Bob naively asks the pharmacist, "Wow, you're a musician?!" prompting him to put on some home-recorded music before going back out front. The old woman with glaucoma complains to David, "I've had to listen to that bullshit song four times already!" When the pharmacist returns, he throws in some pot brownies, a freebie for the old lady — "they'll fuck your ass up!" Cops charge in and bust him for crossing the line. They thank Bob for being a good citizen. Bob reveals that he was wearing a wire — but for warmth, "like electric underwear…and speaking of electric underwear…." Bob holds out two tickets to the Electric Underwear concert. David jumps up and down like a kid ("Me! Me! Me! Me!").

Electric Underwear Link (video)

At the rock concert, Bob points out that with his wire, he can record a bootleg of the Electric Underwear. A slob (Brian) watching TV in his underwear wears a wire, as an announcer pitches wearing a wire to record your favorite show — "Students can use it as a memory helper to record boring lectures." The same shirtless slob is sitting in a lecture hall, drinking beer.

Law School (live)

A bitter, cranky, law professor (Michael) scares the new law students on their first day with his standard speech that only one-third of them will make it to graduation. He has to leave and places the class in the hands of his student-teaching assistant, Gerald (Bob). Gerald nervously tries to carry on the professor's intimidating lecture, but his predictions for the students are strangely specific. ("By the time this class is over, two of you will be murdered, one of you will commit suicide…two of you will quit law school and go off to run an apple butter farm."). The real Gerald (David) appears in his underwear and accuses the "imposter" of beating him up and stealing his clothes. He pulls out a gun, but he accidentally shoots a student (Jerry). The ensuing chaos fulfills the prophecy of the faux teaching assistant. Dead students strewn about, ominous music plays, and Gerald cries, "What have you done to us?!" The professor returns to declare, "He's told the truth! That's all!"

Apple Butter Link (video)

In a TV ad, the faces of Gerald (David) and Imposter Gerald (Bob) are on the label of Hennesy Brothers' Apple Butter — "The only apple butter still sold in old-fashioned, breakable glass jars." An apple butter jar breaks in a park….

Cloning Hitler (video)

Two men who look like Hitler play casually with children at the park. "Hitlers seem to be popping up everywhere," says the reporter. Where are they coming from? Cloning. The Committee for Holocaust Reparations has cloned Hitlers to serve the relatives of Holocaust victims. "And, quicker than you can say 'L'Chaim,' Hitlers have become an integral part of Jewish life." We see Hitlers tending at a Seder and being used as playthings at little girls' slumber parties. But what is life like for the Hitlers? They complain they can't get a date — "as soon as they find out you're Hitler, forget it." If their "master" dies before them, the Hitler is allowed to live as a free man. A sad sack, older Hitler (David) describes his post-service life. "Oh, I keep busy…I clip coupons…I watch my stories, which I love…" His living room wall is covered with invasion-strategy maps ("lazy man's wallpaper"). "I'm Hitler. I can't not be Hitler." The camera zooms in on southern Florida….

(top left) Rehearsing Lifeboat; *(bottom left)* Bob on the lake shooting the local weatherman's fanfare'd intro. (© Adam Timrud Photography); *(middle)* Scott Aukerman in "Hitlers" lab. (© Adam Timrud Photography); *(right)* The Electric Underwear's ridiculous electric violinist (Jay). (© Adam Timrud Photography)

Lifeboat (live)

Sole survivors on a life raft: talk show host Todd Linder Floman (Bob), panelists, and one member of his studio audience are awaiting rescue, eight days after a hurricane sank their cruise ship where they were taping their show on relationships. A white trash love triangle (Karen, David, Jill) continue squabbling: mother and daughter in love with the same man. The audience member guy (Jerry) tells the sad group what's what, starting with the pregnant mother — "You need to respect the baby, 'cause life is precious, and God, and the Bible." He puts a shout out to figuring out how to survive without food and water. Two-timing Derwin's (David) "super-secret lover" Fabian (Suli) climbs into the raft. He was on an island, but he refuses to share the info ("I ain't savin' Mr. Three-timing Whore of the Universe!"). Todd gives his "final thought" after white trash momma mindlessly punctures the raft with her "lady of the manor engagement broach." Derwin, also facing death, has final thoughts — "I knew I'd never make it to 30, 'cause I'm a wild man! Before I die, I'm gonna fuck me a fish!"

Final Thought Link (live)

A desperate man with a gun (John) contemplates killing himself — "I'm getting on the news tonight. That's probably my final thought." He is interrupted by a countdown, and he goes back to anchoring the news.

Scams & Flams (live/video)

Special interest segment of the news, complete with a cartoony jingle open, reported by feeble Yale Hadderity (David). He investigates local businesses and determines if they are legitimate or fraudulent. This week, it's Barnaby Hutchman's "Wishing Well 'n' Such" shop, "where a person can, for a fee, make a wish." The barren shop features only a wishing well. An old woman stands, tossing in dollars. The cameras are an unwelcome sight, and proprietor Barnaby (Bob) quickly ushers them toward the door as Yale fires off the questions. Barnaby vehemently denies it's a scam, which concludes Yale's tame investigation. Yale adds a plug for the store on his segment. Another investigative reporter (Jay) descends upon the scene. Barnaby is really an actor, and the wishing well shop was a trap for Yale's spineless, fraudulent scam reports. Yale begins to cry at his world falling apart. "Barnaby" takes pity on him and tells him it was all a prank — the mean reporter is the actor, "and this is my real hair," replacing his ridiculous wig. Yale is pacified, and concludes his report, "What seems like a scam may not be a scam, but somebody might turn it into a scam."

Weather Close (live/video)

Next is the weather, with low-key weatherman Turk Finnery (Bob). The segment opens with another musical cartoon — which Turk bursts through, replete in barbershop stripes, hat and cane, announcing "That's me!" He starts with the weather, but is interrupted by the showman Turk doing a huge, show-stopping number — with girls, a kick-line, and a champagne cocktail on the lake. The number is upstaged by a live production, Turk now in a red, white, and blue glittery vest, bringing it home: *"I'm talking 'bout the weather report! Oh, yeah!"* Credits roll over the finale, with showgirls, jugglers, animals, and monsters (and Michael McKean).

Notes About Episode 401

Brian: *"Medical marijuana had been in the news recently, a place in San Francisco was giving out herb to people who pretended they were sick and actual sick people. I was joking around that I needed pot to work with Bob, and that my doctor should prescribe some sweet weed. I saw the joke and pitched it as an opening bit. We wrote it together."*

Bill: *"The first time we shot the Pharmacy scene was at this actual pharmacy near Larchmont Avenue. And it didn't work because of the sound. We had to reshoot it, the whole thing. So, we set up a pharmacy set at the women's prison, where we were shooting the opening for #405 [of the new boss running the show from prison]. And the footage that we use of Bob and David going in is from the actual pharmacy at Larchmont, and then when they enter the scene, that's all from the women's prison."*

David: *"We were at this pharmacy, and there was no security. I couldn't believe it! There were these huge jars of everything. I had a backpack, and I was loading up on diazepam, Valium, Klonopin. And I had hundreds and hundreds and hundreds of pills. I'd grab a handful, and walk them out to Dino who had his helmet case on his motorcycle seat, and I would pass it to him. Man, we made out like fuckin' bandits. Probably the best perk we had in the four years of shooting."*

Bill: *"Electric Underwear is my favorite transition piece ever. We needed a transition from Pharmacy to Law School. David lazily offered this rock band name; he was just joking around, making a fake, phony pitch. My head exploded! And we said, 'Let's do that, let's really do that!' But then we resisted using this link because it felt like we were giving in too easily. It is easy to give in to genius! And so we did it. It was a fun, high-energy, stupid, dumb, dumb transition. But it was so worth it."*

Bob: *"The Electric Underwear's performance is partially based on a clip I saw once of the Electric Light Orchestra. They were the first band to be caught using pre-taped tracks in live concerts, and from the clip, I saw it was obvious, with the violinist jumping around with great gusto as he was 'playing.'"*

David: *"Law School, while not that great of a sketch, was another one of those sketches that Bob and I had a blast writing. The guy who takes over and assumes he has to maintain the authority of professor. We loved writing those Paper Chase-esque lines."*

David: *"Apple Butter is a dumb, retarded, bullshit link. It was clearly one of those things where we just gave up."*

Bill: *"Along with many of the other writers, I am featured as one of the 'Hitlers' in this piece. We needed as many as we could get, and everyone was enlisted to slap on a square mustache. In the scene with the elderly Jewish couple settling down for the night while Brian and I were the Hitlers at their bedside, they were told to improvise some dialogue. In the first take, the old man said something to the effect that the weather was improving. The old lady agreed and declared, 'Spring has sprung!', as though it were the topper to some ripping exchange. Brian and I both exploded with laughter the first time we heard this line and then every subsequent time as well. In the show, you can see me just beginning to break up immediately before the cut."*

Bob: *"Janeane wanted to be in the Lifeboat scene. But she is too 'famous.' At first we said yes, then we realized her presence would pull people out of the scene. She would have been doing a Southern accent, she wouldn't have been lost in the scene. We would have only used her again as herself [like Vince Vaughn, Jon Cryer], or we'll use her in a cameo like Brian Doyle Murray."*

Brian: *"Lifeboat was one of those scenes where the room [pitch session] made the sketch work. I went in there with two other ideas and a vague version of this scene. I pitched that Jerry Springer and his guests were stuck in an elevator during an earthquake. The guys riffed on it, someone brought up the movie Lifeboat, and we all liked the idea of that. The guy that Suli played, who climbs on the raft came from a 'real*

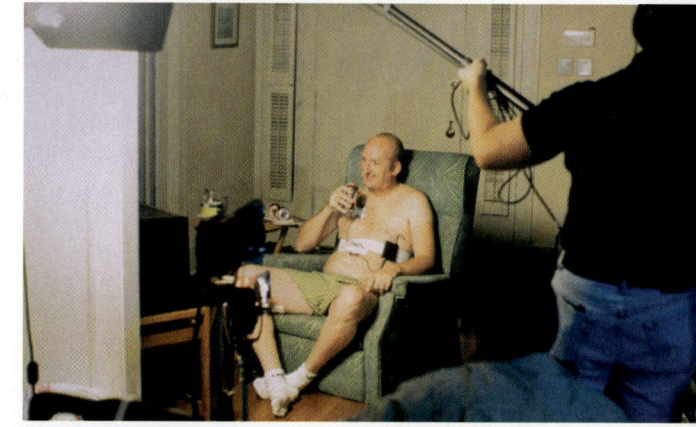

Brian shooting the link from Pharmacy to Law School. (© Adam Timrud Photography)

guy' on Springer's Too Hot video. The weirdo comes running onto the Springer set with his crazy wig and his crazy arms swinging, it was an obvious fit. David's line, 'I'm gonna fuck me a fish,' is one of my favorites, it still makes me smile. A year or two after the sketch aired, a couple of us saw a Springer episode where a jackass kid stood up in the audience and quoted the scene. The guy was obviously a Mr. Show fan and was smirking when he said, 'Life is precious and God and the Bible.' It was hilarious to me because nobody reacts when he says it, the joke was for no one. How many people were watching Springer and said 'Holy shit, Mr. Show, episode 401'? Not many."

Bob: *"I cannot sing. Listen to the crescendo of Scams and Flams for incontrovertible evidence."*

David: *"The wishing well idea in Scams and Flams came from an old idea, when Bob came with me to buy a used Volvo. We went to this little rinky-dink place on Fairfax Ave. This guy was such a classic used-car salesman. 'This baby's a tank!' and hitting it on its side. After we left, Bob and I were talking about shitty salesmen, just selling people anything, people are so gullible. And one of us came up with just having a wishing well — 'Yeah. Anybody who buys a Volvo gets a free wish!'"*

David: *"The thing where I wheel in and sing, 'Oh, my scammy flammy Mammy!' I was supposed to pop my head and arms through this green-screen and sing it to the camera, but we couldn't get it. That took like seven different takes where something went wrong, and each time I got hurt in a different way. The wood broke, the big wood boards were falling on top of me. We went through all the screens we had, and we said, 'Well, we can't do this anymore.' So they got the dolly and tried wheeling me across. I would go right out of frame, I would never stop. It was a funny mess; we were all punch-drunk at that point. It was so late."*

Bill: *"In addition to two police officers and a Hitler, I played the front end of the pantomime horse in the Weather "report" musical finale. I couldn't see a damn thing with that head on and, frankly, the horse's dancing shows it."*

EPISODE 402 — IT'S PERFECTLY UNDERSTANDABLE

written by:	David Cross, Bob Odenkirk, Scott Aukerman, Jerry Collins, Jay Johnston, Bill Odenkirk, B.J. Porter, Brian Posehn
location segment director:	Jonathan Dayton, Valerie Faris
live show director:	John Moffitt
cast:	Bob Odenkirk, David Cross, John Ennis, Jay Johnston, Karen Kilgariff, Jerry Minor, Brett Paesel, Brian Posehn, Jill Talley, Becky Thyre
featuring:	Gerald Jann, Victor Kobayashi, Dennis Lee, Jerry Messing, Sam Sarpong, Ken Takamoto, Preston Wainsley
special appearance by:	Jon Cryer, Brian Doyle Murray, Vince Vaughn

Mr. Show theme song and logo. Psychic (Becky) introduces.

Rehearsal Open (live/video)
Bob and David run the "rehearsal reel" because Bob can't remember his lines. In the taped rehearsal, a trainer with a whip (John) ushers them back to their cage, like animals.

Those Amazing Actors (video)
Lane Wellesby (John), "trainer to the stars," explains about this seeming abuse on reality program, Those Amazing Actors: "They like to get hit. Performers aren't like you and me, they have thick skin." His tricks include smearing peanut butter on soap actors' faces to ellicit a passionate kiss and cuing actors by banging his riding crop next to the correct prop — "There's a reason for the phrase 'as dumb as an actor.'" He predicts one day actors will be trained "to be useful to society." Vince Vaughn is herding sheep, another Hollywood actor (Jay) serves as a "guide dog" for the blind (Karen).

Blind Girl (live)
Karen, a blind girl, welcomes her friend Jonathan (Bob), who volunteers to read to her every night. His steamy selection has Karen asking for sex. They're interrupted by Stephen (David), a man who (lamely) describes the sunsets for her. The boys become competitive and each tries to out-do the other, describing outrageous phenomena in the sky. ("An eclipse? He's not telling you about the nuclear mushroom cloud!") The guys start insulting each other, and Karen confesses she's not blind. Stephen confesses that he is blind. Karen feels sorry for him, and the two go off together. Stephen takes off in his car before Karen can get in and crashes in two seconds. The woman (Brett), bulldozed by blind (and dead) Stephen, uses her cell phone to call for help.

Emergency Psychic Hotline (live)
Emergency Psychic Hotline, where psychics come to your aid in a crisis. Host Janey Paff (Jill), audio psychic Mystique (Becky), and small-time recording artist Maple Syrup (David) take calls. Panicked callers needing help, including a father with a drowned baby, receive useless psychic approximations of their emergency situation. All forecasts aren't gloomy — the bereaved father can also expect a raise at work. Other accident victims get similar psychic help: a man with a mangled body (Jay) smiles, "Wedding bells?" The Dalai Lama dies just after hearing he will be reincarnated.

Dalai Lama (video/live)
(video) Tibetan monks search for years for the next incarnation of the Dalai Lama and find him in Indiana high school senior, Dougie Bendell (Bob). Torn away from his best friend Derek (David), they keep in touch through letters, with Dougie's responses sounding ever more enlightened. ("It is good news about Van Halen. Like the lotus, they bloom for you again and again.")

(live) Dougie Dalai Lama gets a visit at his mountaintop retreat from old pal Derek. The reunion is strained, having nothing in common any more. Derek hits him up for work. ("I thought maybe you could hook my shit up with a jiz-ob.") The Dalai Lama gives in to sentiment, and Derek is made monk shift-supervisor.

(video) Derek screws up on the job (prayer book concealing comic book; hiding porno backflipping into the reflecting pool).

(live) Derek packs to leave, but the monks stand up for him. Their joyful reconciliation is cut short....

Monk Academy (live/video)
(live) The Dalai Lama (Bob) shifts gears: "Okay! Cut the shit!...We've gotta figure out how to beat those rich snobs from the fat kids camp!" William Van Landingham, the portly spokes-kid from the rival camp, shows up to boast on the fat kids' 500-year winning streak. The Dalai Lama and the chubby kid have an angry stare-down.

(video) The referee (Brian Doyle Murray) signals the start of the games

"I could get used to this!" Indiana high school senior Dougie (Bob) is led to his destiny.   photos © Adam Timrud Photography.

("All right, let's keep it clean this year!"). The fat kids cheat to win the water balloon carry. But the monks score in the bike race, thanks to Derek (David) sidetracking the chubby cyclist with chocolate, then slashing his throat. The fat kids bring in a ringer, Professor Murder, for the rap-off. The monks resign to losing again, until the Dalai Lama steps up to the mic, head to toe in Adidas, and raps ("a rap, a rap, arappity, rap, rap!"). "Damn, his science is too tight!" laments an outdone Professor Murder. The monks are clearly the winners! Jon Cryer drives up in a fun convertible with a babe and a monkey (Dr. Baloney). "Duckie!!!" the two friends cheer. They get in and drive away to the *Monk Academy* song.

Chimp Close (live)

Back onstage, Bob and David provide the epilogue to the *Monk Academy* story: "And that's how it happened," they moved to Hollywood, changed their names and started this show with Dr. Baloney, who gives his seal of approval (farty noises). The guys high-five. Credits roll, and their trainer (John) wrangles them back into their cage.

Notes About Episode 402

David: "It was so cool that Vince Vaughn came out for Those Amazing Actors. We were shooting up in the hills, and he had an hour drive to get out there, for four seconds of silent screen time. Pretty decent of him. But upon reflection, everybody who did cameos for us was great. Nobody complained, they did it happily, they, they would drive an hour away to be in a hot, shitty place, with no trailer. Everybody was cool. So, much love goes out to my superstars who helped us along the way."

Scott: "Blind Girl was an old Fun Bunch sketch that I pretty much adapted to be a Mr. Show sketch. Much more successfully, by the way; our Fun Bunch sketch wasn't very good. Our original sketch, B.J. wasn't actually in. It was me and the girl was Rachel Quanitence. The first part of the sketch, up until David's character comes in, was pretty much the old sketch. And then when I was trying to think of how to turn it into a Bob and David sketch, I got the idea of another guy coming in and they have competing descriptions. I remember during Blind Girl it was really written for Bob, at a certain point, to do his patented 'Bob Yell.' And he wasn't doing it, and I asked him, 'Hey can you just let out a yell during this line?' He said that he was kind of tired of doing those. And, of course, he gets in front of an audience, and he starts yelling immediately."

David: "Every once in a while, there are things that someone on the cast just can't get right away. Bob had a monster of a time with Spunk (#307), it was driving him fucking nuts. My thing was Hunger Strike (#306), I didn't get that until the very end, right before we did the show. Everyone has one of those things that becomes a bane, and it's hard to get past. And for Jay it was playing the Dad calling into the psychic hotline about his drowning daughter — playing the balance of being urgent and trying to get the info from the psychic, getting that joke and playing that joke. We were too down to the wire, so we had Bob play that off-camera voice of the dad."

David: "A little tidbit — Maple Syrup, that outfit was designed so I can hold my throat, which I did the first season when we did Screwballz, 'I would love to.' That soulful black voice that I can only do by holding my throat. Paula [Elins, costume *(top left) Vince Vaughn!; (top right) Brian Doyle Murray as the unbiased ump in the age-old rivalry between the Monks and the Fat Kids Camp; (bottom right) David with frequently featured kid, Jerry Messing; (bottom left) Brett Paesel in mid-emergency; photos © Adam Timrud Photography.*

designer] designed this outfit that was big enough, and I actually have a fake arm, and it covers my neck, so I can hold my throat as Maple Syrup."

David: "That hurt like a motherfucker when I back flipped into the monk's reflecting pool. That was a bummer. First of all, it was like two feet of water — you can see when I get up, it's basically at thigh-level. And I also landed on my back. That flapping sound was not enhanced. That was the reverse belly flop. And if you watch the rest of the tape after the cut in the show, I do that little weird dance for a couple seconds, and then I just grab my back and I yell, 'Fuck!! OWW!' It was also really nasty, still, pond-scummy water."

David: "For Monk Academy, we needed to get a legitimate rapper. So Flava Flav came up as an option. And we thought, 'Oh, great. He'd be perfect for this.' But part of the joke is that he loses to Bob (as Dalai Lama). And he realizes he is going to lose and thinks Bob's great, even though he's really bad — it was written in the script that Bob's rapping was really goofy, and it makes no sense, he's just rhyming stuff just to rhyme. A very white-boy version of rapping. We send Flava Flav the script, and it came back that he's very interested, but didn't like the script. And that made me laugh, because you either like the script and you get it, or you don't. And the next day, we heard back from his agent that Flava Flav wants to be shown in a positive light. I asked, 'What does that mean?' He wants to win the rap contest. It was just such a great example of someone not getting it."

Bob: "I felt the Monk Academy scene was too long, especially since it folds into what is essentially a parody, not what we do or strive to do on the show. I thought it was good idea, let's shorten it. And David defended the scene. It was particularly frustrating because I had to remind them that I was the one who came up with the idea, with the transitional line — 'Okay, now cut the crap!' — and into the fat kids camp rivalry. I wasn't putting down someone's scene. Now it's one of our weakest shows, and we have to live with it."

Scott: "I was one of the principle writers on the fat kids scene, which is my Waterloo. First of all, none of the kids' parents knew that there would be so much cursing in the rap. So he's out there, just practicing his rap on the mic — 'If the nigger gets paid he gets all the riches, he never gets enough motherfucking bitches.' The moms are horrified. The kids are waving their hands, they love it. And when we were filming the movie part of it, I was just getting into the groove — 'Hey, I'm pretty good at actually helping out on the set.' So all the fat kids are there. And I swear that it said 'Fat Kids' in the breakdown [which lists the roles up for audition for actors], that they must have been hired knowing this sketch was about fat kids. So I was giving direction to everybody, telling them where to stand, 'Monks, you do this, and all you fat kids, I want you to…' and I said it about three times. And everyone was looking at me. I was thinking only as a writer, I wasn't trying to insult them. So kids started crying, and parents got upset. It's just one of those mistakes you make."

403 SHOW ME YOUR WEENIS

written by:	Bob Odenkirk, David Cross, Scott Aukerman, Jerry Collins, Jay Johnston, Bill Odenkirk, B.J. Porter, Brian Posehn, Dino Stamatopoulos, Mark Rivers
location segment director:	Jonathan Dayton, Valerie Faris
live show director:	John Moffitt
cast:	David Cross, Bob Odenkirk, Scott Aukerman, John Ennis, Jay Johnston, Tom Kenny, Jerry Minor, B.J. Porter, Brian Posehn, Jill Talley, Becky Thyre
featuring:	Gabriel Arabia, Raylene, Charlie, Brandi Sommerville

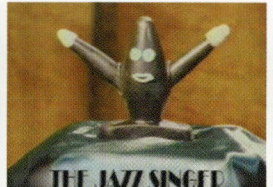

Mr. Show logo and swinging big band theme song. A "Mr. Show Object" introduces: "Hey, bachelors! It's martini time with Bob and David!"

Rat Pack Open (live)
Bob and David come out in smoking jackets (and smoking) with the other guys, onto a stage that is a plush after-hours lounge, with sexy "Mr. Show Objects" (in skimpy outfits with cute, fuzzy antlers and a rum barrel around their neck). Bob and David announce tonight's special guests: Senator Drinks-A-Lot and their dancers, The Itty Bitty Titty Committee. Jill, dressed as an Object and hating it, brings out the 'Ballbuster Hotline" with a call from David's wife, who's got "diarrhea of the nag!" We hear their thoughts — Bob and David have noticed Jill's bad attitude. Jill joins in with her thoughts: "Mr. Show is nothing but a boys' club! Boys write the show, boys get the best parts…girls aren't included."

Mr. Show Boys' Club (video)
Bob's thoughts continue in voiceover, as he defends Mr. Show — "Mr. Show Boys' Clubs of America have always included girls." It's a club where boys and girls can learn all kinds of fun activities — play basketball, take day trips, ballroom dance lessons — but the girls sit to the side while the boys participate. Even when "reaching out to their elders," the girls (and the elderly women) are allowed only to watch through a window. The women who have learned their potential through the Mr. Show Boys' Club include: a magician's assistant, a pro-football player's girlfriend, and Morgangeline the Puckering Moron (John), who kisses fans at sporting events.

Stealing News (video)
Morgangeline's latest caper led police on a two-hour chase, and we are live on the scene. Channel 7 reporter Lane Johnson (Jay) reports on the tragic death toll of the chase, as Channel 6 reporter Chip Curson (David), sneaks in his microphone to catch Channel 7's report. Lane angrily pushes him away — "Curson, would you please get your own news!" Curson turns to his own news camera: "Reporters are being very tight-lipped. We may never know what this was all about. But it seems very important." "Nice try, Chip," says the anchorman (Bob), "Action 6 News — if somebody else is there, we're there, too."

Toenapper News Intro Link (video)
Next on the news: an update on the Hibbert kidnapping story. A reporter from Channel 6 (B.J.), hunched under Channel 8's anchor desk, slyly sneaks his microphone up to catch the story delivered by their anchorman (Tom).

Toenapper (live)
The Hibbert family is relieved to be reunited with their son, who was returned from the kidnappers for no ransom. The kidnapper "Xavier" (Bob) calls Mr. Hibbert (David) to see if he found his son's toe at the drop point, then realizes his fuck-up. He excuses himself and chews himself out. He improvises "Phase 2" — "bring the kid back to the drop point…return in one hour, and you will get the toe." It is revealed that the kid is not missing any toes. Xavier can't help but see the humor when he see his own bloody foot — "There are days and there are days." As he sets ransom for his own toe, the police arrive, laughing as they arrest him. "We've got a killer party tape," they say of their surveillance tape.

Underground Tapes (video)
Students listen to the toenapper's foible at an actual three-person "college" party in this commercial for "hard-to-get" underground tapes. Join the Underground Tape Railroad, and, each month, a college student will deliver a new, infamous tape, featuring such titles as: Train Hits Dumbass, Dick Cavett Lights Fart, Dick Cavett Poo Party, and the newest, The Wyckyd Sceptre Party Tape.

Wyckyd Sceptre (live/video)
Record execs (Tom and Jay) view the now infamous Wyckyd Sceptre tape in disbelief — within the milieu of the raucous party, the lead band members (Bob and David) enthusiastically butt-fuck. The guys from the band (John, Bob, David, Scott), idiots all, arrive at the record company for a meeting. They're shown the tape. They whoop it up at the sight of themselves partying, oblivious to the fact that it was a drunken, gay orgy. They take offense when the execs suggest that they are gay — "Dude, stop saying that, it was just a party!" To help explain, exec Jay announces

(left) "Benny Hill" close with the girls of the Mr. Show Boys' Club; (right) Ignorant rockers Wyckyd Sceptre (David, Bob, John). (Photos © Adam Timrud Photography)

he's gay, and he points out that what they did on the tape is what he does with his gay friends, "because *we're gay*." The band takes this in — "Faggot." Tom tells them their careers are over, but Jay has an idea…they play to stadium full of leather-clad gays at Fire Island with new hits such as "Getting the Shaft Again."

Butt Plugs (video)

The Fire Island concert is sponsored by King Royal Butt Plugs, with something for everyone: the Speed Demon, the Jazz Singer, and King Prong. By Menocu. But what else is Menocu up to? Stiff pitchman (David) escorts us…outside, across a river, over to…

Blind House (MENOCU) (video)

The House of the Future, designed for the blind. In a low-low budget industrial film, Buck (David) greets Dr. Finn Barston (Bob), designer of the house's new technology, which will help the blind avoid "the mess of blind-caused accidents." They go inside, and Buck asks obviously scripted questions about Dr. Barston's voice-identification furniture he developed for "the blinds." In a sparse living room, Dr. Barston demonstrates — he covers his eyes and clumsily bumps around. The furniture announces itself as he collides with it ("I am a couch! I am a couch!"). "So you see, blinds are like regulars now." A deluxe model features celebrity voices. ("Go out and get 'em Rocky! I'm a lamp. Burgess Meredith.") Buck thanks us for joining him, and thanks Menocu…"Oh, great leader!" He bows to a picture of a terrifying space monster.

Racist In The Year 3000 (live/video)

The divine beast Menocu is in his spaceship preparing to blow up Earth. Suddenly, his evil tendril is shot off by a laser gun. "Take that Men-o-JEW!" The bigoted space cowboy is Byron D. Labockwith the VIIth (David), and we are watching his adventure show, *Racist in the Year 3000*. Tonight's episode finds Byron lamenting that he is the last pure white human in a galaxy full of mixed-breed minority alien robots. His master plan of "propergatin' the species" with meek sidekick Dougie (Bob) goes awry when Dougie drawls that he is 1/80 black. Furious, Byron sends him packing. ("I cain't believe I've been makin' love to a man who's part Negro!") In a teaser for next week's episode, Menocu creates a polybreed monster that is "the perfect combination of all the human races and just a pinch of sandcrab." He sics the hideous beast (with one huge claw) after Byron, who has just reunited with Dougie in a desert wasteland. "Quick! Use your magic bean!" screams Byron. Dougie and Byron rub the little lucky bean on their feet, and they run!

Benny Hill Close (video)

The monster chases the boys on the space desert, with sped-up film and *Benny Hill* music. The chase gets wild when Dougie's (Bob) spacesuit snags and is ripped off, leaving him in a shiny blue bikini. Morgangeline the Puckering Moron (John), and an English bobby (Jay) pop up from behind some sand dunes and join the chase. The kids from the *Mr. Show* Boys' Club join in, too, but Byron (David) pauses to shun the little girls. The disappointed girls sulk, talk it over, then leave.

Notes About Episode 403

Bill: "Toenapper came out better than I thought it would. Bob was really great as the confused kidnapper. Only an Odenkirk could have pulled off that explosive rage this character has to have. At one point during the scene, Bob turns to yell at himself in the mirror, and I swear his blood pressure is actually visible on camera. It was a complex piece to do live in the studio, because we had to have two separate sets prepared, a split-screen for the audience to watch, and there was a voice-alteration 'thingy' on the kidnapper's phone. It was a technical tour de force!"

Bob: "People say my anger in Toenapper is exquisite, and 'quintessential Bob.' But, for me, it's just business as usual. I just channeled my anger at the audio department, and voila!"

David: "Half of the Underground Tapes available are based on real things — Famous Model Fistfuck is Jane Kennedy, Senator Suicide is Bud Dweyer, who wasn't a senator, but he shot himself during a press conference, Angry Drunk Black Guy Gives Directions is another real tape, and Train Hits Dumbass was Brian's joke. Not that I don't love it, but that, in the four years of Mr. Show, might be the most offensive thing we ever did, because it's a real tape. It's horrific. It's this woman who's, like, 50-years-old, and a train is stopped and she just goes to walk past the stopped train onto the other track, and a train comes by, and she's dead on impact, she goes flying. Train Hits Dumbass. If it's not offensive, it's certainly the most insensitive thing we've ever done."

David: "Wyckyd Sceptre was an idea that Mark Rivers and I came up with, not as a sketch, but we were talking about the Pamela Anderson/Tommy Lee tape that had just come out, and the ridiculous dialogue. And I think the kernel of the idea came from Mark, about how stupid they are, and they could be fucking another guy and saying the same thing. And that turned into one of the most popular sketches we ever did."

David: "When we were shooting Wyckyd Sceptre, there was no script for when we were partying in the apartment. It was just, go and act drunk and fuck around. That stuff in the hot tub, there was no real dialogue, there might have been something written, but you're in a hot tub, and you're just shouting over each other. You don't really stick to the script, because that's not what real people do."

B.J.: "The 'Fire Island' audience was just seven or eight guys — the writers, Peter Giambalvo [coordinating producer], and I'm pretty sure Vahe Manoukian, crew member, Devo aficionado, and occasional Mr. Show bit player. Even if we had the budget to hire that many extras, we couldn't have acquired that many leather outfits, which is apparently some kind of uniform that the gentlemen wear on Fire Island. Groups of four or five of us at a time would stand in a certain place in front of a large green screen and jump around like "gay" versions of our idiotic selves. We'd do this for a minute or so, then the grouping and costumes would be changed to jump up and down in front of another section of the green screen. The editor then cut these little scenes out and pasted them together in his fancy editing machine to make us look like a large-ish audience. So, if you want to, you can stop the scene (top) Sold Out Crowd on Fire Island! Composite shot of same guys in different leather configurations. (bottom) Wyckyd Sceptre's new following. (© Adam Timrud Photography)

where the Fire Island audience is cheering and dancing while Wyckyd Sceptre is playing, ten of those guys are the exact same footage of me, jumping up and down, and falling all over writer Jerry Collins and Vahe. I'm not sure I was supposed to be doing that, but those two sure knew how to wear that leather."

David: "One of my favorite things — it is my idea and I'm proud of it, even though it's a tiny little subtle thing — in the Wyckyd Sceptre live at Fire Island composite shot, I thought there should be a guy in a wheelchair, because there's always one or two guys, and it's sad but true. And so we got Vahe in the wheelchair, but he cuts the composite shot, and there's six guys in wheelchairs scattered around the frame. It just cracks me up. It's kind of hard to see, but it's really rewarding."

Dino: "One of the butt plugs was supposed to be a cactus, I believe, but ended up looking more like Al Jolson in 'Mammy!' pose, so I suggested painting it black like a minstrel, and I think Jay came up with the name 'The Jazz Singer.' A quick, easy fix that probably worked better than the original joke."

Dino: "Blind House was a scene written by Jay about talking furniture to aid blind people. He wrote the whole thing pretty much as it is about some company called Menocu. At the first reading of the scene, David began saying his lines in a stiff, droll 'bad acting' fashion, and Bob quickly caught on. The idea to shoot the whole piece as a bad industrial followed."

David: "Everybody, Bob and myself included, would bring in a piece that was specific to their kind of humor, a sketch that was unique to them, and it needed work to be on Mr. Show. And Blind House was one of those very typical Jay pieces. And we got it. We were reading it and, about a third the way into it, it was pretty clear — it was kind of dying in the room. It was not really going anywhere, wasn't really getting many laughs. We had been up for how ever many hours. And it was just this unspoken thing between Bob and me, I just started reading it in this very stilted, strange way, and Bob picked up on it immediately. And we just sort of went off in that direction. Everybody started laughing at the silliness of what we were doing and the way we were performing it. All of a sudden, it had this whole different context to it, without ever changing a word in the script. It all started making sense. I honestly didn't start reading it that way to try and make the piece work. I did it to kind of entertain myself and everyone else in the room. It went from not working at all, to working really well. And it gave this piece a context that none of us had really envisioned. We were just goofing around, and it was like, 'Oh this works, this is great.' It's silly and funny. Gives it that whole other layer."

Jay: "Blind House was my answer to 'comedy of understanding' for those unable or too lazy to see. And for those of you out there who are blinds, don't be offended when you feel this. Because all I really wanted to do was write a scene, not hurt anyone. Also, a side note (I don't know if I even told anyone), that the corporation Menocu, also the name of the creature in the spaceship, was simply: ME + NO + SEE + YOU. By the way, clever license plates are the highest payment of respect to our language. I told no one because it would've produced the embarrassment I feel now, but face to face."

Bob: "I love that sketch, Racist in the Year 3000. It didn't get as many laughs as we thought it would, but I think it's a brilliant sketch. And I get a lot of people's comments on it. And one of the lines David gets the most from the show is, 'Keep 'em coming, Gleep Glop!' Some sketches work better on TV than they do live, and I think Racist is one and Philouza is another."

Jay: "In Racist in the Year 3000 I was 'Gleep-Glop' the robot bartender. Under the bar, on a mechanic's creeper, I worked the arms of that little motherfucker, and, for no discernable reason, was obligated to wear a black, skintight full-body unitard. I looked very sissy."

Bob: "I pledge that every show I write on will have a 'Benny Hill Running' segment on it at some point. (Previous to this, there was one in a Get A Life episode that I was on staff for, though it wasn't necessarily my contribution.) Because I watched a lot of Benny Hill. What can I say, I like to be made angry."

Jay: "Shooting the Benny Hill Close was a near-heart attack festival for all involved. A lot of running around. It sucked tremendously, but was for a damn good cause. And, in the end, to me, was well worth it."

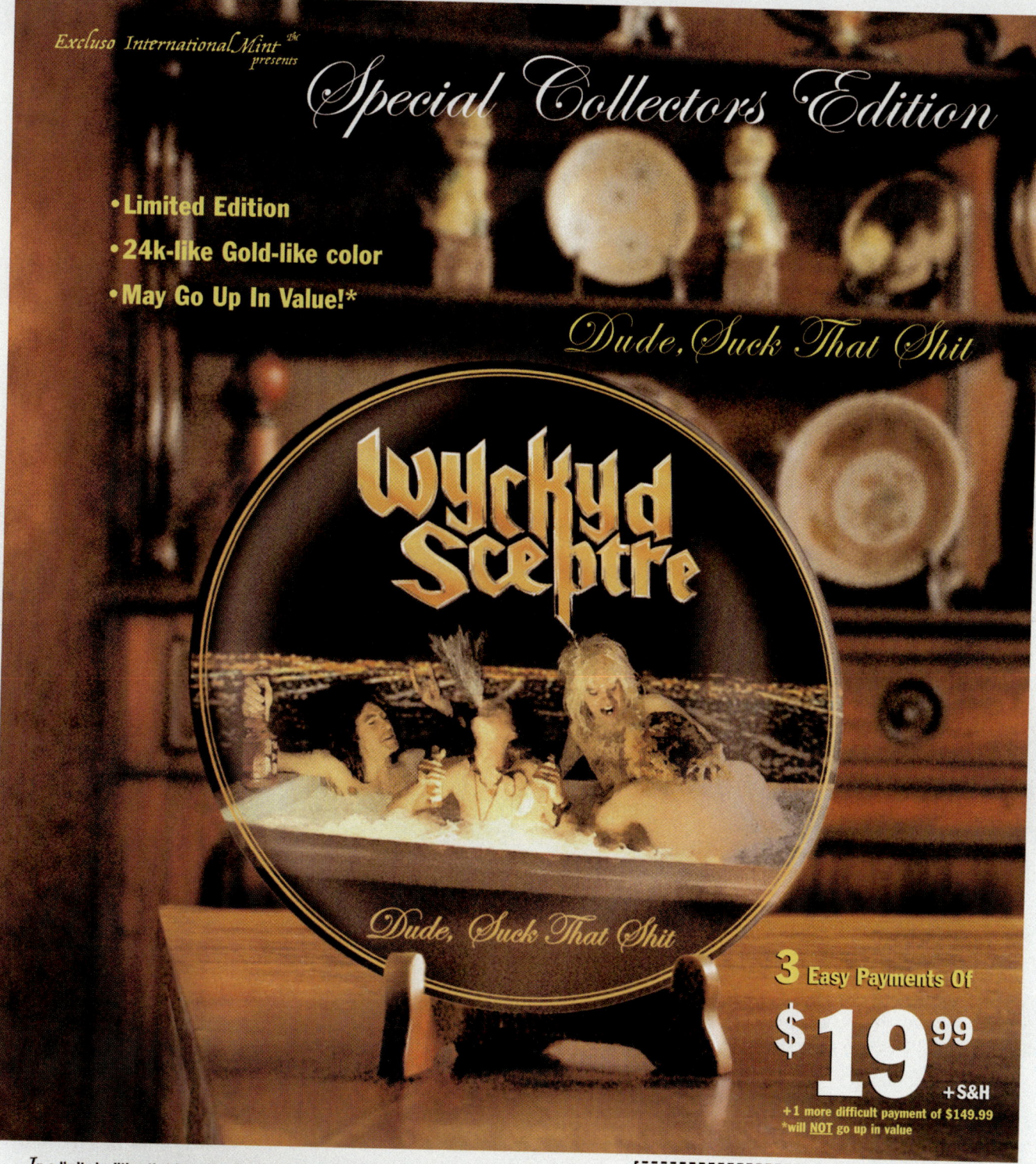

Excluso International Mint the presents

Special Collectors Edition

- **Limited Edition**
- **24k-like Gold-like color**
- **May Go Up In Value!***

Dude, Suck That Shit

Wyckyd Sceptre

Dude, Suck That Shit

3 Easy Payments Of
$19.99
+S&H
+1 more difficult payment of $149.99
*will **NOT** go up in value

In a limited edition that has already been pulled from the market, this delightful keepsake is now available. The Excluso International Mint has commissioned these beautiful plates commemorating one of the world's most beloved group of gentlemen rockers. "Wyckyd Sceptre" have taught generations the meaning of togetherness through music and various other activities. Literally bursting off the plate and bathing your eyes in vibrant color, the plates depict "Wyckyd Sceptre" in a time of great reflection. Each plate is lovingly machine-crafted in Juarez, Mexico, then edged in a pure, 24 karat-like, gold-like color, reminding us all of the pleasant, and comforting look of real gold on the edge of a plate. For 3 easy payments of $19.99 and then one last, more difficult payment of $149.99 this insanely fantastic collectors** item can be yours today. And be assured that 100 percent of the proceeds are donated to The Excluso International Mint Accounts Receivable Office. **Order now!**

**Please note: The word "collectors" is mis-used.

Excluso International Mint **Special Collectors Edition**

☐ **YES!** I want to suck that shit!
Please send me my Limited Edition Wyckyd Sceptre collector's plate entitled "Dude, Suck That Shit". Please bill my credit card $19.99 for 3 months, then $149.99 + shipping and handling.

NAME _____
ADDRESS _____
CITY/STATE _____ ZIP _____

EPISODE 404
RUDY WILL AWAIT YOUR FOUNDATION

written by: David Cross, Bob Odenkirk, Scott Aukerman, Jerry Collins, Jay Johnston, Bill Odenkirk, B.J. Porter, Brian Posehn, Dino Stamatopoulos

location segment director: Jonathan Dayton, Valerie Faris

live show director: John Moffitt

cast: Bob Odenkirk, David Cross, Scott Aukerman, John Ennis, Jay Johnston, Jerry Minor, Brett Paesel, Brian Posehn, Jill Talley, Becky Thyre, Paul F. Tompkins

featuring: Laura Milligan, Dino Stamatopoulos

Mr. Show theme song and logo. The Royal Dutch of Dukes (Jay) introduces.

Blooper Open (live/video)

Bob and David come out in tuxedos and present "Blooper Night." David has fun with the first blooper of Bob throwing up. Bob's upset and shows a private moment of David's: he's dressed in leather, and singing "Emotion Lotion!" into a hairbrush in the men's room mirror ("'Cause I'm a superstar in a superstar machine! Taking it to the staars!"). The guys show hurtful clips of one another. Bob shows more of the same men's room scene, but David has an arsenal (Bob hustling men on the street, Bob's parents disappointed it's too late to get an abortion — "Your son is four years old.") Bob's upset, but ultimately he's a good sport, announcing the winning clip: "Secret Superstar."

Superstar Machine (video)

David continues his performance in the blooper clip, and a talent scout (Dino) comes out of the stall — "Let me tell ya kid, you got the goods!" "Superstar Machine" tops the charts, and is covered by scatty jazz house musicians, parodied by Daffy "Mal" Yinkleyankle, and turned into muzak heard on hold by….

Phone Sex (live)

Mike (David), hanging at home, wasting time on the phone with his friend, Glen (Bob), who's at work. Glen loses a stupid bet and owes Mike two hours of free phone sex. Mike calls back, "I want to talk to the hottest, horniest slut you got." Glen tells him he's supposed to call a service and send him the bill. Mike bullies him. "You lost the bet! Now I'm calling back, so disguise your voice, you dumb dick!" When Mike calls back, he gets to talk to "Peppermint" and finishes in under three minutes. (1 hour 57 minutes of phone sex to go). Office co-workers (Jerry and Jay) catch on, and Jay gets some phone-action going. When Glen realizes it's not Mike, he's pissed, but then easily seduced to put "Peppermint" back on the line. ("You're good. You say all the right things.") Glen is busted by his boss (Brett), and is fired. He snaps back at her — "You're just jealous because I'm more of a woman than you'll ever be!"

Dude's Dude Link (video)

Glen (Bob), in business attire, chats playfully on the phone as light porn music plays. A sexy woman announcer: "Guys, if you're in the mood for some steamy sex chat, there's only one Glen Peterson!" An actor's (John) endorsement: "Glen's a dude's dude who knows what other dudes want to hear when they're imagining talking to a chick." Pull out to reveal the actor is rehearsing for his audition.

Audition (live)

Denny Woodkin (David), another actor, gets called in for his audition. He greets the producers (Dino and Bob) and tells them his audition monologue is from the play *The Audition*. "Can I use this chair?" he asks. They say yes, and he explains that he'd already begun — the question was the first line of the scene. He starts again, "*Can* I use this chair?" They feel awkward holding their tongues, because he seems to be waiting for their reply. "Helloooo! I need it. For the audition. . . Will somebody answer me?!" They say, "Yes, use it." But, "Noooo!" they interrupted his piece. He tries it again, and the producers do their best not to respond to his very specific insults ("You guys sit there — you in your stupid designer tie, and your dumbass glasses and imported bottled water!"). He tells them to fuck off and storms out. The producers are freaked out. "And, scene," Denny says when he returns a moment later. They are surprised and applaud his audition. "Nooooo!" He wants to start over, and they stop him — "Kid, you got the goods!"

Dad & You (video)

Denny Woodkin gets his own TV show, starring as "Dad" in *Dad & You*. In the crappy sitcom, Dad screams and screams at his son to turn off the TV and help with dinner. "Do it! Go!" A viewer (Bob), watching the show from home, nervously abides by the orders screamed by the TV dad and poises his remote to switch it off. "Noooo!" Dad screams, seemingly at the home viewer. "He got me!" the docile viewer chuckles at being fooled again.

(left) Rudy awaits diner David (© Adam Timrud Photography); (right) Bob as Dell Crow, the overworked sap.

Prenatal Pageant (video)

The docile viewer is a run-down Dell Crow (Bob), from his trailer home. He and his pregnant wife, Rhonda (Jill), are entering their unborn baby into a prenatal beauty pageant. Pageant director is cosmetic surgeon/ob-gyn, Dr. Yoburg (David), who surgically applies makeup and liposuctions baby fat, turning ordinary unborns into "beautiful, sexy, award-winning fetuses…they can't wait to be born!" To afford the contest expenses, Dell holds several jobs (pork rind factory worker, proprietor of Toilet-on-Wheels), and is forced to take a fourth job, kissing elephant asses at the circus. But not for naught, because the Crow fetus takes the crown, and Dell's family will receive a year's supply of mac and cheese. Dr. Yoburg buys another Corvette.

The Burgundy Loaf (live)

Romantic couple Chuck and Becky (David and Becky) comment on the excellent service at the very swanky restaurant, Burgundy Loaf. Things get a little too classy for Chuck (David) when Pierre, the maitre d' (Bob), informs him that bathrooms are too "crudite" for the Burgundy Loaf, then removes the cushion from his seat to reveal a toilet/chair. Pierre places an open, velvet-lined box under the seat — "Monsieur may sit, enjoy his meal, and perform his task at leisure" — and when he's done, his box will be sent to his home, first class. Shocked, but not wanting to appear gauche, Chuck shyly pulls down his pants and sits. The maitre d' calls Rudy (Jay), a busboy who, on hands and knees, "will await your foundation." Chuck and Becky awkwardly continue their date with Rudy cracking wise ("Hey there, General, you deployed any troops yet?") Chuck finally succeeds and is hushed when he requests toilet paper. "Frenchie!!!" Pierre cries, and, out from the kitchen, comes the jolly, Cockney chimneysweep (John). He sacks Chuck's poo box and scrubs him clean with a huge, rusted metal brush. ("How about Molly 'ere? She's always nice and mild for the bum of a gen'lman!") When done, Frenchie gives "Molly" a kiss and flies away on his flying bum brush.

Frenchie Delivers (video)

Credits roll, as Frenchie (John) flies across the sky and sings a merry song (to the tune of the *Mr. Show* theme song) and delivers poo boxes from the Burgundy Loafe.

It's me, Frenchie. Flying over the neighbor'ood
'andin' out the boxes, because Frenchie's got the goods!
If you see me comin', give a wink, and a nod.
Here's a little gift that came out of bod.

Happy poo box recipients: pageant parents Dell and Rhonda, phone sex hottie Glen Peterson, the lounge singers, and Bob while he and David are onstage saying goodnight. Bob opens his box and throws up — the clip from the blooper open.

Notes About Episode 404

David: "This was our Emmy submission show. And it might be my favorite show that we did. I have a lot of favorite scenes, and a lot of favorite ideas and moments, but as far as a show in its entirety, this has got everything to me. It's really smart. The performances are great. And I'm glad we lost the Emmy, in retrospect. I had this idea that Bob wasn't that into it at first, and it took a little bit if convincing, but if we won the Emmy for that episode, we were going to all jump up, shout 'yeah, hooray!' Run up onstage, run right past the podium, run right off the stage and up the other aisle and out the exit and never come back. On live TV. But we didn't win and America was deprived of that event."

Brian: "Blooper Open, I pitched. Dino didn't like it right away because he thought it was like stuff he'd seen on late-night talk shows. And doing a blooper idea isn't genius. But it's what we do from the premise, where we take off. I think shooting down premises because they seem kind of hacky can be bad."

David: "The Bloopertron 3000 — the thing we pulled. My idea was, I want to be recognized as the first example of how we've switched because of the new millennium. How we've switched from the 'something-something 2000' to the 'something-something 3000.'"

Bill: "Weird Al — we would see him in the audience; he came to some of our tapings. For Superstar Machine, the joke was there, of the song becoming a hit and spawning different versions of it, the disco version, etc. We had already shot it all. The show was being taped that night. Bob mentioned that we should do a Weird Al version. And everybody was excited — if we do nothing more today, we have to do that. Everyone was rehearsing for the show that night, and David hopped in a car and drove to Eban's, and they spit out this brilliant Weird Al thing, 'Sushi Bar in the Sushi Bar Machine.' And then David came back, and we shot it all before the audience came in for the show that night."

Eban Schletter (music director): "For the Weird Al thing, I scrambled — I was really luckily, some friends of mine had stayed in town, and they had a little accordion that was left there, that was broken. So I just happened to have this real accordion lying around, and I was able to get the chords out of it that I needed. One of my few vocal pieces that got left in, my Weird Al impersonation."

Bob: "The lounge singers who do a cover of "Superstar Machine" are Marty and Elaine — a couple who perform a couple times a week, I think, at the local club called The Dresden Room. And they were featured in the movie Swingers. And they are popular song-stylists among the young intelligentsia of L.A. They create these jazzy songs out of pop lyrics and Elaine scatting. We were not making fun of them. We were using what they do to show another extension of what happens with a popular song. Different small bands interpret those songs. You go to Vegas and hear a Britney Spears song done by a 40-year-old lounge singer, Cook E. Jar."

"Weird Al" Yankovic: "Daffy 'Mal'Yinkleyankle, it was flattering to be yet another pop culture reference in Mr. Show. It was pretty scathing, I have to say. But that's just part of their brilliance. I think Bob encapsulated everything that was irritating about me. Particularly in the early part of my career, way too broad and nasal and just grossly irritating. It was kind of painful to watch because he was too dead on."

B.J.: "Phone Sex is my favorite scene I wrote that made it in — it was the closest to what I had come out of my computer with very few notes. It felt great to get that one in."

Bob: "Audition is another great scene. I wish we had done it without any swearing. I feel like the swearing hurts people's appreciation of the perfect mechanics of the joke, a lot. It obscures the guy's frustration, because he is lashing out so harshly. A mistake in tone."

Troy: "One of the best sketches was a sketch I was around for — Prenatal Pageant — there's tons of stuff that I saw in the dailies of Bob and David just riffing with the other cast members, that's a movie. I've never seen anybody else have that ability that these guys have to go off book and just stay in character. And even when they're just playing around, it's still tracked with story, and do call backs and keep it building. They're able to take those characters into story and into a different level."

Bob: "Prenatal Pageant was really fun to perform, since we left room for ourselves to improvise. There was almost no improvisation on Mr. Show, this is probably the most you will see in one chunk. We had a good cast for this level of characterization. I hope to do a show that incorporates this type of performance someday."

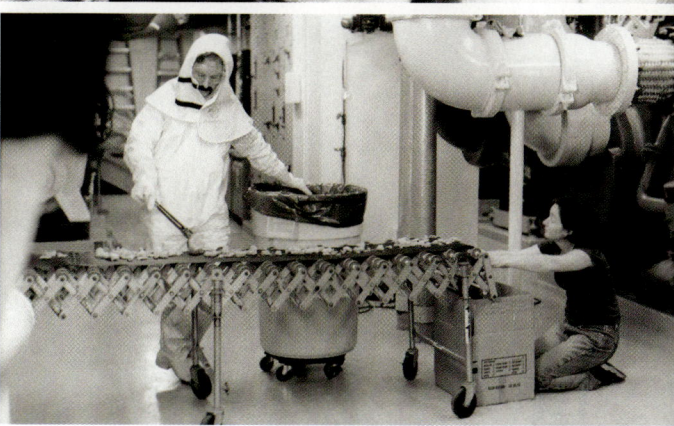

(top) David offers Peter Giambalvo (coordinating producer) a pork rinds snack between takes; (bottom) Dell Crow (Bob) spotting the bad ones at the rinds factory. (Photos © Adam Timrud Photography)

David: "People keep asking me what my favorite scene is, and it's hard to narrow it down. I have a bunch of favorite scenes, but I think Prenatal Pageant is my absolute #1 favorite. It's a really smart idea, it's funny, and it's also really human and poignant at times. And the poignancy is not in the writing, it's in Bob and Jill's performances. What I really like about the scene, it's a good example of what we did really well on Mr. Show, which was taking this already absurd thing that exists, and doing a logical, yet absurd, extension of that idea. And I think it's one thing that makes us stand out from other comedies."

Bill: "There was an argument about the poo box in Burgundy Loaf. I had a different conception of what the poo box would be. People would mention props and stuff, and we're talking about it, and everyone thinks they have the same idea on what something looks like. And then it comes to the art department time, and then it's like, 'Oh, no.' And then we legitimately argue about what the poo box looks like. I wanted a simpler, smaller poo box. But, ultimately, I was not disappointed with the poo box."

Scott: "We were at the offices of Brillstein-Grey [the company that served as the production studio for the show], and I really had to take a shit. And I asked Brian if this place had a bathroom, or was it too fancified. We started laughing, and we started talking about how funny it would be if a place was too fancy to have a bathroom. But we didn't want to pitch it. We had to pitch stuff the next day. And the stuff we thought was going to kill, died. And so, I was like, 'Well, we have this idea,' just expecting to be met with stares, and it went over really well. Totally surprising."

Scott: "The Burgundy Loaf scene originally ended at the Emmys, where Brian and I accepted our award for Best Comedy Scene Ever Written."

EPISODE 405 STORY OF EVEREST

written by:	Bob Odenkirk, David Cross, Scott Aukerman, Jerry Collins, Jay Johnston, Bill Odenkirk, B.J. Porter, Brian Posehn, Dino Stamatopoulos
location segment director:	Jonathan Dayton, Valerie Faris
live show director:	John Moffitt
cast:	David Cross, Bob Odenkirk, Scott Aukerman, Jay Johnston, Jerry Minor, Brett Paesel, Brian Posehn, Jill Talley, Paul F. Tompkins
featuring:	Stephanie Courtney, Jerry Collins, Freeze Luv, Daniel Henson, David Higgins, Gina Morelli, Robert Munns, Vernee Watson-Johnson

Lethal Logo Cold Open (video)

Rap music underscores a soulful woman's voiceover — "*Mr. Show* is a Lethal Injekshun Production." Part of its conglomerated interests: "...record labels...international drug trade...movies...taffy apples...TV shows. All that shit, yo." All run by 'Sweetie Pie' Jonus, from his cell in the new 3-to-5 years headquarters.

> Mr. Show *theme song and logo. 1920's mountain climbing explorer (Jay) introduces.*

Sweetie Pie Open (live/video)

Bob and David's new boss, Sweetie Pie (Freeze), breaks up their hokey *World's Horniest Mad Scientist* sketch. He buzzes in on the big screen, pissed off: "Yo! Bob and Dave! I cut that scene, fool!...I got the motherfuckin' revisions for this week's episizode, bitch." From a jail payphone, he orders the guys to "funny this shit up!" He hangs up to chew out a guard about office supplies.

Family of Five Link (video)

A narrarator informs, "It now costs $800,000 a year to jail just one criminal" — enough to send a family of five to college. (Parents, two young kids, and a grandma hold textbooks and cheer, "Yaaah!") Or enough to send that same lucky family on a 79-day rafting expedition." ("Yaaaah!" they cheer from the river's edge.) But Pembleton State Prison has a solution where criminals can support themselves on the outside while serving their terms....

Rapist (video/live)

(video) Mild-mannered Larry Kleist (Bob) is a convicted rapist, who is allowed to live and work as a free man as long as he's accompanied by "friendly reminders" of his crime. His front lawn hosts signs that read, "BEWARE OF RAPIST." Where ever he goes, he's shadowed by a "state licensed public warning engineer" (Jay) wearing a sandwich-board bearing the warning, "I'M WITH A RAPIST!" "Rapist coming! Don't get raped!" he announces from his van's P.A., following Larry to work. On the job, Larry is hard at work as an insurance salesman, finding creative ways to slip in the mandatory information about his offense. ("Hello! Insurance is my game, Larry is my name! Raping was another game of mine...." Dial tone.) "I think the industry is in a slump," he concludes. Other Pembleton convicts are shown in society: a reporter (David) at a press conference breezes over the fact that he sodomized his nephew before asking a question.

(live) A man (Brian) with his hooker date (Stephanie) tells the restaurant's maitre d' (David) to look under 'strangled seven prostitutes' for his reservation....

Clumsy Waiter (live)

On a business dinner, John gets a suit-full of his entree, spilled by the clumsy waiter (Bob). The maitre d' (David) quickly steps in and insists on paying half of the dry cleaning bill. John's associates (Jill and Jerry) protest, saying the restaurant should pay for everything, but the maitre d' implies that John is responsible because he ordered it. John is uncomfortable with the situation: "Listen, this suit is insured, and I'm only supposed to wear it at the office...my premiums are going to shoot through the roof." He wants to handle it quietly — dry cleaners will only create too much "messy paperwork." The waiter has a solution: he knows a couple of guys who can handle this...

Pallies (film)

Three Mafiosos bury the disgusting soiled suit in the woods by the light of their headlights. It's a Scorsese-type ultra-violent Mafia flick, *Pallies*, with Tommy "Wommy" O'Meara (Bob) narrating about living the glorified gangster life. He's with Jimmy "The Businessman" Idiglio (Jay) and Anthony "One-time" Branca (David) ("Called that because he said everything one time"). The movie has been edited for television. The sweaty and tired wiseguys eat a late-night dinner at Anthony One-time's mama's house, and the obscene language is poorly overdubbed, with ridiculous replacement words. ("The both of yous can grab onto my *(balls)* book, you *(motherfucking)* mother-father *(cocksuckers)* Chinese dentist!"). The violence is also edited out — a gun, a gunshot, cut to Jimmy, dead and face-down in pasta. At another heightened moment, the film cuts to a station break....

Food Ads (FAIRSLEY FOODS) (video)

Len Gibbons (David), third-generation owner of Gibbons's Old-timey Market, makes the mistake of calling huge supermarkets on their high prices in his commercial. Fairsley Foods, a grocery behemoth, hits back hard with a commercial insinuating that Gibbons's Markets have rats, forcing Gibbons to deny it his next ad. Subsequent Fairsley ads promote the highlights of the "Fairsley difference," things like apples always being in stock, stores taht are not constantly on fire, and no homeless people defecating in the aisles. Fairsley also promises that "you can shop comfortably knowing your children will not be abducted, then shipped off to a Pakistani whorehouse, where they'll spend the rest of their lives in homoerotic servitude." Poor Gibbons spends so much on defensive commercials and state-of-the-art security systems, he soon closes all his markets. He's reduced to selling fruit on the streets out of the back of a truck, just like his grandfather did. In black and white, a little Len defends his future failure to his grandpa — "...Fairsley Foods lied!" "Oh, shut up!" he's told. They are greeted by neighbor Thomas (Jay).

Everest (live/film)

(live) Thomas (Jay) reunites with sweet, elderly parents (Bob and Jill), who eagerly listen to the tale of adventurous climbing Mount Everest. As Thomas acts out his suspenseful journey, he mindlessly sits on a beverage cart and falls backwards, knocking his mother's beloved thimble collection off the wall. They all laugh and laugh, and then pick up the tiny thimbles. Thomas's brother, Richard (David), joins them, and they make Thomas tell him the story" — not about Everest. About you, slipping." In demonstrating for Richard, Thomas makes the exact same mistake. "Once was funny, twice is just not being careful!" snaps Mother. After painstakingly replacing the thimbles a second time, he's ready to tell the Everest story again, and again he falls. He flails and knocks the thimbles down so many times that his parents see no humor in it, and they no longer care about his conquering Everest. Richard runs in with the good news that people in New York City want to make a "moving picture" of his story. "Finally!" says Thomas, redeemed. "The story of Everest will be told!"

(film) A silent B&W film, *The Story of The Story of Everest,* plays to a full house, as Thomas proudly watches on. In the film, a young man (a Fatty Arbuckle type) returning home from conquering Everest tells his incredible story, with dialogue on title cards ("The wind!"). He slips and knocks down a thimble collection hanging on the wall. The accompanying music shifts to clownish circus tunes, and the audience roars with laughter at the folly. "Whatta boob!" reads the mother's title

Len Gibbons (David) selling out of a truck after failing to keep his Old-Timey Markets open. (© Adam Timrud Photography)

card. Thomas leaves the theater, devastated that no one takes him seriously. "I, who conquered Everest, am portrayed as a bumbling fool." He slips on the curb, and a car runs over his hands. He holds up his flattened, huge, cartoony hands, and screams in horror, as passers-by point and laugh. It is the end of the *actual* film, *The Story of The Story of The Story of Everest*. Credits roll.

Sweetie Pie Cold Tag (video)

Post-show video teleconference, Sweetie Pie (Freeze) dresses down Bob and David for the weak show. ("How many motherfuckin' times is that motherfucker gonna fall down? That shit ain't funny.") He fires the guys, and their dog, Todo, runs behind the curtain to expose that Sweetie Pie, the jailed gangster, was really their tiny kitty cat. "We're gonna spank you with our lips," they warn and cover the little puff of fluff with smooches.

New boss Sweetie Pie Jonus (Freeze Luv) video teleconferences from his prison office. (© Adam Timrud Photography)

Notes About Episode 405

David: "The woman's voiceover in the beginning of the episode, that is Vernee Watson-Johnson. And she is, among other things, the girlfriend of Freddie 'Boom-Boom' Washington in Welcome Back, Kotter. I love that."

Bob: "*Rapist*, like *Titannica*, features a hang-dog loser character with an inexplicably positive attitude. I think this dimension on these comic characters makes them empathetic, and not just pathetic, which is one thing that separates our characters from characters on such shows as NBC's *Saturday Night Comes Alive!*, etc."

David: "*Clumsy Waiter* should have been called 'Clumsy Sketch.' That slowly surprised us, in that when we were reading it and the first time we walked through it, we were having fun with it. And then, I don't know what happened, but it's just not good. And we all knew it. I remember Dino and Bob wanted to do this thing, that I fought against and ultimately convinced them not to do, but now, in retrospect, I wish we had done it — because there is such a difference in something that's of the moment that's going to be presented and the posterity of something and enjoying it in later years. But they wanted to put a clock at the bottom of the screen with a countdown from when the sketch started that said, 'time remaining in the sketch.' Which is funny, but you don't want to tell people at the beginning of the sketch that it sucks. But now I look back and think that would have been nice to have there."

David: "Audio mix — one of the shittier, slow-paced, uneventful things we had to do in post-production. Dino, Jay, and I were adding the fart noise for Brian for the Food Ads scene. Man, we laughed so hard on two different levels — at the actual sound of all of the farts and watching Brian do it onscreen, and at the absurdity that we were sitting in this audio-mix room, running through about 107 different fart noises. And they were all making us laugh. Every time the guy would play one, we'd giggle like little kids. Even the audio guys, who were pretty stoic, were giggling a lot, too. 'Let's hear the next fart.' After like 15 minutes, you go, 'All right, that seems fine. Let's just move on and let's use that.' And then you think, 'You know what, that sounds like we're trying to make a joke out of the fart, instead of just letting the concept be funny.' And then we'd go back: 'All right, let's not make it as long or as wet. Do you have something dry or shorter?' And it was three hours of our day, listening to get the perfect fart."

Bill: "To my recollection, the scene we talked about more than any other scene in the show, in more detail and at more length, was Everest. We had enough discussion to put man on the moon again. There was so much analysis. We looked at that scene 15 times in the writers' room. Over and over and over again. And it's a good scene (I like it, not love it), and it was worth doing. Reading it on the page, it does not work on the page. You see it and you get it. It sells itself by being presented, not by being read."

Jay: "Everest was actually based on a true story. I've mentioned it before to people, but nobody really cared. Now I will bore you with the tale. One day in a pitch meeting I got on some tangent and told a story of a third or fourth cousin of mine, Clarence Tamalunas. He is an imposing figure of a man, 6'6", long hair, and a big red beard. He would periodically show up at my mom's house in the summer in Chicago, as we lived two blocks from Wrigley Field. He would drop in having just been to a game and he'd usually be a bit drinky, you know, thirsted…drunkle. This one particular day, he showed up and was regaling us of a story that was less than memorable. What occurred next, though, would be the stuff of what I am writing about now. We kept our Weber grill in the kitchen as opposed to the back porch because, otherwise, 'the people that take' would come. So, as he talked, he noticed that we all sat upon kitchen stools. Now, I have never gotten drunk at a Cubs' game, but I imagine it can be pretty exhausting, as he seemed to desire a place to sit. Out of the corner of his eye, I guess, he saw the grill beside him and decided to rest his lumbering frame. Well, he sat upon it and it took off. As he fell to the floor, he reached back to catch himself only to grab onto two large wooden printer trays that were being used to house an untold number of trinkets and baubles. He ripped them both from the wall, and they both emptied and flew all over the kitchen floor. After about ten minutes of picking up all the pieces and setting them carefully back in the frame, we all had a good honest chuckle. Shortly thereafter, my grandfather, Bud, entered from the other room and asked what the huge crash had been. My cousin Clarence took the reigns and began to explain that he was telling this story, and, in the middle, he went

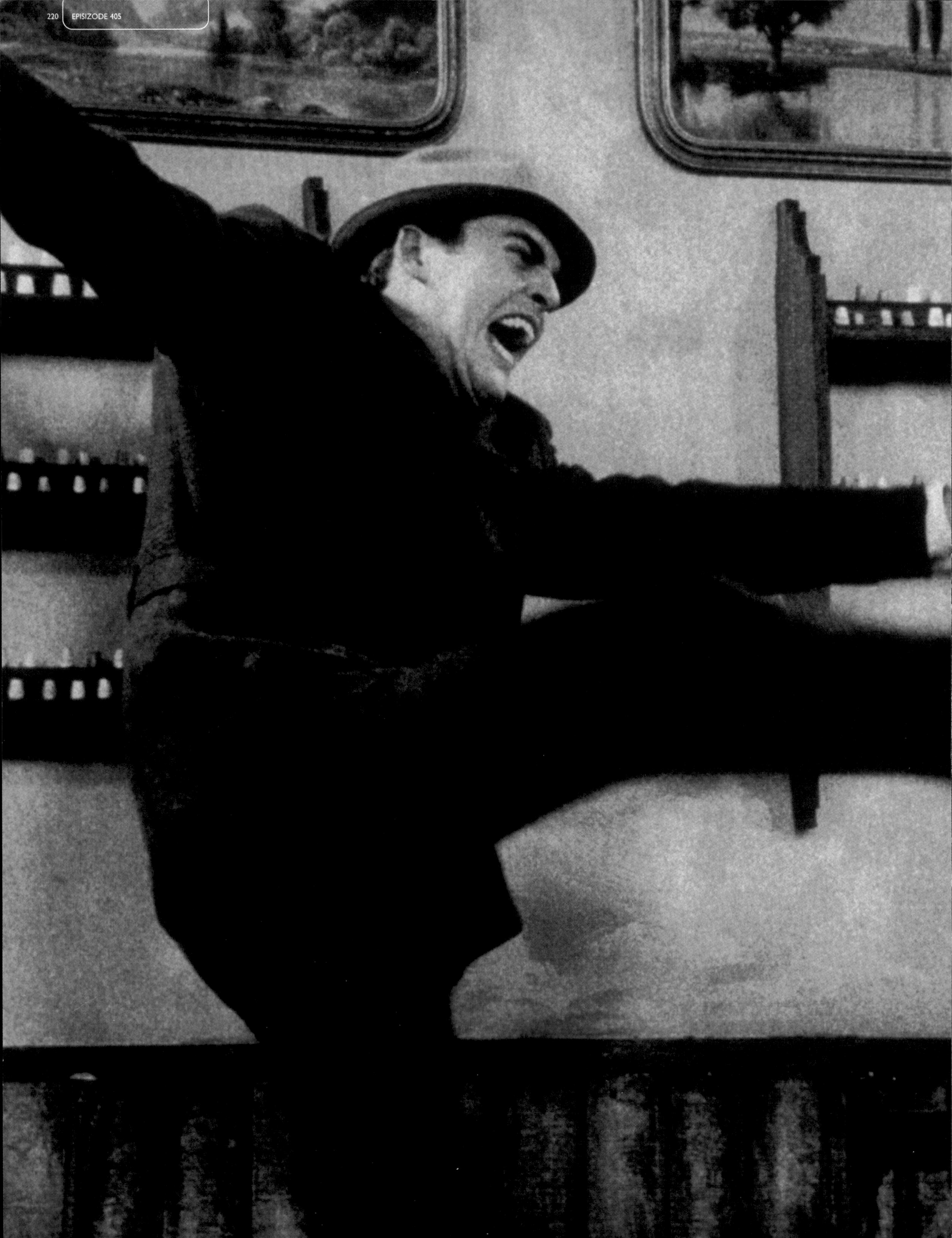

to sit back on this stool that was not a stool, and, in the midst of his explanation he acted out sitting and lost his balance and did it again. The grill took off, and he fell back grabbing at the wall and knocking everything down again. We laughed until we had to pick the little fucking things up again. So, that is the real story of the story of Everest. Do with it what you will, but, always remember, wear a rubber. Always. Everyday."

Bob: "Everest is a magical, mystical marvel. It really turns some people off. But this kind of indefatigably dumb, persistent joke is rare and done well by Jay here. I think it's really funny. I feel it's one of those things, the more you do it the funnier it gets. It passes the baton between annoying and funny. Some people probably just find it annoying. But the most fun is when people find it mixed between the two."

David: "When you see Everest on TV, it's all cut together quite nicely. But when you're shooting it — there's 115 thimbles scattered around everywhere, and people have to come, pick them up, then reset the thimble rack to the wall. We did four or five of Jay's falls, I can't remember how many, but at least one more than you see on the show, because we cut one out. So you're stooped down for seven or eight minutes in between each fall. It really heightened the sense (way more than it does on TV) of, 'Oh, you've got to be fucking kidding me, they're doing it again?!' But that's what we loved."

(top) Bob is Larry Kliest, rapist. Jay is a state-licensed public warning engineer; (bottom and opposite) Jay working it in "Everest." Based on a true story of a story. (Photos © Adam Timrud Photography)

EPISODE 406

written by:	Bob Odenkirk, David Cross, Scott Aukerman, Jerry Collins, Eric Hoffman, Jay Johnston, Bill Odenkirk, B.J. Porter, Brian Posehn, Dino Stamatopoulos
taint segment:	Bob Odenkirk
location segment director:	Jonathan Dayton, Valerie Faris
live show director:	John Moffitt
cast:	David Cross, Bob Odenkirk, Scott Adsit, Scott Aukerman, John Ennis, Jay Johnston, Jerry Minor, B.J. Porter, Brian Posehn, Jill Talley, Paul F. Tompkins
featuring:	Colin Malone, Curtis DeMartini, Dino Stamatopoulos

Speakers Cold Open (DEAD CREW GUY) (live/video)

Bob and David don't start the show, out of respect for a crew member who died. They ask the audience to hold their breath "in honor of him who cannot breathe." A smarmy guy (Jay) pokes his head in. He's "got a line on some speakers." The guys slip in his van and out the back, into Speaker Town. Jay prices speakers with the salesman (Paul), then whispers to the guys, "Dudes, check it out, I know this guy...he can hook you up for $400." Next, he scores tires for them at Tire Town and hooks them up with some mashed potatoes at his mother's dinner table. ("Primo stuff, from Idaho, it's the shit!") But the guys want gravy, and the shit goes down. "That wasn't part of the deal," says Mother. Jay panics and knocks her out. Flitty cartoon birdies circle her head, then fly out the window.

Blind Date Link (video)

The birdies flit about John, all fancied up in a tux and skipping down the street, singing, *"Oh chirpity doo da, shiminy shake! Look who's got his very first date! And if fate dictates, we'll get naked and mate! You just wait!"* He pulls out his waistband, and the cartoon birds dive in. He rings the doorbell....

Intervention (live)

John's blind date was actually a ruse to get him to come to an intervention — not for him, for David. A flabby, beer-bellied David arrives and heads for the snacks. His friends (Bob, John, Becky, Paul, Jill) confront him about his weight gain, but the "truth" quickly turns into a contest of hurtful one-liners. Turns out that David's intervention was actually a set up for Bob's intervention — the group is confronting Bob about his insult-driven interventions. Bob reminds them, through a series of cheap "flash-backs," how much fun his insulting interventions have been. Bob flashes forward to preview next week's fun intervention and is shocked to discover that his friends will bludgeon him to death. Ever helpful, he tells them how to destroy his future dead body to avoid jail. Back in the future, the kerosene can he instructed them to find is empty. Becky anticipated Bob's moves and came prepared. The group sets fire to the corpse.

Ka-Ching Link (video)

In front of Bob's burning house, a fireman smiles at the sweet opportunity, and his eyes turn to dollar signs ("Ka-ching!!"). The same happens to Mother Theresa, when she spies a beggar child, and to a dog that sees a cat, and....

Stop, Change Thieves (video/live)

(video) A car wash employee spies some change left on the dash. Ka-Ching! He grabs it. It's a consumer safety show: *Car Wash Change Thief Action Squad.*

(live) Chief crime stopper Zach Welch (Bob) and his Action Squad, Chuck and Lisa (Jay and Jill), set up car wash sting operations to catch change thieves in action.

(video) Mustached Chuck and blonde-wigged Lisa pose as vacationing husband and wife. They leave the car with twice-busted car wash worker Julio (David), who goes to scoop up the bait when the camera freezes, and we cut to commercial for *Car Wash Change Thief Action Squad...Too Hot For TV.*

(live) Back at headquarters, technical difficulties with the actual footage force them show a reenactment of the crime

(video) With Chuck as "Joolio" and Julio hired to play the vacationing husband. Alas, "Chuck attempted to portray Julio's recent crime, but was foiled by Julio's even more recent crime," reports Lisa. The change is gone before Chuck can reenact stealing it. Confronting the car wash manager and Julio about it, they are roughly turned out of the establishment — "and we were threatened with police action...and sponges."

Men's Club Of Allah (video)

Logo for the "Men's Club of Allah," who provided security for the previous program's loose change. They also provide security for boxers, suburban moms' secret recipes, and generally insecure guys.

Be Kind, Rewind (live)

At the Men's Club of Allah rally, the Honorable Reverend Kulunda (Jerry) attempts to clarify statements he made which he feels were

Car Wash crime stopper (Jay). (© Adam Timrud Photography)

twisted by the media. "The Jew-run media!" parrots his little sidekick (David). Through a lengthy explanation involving mirrors and working late hours, his prior statement that "Korean shop owners are vampires" takes on a complimentary meaning. And when he called for the beheading of all white women, he explains, "I was merely suggesting that the white women put the hair on their *heads* in a beehive..." ("Where you going with this one?" sweats David.) "...Or, '*behead*' themselves!" He next unveils his new succinct catch phrase, "Be Kind, Rewind!"

The Windbreaker (live/video)

(live) The Reverend (Jerry) sermons about rewinding tapes then begins deducing like Batman, and eventually pieces together clues to an impending jewel heist at the Gotham Museum of Valuable Items by arch enemy, "The Windbreaker." ("Rewind...re-*wind*...who fights the wind?...The Windbreaker!") He and his "young ward" (David) rush off to fight crime.

(video) Just as the Windbreaker and his two henchmen (Jay, Bob and B.J.) are about to grab the huge "Mother of Pearl Diamond," the Reverend and his sidekick appear on the scene. A huge Batman-esque fight breaks out, complete with music and cartoon words accentuating each blow. ("Bam!" "Baf!" "Flaggle!") A moment with legs splayed leaves the Reverend wide open for a kick in the crotch..."TAINT!"

'Taint (film)

A wide-eyed boy stares at the cartoon image of the Reverend taking it in the "'taint" in his comic book. "I remember the first time I ever noticed it," starts a voiceover, and we flash forward to a flashback of a 1970's porn photo shoot. The young male model, Theo (Scott Aukerman), is the (nude) picture of innocence acquainting itself with sleaze. Our narrator, Garry Flank (David), publisher of *'Taint Magazine,* demands a very "wide" shot. The photographer (Scott Adsit) argues, "We can already see his bing-bong, and his flabby habby-babby." But Garry wants the space in between — "The 'taint! It's beautiful! That's what people want!" Garry's ex-high school principal and manager of sorts (Bob), sings Garry's praises, crediting him for having the foresight to predict that the 'taint could carry its own magazine. An industry party at Garry's "'Taint Mansion" consists of six people in his shitty tenement apartment. "These are the days, people," he shouts. "THESE ARE THE PARTY DAAAAYS!" He spins in slow-motion, underscored by sexy porny music. When he stops, so does the music. Nobody noticed. The party loses control when the gang decides to get Theo high — blindfold, spinning turns, straight sugar, and a lemon wedge. The young star of *'Taint Misbehavin'!* gets lost in the psychedelic haze. Later, tragedy strikes — conservative pro-wrestler Captain Tragedy (Jay) jumps Garry in an alley. At the hospital, Principal Hayward demands news from the doctor (Jay). "Look, I don't care if his head is in a fucking fishbowl, just tell me he's alive!" With relief, the doctor shows him and Theo to their friend Garry, whose head is in a fishbowl (complete with decorative pebbles and a treasure chest). Theo's and Principal Hayward's jaws drop; the doctor impotently rambles on about his own shock. Credits roll as Garry stares out from his new home. "Dream Weaver" underscores.

Dream Weaver Close (live)

The boys groove to "Dream Weaver" on their awesome new speakers. "I really feel like a dream is being woven," offers David.

Notes About Episode 406

Scott: *"We were trying to come up with something really important that the Speakers guy could interrupt, that was an argument we had for three days. We felt it would only work if he were interrupting something really serious. The original opening we wanted to do was a 'Final Episode' of* Mr. Show. Seinfeld *was doing a final episode, and a lot of shows were doing final episodes at the time. We all thought it would be funny if for #406, in the middle of our season, we did a final episode. And Bob insisted that no one cared about final episodes. And I always thought that was a funny stance to take."*

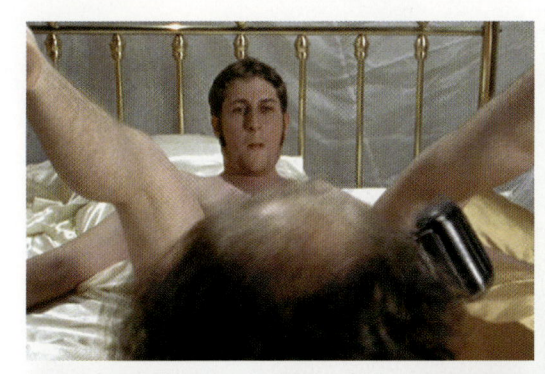

Clockwise from top left: Theo's (Scott Aukerman) wide shot for 'Taint Magazine; Theo's trippin' on straight sugar and lemon (© Adam Timrud Photography); The lost "cold tag" at end of the episode — a eulogy for the entire audience (© Adam Timrud Photography).

B.J.: *"The main thing with interventions — if anyone ever staged an intervention for me, all I would hear is people insulting me. So, I wrote a scene where people enjoyed insulting you and making you feel bad. At one time or another, this sketch was supposed to be in every one of the first five shows of the season and was taken out. And I had no experience with that. It was really heartbreaking every time. Every time they were organizing a show on the boards, they take the little cards, and they piece together a tentative show, with sketches or ideas for sketches. So, very early on, in the very first show, Intervention was placed on the board, and I felt like, 'Oh, what a great victory! I'm going to have a sketch in the first show!' But, no, it was taken out. But I was okay, because it was quickly in the second show. Same deal. Third, fourth, fifth. And so it was placed in the sixth show, and I was very skeptical the whole way. I just knew it was going to be taken out."*

Dino: *"Ivy [the dog] and that cat stunned me when they got Ka-Ching in one take. I thought we'd be there all day."*

Bob: *"I directed 'Taint. Do you like it? The thing is, directing for Mr. Show was a joy and a drag. It was a joy because the director's got to emulate all these clichéd styles. It was a drag because all you are doing is copying other people's clichéd styles. And all the important directing choices are outlined very clearly in the script. So it giveth and it taketh, at the same time. No wonder every single director we used was initially excited at the task, but then quit when they realized they were just tools to execute the writers' visions."*

Scott: *"The idea for 'Taint came from how funny I thought it was that men (and certain hot lesbians) fetishize vaginas. There's huge pictures in porn magazines of just vaginas. No faces, no other parts. I just thought how ridiculous it is to masturbate while looking at a flap of skin between a girl's legs. When I was talking about it to B.J. one day, I just blurted out about how funny it would be to have a magazine that just showed what's in between a dude's legs. That's how a lot of the best scenes were thought up — talking at length about something real, until you come up with a good take on it. The People vs. Larry Flynt stuff came naturally out of that, as that movie had just come out when we wrote the first draft. And a lot of the Boogie Nights/Scorsese filmic touches were stuff that Bob wanted to do. 'Taint originally had a whole live scene prequel, where the model character (originally Bob) was to slowly take off his clothes, revealing horrible things on his body, freaking out the photographer. I think it started off with bad tattoos (that he got when he was six — stuff about Pac Man and Sesame Street), then you saw huge,* ugly birthmarks, and, finally, a conjoined twin that fed off the digested food in the model's stomach. Needless to say, I think the scene works a lot better without it."

Scott: *"The part I played in 'Taint was originally written for Bob. He acted like he was doing me a big favor when he said I was going to get to play it, but I've always suspected he just didn't want to be flashing his balls around, yet again. Still, it's the one thing Mr. Show fans always shout at me, so let me take this opportunity to tell them to go screw."*

Paula (costume designer): *"Disgusting location for 'Taint. We were at Lacey Studios, where they shot Cagney and Lacey — and they shoot a lot of pornos there. It was really disgusting."*

Steve Welch (editor): *"Bob directed this, and he sort of had an idea what he wanted, but he wanted it very over-edited, like Boogie Nights. So he gave it to me and let me hack away at it, which was a lot of fun."* (Steve added the acidy moment of Garry opening the 'mansion' door over and over.)

David: *"My only contribution to 'Taint was Bob's character was written in as some sort of manager-type, and I suggested making him be Garry's high school principal. That would be really strange."*

Author's note: Episode 406 ran six minutes too long, and several things were cut. Among the casualties was a pre-taped piece at the end of the show, set in a cemetery, with a headstone for all the members of the audience. Apparently, no one told them they could start breathing again after they held their breathe in tribute at the top of the show. I vaguely recall this cold tag, and I cannot get a straight answer about this bit from the people involved. Sorry. Here's a cheeky, if inaccurate, reply from Jay Johnston about why it was cut:

"I think a small crippled boy was killed while shooting it, so we were all like: 'Fuck it,' and decided to not show it so his asshole parents wouldn't be all like, 'Boo hoo, boo hoo.' That's why."

EPISODE 407 EAT ROTTEN FRUIT FROM A SHITTY TREE

written by:	David Cross, Bob Odenkirk, Scott Aukerman, Jerry Collins, Eric Hoffman, Jay Johnston, Bill Odenkirk, B.J. Porter, Brian Posehn, Dino Stamatopoulos
location segment director:	Peyton Reed, Troy Miller
live show director:	Keith Trusdell
cast:	Bob Odenkirk, David Cross, Scott Adsit, Scott Aukerman, John Ennis, Jay Johnston, Karen Kilgariff, Jerry Minor, Brett Paesel, B.J. Porter, Jill Talley, Becky Thyre, Paul F. Tompkins
featuring:	Ashlie Chan, Stacie Chan, Stephanie Courtney, Eric Hoffman, Freeze Luv, Leif Anders, Tom Jackson, Mark Matthews, Evan Richards
special appearance by:	Chris Rock

Mr. Show Water Cooler *logo and jazzy theme music.*

Water Cooler Open (live)

Mr. Show Water Cooler, a political roundtable with "absolutely no experts." Their guests are Xona Chiffon (Becky) from porn, and skydiver Keith Minders (Jay). Their discussion is based on "information" gleaned from comedians' monologues ("Did you know that some senator had surgery where he had the NRA's lips removed from his ass?") As Keith points out that those are not real issues, he reveals that he actually reads the papers. They berate him for being an "Einstein" and sentence him climb into the "SMARTY-PANTS!" a super-huge pair of pants filled with vanilla custard), where he must watch the all-news channel. Meanwhile, David, Bob, and Xona party down in a money-spouting "Disco Booth."

Marty Farty (live/video)

The international all-news channel reports on world disasters, such as the American President allegedly farting. At Dominican Ambassador Martif Pharti's big Washington party, the source of a foul odor (a beauty") was traced back to U.S. President Truman Theodore "Two-T" Fruitty (Jay). The fart has captivated the entire nation. (Late-night host Chris Rock quips: "For the next State of the Union Address, the Vice President and the Speaker of the House asked if they could stand *in front* of the President!") Despite the President's initial denials, he accepts responsibility in his national address: "Marty Farty threw a party, and everyone was there. I, 'Two-T' Fruitty, let a beauty, and everyone went out for air…for now, this matter should be between me, my wife, my pants, and our God." The reaction of children around the world is universal — glee and giggles ("He farted!") In England, a palace guard (Bill) loses his composure as two Brit brats make farting sounds. The Queen (David) pokes her head out and reprimands him: "Stop it! You're not supposed to laugh!"

Date With Queen (live/video)

(live) To liven up her tedious party, the Queen (David) decides to play a wicked game on the new footman (Bob). as she individually greets her dull guests (Adsit, Jill, Jay, John, Paul), she tells each of them to stay after the party's over, "for that the twain of us may brandy titherings." At the Queen's request, the footman announces her royal tiredness, and the group bustles about, saying goodbye, yet none leave, each thinking they're special to the Queen. "Are you on the world's longest coffee break?" the Queen belittles the footman. He herds them out again, but they return and "tarry" with pathetic excuses. The flustered footman berates the guests for not leaving the Queen in peace, but soon notices she is gone ("That bitch!").

(video) The Queen gives chase on her moped, and shoots at the footman, who is on her tail. The newspaper account of the chase is cheaply plastered on the wall in an Anglophile bar.

Spite Marriage (video)

Two sleeveless-T'd assholes, Larry (Bob) and Tom (David), bump into each other, and both are too macho to let it go. Their girlfriends (Becky and Karen) tell them to forget it, but they're way too stubborn, each trying to out-tough the other: "I'll stay in your fuckin' ass all fuckin' night!" "I'm in it for the long haul. I'll marry your stupid ass!" Cut to the two at the altar in tuxes with the sleeves cut off, swearing to "not chicken-shit out until you admit that you're a pussy! Or until one of us dies!" Proud parents look on. The stubborn couple make a life of common activities filled with tough-guy aggression (mowing the lawn, serving up lemonade, exchanging Christmas gifts). The happy-to-be-pissed couple breaks up over hurt feelings, when it's revealed that the sweater Larry made for Tom's "dumbass birthday" was actually store-bought. Each is tragically sad and lonely without the other, until they tearfully reunite, instantly resuming their in-your-face stance ("It's on, asshole!"). Still going at it as old men, Tom on his deathbed, they continue their pissing contest until Tom dies. Larry reassesses his opinion of Tom, "I guess he wasn't such a chicken shit after all." "Bartender," he turns to order a drink and realizes where he is — "Oh! My life!"

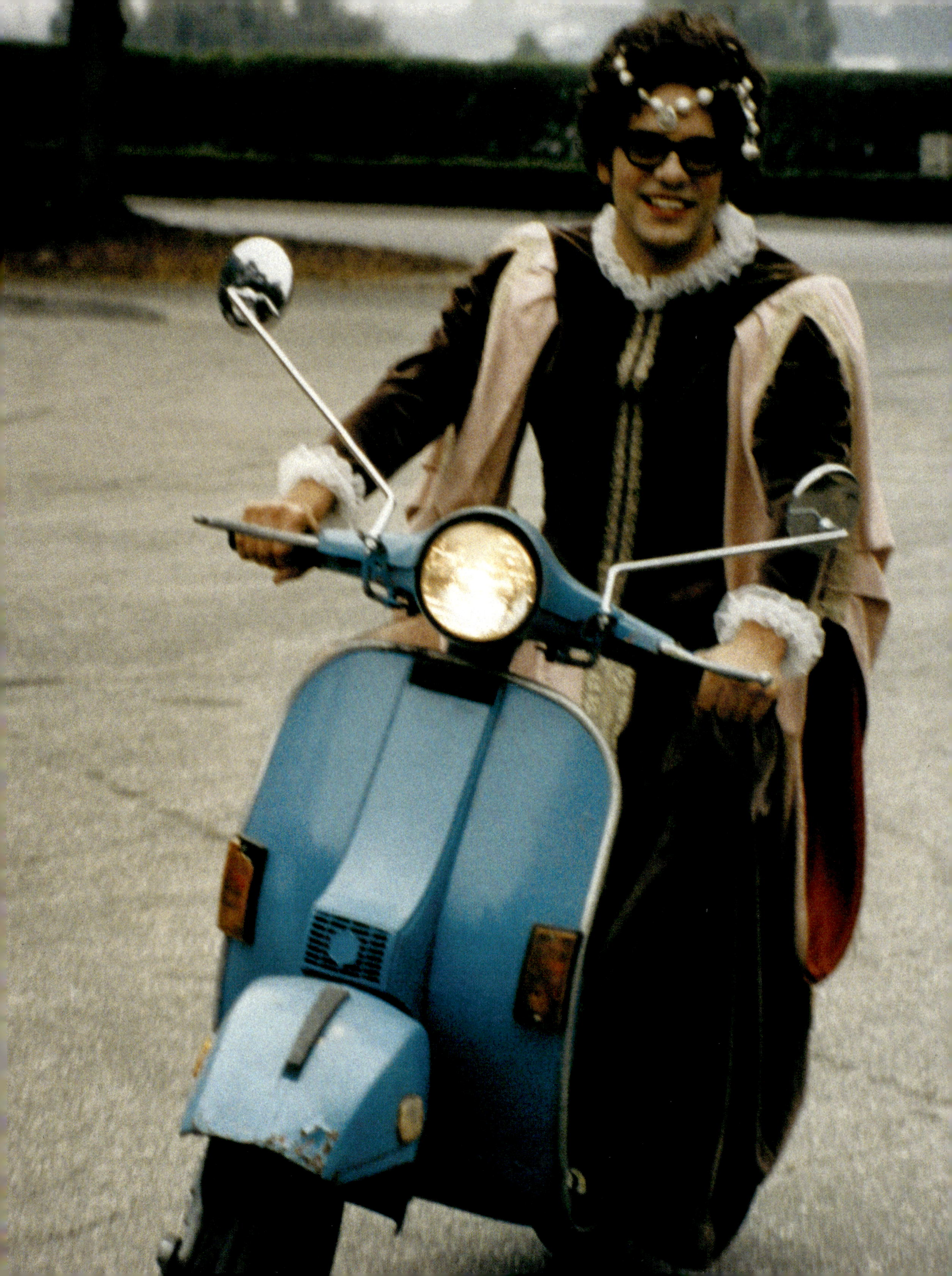

Heaven's Gate Link (video)

Now-dead Larry (David) "wakes up" and finds himself surrounded by a bunch of hip nightlifers (and a few oldies), all excitedly screaming for the attention of St. Peter, who holds a guest list and selectively picks people for admittance to the exclusive nightclub that is heaven. God (Bob), with the tan and swagger of Hollywood producer Bob Evans, emerges from the action inside and tells bouncer St. Peter that he is going down to earth to "make some magic."

God's Book-On-Tape (live)

God (Bob) appears in a recording booth to set to tape his book *My Life in the Fast Lane: God's Autobiography*, his alternately boasting and self-deprecating tell-all, which he dedicates to his son — "Jesus, you're tops, and you teach me new things every day." He comments on the Bible, "Too many cooks…nobody caught the attitude, the swagger, the little-kid wonder." In truth, he has only one commandment: "Sundays are my day…no prayers, no calls, faxes, no nothing." He tells the story of Steelers' quarterback, Terry Bradshaw, praying on Super Bowl Sunday, 1974. "'We're six points down. You gotta help me make this pass.' Boom, I go shithouse on him…You are one pussy-hair away from eternal hell-fire, my friend." Bradshaw makes the pass anyway — "Terry's just that good." He finishes up for the day and gets into his limo, which levitates into the heavens.

Monster Mash (video/film)

An ancient tapestry depicts peasants pointing to a limo in the sky on *Probings*, the TV reality show that probes supernatural phenomena, as the announcer ponders the inexplicable — "Do mysteries really exist?" Tonight's enigma is "Monster Parties," and the only "expert" not too upset by the topic is Dr. Retarded (Bob), novelty record collector, who, from his mother's house, shares with us his favorite monster party tunes, including "Dracula's Pajama Party" by Jerkin' James Whitcroft. The idea of Dracula's purported party is called preposterous by Cambridge professor Chance MacPhearson (Adsit): "If they get together, it's going to be a *terrifying battle*!" Sad-sack songwriter Whitcroft is disappointed at the criticism, because everything in the song is true. It happened to him, and it screwed up his whole life. Under hypnosis, Whitcroft relives the horror (which *Probings* generously reenacts): "The Wolfman is dancing with Frankenstein's Bride. Frankie got mad and nearly re-died. It's horrible!" The lie-detector operator (B.J.) confirms that Whitcroft is telling the truth, except for the part about the monster party. *Probings* follows persecuted Whitcroft to a coffeehouse open mic, where he will take the stage for the first time, as his final step in therapy, and daringly perform the song about his experiences.

Coffee Hunt Close (live)

Whitcroft (David) tentatively begins his song for the coffeehouse audience, but freaks out from horrifying flashbacks. Credits roll, as he tears over tables and audience members, screaming and sobbing in fear.

(above) Bob as the Robert Evans-inspired God, in make-up chair; (opposite) David as Queen on the run. (Photos © Adam Timrud Photography)

Notes About Episode 407

Dino: *"I've always been pretty apolitical, so I was excited that I actually made a contribution to this type of bit…although, it is all about uninformed morons, which is what I am. Witness: when I was working on Conan's show, I came in one day and actually repeated a punchline of some comedian's that I thought was a fact about the President. To my embarrassment, I was justly ridiculed for my error. I remembered this for the Water Cooler sketch."*

Paul: *"Although I was no longer a writer on the show, I did contribute one joke in Season 4: when Bob and Dave are about to sit down for the Water Cooler show, I suggested that a bit of the Water Cooler theme should play as they walk to their chairs. I always found it ridiculous that, on Politically Incorrect, music would play for the three seconds it took Bill Maher to walk to his set after his monologue."*

The start of a beautiful, lifelong relationship. (© Adam Timrud Photography)

David: "For the 'smarty-pants' penalty in the Water Cooler show, there was a fuck-up: the egg wouldn't open. It was hilarious. Jay was standing in the big thing of goo — it really was pudding, industrial-size cans of that crap you get at public school lunch — and we're all anticipating this giant egg to open, and it doesn't. Instead, it's drizzling and dripping on him. And he was just sitting there, and it wasn't anything you could show on TV. It was taking like 17 minutes, and Bob was reaching up and pounding it with his fist, and there was a guy — a scraggly technician with a hammer, going 'donk, donk' — trying to open it up. Everybody was laughing. The studio audience was having a great time. And we're all joking. It just got funnier and funnier. It was one of the funniest fuck-ups that ever happened on Mr. Show."

Dino: "This was a hilarious bit David used to do at parties he actually hosted. Sadly, that's where the bit should have stayed."

David: "That's where the idea for the Queen scene came from — I've never done it. It was a great idea for a practical joke. But, as it turns out, a shitty idea for a sketch. It's just so flat. And nothing more than the concept. We tried so many ways to goose it up. We have really good physical comic actors performing, and after about a minute and a half of watching that scene, you go, 'What? C'mon, man, enough!'"

Paul: "What happened? This scene was so much fun to rehearse, and, then when we were actually taping it, something went wrong. All the fun confusion just became kind of confusing. We cut a number of beats between tapings, and it was cut even more in editing. Also, Bob's Beefeater hat threatened to fall off at any moment. It's still pretty funny, but something got lost somewhere. I modeled my performance as Count Pleasantham on Terry-Thomas."

Dino: "This [Spite Marriage] all began with Bill and I doing a drunken bit at the Cat and Fiddle [pub]. Of course, that's all I really remember."

Bill: "Dino was drunk after a live show at the Cat and Fiddle. We were doing a bit, we totally riffed it. We were in each other's face — 'I'm not gonna let you go!' 'Yeah, well, I'm gonna marry your fuckin' ass!' Guys who get married to be spiteful. We pitched it drunk at the Cat and Fiddle; Bob and David were also drunk. We pitched it again the next day in the office, sober. They liked it. It has great energy to it. I'm excited about it. It's not presentational or a parody of TV and film. It's slice of life."

Dino: "In the Spite Marriage scene, there's a montage with a whistling song. That song used to have lyrics. It was supposed to be in the style of a happy Tiny Tim song, played on ukulele. One of the lyrics was 'Eat rotten fruit from a shitty tree.' The words were cut because there was too much going on. It got to be too busy with lyrics."

Bob: "Robert Evans, the famous movie producer, his book The Kid Stays In The Picture — I got the book and everybody in L.A. was listening to the tapes, because he has such a distinctive voice and delivery. And I was talking to Bill about it on the phone, and we started doing him as God. Then we wrote up four or five stories that God would tell in that swaggering, sexy, 70's kind of slang."

Bill: "Bob and I originally wrote up God's Book-on-Tape, as an idea Bob wanted to do at that year's Aspen Comedy Festival. And people liked it; many people came back from Aspen and commented on it. And then it was just a question of finding place for it on the show. We also had to shorten it way down, because we had a whole bunch of beats to it."

Author's note: *I was at this show in Aspen where Bob first unveiled God's Book-on-Tape. It was surprising and hilarious. I was sitting at a table with David Kissinger — head of a major television studio in L.A. and son of Henry Kissinger, who is famously close friends with Robert Evans. Kissinger immediately recognized the story "God" was telling, as Bob and Bill had lifted them directly from Evans's book. He turned to me and said, with true excitement, "That's my father he's talking about!!"*

Dino: "During the filming of Monster Mash (when David was in his underwear washing his clothes in the sink), Scott Adsit (who played the university professor) was watching the scene on the monitor. He stared and stared at the pathetically grotesque sight of that ridiculous character [David] wringing out his pants in the sink, and finally Scott blurted out, 'Oh, God! He looks just like me!' And he did."

Tracey Krasno (production manager): "You see David washing his clothes in the sink, and he gets in them right away and goes to the coffeehouse without letting anything dry. And we had to soak him, and all we had was a garden hose, and it was 6 o'clock at night, and it wasn't that warm out anymore. We gradually start getting him unbelievably wet, and he's just dying, he's so cold. And you look at him, and you couldn't tell he was soaked. We threw three buckets of water on him right before we started rolling each time. And we did three takes. And he's freezing and he's so miserable. We called up the local cab company, to take us to the Martini Lounge, our location for the Coffee Hunt part of the scene. David got in dripping wet. The driver had no clue what was happening; I don't think he spoke any English. When we got there, the lounge was closed, and we couldn't get a hold of our contact. So, they regrouped for about 20 minutes, and rewrote the scene and shot the way you see it, where he just can't get into the club, and he's waiting. And we did the interior club stuff in the studio, in front of the audience. It wasn't meant to be that way at all."

Paula Elins (costume designer): "David was freezing cold, all wet. He could've been wearing a wetsuit under that, so he could be warmer. And when we did the live portion [in studio] we got him a wetsuit."

David: "The Monster Mash guy was based on this guy, who was a stand-up comic in Boston, and he claimed that he had been abducted by aliens, and he had already been considered quite eccentric and a complete fuckin' pot burn-out. One day, he came back from a gig and claimed that he'd been abducted by aliens. And he had some very specific, trite information. Every detail was exactly as you've ever heard anybody else describe it. The aliens looked like a Close Encounters alien, and their spaceship was kind of a 1950's sci-fi movie space ship, etc. And he just wouldn't get off of it; he just kept insisting. Then I was doing a gig somewhere in the middle of the country, I was at the Holiday Inn at two in the morning, and there was a show called Top-X. It was about alien abductions, a cheesy, poorly made, sensationalistic show. I saw this, 'Oh, my God, it's that guy! What the fuck!' And it was very dramatic, and there was a lot of histrionics about how he wasn't able to do his stand-up for years, he was traumatized, and he couldn't take the stage, and then the camera follows him back to his first gig in over two years. And they show him practicing his act in front of his mirror at home, it's just absurd. He gets hypnotized, you can tell he's acting as if he's hypnotized. A lot of the stuff in the sketch was inspired by very similar scenes, we just obviously made it funny."

Paul: "We were in a real cemetery for this sketch and, at one point, actually knocked over a headstone!!! We somehow did not get thrown out. Maybe these things get knocked over all the time. Be careful in cemeteries! I like to think of someone watching that sketch and recognizing the grave of a loved one on TV. Would you be happy about that? I don't know. But, I do know this: I was thrilled to be playing the Mummy, a monster I have long been obsessed with."

David: "There was a cold tag at the end of the show that was cut for time. It was something that I wrote, and rewrote about three different ways, and kept pitching, but Bob didn't like at all. But I still like it. There's the question in the middle of the Monster Mash scene where the announcer says he drove 'X' miles per hour at 'Y' amount of time. 'Do you know how long it took him? Answer at the end of the show.' And what I wanted to do was a cold tag after all the credits had run: I'm on stage in a bathtub, just taking a bath inexplicably, and then I look into the camera and say, 'Oh, hello. So the answer to the quiz is eight.'"

EPISODE 408
...LIKE CHICKENS...DELICIOUS CHICKENS

written by:	Bob Odenkirk, David Cross, Eric Hoffman, Jay Johnston, Bill Odenkirk, B.J. Porter, Dino Stamatopoulos
location segment director:	Troy Miller, Peyton Reed
live show director:	John Moffitt
cast:	David Cross, Bob Odenkirk, Scott Aukerman, John Ennis, Jay Johnston, Jerry Minor, Brett Paesel, B.J. Porter, Becky Thyre, Paul F. Tompkins
featuring:	Eric Hoffman, Vahe Manoukian, Bill Odenkirk, Rachel Grate, Michael O'Lasky, Bradley Pierce
special appearance by:	Jeff Goldblum

Mr. Show *theme music and logo. Lincoln (Vahe) introduces.*

Reparations Open (live)

David's all dressed up in a tuxedo-on-a-shirt and top hat, passing out cigars (fake poo, really) in celebration of the reparations made to Jews from Switzerland. His riches arrive, but David is disappointed with his 82¢ "Rip-off!" But he agrees with Bob that the card it came in is nice, (a kitten and spilled milk, "We were bad little kitties and we wuv you!").

Mississippi Fun Bucks (video)

At a reparations ceremony in Mississippi, a big cracker Governor (Adsit) announces the distribution of a card to all the blacks ("Uh, oh! Somebody made a mess!"), and Mississippi Fun Bucks, which he hands over to the black man (Jerry) joining him at the podium. They're good for "any one-way ticket" out of the state on a Mississippi Fun Bus. A bus pulls up, and, with a politician's smile, the Governor pushes Jerry on, and it drives away.

> "Mississippi Fun Bucks are not legal tender but may be used to leave Mississippi, and for discounts at Lucky Lady Motor Courts not in Mississippi."

Bugged Drug Deal (live)

In a room at the Lucky Lady, Jim (Bob) and Kevin (David) sit on a huge stash of drugs, awaiting the transaction. Kevin is very nervous, and for good reason. His business partner is acting very suspicious: he recites factual details as he speaks, he can be heard talking in hushed tones in the bathroom, he is wearing a gigantic flower in his jacket lapel, and he puts on a huge sombrero — "Hey, you just took a picture of me with your hat!!" Jim condescends to Kevin, that he is being paranoid ("My magic hat?"). Jim further patronizes Kevin by turning off the lights to reveal the cops behind the "fake painting." Kevin doesn't want to seem that paranoid, so he doesn't turn to look. Finally, to pass the time, Jim entices him with a game of thumbprint tic-tac-toe….

America's Dumbest Juries Link (video)

In Kevin's trial, his tic-tac-toe prints are one of many pieces of incriminating evidence tying him to the drug crime. Will he be found guilty? A clip from next week's *America's Dumbest Juries* gives us the answer: "Not guilty." Even Kevin is surprised.

Rich Guy Negative Ads (video)

Campaign-style commercial promoting the virtues and successes of a Fortune 500 businessman/family man, Charles McHutchence (David), who's not running for any office. He seems like a swell guy. A counter-ad, paid for by rich guy Harrison Greeley III (Bob), wants you to consider Harrison Greeley III, a super guy. The "opposition" continues with each party's ad reacting to the other's latest claims of being a great guy, even attacking the other as a liar. A group of Citizens Against Negative and Unnecessary Advertising, fronted by a Reverend Anders (B.J.), in their own ad, plead "Enough!" with the petty, public character assaults. The rich men, now united, release an ad, flush with Nazi references, to "crush Reverend Anders." The two new allies' latest promo spot features them as friends, having bonded over growing up rich and destroying a common enemy. "Fact: The two have made specific plans to do things together in the future." They're shown taking their wives to the Upper Class Hunt Club where E. Premington spoke in 1923.

The Great Hemingway (live)

In 1923, an elite group (David, Jay, Jill, Paul, Scott) gathers to be regaled by novelist/hunter/explorer Edmund Premington (Bob) and his tales of his African jungle expedition. In describing the lion's roar, his language gets a bit salty ("You feel it first in your scrotum."). All chilling effects are described as affecting the scrotum — in fact each one of a man's scrotums and the nipples on your ass. His admirers have become upset by his description, which he concedes is "not for the faint of scrotum." He argues that he is not speaking metaphorically, and they question his grasp of vocabulary. He insists he experienced all he claims, and to prove he's not a liar, he reveals his freakish scrotumed and nippled bod. Next, we see he has enlisted in a circus sideshow as a the "Multi-scrotumed, Ass-nippled Adventurer." Three little newsies hawk the Premington horror in the paper's headlines.

(above) "The Great Hemingway," not for the faint of scrotum; (below) Rehearsing "Bugged Drug Deal."

Most Trusted News Team (video)

The three grow up to be a team of news anchors, Bennie Drummond (David), Margaret Holden (Jill), and Otto Bergher (Bob) — "The team you trust." They have been the local anchors since 1925. The opening montage shows the team throughout the years, becoming sophisticated, experienced, and, ultimately, elderly. Today, they are liver-spotted and extremely frail. The crew must prompt them over and over, but they couldn't read the stories if they wanted to, and it doesn't seem like they want to. A field reporter (David), familiar with the incompetence, takes over with his report of a plane crash.

Fat Survivor (live)

Reporter Mark Treems (David) is at the scene in the Andes, where searchers found a plane that crashed. Of the 234 people onboard, there is one survivor, Todd Benley (Bob), who has survived by eating his fellow passengers. He is huge and sprawled, relieved and satisfied. "I ate them all, showed no favorites, and here I am, full as a tick, the living legacy of their deeds." It was only 30 days, but he ate all of them. "When I get depressed, I eat; it's my outlet," he says flippantly. His story of the cause of the crash (eating the pilot) has the other reporters laughing, which doesn't go unnoticed by Treems….

2000 lb. Old Man Link (video)

Treems (David) and Benley (Bob) team up for a Vaudevillian act, *The 2000 lb. Old Man*, from Carnegie Hall. Their live show features classic lines such as: "Now, I understand you met Napoleon?" "Met him? I *et* him!" Showing on PBS. Funding for this program provided by Southern Historical Preservation Society and Ragtime Band.

Civil War Reenactments (video)

A *Civil War*-type documentary explores the history behind the reenactment of the Battle of Turner Springs, one of the "fake bloodiest" in history — thousands came "to pretend to be brave." In the reenactment, brother would be pitted against brother: Travis (David) and Lamar (Bob) Kittle left their mother, for the first time in ten years, to attend the reenactment, over 50 miles away. Civil War Reenactment Historian, Chilton Burr (Bob), explains that on the historic day two Lincolns showed up. Two too many, as Lincoln wasn't even there in the real battle. The park ranger (Paul) has to settle a dispute between the reenactors and Renaissance Faire players (Jill and John), who say they have a permit. Two Trekkers appear (Bill and B.J.) for their annual crashing of the annual Renaissance Faire and, to their delight, stumble onto "two different time periods." The Civil War geeks are reduced to re-staging their battle in the parking lot. Cries of war are interspersed with screaming car alarms. Burr's recounting of the day is interrupted, and the camera widens to reveal he'd been in a doctor's waiting room.

Pledge Drive Close (live)

Bob and David are back onstage, asking for pledges to keep *Mr. Show* Educational Programming going. They promote the premiums available for a pledge (The Civil War Reenactment Chess Set and *The 2000 Lb. Old Man* Inspiration-A-Day calendar), but still no calls…until Bob offers the fake poo cigars. The credits roll over an inpouring of callers, offering strange personal information, before getting to the point — "Y'all got fake poo?"

Notes About Episode 408

Paul: *"They did a live show at the HBO Workspace [a small theater in L.A.] to work out some rough sketches. They learned that the Queen scene (#407) is too long, that the Debate scene (#409) can be really funny, and that the Bugged Drug Deal scene really works. They threw out another scene involving a forensic sketch artist and a witness who would not describe the suspect by skin color, because he doesn't see color, he sees people."*

Jerry: *"I was the first recipient of the Mississippi Fun Bucks, good for one ticket out of Mississippi. Adsit, as the Governor, says, 'Ooh, there's the bus right there.' And the bus drives up, and we had all these extras — it was supposed to be a bus-full of all these black people going off to who knows where out of Mississippi. And all the extras were so tired, and all they were doing was sitting on the bus, that they were all sleeping. They slept through the whole thing. So it looks like they're all going off to who knows where — their deaths. And David was like, 'Yeah, leave them alone. It's just as well.'"*

Bill: *"The Reparations scene exists just to see David hand out fake poo."*

David: *"Reparations into Bugged Drug Deal was one of the hardest links we ever had. It had to get you from the courtroom steps in Mississippi to a motel. It was especially difficult, because we were at the end of the season when you can see the light at the end of the tunnel. We were really sweating this one out. Two days we spent on that link."*

David: *"I feel like Bob and I should have switched parts in Bugged Drug Deal. I think it would have been better. I think that Bob would have played my part in a more interesting way. I didn't say anything because it seemed to be okay, and I didn't want to feel like I was asking for the more fun role."*

David: *"The Great Hemingway, I can honestly say I was never a big fan of. And those guys loved it. I think Bob and Dino wrote it. It's just one idea. The guy gathers people around, and he keeps using the word 'scrotum,' and it's their reaction. That's all it is. It's like the 'awkward guest sketch.' It has no build or travel to it at all. I don't think it's a bad sketch, but it really feels like we borrowed it from SNL. Like we went over there late at night, when nobody was there, and broke into somebody's office and stole it and put it on our show."*

Paul: *"I remember that I almost broke (I did break every time in rehearsal) during the Hemingway sketch when Bob, accused of speaking metaphorically, cries, 'I am no symbolist!' and then says, in a very low monotone, 'When the African lion attacks....' Also, I thought maybe Jill was supposed to be my wife, so I comforted her every time she began crying. But then, at one point, John comes over and comforts her, and then we both comfort her. Then I thought, maybe she's John's wife, so I didn't comfort her any more after that."*

Bob: *"The Great Hemingway is my own idea, drawn from an actual Hemingway sentence I read in Vanity Fair. It was part of the unfinished novel that his executors released at this time. The line about 'feeling' the lion's roar in your 'scrotum' struck me as a really terrible, desperate effort of description. More like des-crap-tion, am I right? I am now going to fire the person who writes jokes for me."*

Dino: *"Fat Survivor — I don't think anyone likes this bit, but I had fun writing it with Bob. The scene still makes me laugh in a purposely hokey kind of way. It's really an old-fashioned, Vaudeville-styled, set-up/punchline sketch with a hilarious premise which I assume was Bob's. We commented on how old school it was when it finally devolves into a Brooks/Reiner parody."*

Bob: *"I wish I hadn't done a 'funny' voice in Fat Survivor. It obscured/ruined the great one-liners that make up the scene."*

Dino: *"I play Lincoln in this, because I look like Lincoln. No, he's not one of our better looking presidents. Anyway, I don't know if anyone notices that — in the stills used in that scene — Lincoln is beating the shit out of a black soldier [Jerry Minor]."*

Bill: *"Civil War Reenactments was the only scene in which I spoke any lines. (Okay, I did some voiceover once.) I was not a performer on the show. Oh, sometimes when a table was too expensive, I would stand in and hold something required in a scene. I was flattered that I was chosen to play 'Nerd #1,' one of the guys who dresses each year in a Star Trek-like costume and confronts the Civil War reenactors as though he's gone back in time. I had to wear a prosthetic piece on my nose, which was held in place by my nerdy glasses. They were my regular glasses. My nervousness about performing, I think, helped lend some nerdy authenticity to my line delivery. I'm glad I got to be a part of this piece, but that was enough. I ain't no one's monkey."*

Civil War Re-enactors. (top) Dino Stamatopoulos and Vahe Manoukian, two too many Lincolns; (bottom) Ken Daly, Mark Fite and Bob Odenkirk reenact awaiting orders. (Photos © Adam Timrud Photography)

Bill: *"With a strong idea behind a scene, you can explore and go nuts because, even if some of the parts don't work, everything is still orbiting in a funny 'space.' The Civil War Reenactment documentary was one of my favorite examples of this. Of all the blasts I had writing on the show, this one was the blastiest. David, B.J., Scott, and I worked on this one for a day or two. By the end, we had tons of material. Too much. I think what we ended up with was great."*

David: *"Civil War Reenactments: the best thing — this is a real thing! I saw this thing on TV where these total Star Trek nerdy guys would go to Renaissance Fairs, and they pretend that they've landed on the planet at that point in time. Fuck! That's awesome! A bunch of Star Trek nerds at a Renaissance fair interacting with the Renaissance people and, both of them getting on each other's nerves! Also, I love the line Bill improvised. Bill and B.J. are the Trekkies, and when John, as the Renaissance king, slaps the phaser out of Bill's hand, Bill turns to the park's guard, he says, 'You saw that.' It's really funny. That's one of those little moments that cracks me up. That was also my extremely poor attempt at doing some sort of Baltimore/Philadelphia accent. And I don't think people know that that's Jeff Goldblum reading the postcards, which is cool. Because you find out later, maybe figure it out on your fifth viewing."*

EPISODE 409
SAD SONGS ARE NATURE'S ONIONS

written by: Bob Odenkirk, David Cross, Scott Aukerman, Eric Hoffman, Jay Johnston, Bill Odenkirk, B.J. Porter, Dino Stamatopoulos

location segment director: Peyton Reed

live show director: John Moffitt

cast: David Cross, Bob Odenkirk, Scott Aukerman, John Ennis, Jay Johnston, Karen Kilgariff, Jerry Minor, Brett Paesel, B.J. Porter, Becky Thyre, Jill Talley, Paul F. Tompkins

featuring: Eban Schletter, Jake Sakson, Cullen Arroyo, Justin Lee Cooper, Isaiah Griffin, Ashley Hughes, Lana Kinnear, Jerry Messing, Logan O'Brien, Lauren Schaffel, Brandon Wengler, Jewelia Zafares

Content warnings appear: "BL" (blue language), "AP" (adult positions), and "MD" (mature delicacies).

Ratings Child Open (live/video)

(live) David, hobo sack-on-a-stick at the ready, prepares to run away from the show. "How am I supposed to trick little kids into seeing my butt with these damn warnings?" he complains to Bob. Suddenly, a little space child, Lucien, zaps onto the big screen. Dubbed with an adult voice, he explains the latest TV warning — "PBD" equals "Potential Buttocks Display." He introduces himself as "he who watches all of television, crowning shows with the warnings befitting them."

(video) They're beamed onto his spacepod and served "Angel's Cloud," a smoking blue cocktail which shrinks them, Alice-style, to invisibility. Lucien laughs maniacally. His parents (John and Brett) storm in and scold him for watching adult-rated TV. "Oh, goodness…the irony is as bittersweet as tears on Turkish delight!" He gets a spanking and is left to lament a future world with no ratings system. "Oh, happenstance!" he laughs. His prophecy is realized when the storybook reader on a children's program is a topless sexpot….

Debate (live/video)

(live) Uncensored children's programming is the grandstanding topic for Senator Hensley (Jerry) at an election debate. He praises the efforts of two TV watchdog parents from his community, who stand and accept applause. Next, candidate Whiteside (Paul) similarly applauds a couple of *his* community-minded constituents. Candidate Fitzpatrick (Bob) is uncomfortable; he's brought no "guests." He arbitrarily picks out a fat guy (David), who "can't be doing too great," and wins over the crowd by making insulting barbs. Fitzpatrick's success provokes the other debaters to do the same, each picking on the same hapless fat man, who tries to remain good-natured until 2Whiteside makes him cry. Fitzpatrick purports to empathize with fatty ("a part of me is a fat man, too") and leaves to thunderous applause.

(video) At his victory celebration, he thanks his family, friends, and the fat guy, taking every opportunity to insult each of them. Victory marching band music plays as his supporters cheer!

Music Offer (live/video)

A commercial for a music offer: a dignified man of taste (Bob) drinks in the victory music ("Philouza's March No. 34") and teases how wonderful it would be to own the world's finest music in one collection. He lists other master compositions, which he associates with the TV shows that adapted them as theme music (Beethoven's Fifth as the theme from TV's *The Gun Shooter*). This music compilation cannot be found in stores, nor through a TV offer, he explains — "This is your opportunity to provide *me* with the songs I love, in one collection." Send your music to "Music for Jerry" at "Jerry's Mansion" in Connecticut. He also needs some milk and orange soda ("My grandkids are coming over.").

Inside The Actor (live)

(live) Cyrus Castilla Tetley (David) hosts *Inside the Actor*. He rapturously introduces his guest, actor Ryan Dorn (Jay). The grungy, mumbling Dorn explains he still has the script from his first commercial for zit cream. "Frame it!" cries Tetley. "Bury it! Walk twenty paces away. Dig it up in 15 years, and teach the world to sing!" During the student Q&A, Tetley screams, "Who dares question Ryan Dorn!" as he gives the actor a footbath. "To gain better insight" into what makes Ryan so great, Tetley and two students (B.J. and Becky) are shrunken and injected into Dorn's bloodstream.

Lost Inside The Actor (video)

(video) A bad 70's Saturday morning TV show, Tetley and his students (David, Becky, B.J.) perilously raft down Dorn's bloodstream. Theme song for their adventure:

> *Cyrus and his students on a routine exploration*
> *Into the greatest actor ever known!!*
> *Plunging through the bloodstream into the glands of a Ryan Dorn!*

Lost in the prehistoric forest inside actor Dorn, and afraid of the ferocious (toy) dinosaur, the students try to start a fire to get their host to sneeze them out. Smitten, Tetley is not so upset, "Oh, what a wondrous world. I shall never leave!" Co-inhabitants include Blinky, the makeshift robot, and Evel Knievel (Paul). Dorn's sneeze propels the students out.

(top) Aside from Bob and David's bare asses, the show's only nudity; TTOMO saying "Goodbye 2 Every 1 Ever." (Photos © Adam Timrud Photography)

They land on some grass, and a huge hand crushes them as it grabs up a handful of earth.

Earth Shoes (video)

Reporter Brink Flanks (David) holds a fistful of earth to emphasize his report on the scientific theory that billions of feet walking every day will diminish the earth by the end of the next millennium. Dr. Todd Bruman (Bob) explains his theory in condescending detail, that each step compacts the earth and also kicks dust into the air, lost forever. The scientist's solution? Stop walking, or walk differently. He impatiently teaches Brink a walk he developed, "loosely based on the movements of the skitter bug." Dr. Bruman defends himself against one of his critics, Dr. Austin Parlmer (John), by alluding to his detractor's habitual gambling and masturbating. Brink sums up the report, skeptical about the switch to skittering, especially if their scientist instructor is so rude.

Dying Planet Link (video)

Earth Shoes is part three in a five-part public-TV series, *Our Dying Planet*, made possible by support provided by The Riffingtons, "a family of oil and energy companies proud to sponsor the final days of planet Earth." R&B sensation Three Times One Minus One's (David and Bob) hit video "Goodbye 2 Every 1 Ever" their homage to everyone who's died) plays.

Teardrop Awards (video/live)

TTOMO is nominated in the Teardrop Award's saddest song category. Other nominees: Willips Brighton (Bob) for his Beach Boys-esque "Mouthful of Sores," and Horace Loeb (David) for his tribute to his young son's tragic death, "Heaven Better Save Some Tears." Loeb is the winner — "I wish my boy could be down here to share this with me, but then I wouldn't have written the song, so scratch that!" In his excitement, he sends his award plunging into the chest of Willips Brighton's son. This spurs Brighton to write a tribute to his own dead son, "Ain't No Fun" (where he compares his sadness to having mouth sores), a Teardrop Award nominee the following year. It ties to win with Loeb's tribute song to Brighton's dead son. Loeb is exuberant, and Brighton stabs him with the award, "fatally murdering him." Loeb made a special video tribute song to himself, in case he died. ("I'll really miss you, Me.")

Shrunken Mr. Show Close (video)

A still-shrunken Bob and David say goodnight from the stage, which is actually inside Lucien's shoebox for class show-and-tell. Credits roll as the space kids in class go crazy for it, commenting with dubbed adult voices.

Notes About Episode 409

Bill: *"There was an old episode of* Star Trek *in which little Clint Howard portrayed some sort of weird space man-child. All I remember of it was Clint wearing a bald cap and dressed in flowing, glittery clothes while reclining on pillows. Some crazy plot line saw Kirk, Spock, and Bones ending up as captives aboard his tiny spaceship, where they were treated as honored guests and plied with exotic space booze. So far, so good. What was really weird was his voice. They had dubbed an effete man's voice over Clint's, and the effect was truly bizarre. When the little boy laughed, it was creepy. Creepy enough to make the short list of things that I remember from childhood. In casting children, you mostly encounter kids from families where the only inherited talent is self-delusion. Few, very few, are genuinely gifted. The little boy who played the Ratings Child was really talented. He had to sit for hours in a bald cap and repeat long sections of dialogue to unseen actors. And it was hot — all of our location shoots were hot — but he never complained."*

Paul: *"*Debate *was fucked up. Jill, Jerry, John, and I all went up on lines. Not only did this never happen with the live sketches (I can think of only one other time, and I will not embarrass the actor by mentioning it here), but for all of us to do it was extremely odd. As we were taping and the lines were being forgotten, a thick sense of dread came over me and, it seemed, the whole studio. Now, I never sleep through the night. I curse whoever wrote that scene. It was clearly haunted."*

David: *"In* Debate, *that was honestly one of the most fun things I did after four years on* mr. Show, *playing that guy who had no lines, but just did that exaggerated mugging thing. I just had so much fun doing it. It's like a mute Robin Williams on lithium."*

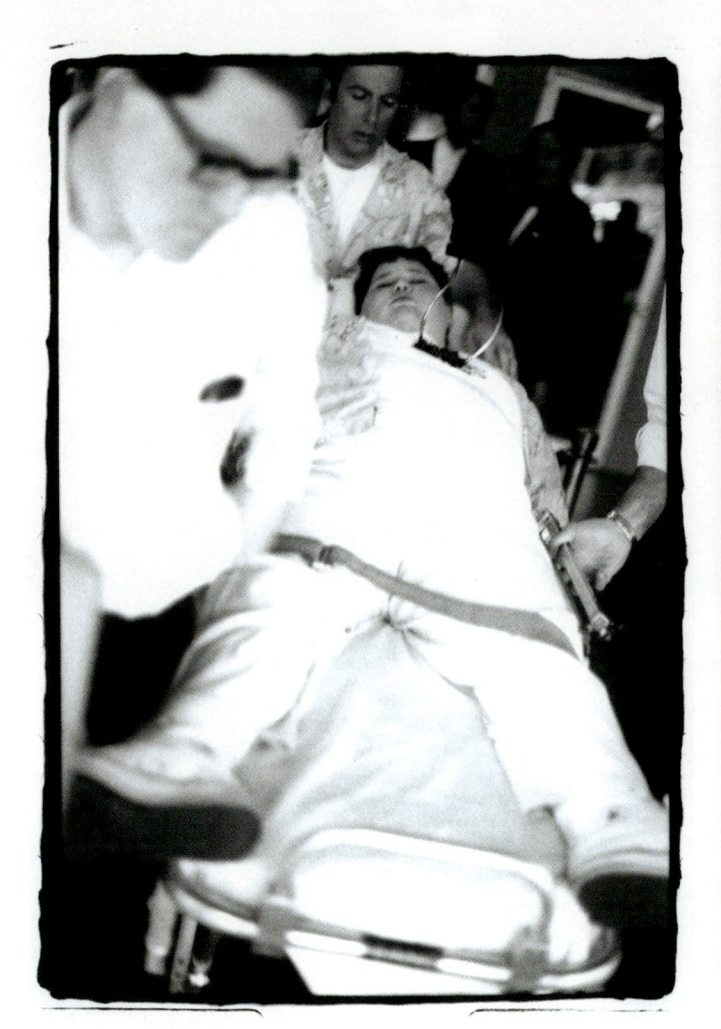

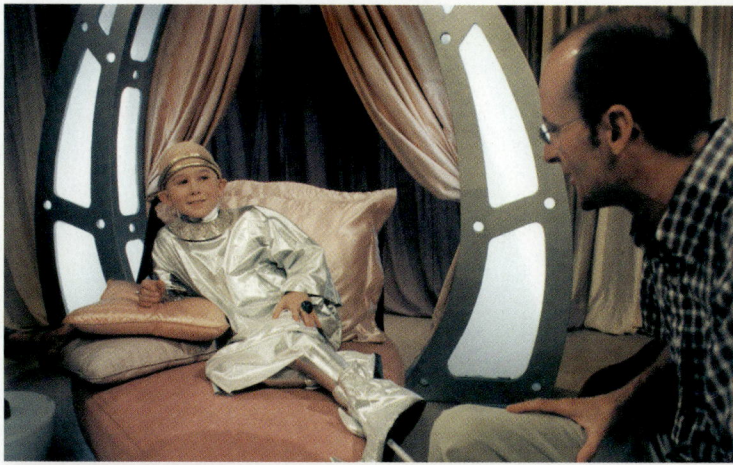

(left) Willips Brighton's son (Jerry Messing) takes a Tear Drop Award in the chest, inspiring at least two very sad songs; (top right) Director Peyton Reed with ratings child; (bottom right) Peyton reviewing shots with Bob and Bill for Debate sketch victory party scene. (Photos © Adam Timrud Photography)

David: "If ever a show and a person was right for spoofing and more, it was that show [Inside The Actors' Studio]. I really have a visceral hatred for that show, and everything it stands for. And I think we were very prescient, if you look at some of the guests they've had on in the last year. We're talking about Ben Affleck, these people who are being celebrated as these great actors and asked to impart their wisdom about the process. And they're talking about people who've done very little. Initially, they had on Sean Penn, DeNiro, Harrison Ford, Glenn Close. And now, they are very quickly dipping into the lesser talented pool. They did something that came close to us talking about the zit cream commercial. He started reading the list of Ben Affleck's awards. 'In 1998, you won the Blockbuster Award for Most Popular Male Actor.' Applause, applause. 'In 1999, again, you won the Blockbuster Award….' The fucking Blockbuster Award?! A fucking write-in award from white people who rent movies? What are you talking about? I get totally apoplectic when I watch that stuff. It's so wrong."

David: "The 'frame it!' line, that he says to the actor, is something James Lipton actually did say regarding the napkin that Billy Crystal jotted his brilliant idea for Curly's Gold on. Frame it? Frame the fucking napkin with the Curly's Gold idea on it? I got a better idea — get in a time machine, go back, take that same napkin, write your idea on it, and then wipe you ass with it, and then frame it. It would be weird, but certainly more appropriate."

Paul: "I was very, very excited to be playing Evel Knievel for this sketch. It was hard not to laugh when I was doing the bad acting. I love myself and how talented and funny I am."

David: "We did Earth Shoes for Troy's pilot, The Big News, before Mr. Show, and we also used it in our live show. We said we would do it for Troy if I got to direct it. That was another example of me saying, 'I'm going to direct this!' And then getting to the set — it was the first thing I ever did — there were so many mistakes. When I look back on them now, they're so obvious. Just being ill-prepared and not figuring shots out, and Troy was so cool about stepping back and saying, 'Um, why don't you try that?' 'Ohh, yeah! That'll work.' So he basically directed that thing. I didn't know what I was doing. We had to redo it for Mr. Show, it wasn't broadcast quality. Unfortunately, the one we originally did is a lot funnier than the remake for Mr. Show. The performances were all better in the first one, I was basically a straight man in that, but Bob and John were really, really funny in the original. That piece was kind of a throw away. That piece stands out to me. It doesn't exactly feel like Mr. Show to me."

Bob: "Teardrop Awards — I actually had a bacterial infection in my mouth that revealed itself as a multitude of heinous sores. Because of that, I was bedridden. Because I was bedridden I actually watched a music documentary about the Beach Boys and was alerted to Brian Wilson's latter-day songwriting technique. Just write about the minutiae of your dumb life. I then found myself on TV singing about mouth sores. Beautiful story, yes?"

Scott: "The day we were shooting the Teardrop Awards, we got a message that HBO didn't want us to do it because they thought Eric Clapton might sue. We all looked at each other, shrugged, and continued filming. No one ever heard from Mr. Clapton."

EPISODE 410
PATRIOTISM, PEPPER, AND PROFESSIONALISM

written by:	David Cross, Bob Odenkirk, Scott Aukerman, Eric Hoffman, Jay Johnston, Bill Odenkirk, B.J. Porter, Dino Stamatopoulos and Brian Posehn
"goodbye" segment director:	David Cross
location segment director:	Peyton Reed
live show director:	John Moffitt
cast:	David Cross, Bob Odenkirk, Scott Adsit, Scott Aukerman, John Ennis, Jay Johnston, Jerry Minor, Brett Paesel, B.J. Porter, Becky Thyre, Jill Talley
featuring:	Eric Hoffman, Laura Milligan, Bill Odenkirk, Mark Rivers, Dino Stamatopoulos, Paul F. Tompkins, Mindy Jovanovic

Resort Cold Open (video)

Mr. Show is broadcast live from Globo-Chem's Employee "Get Motivated" retreat at La Questa Resort in Scottsdale, Arizona.

Exec Open (live)

Bob and David entertain at this corporate gig, tailoring their "jokes" with employees' names and personal info. It's a big hit, until they get a little too personal. David teases that during tug-o-war, he was behind Jeff Teasdale (Scott), and "his adult diaper broke, and I slipped in his shit." Another employee, Larry (John), is furious when the boys joke about screwing his wife, and he runs off to find Carl, the culprit who gave up the gossip. Next up is motivational rock band "Honesty in Motion" (Jay, Becky, and Jerry), led by singer, and C-level celebrity, Josh Fenderman (B.J.).

Money Warning (video)

TV's *Genuine Hollywood Factual Report* covers the rise and fall of 80's pre-teen idol Josh Fenderman (B.J.). We see slow-motion footage of him doing his Michael Jackson dance move, in front of tens of adoring onlookers. The same footage is replayed throughout the report. Winning the hearts of America as a tiny commercial actor ("It's Pumkinninny!"), he was "one of Hollywood's toppest young stars" by the time he was 12. He made shitty movies and "tens of millions of thousands of hundreds of dollars." But by the end of the '80's, he was broke. Josh blamed the money for his losses. "I didn't realize that if you exchanged it for property and services, they would take it away for *good*!" Josh took the Treasury Department to court and won. All newly-minted currency contains a warning: "THIS DOLLAR IS NOT YOURS AFTER YOU SPEND IT."

Warnings Link (video)

Josh's victory leads to an explosion of similar consumer warnings:

"ENTERTAINMENT NEWS IS NEITHER ENTERTAINMENT NOR NEWS"
(on car mirror) "OBJECTS IN MIRROR ARE NOT REALLY IN MIRROR. LOOK OUT!"
(on heart-shaped box of Be Mine candy) "CANDY IS NOT REALLY IN LOVE WITH YOU"

(top) Bob and David custom-tailoring their material for this private corporate gig; (below) B.J. Porter as Josh Fenderman as seen in his "Genuine Factual Hollywood Report." (Photos © Adam Timrud Photography)

Weeklong Romance (live)

In a restaurant, a girl (Jill) gets a box of candy from her boyfriend (Bob). They are very happy to be reunited after a week long break up. In that week, she says she was depressed and signed up for a Tex-Mex cooking class. He says he cried and barely left the house. He lights up a cigarette. "Since when do you smoke?" He took it up last week and has even tried to quit, twice. As he continuously tries to deflect the conversation back to her ("Tex-Mex. Now, that's Texas and Mexico?"), the depth of his activities during the past week are revealed as, one by one, angry people confront him with a sock in the jaw. He was engaged and stood up the bride at the altar; he joined, then got kicked out of, a Christian rock band ("2001: A New Wave Godyssey"); and he beat out a porn star in a blowjob competition. Jill ultimately has trouble accepting Bob's activities, and he gets defensive and accusatory — "I'm sure you did a few things that you're not very proud of, Miss Tex-Mex!" She gets up to leave, and she's busted. There's mesquite sauce on her sleeve — "I thought you said that class hadn't even started yet." He socks her and rejoins his friends from "Godyssey" (David and Scott).

Godyssey Link (video)

In the Coffee Dome, 2001: A New Wave Godyssey (Scott, Bob, David) are performing their original tune, "Praying Machine." They are drowned out by the thumping Satanic beat of Marilyn Monster, performing to a capacity crowd in the adjacent Octo-Dome Arena, where he whips them into a frenzy by pouring a bucket of blood over his head.

Marilyn Monster Pizza Parlours (live/video)

(live) Backstage, Marilyn (David) is tickled by the video of his rocking performance. He takes off his red hair, revealing a David Cross bald head, and introduces himself as Larry Turnaur to the new "funployees" watching this training video for his chain, Marilyn Mozzarella's Pizzarella Pie Parlours.

(video) Hokey, friendly music underscores. His family restaurant features employees with Marilyn-like white painted faces, red contact lenses, and wigs of black stringy hair. There are many rules and strict penalties. Fred (Bob) — the employee who does all the video's "don'ts" — gets a "green level-two punishment," the bloody diaper. He is made to stand naked, but for his dripping, bloody diaper and cape, in the middle of the restaurant as patrons and other employees ridicule.

(live) Larry lists the 16 "P's" to success: "Poise, personality, professionalism, positive mental attitude, (im)press the customer…please don't flush sanitary towels down the toilet, phreeze plenty of ice, placate, pomp and circumstance, patriotism, pepper, and professionalism." He encourages the new employees to have fun and remember to break some rules. "But, *don't* break any rules." A P.A. with a clipboard and headset (Mark) signals to Larry that it's time to go on stage.

Info Jimmy (video)

The P.A. (Mark) goes down his list to cue people on their activities. He walks down the street to a bus station, where a kid is slurping on his empty soda cup — "Okay. You're done with that, you can throw it away." "And, pull out…*Now*," he tells a couple getting it on in a sleazy motel. He shows up at a local bar to announce it's closing for the night.

(top to bottom) Weeklong Romance — *Jill reunites with her beau after a long week apart; Becky in wedding dress and still pissed, in a beat that was cut from sketch [see script pages opposite]; Scott and David, Bob's ex-Christian rock bandmates; 2001: A New Wave Godyssey play the Coffee Dome (Photos © Adam Timrud Photography)*

30 CONT'D (4)

> JILL
> Oh my God, are you okay?

> BOB
> Yeah, that's Crystal's boyfriend. I guess he's mad because I beat her in the competition.

> JILL
> You gave people blowjobs?

> BOB
> The most people. That's why they've named a drink after me here.

> JILL
> They have a drink called a Todd Hindley?

> BOB
> No, it's called "The Ultimate Dicksucker". You know, Tex-Mex seems hard, does that use mesquite?

A WOMAN IN A WEDDING dress steps up and punches BOB.

> WOMAN
> Dick-sucker!

The WOMAN turns to JILL and punches her.

> WOMAN
> You thieving bitch!

> JILL
> Jennifer? I didn't steal him, he...

> WOMAN
> Steal him? What are you talking about? You stole my clothes and I've had to run around in this damned old wedding dress.

She exits.

> BOB
> I stole her clothes. Gave you some, that sweater.

"Weeklong Romance" script pages with cut scenes.

(CONTINUED)

                    JILL
          But you gave me this sweater for
          Christmas.

                    BOB
          Oh, this happened months ago,
          not this week. Now, when does
          this Tex-Mex class start?

                    JILL
          Look, this is very hard for me,
          I thought you said you were
          crying all week.

                    BOB
          I was! Okay?! Then I was born
          again, joined that band, met
          Jennifer, got engaged, quit the
          band, lucked into that porn
          film...

A PHILLIPINO DAD and his TWO DAUGHTERS are passing and notice
bob and break out into laughter and shouting a phrase.

                    PHILLIPINO GIRLS
          Le-dai! Le-dai! Hut Hut Hut!

                    BOB
          (WITH A SMILE) Le-dai! Le-dai!
          Hut hut hut!

He smiles and waves as they pass, giggling.

                    BOB
          That's my catch phrase. I host
          this kids show in the
          Philippines, it happened last
          uhhh, Wednesday, or Thursday
          morning, I don't know, the
          international date line's got me
          all confused...

                    JILL
          Jesus, Todd!

                    BOB
          Look, I'm sure you did some
          stuff you're not very proud of,
          Miss Tex-Mex!

Cut

(CONTINUED)

Goodbye (film)

Casual friends (Bob and Jay) catch up at a bar after five years. Unsure of their friendship status, they awkwardly hug goodbye, then awkwardly walk the same direction. The uncomfortable moment repeats itself, because they are parked in the same garage, and then they run into each other at the Quik Mart. At a filling station, Jay thinks he hears Bob, but it's a different guy. Jay suddenly panics — "Where is he?!" He tears apart the Quik Mart, then races back to the parking garage, and then to the bar where there is no sign of him. Depressed, he camps out by the bar, until morning, when the A.M. paper delivers the news that "Friendly Acquaintance Dies." A related story, "Friend is Sad," features a photo of distraught Jay. At the funeral, a bereaved friend laments she never got a chance to say goodbye. "I did…a lot," whispers Jay. Bob's tombstone reads "R.I.P. 'A Good Friend'."

Tombstone/Vendetta Link (video)

Other tombstones in the graveyard include one for Van Hammersly, and "R.I.P. I'm Dead Without My Coffee In The Morning," which is also a paperweight on the desk of….

Vendetta (live)

Carl Peters (David), the culprit who divulged co-workers' personal info at the company retreat, is confronted by an irate Larry (John) for doing his wife. Carl insists that it's not what Larry thinks — "We didn't do it for fun, I swear. We were making amateur porn films." The scene gets screwier, revealing the involvement of the office super (Bob) — "You taking credit for my work?" — and co-worker Todd (Jay). As the farce takes more twists and turns, the P.A. (Mark) peeks his head through the door. "Okay, this scene is over. Let's roll those credits, please."

Info Jimmy Close (live)

Credits roll over P.A. Jimmy (Mark) walking toward the outside of the studio. He lights a smoke, and relaxes. When the music ends, he looks at us — "All right, that's it. The season's over. Beat it."

Notes About Episode 410

B.J.: *"So both David and Scott saw the E! True Hollywood Story on Corey Feldman and were laughing about it, and Scott shows up to the next writer's meeting having written this entire sketch, to my knowledge without ever even officially pitching it at the table. Maybe I've simply forgotten, but I cannot remember him ever pitching Money Warning, as it became known. I also remember it being one of the least re-written sketches of the entire season. There were edits to make it shorter, but almost no changes. Unlike Everest, for which we read a new version of twice a week, for well over a month. One of the biggest and most pleasant surprises for me, during Season 4, was being chosen to portray the thinly-if-at-all-disguised Corey*

(above) David as Marilyn Monster on stage at the Octo-Dome Arena.
(below) Larry Turnaur, the man behind Marilyn and the chain of pizza parlours. "But, don't break any rules." (Photos © Adam Timrud Photography)

Feldman-based character Josh Fenderman. I found out the night before filming it that I was going to do it. Down to the last minute, they were trying to get Seth Green, who undoubtedly would have been perfect for it. But he couldn't get out of his Buffy the Vampire Slayer commitment. This gave me no time to study Corey — and maybe I was ultimately better off — but I did wish I could have gotten some more specifically Feldman-esque qualities into my performance. We were watching one of the first edits of the piece, just before we taped the live show. It was good, but Bob had a suggestion that really made it one of the strongest sketches in that show — to repeat the footage of me dancing in my 80's costume outside of a premiere as many times as possible. People still ask me if I'll 'do the dance.' I always just smile and say, 'Seriously. Fuck off.'"

David: "I had seen Corey Feldman's band, The Truth Movement. And that truly was one of the greatest, most exciting experiences of my life. I've seen him twice. When I saw him, I was moved to tears. You gotta see it. If you ever get a chance to watch Corey Feldman and The Truth Movement, he's really got something to say about being a celebrity, and he says it in a really magical, beautiful way. I was at home, and Ken Daly called me, and he's frantic — 'You've got to get to the Derby right now! Corey Feldman is having a birthday party, and he's introducing his new band!' I grabbed my camera, even though I knew I had shot film in it, and I just rewound it, and I ended up double exposing all the film, but I had to have all the pictures of him in his Michael Jackson-era hat. At one point, he took all that stuff from his Michael Jackson look that he had for a couple of years, and he puts it in a trunk, and he sings a song, something like, 'Who do you want me to be? Is this who you think I am?' And then he sets the trunk on fire. He pours a little rubbing alcohol on it that kind of burned off, and that was it."

B.J.: "After burning the trunk of clothes, for the rest of the 'gig' — to use the musicians' parlance — Corey performed as himself, whatever that means. It was this confused rejection of Corey's former image that inspired the lyrics Josh Fenderman sings with his band Honesty In Motion:

> Is this who you think I am? / Who do you want me to be?
> Am I your dream-faker? / Why can't you let me be me?

Beautiful, huh? You said it. Yes, you did!!"

David: "Money Warning was also inspired by the M.C. Hammer Behind the Music. That's an oft-told tale, of the person you thought was a multi-millionaire, but then they got screwed by their accountant, they never read their contract, etc. But there were a couple things specifically in the Hammer story, where he earned all this money, and, clearly, he's not very bright. He gave his uncle a million bucks to buy a horse or some shit. And then, walking through his house, it's just this physical monument to vanity, there's fountains, and he's showing his foyer, 'All this floor is imported Italian marble….' And then he's sitting there crying poor. And you're thinking, 'What an asshole!' And the actual line that Jill says in that sketch — 'We built the house on the hill, so the poor people could be inspired,' is actually something that M.C. Hammer did. He made this big point about going back to the poor section in Oakland, to the 'hood, and building this mansion at the top of the hill, 'so all the poor kids could look up to it and be inspired.' I mean, how fucking out of it do you have to be?"

Bob: "Weeklong Romance — brilliant idea. The guy and girl split up for one week, the guy does loads of stuff, and the girl doesn't do anything. And they want to get back together, and it starts coming out what he's done with his week. The punching is very old-fashioned-y. It could've been done on Your Show of Shows. Just change what he did with his week. I love scenes that are Vaudevillian, like Shampoo, Audition, Weeklong Romance, Lie Detector. All of those could have been done 50 years ago, and, who knows, maybe in one form they were."

Bob: "Marilyn Monster is a great piece highlighting the merchandising of any and every form of teenage rebellion. A point that is so trite, it's hard to make to any real effect. But a pair of bloody diapers will get people's attention every time."

David: "The whole shoot with me onstage as Marilyn was awful. That was all Kyro Syrup. It was the middle of the summer. We were at the Palace on Vine Street, it was a ridiculously hot day, and that outfit was not comfortable. Those shoes were not comfortable. I had those silly contacts in, which are also not comfortable. And they are not my real prescription, so now I can't see a fucking thing. It's hot, and I have to keep pouring sticky liquid corn syrup on me over and over again. Luckily, we got it all in three takes. I think everyone knew we weren't going to get more than three takes of that one."

Tracey Krasno (production manager): "For whatever reason, unfortunately we got some ultra-Christian parents of the kids in the pizza place, who just flipped out and lost it, and would not allow their kids to be in that scene and see him. They would allow their kids to see him in the diaper, but not the bloody diaper. So we had to shoot creatively to get a shot like the kids were reacting. When you see the reverse

*(above) Tonyia Verna (hair/makeup) giving that Goth look.
(below) David setting up a shot as director of the "Goodbye" segment. Photos © Adam Timrud Photography*

EPISODE 410   247

(top) Mark Rivers is "Info Jimmy"; (center and right) Bob and David say goodbye and thanks from stage after final show. Photo © Adam Timrud Photography; (bottom) Corey Feldman and his band The Truth Movement provided entertainment at the Season 4 wrap party. Photo © Adam Timrud Photography.

shot, with Bob in the bloody diaper, there's just me and Tonyia and couple of the grips, there's no kids."

Paul: "I make two brief appearances in the last ever episode of Mr. Show. I am seen in a photograph as the moderator in the corporate seminar open, and I am seen playing pool with Eric Hoffman and Tracey Krasno in the Goodbye sketch. As we filmed the part where we were all leaving the bar (I believe the name of the place is Hank and Frank's), we had to exit and enter the bar over and over again. By this time, the bar's regulars were there in full force. After a while, a few of us started ordering beers and would drink as much of them as we could each time we had to go back inside the bar. Back by the pool table, the scores from a real pool match were on a dry-erase board on the wall. The folks playing were, apparently, Chilito, Guapo, and Kmoa. In the credits at the end of this episode, Eric, Tracey, and I have these sobriquets inserted into our names. Look for them! I swear they're there! I can't promise you it's worth it, but I am no liar!"

BOB ABOUT THE LAST SEASON

"The best season overall. We did everything we were known for and at the same time this season plays to a wider audience. There are fewer digressions into absurdity. We were more confident, had a schedule which kept the shows strong from beginning to end, every episode. A great time, and everybody at the top of their game.

The show really did grow every season, from something only a comedy writer could love, to something any intelligent, aware person with a sense of humor could get and enjoy. A scene like Civil War Reenactments would work for anyone who was even marginally aware of pop culture notions of that time. And the live scenes; *Audition* (#404), *The Burgundy Loaf* (#405), *Toenapper* (#403), *Lifeboat* (#401), *The Great Hemingway* (#408), *Bugged Drug Deal* (#408), *Weeklong Romance* (#410), *Phone Sex* (#404), holy shit, I just listed eight awesome live scenes, that's like eight seasons' worth of any other sketch show. So, maybe we didn't need any more seasons…

Who decides what's successful? On some level, there is a shared awareness and acceptance that a celebrity, or a TV show, or whatever is a 'success' and deserves support and focus. Somehow it never came around to us. We're in some good company, though. It's weird, but at the HBO Aspen Comedy Festival in 1997, when *Monty Python* were reunited (minus the dead guy) and given an award, John Cleese held it up and said, 'Thanks, but why didn't you give us this when we could have used it?' That surprised me, and I asked around, and I guess they were never that big a deal when they were on the air. Of course, they certainly weren't in America (the show wasn't even on until the series had ended), but neither were they big in Britain. So…in that way, I guess we deserve the compliment, 'Your show reminds me of *Python*.'"

Try Again (Adam's Song)

WORDS AND MUSIC BY TITANNICA

Moderato Aggressivo

Now say goodnight little one "Try Su-i-cide" we once sung Your parents sued we fuck-ing won. Pulled sheet back hurt my eyes Wet ci-gar, you should have died Did we mention, we fuck-ing won?

(Spoken) Like my dead Grandpa told me, if at first you don't succeed Try try try again

---

Try Again (Adam's Song)

Now say good night, little one
Try suicide, we once sung
Your parents sued, we fucking won

Pulled sheet back, hurt my eyes
Wet cigar, you should have died
Did we mention, we fucking won?

solo

(Spoken)
Like my dead Grandpa said to me...
If at first you don't succeed...

(Chorus)
Try, try, try again...try, try, try again...head first next time...dive right in

(pre-chorus)
Shush, little Adam, don't say a word
Your body looks like a greasy turd
When we saw you in that bed
Should have thrown acid on your head

(Chorus)
Try, try, try again...try, try, try again...
head first this time...dive right in

solo

End